★ ★ ★ ★ ★

"This globe, at some undescribed period, having been convulsed and broken up,
was a dark and watery waste for ages perhaps, till out of this chaotic state,
the present fabric of the world was made [by God] to arise."

– Jamieson, Fausset, and Brown Commentary, 1871

BEFORE
GENESIS

THE UNAUTHORIZED HISTORY OF TOHU, BOHU, AND THE
CHAOS DRAGON IN THE LAND BEFORE TIME

DONNA HOWELL
DR. THOMAS HORN

DEFENDER

CRANE, MO

BEFORE GENESIS: The Unauthorized History of Tohu, Bohu, and the Chaos Dragon in the Land Before Time

by Donna Howell, Dr. Thomas Horn

Defender Publishing
Crane, MO 65633

ISBN: 978-1-948014-72-4

Printed in the United States of America.

A CIP catalog record of this book is available from the Library of Congress.

Cover design by Jeffrey Mardis
Interior design by Pamela McGrew

All Scripture quotations are from the King James Version unless otherwise noted.

Donna and Tom's Dedication

First and foremost, to the one God and Creator—existent in three Persons: Father, Son, and Holy Spirit—from whom we have all been given the planet that has become the chief focus of this book. Thank you, Jesus, for the sacrifice on that cross two millennia ago that paved the way for reconciliation between God and mankind, and for all the souls who have come to know you since that event.

Second, to the following people, who assisted in constant prayerful and emotional support during this project, and who endured many occasions of after-work-hours' "parsing" of complicated research in the evenings: Nita Horn, James Howell, Joe Horn, Allie Anderson, and Donna's sweet "little scholars," Joee and Althia.

Third, to all our friends and partners at SkyWatch TV and Defender Publishing, who always make us look better than we are: Angie Peters, our book editor; Derek Gilbert, Sharon Gilbert, Gary Stearman, and the late Chuck Missler and Dr. Michael Heiser, whose past research and conversational contributions helped the direction of this book take form; the Jacksons, Brittney and Dakota, whose social media and video editing experience gives us the promotional advantage in "getting the word, and the Word, out there"; Charisse Parton, Pennie Dutton, Katherine Horn, and a long list of other precious folks whose leadership in many departments of the company keep things operating smoothly so Donna and Tom can write.

CONTENTS

Introduction: The "War" I've Started
Will It Be Worth It in the End? 1

PART I: THE DEBATE

Chapter 1: The Two—*Yes, Two*—Views on Cosmology 11
Chapter 2: Ussher Chronology
A "Powell Doctrine" for the Church? 53
Chapter 3: The Bible Says…*What?!* 87

PART II: SUPPORTING EVIDENCE

Chapter 4: Either All These Scientists Are Wrong,
Or God Is "Tricky" 119
Chapter 5: Mystery History 153

PART III: THE SERPENT KING

Chapter 6: Earth between "Void" and "Good" 237
Chapter 7: The State of the "Void" 267
Chapter 8: Lucifer's Fall and Extinct Animals of the "Void" . . . 287

Conclusion: The "War" I've Started
It Is *Worth It in the End!* 323

Notes 333

The "War" I've Started

Will It Be Worth It in the End?

"YOU'RE GOING TO START A WAR," the theologian said. "If you write this book you're planning, you *will* start a war. What you are saying—your approach to cosmology in light of all parties currently involved in the debate—is not one the world is ready to hear. And it doesn't matter what your reasons are. As driven as you are to reach the lost through this message, if you write what you're planning to write, you are literally begging for an unfathomably deep pool of argumentative agitators to surface from out of the woodwork on all sides and argue with you. Are you prepared to respond to *all* of them?"

This was the warning given in person to me and several other researchers from our Defender Publishing team a few years back. We were out to dinner with one of the most respected theologians of all time between presentations at a local conference. His chopped-steak-and-onions dinner was half-eaten, and then abandoned, halfway through the conversation, when it became clear to him that we were actually considering publishing a book like this.

"You can't be serious," he said, shocked by the implications of this research possibly being distributed across the US.

For a moment, I allowed myself to become intimidated by his cautionary words. I glanced at Dr. Thomas Horn—simply "Tom" to his

1

inner circle—who was nonchalantly stabbing about his salad with ranch, unfazed.

"Yeah," Tom said, poking at a cherry tomato. "Yeah, I'm serious. And yes, I know. This book will make some folks mad, but that's true of anything we would attempt to write, anyway. SkyWatch Television and Defender Publishing have always been about addressing that one neglected subject. You know, the 'topics the Church won't touch.' We've put our necks on the chopping block for years with media that tackles all kinds of bizarre subjects—aliens, UFOs, the Vatican and the pope, occultic symbolism embedded in the blueprints of the nation's capital city, Deep-State deception, all that edgy stuff—and what, if anything, the Bible says about it all. We try to be fishers of men, *all* men, and that can't be done if our end goal is to only speak or write about what has already been well covered in the scholarly world up to this point, right?"

"Okay, but," the theologian interrupted, shaking his head. "I mean… you can't possibly know how wildly you would provoke both the scientific world and the Body of Christ if you do this thing. I mean it. There's 'edgy' and there's 'war,' and *this* will be war!"

"Well," Tom said with a smile. "A lot of people out there could potentially come to faith in God if they were equipped with the information this book would present. And, to answer your question: No, we would not feel obligated to respond to all the agitators. Christ didn't in His day, did He? He simply gave people the truth and allowed them to accept or reject it, but He didn't stand around arguing. Though it's true we're not perfect like He was, we can attempt as best we can to follow His model: Shed as much light on truth as possible and hope it reaches those who need it."

The theologian blinked, took a sip from his iced tea, and nodded. "You got me there, Tom."

"Besides," Tom said with a chuckle, "don't you agree that this radically different approach to the subject of Earth's origins could be correct?"

"Oh, absolutely!" came the response. "It's more than possible, it's likely!"

"Then why can't I convince you to write this? With your five thousand degrees in Bible studies and theology," Tom sarcastically said with a wry grin, "you would be more than qualified."

"Five thousand!" the theologian laughed. "It's not quite to that number *yet*, but I'll try not to disappoint you, Tom." After the exchange of a few chuckles, he finally returned his attention to his meal. "No, sorry. I respect you and your team, Tom, but *this* ain't my thing. You have no idea what kind of fallout would blow up my desk, my career, or my ministry if I tried to take this on. The compatibility between the Bible and science—from the angle you're all coming from—would be a death knell."

His answer was accepted, and that was the end of Tom's attempt to recruit this individual in the project. The rest of our dinner was quite fun, and I felt honored to be in the presence of those brilliant minds who have more of my personal respect than any earthly language could articulate. But as the conversation went on regarding the relationship between science and the Bible, I couldn't help but wonder why these words were being treated as two *unrelated* subjects.

They're *not* unrelated, just so you know.

Years passed, and Tom continued to propose this book to others. Each time, the answer was the same: These learned men of God with multiple doctorates in theology, who can quote and exegete with linguistic expertise the Bible's most obscure and confusing passages, agreed the ideas presented herein were not only *possible*, they were likely. Some of the most respected scholars in all of Christian academia acknowledged that we were "onto something," that "this explains *everything*," that "it all fits," and that "this cannot be left unwritten!" Yet, when they were given the opportunity to be the chief author, they were either too swamped with their own ministry demands (which was most often the case) or they felt the subject would "be too edgy for their ministry."

I, however, kept digging…

Perhaps it was my passion for the deep research and dramatic conclusions we've drawn about the true origins of the Earth that led Tom to eventually choose *me* to write this…and I knew one thing to be true from the very start. It is an irrefutable fact of human nature—proven by repetition throughout history, and well captured in the following famous statement frequently attributed to English psychologist, philosopher, anthropologist, sociologist, and biologist Herbert Spencer:

> There is a principle which is a bar against all information, which is proof against all argument, and which cannot fail to keep man in everlasting ignorance. *That principle is condemnation before investigation.*

Let it sink in: A "bar" that stops the flow of "all information." A rebuttal against false "proof" that obliterates "all argument" and destroys rare, priceless objectivity in the quest for transparent truth. A component of human communication that "cannot fail" to preserve and maintain the prison cell of man's "everlasting," yet familiar and comfortable "ignorance."

What could be so powerful?

"Condemnation before investigation." In other words, sacking a possibility before allowing the evidence to speak for itself, because people assume they already have all the answers, and those answers are incompatible with the posed theory. That is, the dismissal of all elements in an otherwise affable or progressive conversation—beliefs, opinions, points of view, contributing evidence, or irrefutable facts of an argument, debate, or examination of any topic—if the listener on one side does not hear what he wants to hear. If this recipient of new information finds his preconceived ideas, former training or education, long-held traditions, ideologies, principles, or creeds threatened by fresh data, he rejects it, embracing the prison of ignorance above that which is genuine. To do otherwise is to allow the investment he has placed in his former worldview to weaken and crumble out from under him, perhaps even damaging the reputation he holds among his peers as the one most knowledgeable on the subject and leaving him stranded, alone, and lonely on the island of enlightenment. To admit he may have been wrong is to admit a weakness and lose some or all of the support he's accustomed to within his surroundings, so

he chooses to keep good company, stay blind, and stand firm on the endlessly unstable ground called "error."

The running narrative surrounding most "Old Earth" books—from
both the secular world and the Church Body—is that the authors are "trying to make the Bible agree with science [or evolution]," *or* the other way
around: "trying to make science [or evolution] agree with the Bible." Both
of these angles inherently miss the most critical and obvious factor in the
room: God, the Creator of the universe, the Master Scientist who personally and joyfully crafted this planet and all the natural laws it bows to, is
the one and only God over *both* science and the Bible. Therefore, neither
true science nor the Word of God is in conflict with the other—once the
emotional responses from all parties is stripped away and replaced with
careful consideration of the mountains of evidence in support of their
potential harmony.

To put this another way: 1) The Bible is God's revelation to humanity, and nobody in the Church would disagree with this. 2) Earth is God's
Creation—His creative and very physical revelation to humanity—and,
once again, nobody in the Church disagrees. If, then, both are *His revelations,* and if He is genuinely the immutable and indisputable God over
both, then both the Word and the world *must be* pointing to one Truth,
and are therefore irrefutably free of contradiction.

Why, then, do we see so many apparent contradictions?

Of utmost importance in the attempt to answer this question is
an accurate treatment of the term "true science." By this, I refer not
to what conclusions within the scientific world have arisen through
exclusively human origin—as the Bible bows to no man-made investigation, discovery, laboratory result, mathematic calculation, or observation of any kind—but to genuine reality as God has ordained it.
Such a "genuine reality" in regard to cosmology and the origins of the
universe is not easily found in any scientific journal or Bible study,
since we remain finite humans whose grandest digs into the Word and
world of God are personal and subjective, and therefore susceptible to
endless error.

Nor do I claim under any circumstance to have been given dreams, visions, or divine revelation from God that makes the conclusions I've come to in this book *the* "genuine reality" superseding all other relative books or studies of this nature. That is absolutely not my purpose or goal.

I merely wish to uproot and set aside the nagging, chiding rebuke from voices on all sides that continuously suggest that taking the Bible and science together is wrong or sinful.

If God personally created the world, *and He did*—and if God personally guided the writers of Scripture to faithfully pen His self-revelation to all of mankind, *and He did*—then weaving these two threads together and seeking to find one accord between them is nothing short of a genuine act of worship.

This seemingly nonexistent and unique approach to harmonizing Scripture and science has been attempted by some in the past, but it has unfortunately been to the chagrin of many skeptics—inside and outside of the Body of Christ. In my humble opinion built from personal experience, this endeavor has (primarily) resulted in three responses: 1) The Church says the Bible should never be interpreted or reinterpreted in light of scientific discovery, because the Bible is the final, authoritative Word of God, and all other pursuits are fanciful, arrogant attempts to usurp His authority and place Him in a box that suits our ever-changing whims; 2) scientists say that because their work is demonstrable, transparent, and visible to all humanity, the incompatibilities of the biblical narrative prove the Word to be nothing more than archaic collections of irrelevant myths and fables that should be lost in the throes of history alongside all other literature originating from before our more enlightened eras of technological advancements and human achievement; 3) Christian or religious apologists—on both the Young Earth (the belief that our planet is around six thousand years old) and Old Earth (the belief that it is far more ancient as science identifies) sides—dedicate an exorbitant amount of time defending their beliefs by showing only the evidence that stacks in favor of their own research, while irresponsibly ignoring (or neglecting to respond to) glaring discoveries that render their conclusions ultimately impossible.

It is therefore extremely bold (and some would say audacious) to attempt a work like this that the first group considers heresy, the second group considers irrelevant, and the third group considers incorrect from every angle that does not complement their own findings.

In today's Body of Christ, Young Earth Creationism is, by far, the leading school of thought—so much so that those whose views and beliefs do not align with the Young Earth group are branded as liberal interpreters, as if they merely pick and choose what they want to believe from the Bible and discard the rest. An author such as myself who sets out to present the case for an old planet Earth is, as we've heard within Defender Publishing circles countless times, "looking to start a war."

From the bottom of my heart, that is not my intention. Much to the contrary, it is *peace* that I seek to spread, though it is a hand outstretched to the lost that I champion even above the comfort of agreeing with my Christ-believing fellows.

But above all else, I seek to make one thing clear: The Bible is THE Word of God, inerrant and infallible, God-breathed, and useful for *all* teaching, including those uncomfortable areas that plague our modern, heavily scientific world. It remains authoritative and relevant in all epochs, throughout human-guided investigation and discovery, and it is the corporate duty of Christ's followers to recognize this. Therefore, it is to the Bible that I turn for answers regarding the question about our planet's age that has unfortunately become the great divide separating believers from nonbelievers, the litmus test of whether a man or woman could ever come to the throne of a God whose Word is (apparently) in conflict with demonstrable, systematic studies in laboratories across the world. I am not driven by the need to "make the Bible agree with science"—as my faith in God is not shaken by even the most impressive of secular pursuits—but by my insatiable thirst to humbly reach out to those who are on the fence about "an unscientific God." If the God of Abraham, Isaac, Jacob, the Hebrews, the Jews, and the Gentiles is truly the God of Creation, too (as I believe He is), then He is the Supreme Scientist who made every observable thing in this world; He is not surprised by anything we find, and whatever lies at the absolute end of "true science"—be it an Old or a Young Earth—points back to Him indefinitely.

No one, of course, is required to agree with my research and findings. But my hope is that readers will see that I've taken great pains to faithfully present a *biblical* case for how the same God who created this planet, and all scientific pursuits within it, ultimately maintains control over what He formed "in the beginning"—however long ago that was.

So, am I "starting a war" here? And, if so, will it be worth it?

That depends on the war I've supposedly started. I'll meet up with you later, in the book's conclusion, to answer that question in a way that is, perhaps, quite unexpected.

PART I

THE DEBATE

Chapter 1

The Two—*Yes, Two*— Views on Cosmology

What we observe is not nature in itself but nature
exposed to our method of questioning.
—Werner Heisenberg

THE ABOVE WORDS were written by quantum physicist Werner Heisenberg, the German 1932 Nobel Prize winner whose work first shifted the world of science from focusing on the incomplete study of old quantum theory to modern quantum mechanics. Though his role in Adolf Hitler's regime has made him the subject of some controversy (he was appalled by Hitler's Aryan race dogmas and despised the political maneuverings of the madman against Heisenberg's fellow Jewish university academics, but he remained dedicated to science in a day when such dedication would brand one as compliant to the Führer's agenda), nobody can question that Heisenberg was one of the most brilliant minds in human history.

Heisenberg's famous quote makes a fundamental, as well as a radical, law of the universe stand out: We finite humans view the workings of nature and our planet with a limited perspective. The more we observe and test from that *incomplete* perspective, the more we render scientific theories that cement themselves in the related fields of research as the

supreme truth by which all other observations will be compared. But even
the greatest and most impressive of all these "laws" we establish about the
universe are still subject to our own methods of questioning and examination and are, therefore, flawed.

I share this early on to express one major element of my study
throughout this book: Though I do believe science is a necessary part of
the human journey in unpacking the mysteries of the universe, I admit
that, at any moment, crucial information could be updated in our research
databases across the world that uproots all we think we know about a
topic today, replacing it with better science tomorrow. But all we can do
as finite humans is work with the knowledge we have now, so I write with
that in mind, respecting sciences that have been deemed empirical for the
moment.

But, to address the fattest elephant in the room right away so most
Christian readers can breathe a sigh of relief and hopefully lower any
defensive walls they've raised in anticipation of my potentially stripping
God of His creative role in the universe, let me also say this: In no way
does this book endorse the platform of evolution that proposes anything
in the cosmos came about randomly, by accident, by coincidence, or from
any other approach that renders us all a result of a glorified cosmic sneeze
or merely the fortuitous side effect of primordial soup. Nor does this book
rest on a Deist (or equivalent) position that views God as having wound
the clock and sat back to watch it tick on its own.

This planet and every living thing on it found their origin in a loving
Father who has a precise purpose for each of His creations. If not even
a sparrow can fall to the ground that He doesn't know about (Matthew
10:29–31)—and if even the lilies of the field that seem inconsequential
are so important to God that He has gone out of His way to dress them
in beauty rivalling even that of Solomon's royal splendor (Matthew 6:28–
29)—then we know God is aware of, and involved in, the formation of,
and plan for, all creatures great and small.

Chuck Missler, one of SkyWatch Television and Defender Publishing's
dearest friends who has now gone to be with the Lord, was an astounding
philosopher, theologian, and quantum physicist. Before he passed on, he

released a twenty-four-session video collection (each session is about an hour and a half long). It's probably the most exhaustive and detailed study of Creation I've seen. Missler's brilliance and understanding of the metaphysics of the universe are so overwhelmingly above the average study of Mosaic Hebrew that if *he* says something definitive on God's handiwork—and proves his theories with mathematics and science—then it's worth having a look at.

I'm going to use an example from his teachings now, but I want to warn the reader first that this following sneak peek at Missler's presentations is *not* how the rest of the book will read! Bear with me to get the gist of this example, and everything that follows will make use of more common language. (And I promise I won't keep talking about math!)

In only his fourth video of the twenty-four, Missler starts with a clever, intentional deception to illustrate a concept.[1] Without telling his audience that he's performing an object lesson, he approaches the microphone wearing a long string of black and white wooden beads. Some of the beads are short and round, while others are long, resembling bone beads common in tribal jewelry. Taking them off and holding them up for all to see, he then says he was messing around with beads one day when he accidentally dropped them to the floor. He picked them up and strung them "randomly" on a string to store them. Then, he got to looking at the beads and realized they miraculously spelled out Genesis 1:1 in Morse code, "all by absolute, random chance." In the audio, somewhere off-camera, one or two people sound like they're sold on the story, as I can hear the faintest murmuring of discussion about the details. The rest of the audience, however, is not fooled, and a few tentative chuckles bubble up. "Why are you laughing?" Missler asks. And, of course, this question spurs another wave of laughter. He continues:

> You know, it's interesting, you haven't done the math, but you know, just from your gut, that this is not possible for three hundred and forty-seven beads to arrive in exactly that order that would represent that kind of *intelligence*.… Could this have occurred by random chance? Well, let's analyze that a little bit.

There are three hundred and forty-seven beads here, and they are either black or white, so there's an "alphabet" of *two*, right? So, the chance of any particular sequence…emerging happens to be two [letters], raised to the three-hundred-and-forty-seventh [bead] power.

[On his slide, he shows this equation as: "$P_{random\ chance} = 2^{-347} = 2.8869 \times 10^{-104}$."] That's roughly equivalent of ten with a hundred and four zeroes after it. Now, that's a big number. It's probably bigger than anyone in this room, including me, can imagine…. You see, any number [that is] more than ten with *fifty* zeroes after it is defined in physics as "absurd" [in the calculations of probability that something happened by coincidence].[2]

Yet, as Missler goes on to point out, a random-happenstance story like his tale about beads is far more acceptable and likely than random evolution could ever be: "This is just a simple string of three hundred and forty-seven elements," he says. "You wouldn't allow me to try to sell your kids [on the idea] that this happened by accident, but you send them to school, where they teach them that *we* happened from an accident. You and I came from a rock."[3] The audience laughs again, contemplating the absurdity of the implied math. Then, he nails his point:

In your blood, you have a thing called a "hemoglobin," right? Hemoglobin happens to consist of *five hundred and seventy-four* elements, not from an alphabet of *two* but [from] an alphabet of *twenty*. [He goes on to show on a slide the twenty amino acids involved in the hemoglobin sequence, and explains that they have to appear in a very specific order.] If you don't get the specific order, it's called "hemoglobinopathy." It's usually fatal. [In other words, humanity would never have existed in the first place if this sequence wasn't perfect; we would have died out with the first humans subjected to almost-certain death caused by blood disease.] The formula for these linear arrangements [in the hemoglobin]…comes out to ten with *six hundred and fifty zeroes* after it!…

What's the likeliness that [the] hemoglobin happens by accident? That's really, *really* absurd, okay?[4]

The "formula for linear arrangements" computation on the slide looks like this: $N=n!/(p! \times q! \times r! \ldots)$. This leads to 10^{650} possible "permutations" in the formation of this single human trait.

(That's complicated mathematics I don't expect all readers to understand. I sure can't follow it; but I do get the point he's making.)

This equation is such an unbelievably high number that the hemoglobin alone argues for Intelligent Design, and that is supported by the timeline:

The possibility of *chance*, now—you need to understand some of these numbers. If you assume the world has been around for eighteen billion years, as many scientists do, that's only ten to the eighteenth [10 with18 zeroes following it] seconds. If you take the entire history of the universe as conceived by the astronomers— call it sixteen, eighteen billion, whatever—that's only about ten to the eighteenth *seconds* in the history of the universe. That is a *biiiiig* number! [With the hemoglobin, we're] talking ten to the six hundred fifty [10^{650}]? You gotta be kidding![5]

In other words, it's a mathematical impossibility that our hemoglobin, with a "random chance" of 10^{650}, could have developed in 10^{18} seconds in the model of evolutionary science's history of the universe since the Big Bang. There simply aren't enough seconds in the millions of years evolution demands for this to have randomly developed—and, as Missler said, this is math that even physicists of all fields agree is absurd, and therefore impossible.

As I indicated, ten to the fiftieth [10^{50}] is "absurd" [to scientists, physicists, and mathematicians in coincidence-probability equations], and the specificity of the hemoglobin is *far beyond* any *rational* comprehension of it being ascribed to "chance." [Missler uses "winning the Idaho lottery" as an example:] I understand the odds are about one in eighty million to win. What's your chances of winning it every day for ninety days in a row?[6]

In case you missed it: According to Missler, winning the lottery ninety days straight—with each win being subject to one chance in eighty million—is the same likelihood required to equal the odds of the hemoglobin occurring by itself, on accident, by chance, or randomly, etc. With this same math in mind, he goes on to discuss other parts of the human body, and the calculations are just as unbelievable. He likewise proves his point by showing code-cracking probabilities in relation to the "code" intrinsic to the human body, the nucleus, electrons, cells, plasma membranes, equilibrium, proteins, atoms, amino acids, gravity and similar laws of nature, and other variables of our earthly reality.

In the sixth session, he uses his wristwatch to illustrate even more concepts kids are being taught in public schools—none of which are mathematically or scientifically possible. The watch is a complicated mechanism, yet even the most impressive one in the world is *rudimentary* when compared to the wrist it's strapped onto. He follows this example by bringing up the invention of a camera, showing that it, too, is quite simple when compared to the human eye. He goes on to discuss what we know of complex system assemblies (cars, for example) that require all subsystems within them to be functional for the whole system's survival: If one part of a car's engine is not operating, the whole vehicle rapidly breaks down. A mechanic is needed to fix it. The human body, however—when its various healing processes and overall functions are analyzed—can be compared to self-modifying, self-programming, self-diagnosing, and self-repairing machines!

Human scientific study and invention, for all of its incredible achievements, has never been able to design a computer or machine that can come close to this performance.

To illustrate the magnificence of the human body's ability to self-replicate its DNA (deoxyribonucleic acid that replicates and stores genetic data inside our cells that essentially makes us who we are), Missler instructs all members of his audience to give him two strands of fishing line, each 125 miles long, shove it through an opening in the side of a basketball, then "unzip it, copy it, and put it back in at three times the speed of an airplane propeller without tangling."[7] In addition, every cell on Earth has derived from another living cell, and no one has ever been able to answer how all cells required for life on Earth could have popped into full function at the same time in order for life to evolve.

Which came first, proteins or DNA? One can't exist without the other, so they had to have been created at the same time.

Of course, scientists theorize that RNA (ribonucleic acid, similar to DNA but instead of replicating and storing genetic information, it converts the DNA data to protein material) was the first "builder" in the sequence, but for as many explanations that surface behind this theory, more questions arise showing it to be impossible *once all relevant details are brought into the picture.* And that's the problem: Scientists claiming to have the answer nearly always share a part of, but not the whole, picture. It's a proof-texting-style loop that will never end, unless scientists do the unthinkable and admit we simply don't know. And just about the time it finally starts to sound believable for *humans*, the whole discussion of evolution starts over when applied to animals.

Missler uses the examples of dolphins, woodpeckers, beetles, giraffes, and several other species of life in the animal/bug kingdom to show that life couldn't have carried on past the first day or week if evolution was the sole source of engineering. For instance, as Missler discusses in the seventh session: The giraffe's long neck is handy for reaching high branches for food, but what about getting water? Its heart is two and a half feet long. Bending down for water would cause an embolism (when the blood vessels burst in the brain) if it weren't for the creature's unique circulatory system, including sponge-like vessels designed to act like a blood-brain reservoir. If the giraffe suddenly raised its head without this type of circulatory system, it would pass out from lack of blood to the brain. If any of the many moving parts in this area of the animal's biology were out of place for even a day, the whole system would fail and the giraffe would fall dead, never surviving long enough to pass its genetics down to its offspring. Again, all parts had to be in full working order at once for the giraffe to even exist in its current form. Yet, we are taught to believe that, somehow, evolution was able to anticipate this long-neck lifestyle in advance and order the development of the whole system over millions or billions of years without the extinction of the giraffe species.

And don't get Missler started on Darwinism. In session seven, he goes down a list of findings that "support" Charles Darwin's monkey-man hypothesis and he shows slides demonstrating that many weren't at all what they were claimed to be. For example: The Heidelberg Man discovery of 1907 was only a jawbone, proving nothing on its own; the Nebraska Man finding of 1922 was a single tooth, which scientists proclaimed at the time to be of the earlier *Homo sapiens* family, but was later discovered to be a pig's tooth; the jawbone of a modern-era ape was the fraudulent platform upon which a "scientist" named Charles Dawson deliberately filed down, treated with salts to increase the appearance of age, and built the monkey-man link called the Piltdown Man in 1912 (his dishonesty was proven in 1953); all evidence of the 1921 Peking Man completely disappeared when questions of its authenticity arose, proving, well, *nothing*; the Neanderthal Man found in the Neander Valley near Dusseldorf, Germany, was proven by the International Congress of Zoology to be the bones of an elderly man with arthritis in 1958; the Java Man remains found in 1922 were a skull cap, femur bone, and teeth, which were kept away from peer-reviewed study until the demand for analysis could no longer be ignored, and aside from the fact that the teeth were eventually determined to originate from an orangutan, the skull cap and femur bone alone showed no evidence of Darwinian evolution.

"The main point," Missler says, "is that, in a hundred and twenty years of searching, no intermediate stages [of man] have been found [to support Darwinian evolution]. The missing link has been a fool's errand."[8]

It's no joke: Our children are being taught only the part of the picture secular educators want to emphasize; they are *not* learning about the probability calculations of Intelligent Design, even though that requires less faith and imagination to conceive.

Though Missler didn't say it outright, I will: It takes far more faith to believe in random evolution than it does to believe in Intelligent Design.

We won't go through the rest of Missler's presentation on this study, as the point has been made: The idea of the natural evolution of humans without the involvement of an intelligent Creator is rubbish. Even if we could argue our way around the miniscule possibility that we *did* develop as a result of the Big Bang billions of years ago, there simply wasn't enough time from the Bang to today for that kind of evolution to take form.

Therefore, this book will not be a study on the sciences of evolution and how they interact with theology.

In fact, though I will discuss science in a few areas (like chapter 4), nothing about this book should be considered anything close to a science manual or a companion to one. I share this brief input from Chuck Missler to illustrate how human-guided, scientific pursuits are flawed— science can be demonstrated, but even the most reliable demonstrations are not the whole picture. I do believe Earth is very, *very* old, but I also believe it has always been under the guiding hand of God: nothing random about it.

Though there are many cosmological views, only *two* ever get any real attention: naturalistic evolution (the Big Bang theory, Darwinism, etc.), and Creationism (God as the Intelligent Designer of the Earth and all its inhabitants). Some popular approaches to cosmology, such as Theistic Evolution, may appear at first glance to be in their own category, but they fall under these two "parent" terms in some way or other, as we will cover at the end of this chapter.

Historically, it has been largely implied (if not directly stated) that the first of these categories is the scientific view, while the second is the theological view. It is assumed by both religious and irreligious folks that these two views *cannot* agree, no matter how we approach the subject, because each cancels out the other: If God created the world, as stated in Genesis, then science is tossed in the wastebasket because it disregards God's eminent role in our planet's existence. The opposite is also true: If our planet came about naturally and on its own, then the whole portrait of Creationism is put to the fire because God is not needed and, by extension, faith in Him as God is questionable or useless. Meanwhile, a barrier is raised, leaving no room for compromise between the two groups: Generally, Christians think followers of science lack faith, while followers of science think Christians are religious fanatics who won't let go of their pet theologies even in the face of true, demonstrable science. Either way, there appears to be a giant "DO NOT CROSS!" line on each side—a "pick what side you're on, but don't ride the fence" position—prohibiting any imaginative mind from blending aspects of the two views into one that reasonably acknowledges elements of truth in *both*. This is a travesty that causes undue division, as the harmony between God and science is not at all hard to find, despite that many have been groomed by modern society to think otherwise.

Most of today's Church is unaware that many potential cosmological explanations do consider God and science together, and in a way that doesn't compromise the scriptural record. The number of scientific theories that are compatible with Creationism is overwhelming; that's not even a shock to those who know what the Bible truly says on the topic and who stay up to date on advancing research in the origins of Earth. But, within the Church, the deficit of knowledge regarding this very compatibility—and in many cases, the staunch refusal to even give ear to any possibility outside the mainstream rendering of Genesis, because to do so would be an affront to God—has made it difficult for believers across the globe to reach those who can't bring themselves to believe in God while "science has all the answers" (a view that's not always reliable but should be addressed with compassion and an open mind).

For some readers, due to the celebrated theories of Charles Darwin (and the near-universal acceptance of his teachings in most schools and universities in many recent decades), potential unity between science and Creationism forces the notion that God used science to gradually develop Adam from a long line of chimpanzees or some similar ape species over millions or billions of years. Right away, we can see how the "ape Adam" hypothesis conflicts with the Creation account in Genesis, which describes God forming Adam from the dust of the ground. "Adam was *not* a monkey!" preachers rail from the pulpit. "Evolution is absurd! Unfaithful! It denies God's handiwork!"

But not all scientific theories related to humanity and Earth's origins rest on Darwin's dated speculations. For example: There is a crucial difference between microevolution and macroevolution, despite the similarity in spelling: Microevolution (with an *i* as the second letter) describes improvements, changes, or natural selection within a species over time based on their biological needs (as one example). Macroevolution (with an *a* as the second letter) describes one species literally *becoming* another over time (such as the "man from monkeys" theme).

Some species of birds that have migrated and settled in colder climates have, over years, produced larger and larger offspring that are more resistant to inclement weather. If we were to study one of these species in a lab, we would determine that the creature is still a *bird* (not a lion or dog or anything else), but that its very biology has changed to adapt to new environments throughout generations of breeding. This is microevolution, and it's not merely a theoretical possibility, it's a scientific reality that is consistently evident in the animal kingdom. In contrast, macroevolution identifies the possibility that a bird species, over billions of years, develops traits from other species it doesn't share DNA with, crossing over and *becoming* something different and new. (I'm not suggesting that any scientist or lab has ever claimed a bird could become a lion or dog. This example is intentionally absurd to help readers get the gist of what's being explained.)

More often than not, even Christians who believe in a literal rendering of Genesis acknowledge the possibility that the human body has evolved through microevolution since the time of Adam. Yet a man is still human, sharing basic traits of the human race with everyone else: two eyes, two ears, two arms, two legs, eight fingers, two thumbs, ten toes, and a belly button that proves he, too, was connected to a human female at the time of birth through an umbilical cord like the rest of us. That is true even if, say, a colder climate has altered a man's biology in some minor way to ensure his survival in a given region. Even though we cannot see under the skin, we are aware that similarities dominate in this area as well: one stomach (not four or more like cows and other animals); regular digestive fluids (not the hot, corrosive liquid that explodes forth from the

Bombardier beetle); one brain (not nine like the octopus), and so on. A Samoan male is likely to be far larger and taller than a Bolivian male who, on average, stands around a foot shorter. Both of these men are obviously human, while microevolution (and a family tree, of course) has played a part in modifying the way their bodies respond to the environment. We don't have to believe either of these men came from monkeys in order to observe *a type* of evolutionary activity within their DNA that makes them different from each other. Our very own power of sight attests to micro-evolution every day, and it's not a shock.

When Christians say, "I don't believe in evolution," those outside the Church who are knowledgeable of such differentiations in science are tempted to ask, "Which branch of evolution are you referring to?" Christians therefore remain unequipped to engage in the debate from a learned position, showing their hand of cards to be deficient from the beginning of the conversation. We have so distanced ourselves so far from having anything to do with "that other, faithless cosmological explanation" that, to the world, we've crawled into the cave of irrelevance. We celebrate our separatist seclusion, pat ourselves on the back, and believe we're being the faithful Body of Christ, meeting every Sunday to congratulate ourselves on being the enlightened ones who reject "that ridiculous monkey idea" (for example), while in reality, *we* are the ones who lack enlightenment when we believe science (and its many related fields of study) represents any kind of threat to God and faith. Keep the following statement in mind as you read through this book:

Willful ignorance is spiritual negligence.

Why? Because, in order to reach the lost, we need to know *how* to reach them. As long as we refuse to engage in conversation about how science and faith *can* merge, we remain disconnected from the very souls we're called to minister to. In the meantime, we continue to argue without knowing the facts, which leads to defending an incomplete and weak position, making us only look more uneducated and foolish when we're confronted with the world's developing sciences.

Microevolution is simply an easy example to build my case upon, as it obviously blends just fine with theology. But are there other areas of the science-vs.-theology battle that can go together just as harmoniously? If so, how far do they go? Can the Word of God finally have as much relevance to the world as the laboratory? And is it possible that God-fearing Christians can at least *appreciate* (note that I didn't say "blindly accept") what labs demonstrate to be true, choosing to praise God for *His* science instead of ironically rejecting a part of His creativity through resistance to it?

And most importantly: Is there, perhaps, an explanation about the origins of our planet that can also identify with and unite *both* Young and Old Earth interpretations of Genesis, while also allowing scientists to have a voice?

Whoa. What? How can Earth be old and young at the same time?

Well, that's not quite what I said, is it? I said the two interpretations of Genesis can merge. And they do, in my theory, while also respecting our developing science and those who study it.

I know that's asking a lot, and it certainly sounds impossible this early on, but when you read the coming pages, I believe you'll see that this is more than just a possibility or mere speculation, though it may not be the Sunday school lesson you've heard before.

This is all well and good, Donna, but what does this really have to do with Jesus? Isn't the Gospel all about Him? Shouldn't we be focusing on the testimony of Christ first and foremost, instead of entertaining the possibility of a merger between theology and science's answer to the great cosmological question about the age of the Earth?

Believe me, preparation in this area is a *powerful* tool for evangelism.

Learning from Galileo: Yesterday's Silenced Heretic; Today's Celebrated Genius

Don't forget, folks, what happened to Italian scientist and devout Roman Catholic Galileo Galilei (1564–1642) when he, too, challenged mainstream biblical interpretation in that age-old debate about what stood at the center of the universe: Earth or the sun.

Galileo's telescopes and research gave nearly irrefutable evidence in his day that it was not Earth standing still in the middle while other space objects rotated around *it* (the geocentric model), but that the planets, including Earth, were rotating around the *sun*, located in the center (the heliocentric model). Despite the fact that countless astronomers had adhered to the heliocentric model since at least the time of Copernicus (1473–1543), geocentrism was the leading Christian belief at that time. Many wise, talented, and learned men in Christendom (including Martin Luther and John Calvin) railed against Galileo, firmly asserting that heliocentrism went against what the Bible says. (In the coming pages, you're going to notice a pattern. The Bible doesn't say, "Earth is in the center and the sun rotates around it," or anything of the sort, but to the closed minds of yesterday, that was "what the Bible says." To almost all Young Earthers, "The Bible, itself, says Earth is a young planet," even though that direct statement cannot be found anywhere in Scripture.)

Some verses, such as Psalm 93:1b, when interpreted literally, do appear to suggest that Earth is not in motion: "the world also is stablished, that it cannot be moved." Galileo, for his "heresy" against the integrity of the Word of God in such places, was brought to Rome to stand trial before the Catholic Church hierarchy in April of 1633. The judgment banned him from ever teaching his astronomic discoveries again, prohibited distribution of all his written work on the subject up to that point, and landed him under a lifelong house arrest following a forced recantation of his work regarding space objects. (Actually, had this trial gone down the way it did for some of our Christian heroes of the Middle Ages, Galileo could have easily been another martyr of the Inquisition, so the house arrest, as harsh a punishment as it sounds for merely attempting to bring scientific knowledge to the world, is mild for this era.)

Today, the majority of Christians aren't in the least bit bothered by believing that Earth rotates around the sun (not the other way around) and that verses like Psalm 93:1 are a metaphor of God's provisionary protection over His people. In part, this is because refusing to allow this interpretation causes at least one major contradiction: Revelation also prophesies about the complete destruction of our planet (and its subsequent replacement with the New Earth). So, if we interpret both Revelation and Psalms literally, we're met with the challenge of explaining how a planet that "cannot be moved" (Psalm 93:1) also completely "passes away" (Revelation 6:14; 20:11; 21:1; Matthew 24:35). (There are many more biblical contradictions than what are listed here that would result from forcing geocentrism.)

Three hundred years passed before Galileo's discoveries would be well accepted in Church circles and allowed to be considered alongside theological pursuits. Yet, when they finally were, far from *harming* the integrity of Word of God, the opposite happened: Allowing heliocentrism to challenge our then-current models of literal interpretation actually led to a more cohesive, noncontradictory reading of Scripture!

As an important note, something else also happened: Science and Scripture *merged*, each allowing for the other to be true. Don't miss this: Neither was threatened by the other; this appealed to people who wanted to believe in God but couldn't at the time because "the Bible says Earth is at the center of the universe." In the end, God was glorified—not for being the One who created an unmovable planet as Luther, Calvin, and others thought, but for being the Author of the Word that does *not* defy what is confirmed through science, math, and the observation of God's own universe.

So…let's visit a hypothetical situation. *If* Genesis allows for an Old Earth, will it take another three hundred years for the Church to accept that reality and apply it to their mainstream interpretations? Or will we, like in Galileo's time, label as heretics anyone who doesn't agree with mainstream interpretations because their conclusions make us uncomfortable?

Perhaps we should answer this question with another: What is our ultimate goal in every interpretational quest into the Word of God? Comfort in keeping traditions? Or *truth*? If we hold tradition above God and His absolute truth, then our motive is wrong, and we aren't really serving Him as we should (Mark 7:7–9, 13). If truth is the goal, then whatever we discover to be true will point to the God of Truth anyway, so where is the threat?

Though we must always, as Bible-believing saints, put what the Bible says ahead of what science says, we should *never*, as Bible-believing saints, put what *we think* the Bible says ahead of what it actually does say. When human understanding blocks or hides what could be the real meaning of Scripture, we've alienated those who may have come to know God and Christ through the genuine meaning of that passage...*and* we've committed a grave sin by "adding to" or "taking away from" what the Bible says, which is, in no uncertain terms, prohibited by the Author of Scripture (Deuteronomy 4:2; 12:32; Revelation 22:18–19; Proverbs 30:6). But when we forego the traditions of men and allow the God of science to relate to the humanity He created through the revelation of what He said in the original Hebrew and Greek—*no more and no less*—we see people come to God.

For many, the "come to God" moment begins—and sometimes, sadly, ends—with the age-of-Earth debate.

That Day at Lucky's

I'll never forget this moment—and many others like it—as long as I live. Experiences like these have been common throughout my entire life, and it is conversations like these that raise a wall between Christians and the rest of the world.

About three years ago, I was shopping at Lucky's Natural Foods supermarket in Springfield, Missouri, for probably the hundredth time since it had opened the year prior. We had just made the wise yet complicated shift from harmful, over-the-counter pharmaceuticals and vitamins to natural supplements for treating most of our family's health needs.

Daniel Belt, a head manager of that branch's supplements department, was sharing his insight regarding my daughter's "mystery cough." (This is what we termed the spasmodic coughing episodes she has suffered since birth. Doctors have never found a cause behind—or a *cure* for—this cough. When risky correctional surgeries were beginning to surface as the only answer offered by Western medicine, my husband and I knew we had to go another route, and Daniel was proving more knowledgeable about the topic than any practitioner we had seen yet.)

We were *not* discussing spiritual beliefs; though, as a child of God and a follower of Christ, I try to remain open to that topic any time the opportunity presents itself organically. In this case, it did.

"I'd love to treat the unknown cause with plants from God's earth," I said, "as opposed to continuing with these meds that don't work anyway."

"Funny thing about God's earth," Daniel responded with a smile, "it's been the answer since the beginning of time for many maladies. Pharmaceuticals have their place and time in the world of healthcare, but they shouldn't be the first go-to for everything like they have been when God *clearly* provided what we need, directly from the soil, to sustain optimal health in most cases."

I was touched to learn that this vitamin and supplement expert I barely knew at the time was—if I understood him correctly—willing to acknowledge the Creator of the universe as the Great Provider of human health. I couldn't help but comment.

"I guess God knew what He was doing, eh?"

"Oh, for sure!" Daniel said, showing an excitement to the shift in conversation. "In fact, it was my journey to optimal health that restored my faith in God. Deep studies into the earth and all it offers to humankind points to a Great Intelligence behind the formation of *natural* medicine, which doesn't have harmful side effects like many lab-created medicines that are marketed to treat the same conditions or sicknesses."

A metallic rattle clinked in the air between us as I tossed six or seven bottles of Daniel's recommendation into the empty cart while I considered how to respond. I was dying to take the discussion further, but I was aware that he was on the clock and I was merely a customer. He had other responsibilities and people to tend to, yet I couldn't help but wonder if his beliefs stemmed from Christian conviction, specifically, or if he perhaps belonged to another religion that allowed for an alternative position on Intelligent Design. Was the Holy Bible his personal spiritual authority? Or something/someone else? Either way, I would always show him respect, but I also reserve the right to do my own inner happy dance when I meet a fellow believer.

I decided to break the ice in this area.

"I agree completely," I said. "I'm working toward a master's degree in theology, and I've studied apologetics and science. Once you see how science and God mesh together, you can't 'unsee' it!"

Had I just touched a nerve?

Daniel broke eye contact and glanced to the floor, clearly contemplating something I perceived from his countenance to be potentially awkward. Yet he and I had already had many conversations that, for some folks, could have become awkward (all related to my own transition to the holistic lifestyle we appreciate now), yet never did. Daniel always held a gentle peace and a trainload of respect in his dealings with others that gave me confidence to open the Pandora's box of the subject of religion without fear of offending him. Needless to say, however, religion and natural supplements are different animals, and it was clear by his hesitation that he was forming a response that, in turn, would not offend *me*.

"Sorry," I said quickly to fill the dead space. "I didn't mean to bring up a touchy subject."

"Not at all." His eyebrows raised in earnest as he shook his head in reassurance.

"I mean, we were talking about my daughter's cough and suddenly I threw religion into it. That was kind of a dumb move."

"No, not at all. Uh…" Daniel proceeded cautiously. "The thing is…" Again, he hesitated.

Daniel had always been one of the most articulate people I'd ever had the pleasure of listening to. His input or answers to health questions were without deviation, quick, confident, and well thought out. Every time. Now, suddenly, I had walloped him with a doozy (or at least that's the fear I had at the moment) and he appeared to be calculating how to structure his reply carefully. Inside, I was praying God would forgive me if I had spoken out of turn, that He would help me find the words to say to avoid further injury in the exchange so my talks with Daniel about vitamins (or God?) wouldn't be hampered in the future. After all, Daniel was rapidly becoming a close family friend and we looked forward to seeing him every Sunday after church during our weekly grocery trips. On this particular stop, my husband and kids were shopping in another aisle. If ever I needed my husband's typical, soft rescue from the "word vomit" I've been known to spew at the wrong times, this was it…but alas, he was unavailable, so I had to try to fix this mess on my own—if, in fact, it was a mess I had created.

"The thing is," Daniel tried again, "Planet Earth is very, *very* old," he offered.

Ahhh…so *that* was it. Whew. Crisis averted. This wasn't going to be a problem after all.

Some readers may wonder where Daniel's comment came from. There we were, dipping into the pool of religious thought, about to launch into whether he believes in God and if Jesus fits into that scenario, then, seemingly out of the wild blue, Daniel says the world is old.

Why? What did that have to do with anything?

The answer to that question—at least as postulated by the modern world and Western culture—is: everything. It has *everything* to do with it. Read on…

My furrowed brow relaxed and I smiled with a nod to set Daniel's mind at rest. Not only was I not at all offended by his statement, I wasn't in the least bit shocked. I had been there many times. I breathed a sigh of relief. For all he knew, I had been getting ready to balk at his "bold assertion" that the world wasn't, as many conservative Evangelicals believe, a mere thousands of years old. I don't typically interrupt people, but I knew I should this time. If he only knew what I was thinking, his respectful apprehension could die on the vine and spare both of us from further concern. Daniel was about to learn we had something in common besides a passion for natural supplements.

"Oh, absolutely," I said with heavy emphasis. "I believe this world is *very* old, and it's a known point of contention between many Christians and non-Christians who spend a great deal of energy defending their positions when, tragically, they don't need to allow the conversation to be the faith deal-breaker it often is."

Daniel was visibly relieved, and we continued a few minutes of casual banter as we wrapped up our conversation about religion.

I'm endlessly grateful that this supermarket moment ended in the peaceful way it did, but, if we're being honest, that's not the typical happy ending, is it? Much to the contrary, these age-of-Earth debates often end in dramatic divisions. As it stands in many Christian groups, we must either choose science *or* God; it's never an option to choose science *and* God. Did He not create the entire universe and the starting points for all the scientific pursuits within it?

There is an understandable reason someone like Daniel would tread carefully in a conversation like that: A majority of Evangelicals adopt the Young Earth interpretation of Scripture and appear to hold as tight a grip upon it as they do their fundamental doctrines of Christ's humanity! Anyone who challenges the Young Earth theory is, as I've heard several times, "going against what the Bible says." The foundation of their faith appears to hang perpetually on what they understand to be the *only* explanation of Creationism. For, if we accept any scientific explanation regarding the great, cosmological question about the origins of the universe, then we must reject God as Creator in the process…because, of course, every Old Earth theory automatically means mankind came from monkeys, which goes against the Creation epic outlined in Genesis 1, right?

Not exactly…

And though I chose that day at Lucky's as my testimony in this case (mostly because it *did* have a happy ending), I've had this same encounter many times; it's a frequent déjà vu experience for me anymore. Usually, it plays out something like this (though this scenario is grossly oversimplified):

"Do you believe in God?"

"No. Are you kidding? Who can believe in God as the Creator of the universe when the Bible itself says that planet Earth is only several thousands of years old?"

"Well, it *could* be that young, and there is evidence that is pretty convincing, but the Bible doesn't actually say that, for the record."

"How do you figure? Every Christian I've ever met has claimed this is the very teaching of Scripture."

For those who are open-minded enough to hear my research and theories, a door to speak about Christ is thrown ajar, *making the cosmological debate the very tool we can use to help people come to know the Savior.* If they can believe God had a hand in the formation of the universe *and* trust the science on the matter, a major point of contention between science and faith is resolved—sometimes in only one conversation (as has been the case for me before)!

Follow this logic: a) If Creationism is true, then God is real, *but* b) if Creationism forces the belief in a Young Earth, then our current science is largely false—a conclusion that appears absurd to many and that makes God, also, appear absurd. The age of Earth, for these millions of people, becomes the very litmus test of whether a person can believe anything else the Bible says. And, if science and faith can merge—getting cosmology and science out of the way for the skeptic listener who would doubt God on that basis, alone—only *faith* remains in the conversation as the focus.

Suddenly, Jesus gets important, *fast*, as He is the answer to every faith-related question from the first human forward to today.

So, you see? For many, the age of planet Earth has *everything* to do with whether they would or would not come to belief in God…and the ability and willingness one has to engage in this conversation with an open mind and knowledge of different sides of the argument is actually a direct tool for evangelism!

Herein lies the crux of this book. Whereas I hope not to offend the seemingly countless numbers of Jesus followers who believe in a Young Earth, I have no choice but to be bold—as Daniel was—and say, "The thing is…Earth is very, *very* old," while following up that claim with an alternative explanation. This is something I must do, despite knowing some will oppose it, because I believe many folks who are currently on the fence about their faith can and will be strengthened by knowing that they don't have to disregard the laboratory's current and future explanations about our planet in order to accept God. By doing this, I am attempting to "gain the more" for Christ, as Paul did in his day (1 Corinthians 9:19).

The other thing is that the evidence does not—*nor will it ever*—refute Intelligent Design and the Creator we've grown to love for the world He's made. He is *the* Master Scientist of the universe. Nothing can strip Him of that title, so approaching the subject of God with science in mind is not a surprise to Him, and it certainly *is not an affront to Him or to faith in general,* as it only gives Him proper credit to begin with. God does not need Christians to "help His case" by silencing the scientific community's proud discoveries and developments.

Keep in mind, with all the beautiful and glorious truths the Bible does share, it happens to be completely silent about Earth's age.

Then why do so many Church teachings claim the world is young or that the Bible, itself, says so?

In scholarly circles, it's called "Ussher Chronology," and it's only *one* way to interpret the Good Book.

Earlier in this chapter (specifically titled for *two* views), I maintained that Naturalistic Evolution and Creationism are the only two "parent" categories of approaching the topic of cosmology and the age of Earth. I hold that most, if not all, other views fall under these, and it's my goal within this book to merge the two views into one.

However, one important caveat must be addressed first that affects every one of the following worldviews.

Blurring the Line between Science and Philosophy: A Critical Error

The statement, "Nature is the only cause behind existence," is not scientific, it's *philosophical.* Nothing is wrong with engaging in philosophy, so long as we remember never to cross the fine line between a) studying the sciences and appreciating what those pursuits show, and b) concluding that science "proves" nature to be the only cause behind everything that exists. Science can show God's handiwork, but it cannot disprove His existence. The minute that line is blurred, we've crossed over from science (demonstrable facts) into philosophy (seeking wisdom about the world and its people). The highly praised scientific model is based only on observation and empirical verification; true science proves and disproves hypotheses regarding the natural order when it is allowed to be tested properly, but suggesting there is no God because of what appears under a microscope, in a petri dish, or within a mathematical calculation cannot be proven and, therefore, is not considered true science. Thus, cosmology—though many scientific branches of study and research stem *from it*—is not inherently a field of science, because until we develop a time machine and travel back to the first moment anything in the universe existed, none of the many origin-of-the-universe theories can be tested against empirical verification, let alone subjected to peer review!

Nevertheless, folks in the fields of cosmological science often do blur this line, making "proof" statements with conviction, showing that a particle over here or a bit of matter over there makes nature our only god and creator. For believers constantly bombarded with "proof that God does not exist" (as I have been many times), remember: Science can be helpful in illustrating what we can see and test in laboratories, but the minute its findings are used to join the debate about "proofs" regarding a Spirit who has been invisible from the beginning (John 1:18) and who is uncontainable within any human-conducted testing facility or mathematical models, we've stopped talking about science completely and moved into the realm of philosophy. Faith is believing in what we hope for, whether we can see it or not, including planet Earth, which was "framed by the word of God" (Hebrews 11:1–3). Science is a different animal altogether. So, regardless of what progressive discoveries and advances ever spring from human research, we have the right to stand firm in our beliefs and philosophies about the untestable, unconfinable, invisible God.

Yet, before we assume that faith is *only* defined by belief in what we cannot see or prove, consider the integrity of the Message God has given us.

The Alternative to Biblical Faith: It's Still "Faith"

The Bible was documented over the course of approximately fifteen centuries and written by about forty authors who ranged from poor and uneducated men to wealthy kings of nations and everything in between: physicians, lawyers, shepherds, fishermen, tax collectors, prophets, priests, and at least one now-famous tentmaker. Not only were almost all the biblical writers strangers to each other, their varying backgrounds and life experiences prepared them to approach God from completely different angles...yet there are no contradictions within the whole of Scripture.

How is that possible?

Some skeptics of the Word nonchalantly claim inconsistencies or contradictions do exist, but they usually make those claims without responsibly considering the primary Hebrew or Greek languages and context. (Actually, and quite tragically, "inconsistencies" and "contradictions" are often pointed out by those who haven't read the Bible at all and are only reiterating atheistic views shared by friends.) I admit that, in *English* Bibles, some verses do appear to conflict with others. This is an unfortunate side effect of variances in translation...but that is another book for another day.

That said, when correct context is responsibly applied to Scripture by observing what the original author intended to communicate to the first audience and in the first language, we arrive at the *unnatural miracle* of what scholars call the Bible's "internal consistency": one God, immutable and unchanging forever, consistently portrayed in the writings of many men from all over the world who experienced Him differently over the course of a millennium and a half.

But even without having to defend the integrity of the whole Word altogether, let's focus on a more concise example: Mathematicians have calculated that, if Jesus had satisfied only *eight* Old Testament prophecies in His New Testament coming, it would be by "one chance in one hundred million billion" that it occurred outside the realm of divine guidance and intervention.[9] Likewise, "the probability of [Jesus] fulfilling forty-eight prophecies [by coincidence] was one chance in a trillion, trillion, trillion, trillion, trillion, trillion, trillion, trillion, trillion, trillion, trillion, trillion, trillion!"[10] As well-known former Jesus skeptic and *Case for Christ* journalist Lee Strobel attests: "Our minds can't comprehend a number that big. This is a staggering statistic that's equal to the number of minuscule atoms in a trillion, trillion, trillion, trillion, billion universes the size of our universe!"[11] This, for obvious reasons, makes the *365-plus* prophetic utterances of the coming Messiah prior to their fulfillments almost unfathomable to even attempt to calculate (and, by the way, 365 is a conservative number).

Of course, we aren't required to believe the testimony of the Bible, but that doesn't mean we are free from having to put our faith in something unseen and unprovable: Though the Bible cannot be irrefutably proven via empirical data or the scientific method, when it comes to cosmology, science can't, either! The unity of Scripture occurring on its own is so unbelievable that, in my opinion, as stated prior, it takes *more* faith for mature and rational thinkers to believe in the randomness of evolution than it does to believe in Intelligent Design.

In January of 1982, in the *New Scientist Magazine*, powerful insight was posed by Chandra Wickramasinghe, who said: "The chances that life just occurred are about as unlikely as a typhoon blowing through a junkyard and constructing a Boeing-747 [airliner]."[12]

If this "chance that life just occurred" scenario is what some choose to put their faith in, I respect their freedom of choice, and I *do* respect their faith…but it is still—unquestionably and categorically—faith that is required to accept and adhere to this human-drawn conclusion that many for good reason have found implausible. We can remove God from the picture and disassociate scientific creeds from all labels resembling "religion," but one thing doesn't change: Both religion and science, when it comes to the great cosmological debate, *require believing in something we cannot see.*

Until we invent the time machine that can handle the trek back to the beginning of all time, space, and matter, that will always be true.

Let's dig in.

Cosmological Views

Naturalistic Evolution and Creationism—the "two views"—branch into subgroups (which, in some cases, overlap at certain points, such as Old Earth Creationism and Theistic Evolution discussed shortly). For those who may be new to this subject, I will list the major categories briefly and follow each with some logic behind why I support them or don't. (Note that the following list only covers approaches to cosmology that pertain specifically to science or Christianity [not, for instance, the "ongoing cre-ation" views from Hinduism, etc.], since the harmony of both is the focus of this book.)

Secular, Naturalistic Evolution

"In the beginning, there was nothing; then it exploded." This statement, though humorous (and often shared from pulpits as a dig against the secu-lar world), is ultimately what the secular naturalistic evolutionary view proposes. (There is a sort of "Christian Naturalistic Evolution" we will cover in the next few pages, though it goes more accurately by the term "Theistic Evolution.")

This view covers most of what is taught in Western government-spon-sored/funded schooling. It is the idea that all life on this planet and in the universe came about via natural means over a great period of time—no Creator involved.

The most common explanation for this is the Big Bang theory, which, in short, claims all the matter in the universe originated in one hot, dense, concentrated point of energy and light (the Big Bang Singularity) upwards of 13.8 billion years ago, then exploded outward (during an event called "cosmic inflation"), making room for particles, atoms, and gases to form and develop what would eventually become stars, planets, galaxies, and so on. Other theories in this category of natural cause do exist and have some following, such as the Steady State Theory (which holds that the universe is infinite, with no beginning and no end, and that the creation of matter is continuous, steady, and always has been) or the Cyclic/Oscil-lating Model (an endless number of Big Bang-style expansion-explosions that, over time, reverse and collapse inward [an event known as the "Big Crunch"], and then rebuild, creating a perpetual, self-sustaining cycle), to share two examples. However, it's fair to say that, by far, most experts in research fields related to space adhere to some strict form of the Big Bang.

Whether it relies entirely on the Big Bang theory or not on a case-by-case basis, Secular Naturalistic Evolution disregards the involvement of any Intelligent Designer (God), and instead seeks to explain all of matter as occurring on its own from nature. The major problem with this approach is that nobody in the scientific world has ever been able to produce a solid answer for what came first. If the Big Bang was the first event in the known universe, where did that concentrated matter come from? No matter what our digs into subjects of general relativity, energy, physics, inflation, vacuums, gravity, or any other space research pursuits produce, we are always left with the question of what caused each of those things before *they* existed or acted, as well as why the natural laws exist to govern them the way they do. If the origin of the cosmos *can* be traced to one event, who or what caused that event? Who first created, then lit, the proverbial stick of dynamite that exploded into the debris we now know as "space"? Each time science provides an answer, another cosmological-origin question forms.

A few years back, an atheist friend phoned me excitedly saying science had discovered the "God particle" (Higgs boson), explaining the formation of particle mass and, apparently for some, placing our origins singularly back into the hands of nature and debunking God as mere myth. When I asked who put the God particle there and who decided it would function the way it did, there was no answer.

We are living in a moving, changing universe, and nothing can move or change without a force or cause behind it, as well as a preexisting element that adequately required movement or change from where or what it was before. (This is why, in apologetics, God is sometimes referred to as the "First Mover.") Science, itself, attests to this—repeatedly and consistently—yet it cannot explain what the very first moving force was. To put it another way: Nothing can come from purely nothing, exploding into existence by itself, yet that is essentially where the Big Bang (and other secular Naturalistic Evolution theories) ceases to make available any explanation that can be proven or even reliably charted. Something—or Someone—*had* to be at least the initial cause.

Italian priest and theologian Thomas Aquinas (1225–1274) said in his work on the cause-and-effect support of God (otherwise known as the "argument from causation"): "There is no case known…in which a thing is found to be the efficient cause of itself; for so it would be prior to

itself, which is impossible."[13] This is complicated, so follow my modern-
ized rewording: "We do not have a single known case in the history of the
universe or science in which something has caused *itself* to exist, because
that thing, whatever it is, would have had to 'create itself,' which means it
existed before its own creation in order to *execute* its own creation." Mind-
boggling… Yet, by that same logic, tracing all things back to the beginning through a secular lens, we arrive at a point where a vast "nothingness"
had to have created a "somethingness" from within itself, illustrating a
creative self-awareness in the process.

What "nothingness" could be that self-aware? Space dust?

…And we're round-about back where we started: Who put that space
dust there?

To quote yet another theological giant from the Church's past, here is
an excerpt from the celebrated *Mere Christianity* by C. S. Lewis:

> People who take [the secular or materialistic view] think that mat-
> ter and space just happen to exist, and always have existed, nobody
> knows why; and that the matter, behaving in certain fixed ways,
> has just happened, by a sort of fluke, to produce creatures like our-
> selves who are able to think. By one chance in a thousand some-
> thing hit our sun and made it produce the planets; and by another
> thousandth chance the chemicals necessary for life, and the right
> temperature, occurred on one of these planets, and so some of the
> matter on this earth came alive; and then, by a very long series of
> chances, the living creatures developed into things like us.[14]

There is no identifiable "first cause" outside of the One whose innate
eternality transcends (and therefore makes irrelevant) "the starting point"
our human minds get hung up on, and Lewis, as advanced as his thinking
was at the time, is actually wrong. It's not even close to "one chance in a
thousand." If we dig into some of the Chuck Missler-type analyses calculating the probability of chance in the earliest moments of the universe,
we see early on that "one chance in a thousand" is far too conservative a
number to take seriously.

And the unanswerable inquiries don't end with what came first: What is time, exactly, and why does it move forward in an irreversibly linear direction? Whose idea was gravity, and why does it work the way it does? Why are there even planets out in space to begin with? Why aren't planets big, blue blobs of a gelatin-like substance—or something else? Without the planets, would there simply be nothing but blackness, forever, since nothing comes from nothing? And if there are planets farther out than our technology can perceive, do they operate under the same laws of physics as Earth? Why does *any* of this exist? Why are any of us here to begin with? Where do the natural laws come from that all of our known creation submits to (gravity, motion, etc.)?

In order for there to even be sustainable life on Earth, our planet needs to be a certain distance from the sun, with just the right angle of tilt; an exact speed of rotation; precisely the correct ocean depths and weather patterns; magnetic fields that stave off fatal radiation levels; water; carbon; atmospheric insulation…and a countless other contributing factors, any *one* of which could have, with the most microscopic adjustment in its earliest development, corrupted all of life and made Earth an uninhabitable, evolutionary catastrophe. Without these laws, patterns, and fixed positions, all of creation would fall into chaos, but the perfection of these laws couldn't have designed, managed, and ordered themselves into existence (no self-aware space dust could have done it), so who or what established the natural order of the universe?

I could give numerous other examples of unanswerable inquiries, but you get the idea—and, generally speaking, they all lead to the same place: We don't know and we will never know. (This is why science, too, is a matter of faith—both in the conclusion demonstrated *and* in the people who demonstrated it, as they don't always address the evidence stacked against their conclusions.) Meanwhile, our presence here only amounts to a giant question mark, giving us a bleak destiny and pessimistic outlook on what we are and how we should live as long as we're forced to suffer this maddening condition called "life" with all its pain and pointless suffering…

…unless there is a God.

The second God is restored as Creator, things click into place: Life on Earth, humanity, creation, all the governing laws of nature, the mysteries of space, and every other imaginable related subject is under the Great Scientist's management—made by Him and for Him, intelligently and with intrinsic purpose and intent, before the Big Bang or any other theories can even come into play. If we rationally accept Intelligent Design, then there *is* a God out there behind all of this, and that same God has a plan for His creation, including humanity, which gives all of human life a role in the grand design. Suddenly, questions like "Why are we here?" have the beginning of an answer. (The rest of that answer, of course, is the individual's spiritual journey to identify whether that belief leads to the Yahweh of Genesis and, by extension, to Christ. This philosophical trail is not herein shared to prove the God of the Bible as much as it is to challenge the atheistic approach that there is no God at all.) Ironically, the acceptance of the reality of an Intelligent Designer satisfies both the scientific inquiry (how/why we came to be created in the beginning) as well as the emotional, psychological, spiritual, moral, and philosophical explorations that feed the deepest human yearnings (the purpose and meaning of all existence).

However, as the more philosophical teachers of the Word are quick to point out, there is yet another sad side effect of adopting Secular Naturalistic Evolution: lawlessness.

If everything that exists is no more than the result of a cosmic accident, then there is no real accountability to any entity higher than ourselves. Every crime, from theft to rape to murder and beyond, is only a "crime" if humankind deems it so. But the moment that one person disagrees with another about what is lawful, the only true authority that can weigh in and side with either one is a judicial system built by other *people*. By the "majority rules" conviction of the human conscience, we can, and have, established some code of moral conduct called "law" and subjected residents of Earth to this system by force or threats of consequences. But because people are inherently subject to making mistakes, even the most virtuous and honest systems of judiciary order are at risk of error, leading them to be rightfully and perpetually challenged.

Further, no one system can objectively be raised above another. Russian law, for example, is not North American law, yet both are enforced upon the people of each nation, so which country outperforms the other in upholding morality? They could argue forever (and such turbulence has resulted in endless warring), but without God, the only moral absolutes that will ever rule are those initiated by the finite minds of *people*, and are therefore fundamentally and permanently flawed.

Secular Naturalistic Evolution thereby not only ends in the philosophical, "I don't know why I'm here" dilemma, it additionally takes on the philosophical, social, political, ethical, and moral question of what authority has its ultimate grip on all things right and wrong while we live in the very existence we've just shown to be pointless. From there, as we've already begun to witness in the Western world, is the development of individualistic truth instead of unconditional, objective reality, wherein folks feel justified saying, "Your truth is not my truth, so I will follow *my* truth."

Two subjective and irreversibly incompatible human judgments *cannot* both be true. Read a book on war and watch how that plays out. The end is always chaos.

Evolution, by itself, allows for the eternal questioning of human decency, since there is no one Creator-system of governance to which all humanity is subject in communal peace and respect. The cyclical, pathetic loop of "do the best we can in our own human strength, power, and reason" eventually climaxes in lawlessness—just like the book of Revelation forecasts.

To contrast this bleak approach, however: God provides a flawless system of law. It was conceived in the foreshadowing Old Testament and climaxed in perfect love in the New Testament—a law under which all people are equally priceless, uniformly deserving of respect, and whose Savior thought of each specifically when He submitted to death for the sake of their eternal joy.

Young-Earth Creationism

Young Earthers most frequently believe our planet is somewhere in the vicinity of six to ten thousand years old. The leading reason for this is that it's one of the most popular ways to interpret and calculate the chronology of events in the Bible, starting with the events described in Genesis. The "days" of Creation are, to this group, viewed as literal, twenty-four-hour periods. And note that they may not be wrong…though, if they're right, it may not be the whole story.

The first question that arises against this group is in relation to how Earth would *appear* to be so old if it is, in fact, young. Answers vary, of course, but here are the two central theories:

1. God chose to make the world look older than it is. (That's not as crazy as it sounds to some. Bear with me.) His *purpose* in doing so is a matter of opinion and theology, but, biblically speaking, I understand the deduction. Assuming the "days" of Creation are literal, then the plants, animals, stars, and even humans (Adam and Eve) were all created with the appearance of age as well. Jumping into a time machine and traveling back to Eden, we could ask one of these two full-grown adults how old they are and be shocked when they express they were born "yesterday" or "a few hours ago"—even though they appear to be full-grown adults. We don't read about God rearing Adam from infancy, Adam waiting for a fruit tree to reach maturation for harvesting, the animals waiting in darkness while the space gases took billions of years to form a sun and stars, or anything of the sort. God created a fully functional, operating world—and, most importantly, He's *God*, with all the power and entitlement in the universe to form whatever He wanted and for whatever reason, whether or not we understand it. (However, *this portion* of the "appearance of age" theory is biblical, because the Bible directly explains Adam's sudden "birth" and subsequent intelligence. Later, in the "Tricky God Theory" section of chapter 4, you will see why this line of reasoning cannot extend to all questions related to Earth's apparent age that are *not* discussed in the Word.)

2. The Flood of Noah's time changed the entire globe, shifting everything on the planet around, relayering the soil and rock, and fluctuating the geological shapes our planet's surface originally

held. This intense event altered the topography of Earth so dramatically that current age-determination sciences will forever be thrown off-kilter and, thus, are unreliable.

But, as *most* Young Earthers stand by biblical genealogies, it would put the time between Adam and Jesus at about four thousand years, and then two thousand years between the birth of Jesus and now, creating the narrative for Earth being six thousand years old. (Much more on this topic in the following chapters.)

Though I respectfully disagree with Young Earthers on the conclusion of our planet's age, it would be unfair to write off the entire group as irrational, irresponsible biblical interpreters. Much to the contrary; they wouldn't be so passionate about defending Earth as being young in the first place if they weren't driven by a sweet, humble, and respectable determination to read God's Word and spread the Gospel message everywhere. Likewise, their research is not compiled by Bible scholars alone, but often by top scientists in fields such as biology, geology, paleontology, astronomy, and so on, which leads to a solid level of credibility behind many Young Earthers' claims.

This group has amassed an impressive array of evidence in support of a young planet, which brings me to a point that must be made in their defense early on regarding the relationship between Young Earthers and a few of their past leaders.

Because a church service or conference isn't necessarily made up of attendees who are experts, it's sometimes easy for pastors, teachers, or speakers to continue presenting information long after that material has become outdated, with audience members not knowledgeable enough to recognize the material as out of date. For example, a man who taught Creationism back in the 1980s might, without ever updating his information, continue today sharing evidences that were relevant forty years ago but that are irresponsible *now* in light of more recent discoveries. For those in the Young Earth circle, this has been an ongoing problem (I could list a few men who are still clinging to their 1980s research at this very moment); a few key speakers have been openly criticized for continuing to represent certain obsolete discussion points as facts. The listeners hear these presentations and write off the whole group as "a bunch of old suits who don't know anything." Whereas outdated information could be, and has been, given from a number of platforms—including those on the Old Earth side (and, oh my goodness, it is also true for science textbooks in schools!)—this remains a major issue for the Young Earthers. There is also the matter of the personal reputation of a couple of the group's most vocal leaders in the recent past. Though I wish it weren't the case, when a Christian spokesperson is drawn into a major spectacle because of a moral problem, the world tends to feel as if *nothing* that leader has said is trustworthy, and his or her theology or teachings get buried under layers of skepticism and doubt. At times, this attitude bleeds into a whole group. A couple of decades ago, one particular Young Earth teacher got into some serious financial trouble when his ministry made some dubious moves on tax reports. The controversy caused by those decisions didn't just affect the trustworthiness of this man's reputation and ministry, but it threw into question the whole Young Earth constituency, casting *many* Young Earth ministries into the same shadow of uncertainty and irrelevance.

Therefore, some hear the term "Young Earth" and automatically associate it with folks who can't be trusted morally or academically, which is unfair. I will therefore steer clear of denigrating the whole Young Earth group as a result of the actions of a few, but I'll *also* avoid reiterating information that should have been laid to rest in the Young/Old Earth debate decades ago (which is quite a load, unfortunately).

However, for the sake of being balanced, I've commissioned the help of a Defender Publishing assistant and *SkyWatch TV Magazine* guest journalist, Brittney Jackson, to illustrate a couple of examples of the Young Earthers' especially convincing discoveries. I asked her to find their most convincing pieces of evidence, while steering clear of the same, tired arguments related to the Flood of Noah's day and what that means for rock strata. (This book is long enough without covering all of those findings and the arguments that attempt to refute them. Curious readers can go to the Institute for Creation Research, Answers in Genesis, or a number of other Young-Earth ministries for further information.)

Here's what Brittney found:

When looking up a list of Young Earthers' most oft-referenced evidence, two major claims keep coming up: the Faint Young Sun Paradox and helium diffusion found in zircon gems. Upon my own research into these topics, several claims were made that were later argued against by other scientists, *or* claims based in opinion without ample proof.

The Faint Young Sun Paradox

When a star, such as our sun, is formed, it is not as hot or bright as it will eventually become. When Earth was formed—whether that means millions, billions, or only six thousand years ago—there was a phenomenon known as the Faint Young Sun Paradox. The sun we see today is too bright to look at. It keeps our planet warm and provides the elements we need to cultivate land and, for the most part, to live upon it comfortably. There isn't a "film," or fogginess, around it on a clear day. But, when the Earth and sun were first formed, the sky would have been a hazy, dusty orange, and the sun would be less visible from the ground.[15] Through this discovery, astrophysicists have found that the solar luminosity shouldn't have been warm enough to support life on Earth, and the globe should have been frozen solid.[16] Yet, sediments in aquatic environments and bacteria found in fossils show that Earth was not frozen and was indeed hospitable, despite the distance and luminosity of the sun. This creates a paradox that has had scientists scratching their heads for decades; no reasonable or viable solutions have surfaced.

The paradox came about in the 1960s, when astrophysicists ran simulations to show that, when the sun formed, it was 25–30 percent dimmer than it is today, meaning Earth's average surface temperature would be about -7 degrees Celsius (or 19.4 degrees Fahrenheit), and nothing should have been able to live or grow. Since this discovery, climate experts have been trying to explain how Earth could have been hospitable, coming up with several theories including greenhouse gases or the sun having a higher solar luminosity. Despite this, there is ample proof that Earth was not this cold, as we can see in discoveries from Jack Hills, Western Australia.

Western Australia has become a place of high interest for scientific discoveries when it comes to the age of Earth. Zircon is a popular gemstone found there that has been used in jewelry as a substitute for diamonds because of its hardness and unique, tawny shine. The beautiful gem, however, is an ancient mineral dated to 4.4 billion years ago that contains oxygen isotopes that had to be formed in a watery environment and could not be shaped in ice. This leads scientists to believe that there was indeed life on Earth over three billion years ago.

Young Earthers claim there is no paradox because the sun, Earth, and solar system have not been around for billions of years; therefore, the sun hasn't had to increase in luminosity.[17] One of the leading scientists with this claim is Dr. Danny Faulkner, who says there is no way to determine the age of the sun, but that if the sun is billions of years old, it should be much brighter today than it is. (I could not find ample proof of this conclusion.) Dr. Faulkner also states that the sun and solar system are "young and consistent with the 6,000-year age of the solar system as recorded by *Biblical chronology*."[18]

Zircon and Helium Diffusion

Along the line of zircons, one of the leading advocates for a Young Earth, Dr. Russell Humphreys, has used the helium diffusion in zircon crystals to support this hypothesis through his program RATE (Radioisotopes and the Age of the Earth). Through accelerated nuclear decay and the high amount of helium left inside of zircon crystals, this model claims the Earth is younger than scientists traditionally believe.

Helium is a gas that can diffuse through solids but, as Dr.

Humphreys claims, it hasn't had enough time to pass through zircons, meaning their presence in the gems proves an Earth age of eight thousand years or less.[19] During the 1970s, the United States Energy Research and Development Administration began researching and drilling into a geothermal energy site in the Jemez Mountains near Los Alamos, New Mexico. They sent the samples from various depths for isotopic analysis and other testing. Within the nuclei of zircon, uranium and theranium are present.[20] As the zircon sits, it begins a process called nuclear decay, which the USEPA (United States Environmental Protection Agency) describes as "the emission of energy in the form of ionizing radiation."[21] When these elements break down, they transform into a different atom or daughter product—which, in this case, results in the formation of helium.[22] Helium is a lightweight element that, over time, makes its way out of tight spaces. Tests on several samples showed that helium was still present, and that if the samples had been there for billions of years, the helium should have already diffused and dispersed into the atmosphere. More specifically, the zircon samples had anywhere from 17–58 percent of the helium originally deposited, confirming that a large amount of nuclear decay had taken place and, therefore, should have not been present at all if the samples had been sitting for millions of years, according to Dr. Humphreys' research.

However, in the same article, Dr. Humphreys claims that "God may have changed diffusion rates by some drastic means, say by adjusting the laws of atomic physics which control diffusion."[23] While God is more than capable of doing anything He wants, why would He change the rate of nuclear decay within these gems to speed up a process that would naturally take place over billions of years so that it would *really* take place within a few thousand? [Readers will see in chapter 4, in the section "Tricky God Theory," that He wouldn't have—in fact, theologically, He *couldn't* have.]

Is Humphreys the only scientist to hold this belief? How accurate are his findings?

Several scientists have spoken out against Humphreys' RATE model, a notable one being Dr. Gary H. Loechelt who, throughout the years, has had a back-and-forth with Dr. Humphreys through scientific articles and journals. Dr. Humphreys claims that in order for the Old-Earth theory to be correct with the discovery within the zircons, they would have had to be exposed to less than 75 degrees Celsius for more than 1.5 billion years.[24] Dr. Loechelt, who believes in the Old-Earth Creation model, claims Dr. Humphreys' experiment was "contrived to fit a preliminary dataset," and is therefore unreliable.[25]

In Dr. Loechelt's interpretation of the helium remaining inside the zircon, he points out that two different states of helium are found: one is loosely bound and the other is tightly bound. As early as 1964, around the time of the zircon discovery in New Mexico, geochronologists have recognized that the age of minerals does not always reflect the rock's forming ages. This is called the multi-diffusion domain (MDD), and is used to explain terrestrial thermal histories.[26] Essentially, helium could still be present within the gems because of the temperature changes throughout the millions of years. As the gems sat in the ground at various depths, the temperature at the Fenton Hill, New Mexico, site rose from 87 to 197 degrees Celsius due to a heating event that occurred twenty-four thousand years ago.[27] Further, the calculations used in Dr. Humphreys' RATE experiment *actually support* an Old-Earth model of 4.5 billion years.[28]

In conducting his own interpretation and calculations of the heating experiment for a two-domain diffusion model, Loechelt found that 30 percent of the loosely bound helium survived heating ramps of up to fifteen hours, and 15 percent at up to 300 degrees Celsius.[29] As stated in the latest update to this research, Loechelt explains that if you take a rock sample from deep underground, crush it, remove the zircon, place the extracted zircon crystals in a high-pressure vacuum system, heat them to high temperatures, let them cool, then repeat the heating process a second time while measuring the released helium throughout the process, the following can be observed:

> After excluding the initial temperature ramp, the high-temperature steps above 350°C accounted for over 22% of the total helium in the system, whereas the four low-temperature steps below 275°C accounted for only 0.0008% of the total helium in the system, or about eight parts per million. What do these eight parts per million of helium release tell us about the age of Earth? Very little, in fact.[30]

Obviously, these are only two avenues of Young Earthers' research. These examples aren't shared as topics of debate, but to show that the group really does come to their conclusions responsibly, tackling technical and complicated issues like the long-ago faded sun or the relationship between helium and zircon.[31]

Theistic Evolution

The Theistic Evolution view maintains that the Big Bang (or other leading theories) did, in fact, occur, but it was *the* means through which God created the universe. In other words, God created science and then guided it supernaturally to produce the world we see today. This appears to answer the otherwise unanswerable questions of who or what came first, why we're all here, who established the natural order, and so on, as everything still assents to the Creator's prerogative without denying scientific discovery.

The Christian's argument against, or in favor of, Theistic Evolution depends on one's approach. For instance, if evolution must mean that man came from monkeys (Darwinism, or at least what most folks believe Darwin taught) instead of from the dust of the ground as stated in Genesis, many followers of the God of the Bible will understandably respond that Theistic Evolution disagrees with what's scriptural. Others interpret

Genesis and the account of the formation of Adam to describe a lengthy process wherein God used the dust of the ground (Earth matter and particles) to slowly, methodically form life—*possibly* an ape species (a detail that can change depending on the speaker) and eventually humankind— in His image, over billions of years of natural evolution (key issues with this interpretation are yet to come). Others don't take issue with matter evolving slowly and naturally over time under God as Planetary Supervisor, so long as monkeys are strictly left out of the picture and Darwinism isn't the sole account of how Adam came to be.

So what, then, is the difference between Theistic Evolution and Old-Earth Creationism?

Initially, it does appear that Old Earthers and Theistic Evolutionists are synonymous, but, because of some of the conclusions closely associated with each, it's not quite that simple. Both agree that Earth is very old, and they do have this major point in common. Where they typically differ, however—regardless of their explanation of the first human and their acceptance of Darwinism and the like—is that Theistic Evolutionists allow the natural processes to have been the *exclusive* vehicle God drove to create. In other words, all pieces, particles, and matter within our known reality can be explained and illustrated by whatever science shows to have happened, and the book of Genesis relates only an allegory of that developing evidence. Logically, this leads to a doubt of the supernatural and *purposeful* elements of God's Creation, as B. T. Arnold of Baker Academic's *Encountering the Book of Genesis* attests:

> Though the theistic evolutionary approach is possible, it is difficult to harmonize Genesis 1–2 with certain evolutionary ideas. The theory of evolution teaches that humans resulted from chance events, the outcome of natural selection and the survival of the fittest. On the other hand, Genesis portrays a first human couple as parents of the whole human race. Adam and Eve were intentionally created by God in his image. This important doctrine, which is confirmed elsewhere in Scripture, is difficult to harmonize with the randomness of evolution.[32]

If the Theistic Evolution school of thought is allowed to go to the extreme, the many miracles recorded in the Bible (an outright defiance of the natural order in every case) can subsequently be disregarded or interpreted away…for how can miracles or supernaturalism remain believable realities when God didn't even employ that part of His nature and character when He formed the very world we live in?

Old Earthers who distance themselves from the term "Theistic Evolution," by contrast, are more skeptical of some aspects of the evolutionary model taught today. They may agree with Theistic Evolutionists that the world is old, but on many other points (often including the speed at which Adam was created), Old Earthers allow for science and nature to bow to the authority of God—not the other way around—while they embrace the supernatural element of God's act in Creation. The term "Progressive Creationists" can at times be stamped on this group, though this branding also covers a collection of people with varying interpretations of certain events. (Note, however, that thousands of Old Earth adherents—among whom are theologians such as Gary Stearman, Tom Horn, Noah Hutchings, and the late Chuck Missler—nevertheless believe there *were* a literal six days of Creation at the time of Adam and Eve; more on this later.)

By now, it should be clear why we aren't including a section on the beliefs of the Old Earth group. Not only is the gist captured in the immediately preceding section on Theistic Evolution and how it differs from Old Earth Creationists, but the rest of this book addresses at greater length what they believe and why. (However, note that even the Old Earthers have never produced a book quite like this one. Wait until we get to the dinosaurs…)

With that out of the way, let's consider when and how the Young Earth chronology was almost irreversibly inaugurated into Christian culture so we can reflect on whether *or not* their conclusions are the only responsible, biblical ones (as many in my experience have said) Christians can reach on this topic.

Chapter 2

Ussher Chronology
A "Powell Doctrine" for the Church?

AN IMPORTANT DISCLAIMER EARLY ON: Many Young Earthers will not recognize the name "James Ussher" or the term "Ussher Chronology," and will therefore believe this chapter doesn't apply to their ministry's evidences for and arguments in favor of a Young Earth. However, *even if it goes by a different name*, the spirit of the Young Earth argument is the same or similar in many ministries, and it just so happens that James Ussher was the first to popularize that argument and make it the most widely accepted cosmological Christian apologetic of his time and ever since.

For instance, a Young Earther might say, "I don't know about that Ussher fellow, but here at [insert name] ministries, we believe in the literal interpretation of Genesis and the Creation epic involving six days of God's work forming the planet followed by a day of rest. Since Adam was the first human, formed from the dust on the sixth day, we can count family generations from certain world events and other Bible characters' family generations all the way back to *him* and narrow down the approximate date or year that God created the world." Through a rather ingenious and logical process of elimination, this person and/or the ministry they belong to has, perhaps even unknowingly, just referred to the precise calculations and methods used by Ussher to establish the Young Earth theory from the onset of its widespread acceptance, while simultaneously admitting they've never heard of him. Certainly, anyone at any time in history—well before Ussher was even born, and for that matter, hundreds of years after his death—could have read the book of Genesis and concluded the same thing on their own: 1) Adam was the first human, and he was made at the same time as planet Earth; therefore 2) Adam's birthday is within days of Earth's birthday; which means 3) identifying the age of Earth is a matter of identifying how long ago Adam lived based on the subsequent ancestry from his life forward. But the difference between Ussher and others who have come to the same conclusion was the supreme weight his word carried in the discussion at the time he lived. As the following will show, Ussher's personal and powerful support for Young Earth deductions was the catalyst that pushed the Young Earth movement to the top of the answer board permanently...or at least for the next four-hundred-plus centuries until the Church began to adopt another apologetic for Creationism.

James Ussher

Chronology is the arrangement of facts and events in the order of time. The writers of the Bible themselves *do not adopt any standard era according to which they date events.*
—M. G. Easton, *Illustrated Bible Dictionary and Treasury of Biblical History, Biography, Geography, Doctrine, and Literature*[33]

It all started with a crucially important man, alive and thriving among Irish scholars between the years 1625 (the year his work reached paramount importance) and 1656 (the year of his death). From early on, James Ussher studied and mastered multiple languages, making himself a polyglot well before he graduated. His Bachelor of Arts degree from Dublin's Trinity College was awarded for his rich theological studies when he was around seventeen years old (circa 1598), and, by the time he was approximately twenty (1600–1602), he had received his master of arts degree, becoming an officially appointed as a fellow of the college as well as a prominent priest in the Church of Ireland. It was throughout these days of instruction at Trinity College that he became fluent in biblical Greek and Hebrew,[34] taking on the role of "respondent" in the realm of philosophy—"a task which he performed with great applause"[35]—shortly before he transitioned into his position as professor of divinity,[36] developing into an astounding lecturer. In 1607, he became professor of Theological Controversies at Trinity College, earned a doctorate of divinity in 1613, and moved up to the remarkable titles of vice chancellor and vice provost by 1616.

In addition to entering academia at such a young age, Ussher had important connections, both politically and religiously. His grandfather on his mother's side was a speaker in the Irish Parliament who had helped establish Trinity College,[37] and his uncle on his father's side carried one of the most influential titles in Ireland's religious history: Archbishop of Armagh and Primate of All Ireland. So widespread was his reputation through the high-ranking religious and political circles that, when Ussher traveled to London in 1609, he made quick (and lifelong) friends with some of the most powerful men in England: "Sir John Bourchier, afterwards Earl of Bath, Dr. Davenant, afterwards Bishop of Salisbury, Sir Henry Savile, Mr. Selden, Mr. Briggs, Professor of Astronomy at Oxford, and many others.... His name was now so well known in London, that some notice was taken of him at Court, and he preached before the household."[38]

By the time Ussher had grown to release his own scriptural interpretations into the world, his opinions and conclusions already—by birthright and association with important people in Church and secular government—held vital weight. Then, in 1625, he, too, became the Archbishop of Armagh and Primate of All Ireland, carrying on his uncle's title, work, and legacy. The honor was bestowed upon him by none other than King James, himself.

Yes...*the* King James of the King James Version Bible translation. The two men knew each other, and, although historical accounts of Ussher's influence behind how that translation was handled by the king, himself, vary from source to source, we know for certain that Ussher Chronology was included in many of the first English study Bibles, perpetuating his apologetics in a tremendously widespread way to both scholars and clergymen.

If this was a biographical work on the life and times of James Ussher, much more could be said of all he accomplished and how his voice gradually became one of the most consequential in the history of the Church to date. Suffice it to say that, when Church leadership, governance, and polity were fractured through the work of Martin Luther and the Protestant Reformation, it would take centuries to sort out the fundamental strongholds that built the theology we now rest on within the Protestant Church, and Ussher's was a key voice during this era. (I don't mean to imply that Luther's work in the Reformation—or the Reformation itself—wasn't necessary. Quite to the contrary, I believe the Roman Catholic Church was corrupted in most of its pursuits at the time [and still is, in some regard], and the Reformation did much in the way of correcting that. But the Reformation also ignited a bomb in the leadership structure of the Church, and believers of that day were forced to pick sides, which of course distracted from the Church's mission and theological training.) Every denomination at that time—from Arminianism to Calvinism to Lutheranism—at least in part developed while Ussher was openly supporting or opposing certain teachings, and his impact on these movements was enormous and groundbreaking, branding him forever as an "answer man" when there was a dispute. Likewise, his stance against the papacy garnered great support for his teachings, as the Church was daily splintering farther and farther away from the Roman Catholic hierarchy. (He was key in the earliest controversial debates about whether the biblical, end-time Antichrist could be the pope. Of course, this drew both support and opposition, but either way, everyone was talking about Ussher as an authority on such matters, heightening his popularity among the clergy.) So, as Ussher's personal interest was Bible study and teaching (as is obvious from his own writings as well from what others wrote about him), his sway within the Church influenced even secular politics throughout Ireland, Scotland, and England during the Wars of the Three Kingdoms, as there was a definite, indivisible merger of Church and State in those days throughout many regions. Amidst these conflicts, he acted as an advisor to kings and Parliament.

By 1639, when Ussher wrote one of many works considered masterpieces of the Church—*Britannicarum Ecclesiarum Antiquitates* (*Antiquities of the British Churches*), which covered the most extensive and significant historical beliefs of Christianity from Christ forward to Ussher's day—his opinion on any biblical topic was so widely and immediately accepted that it would take centuries and thousands of polished scholars to challenge any theology or scriptural interpretations he released into the world of Christendom. Those who would have opposed his claims at the time were likely written off as conspiratorial troublemakers.

However, more than any other area, and from his entrance into the education system at a mere eight years old, "the decided leaning of his mind was to historical and chronological inquiries."[39] In other words, the chronological order of biblical events was Ussher's passion; one might even say it was his obsession—likely an accurate assertion in light of the fact that, at around eighteen years old, he absolved himself of any property inheritance after his father's death, signing over all the land he was entitled to in order to pay for his college fees and study materials to further his research in this area.[40] In fact, "so rapid was the progress made by the youthful student, that, ere he reached his nineteenth year, he had drawn up, in Latin, a chronicle of the Bible, as far as the Book of Kings."[41] Chronology was the meat Ussher fed the mind throughout his entire life, and it resulted in his writing so many works that the complete collection has, today, been crammed into a massive library of seventeen large volumes of books, dissertations, sermons, and other documents. Though not every one of these masterpieces centers on chronology, *all* are at least inspired by, and originate from, his work in sorting out what and who came first in some aspect of human history.

I find myself tempted to go on and on about James Ussher, reflecting not only on the monumental impact he had on society and the portions of his theology that cling on in modern Christianity, but about the man, himself. Despite the ceaseless line of governors, rulers, statesmen, lords, and a long list of other elite and prominent men across the globe who stood before him to seek his council or ask his opinion on matters then reserved for only the highest-ranking officials, Ussher's nature and character are frequently described by his biographers to be driven by a heart for the Gospel. He wasn't always a perfect man, and at times he bumped heads with others (of course, that could certainly be said of anyone alive in his day who opposed the Roman Catholic Church), but overall, he is remembered as a God-fearing and upright man who prioritized correct theology and scriptural interpretation every day of his life. Much less could be said about most average Christians today, so his example of passionate ministry is humbling…and inspiring.

I hope his mark on the world of theological pursuits echoes forever throughout the universe, stirring men and women of God, everywhere and in every age, to follow in his footsteps and model their own Bible studies after those of such a devout man as he. I truly mean that, and it must be stated here and now, because what I'm about to say of him would otherwise sound harsher than I intend.

As we proceed through the next few pages, please remember Ussher as a man with only the holiest and most sincere intentions…but in order to approach his chronology with accuracy, we must also remember him as *any other mere man* who is ultimately, despite his best efforts otherwise, capable of error.

The Weight of Ussher's Annals: It's Happened Before

Book titles in James Ussher's time were often incredibly long. Unlike today's titles chosen for eye-grabbing marketability, antique works were named for their subject(s), as well as for the author's "angle." Such is the case for Ussher's 1650 Latin magnum opus and the very book behind many Young Earthers' chief arguments: *Annales Veteris Testamenti, a prima mundi origine deducti, una cum rerum Asiaticarum et Aegyptiacarum chronico, a temporis historici principio usque ad Maccabaicorum initia product.* In plain English, this title reads: *Annals of the Old Testament, Deduced from the First Origins of the World, the Chronicle of Asiatic and Egyptian Matters Together Produced from the Beginning of Historical Time Up to the Beginnings of Maccabees.* (A mouthful, I know.)

In many modern references, Ussher's most important work is shortened to *Annals*, which is how we will proceed as well, but early on, there is something in the title I hope to draw attention to: "deduced from the first origins of the world." Meaning no disrespect to Ussher, there is a misnomer in this string of words that assumes the writer of *Annals* was personally present at the world's origins in order to "deduce" what occurred at that moment—or, that he had a personal, supernatural revelation from God regarding the origins of the universe that led to an irrefutable, God-given deduction. I realize that's not literally what the work states, but placing Ussher's influential name alongside something that has been "deduced" (narrowed down to a solid conclusion)—and believing that very conclusion to have been backed by the authority of the Bible, itself—infers a sense of weight that the information is absolute. More simply: *Annals* has the ultimate, matchless, most sovereign, indisputable, and *supreme* answer to history's grandest question regarding how and when we all got here. Some Christians today haven't even heard of Ussher, but while he lived, a work by a man like him would have leapt across the lecture hall of the greatest universities and slapped any skeptic upside the head, wagging an invisible finger of shame to any who would be bold enough to doubt his work. Though not every Young Earth ministry or spokesman claims to base their evidence upon only what Ussher taught (especially when his findings came under harsher scrutiny in the nineteenth century, and since then, Young Earth groups have distanced themselves from his name), without Ussher inaugurating these apologetics into the Body of Christ when he did, we may never have had such a huge movement of Young Earth apologetics in the first place. Had it not been for Ussher's work, we *may* have simply approached theology and science *together* from the beginning, allowing the Great Scientist and His Creation narrative to harmonize, instead of placing ourselves in a position to be "the weaker argument" to the unbelieving (or skeptical) world outside.

Needless to say, there was a sort of unassailable "authority fortress" (I'll explain this term in a moment) this particular manuscript held from the beginning.

Interestingly, I've come across this before...

In 2016, Tom Horn approached me to assist with the research behind the book, *Unearthing the Lost World of the Cloudeaters: Compelling Evidence of the Incursion of Giants, Their Extraordinary Technology, and Imminent Return*, which he coauthored with Stephen Quayle. Most of my findings were included in the eleventh chapter, entitled: "The Truth about the Great Smithsonian Cover-Up." One central purpose of the book was to investigate the concepts and potential proofs that giants existed upon the earth at some point, as Genesis 6:4 states, and to consider what that might mean for science. (Important note: Sometimes, when people hear the word "giants," they think of a massive, humanlike entity standing hundreds of feet tall, with a head towering above the clouds and feet that could simultaneously crush the Taj Mahal and half of India in a single step—resembling something straight out of a fairy tale like *Jack and the Beanstalk*. However, when *we* say "giants," we're referring to the beings whose bones were found in earlier archeological digs measuring closer to the size of a very large human, as we will see in chapter 7 of this work.)

The research from *Unearthing the Lost World of the Cloudeaters* is relevant here for two reasons: 1) It illustrates what I mean by an "authority-fortress" theory that cannot easily be struck down once introduced by the right man in a position of power (which is what happened with Ussher, though his intention was pure); 2) it contributes to this book's message by showing how, in the past, discoveries on our planet were hidden under layers of red tape that prohibited the general public from knowing scientific and archeological facts that would debunk everything we *think* we know about evolution (including Darwinism).

The trail in that chapter begins by noting the almighty super-museum, the Smithsonian Institution, frequently spreads misinformation through erroneous artifact displays, discovery reports, conferences, educational materials, and other outlets. One area in which this was particularly applicable to the *Cloudeaters* study was a great number of bones that had been unearthed in Native American burial mounds. Remains of an ancient race we know hardly anything about (even still) were dug up at multiple sites across the US, showing that something, some humanlike race of *very* large proportions, had walked the earth alongside man in the distant past. (These findings will be discussed in a later chapter. For now, pay close attention to how easily the truth about Earth can be concealed from the public through only one person with impressive connections.)

To those initially wondering why a museum matters in the discussion of power, it must be explained that the Smithsonian, despite the fact that it's long been a popular destination for vacationers to see many famous exhibits at its New York or Washington DC facilities, it's always has been much more than just a tourist attraction. In the mid-1800s, a wealthy chemist named James Smithson designated in his will an enormous sum of money in to go toward furthering knowledge in some aspect on US territory. He didn't stipulate the "how" and "what" behind the way the money should accomplish that goal, so our government went back and forth for eight straight years debating how "knowledge" could be increased through this great donation. Among the many ideas offered by US government officials were the establishment of "school grounds, libraries, observatories, gardens, zoologist research centers, agricultural hubs, art galleries, and science discovery centers."[42]

Gradually, the idea that morphed from so many conflicting angles birthed a one-of-a-kind establishment in that it eventually encompassed all the ideas together into one central focus: the assembling of a collection of artifacts, specimens, artwork, and educational materials and aims of every kind into newly raised buildings where they would be preserved and arranged for the purpose of public education. These buildings would also house many educational conferences, lectures, and seminars given by celebrated professors in fields relative to: astronomy, geography, geology, minerology, philosophy, science and chemistry, agriculture, natural history, American history, fine arts, antiquities, and the study of cultures around the globe.[43]

Whispers of this new establishment spread quickly across the States, and the word "Smithsonian" gained an immediate reputation as being one of the most innovative, advanced, technological, and state-of-the-art educational centers in the world. So far more than mere "museum" was what the Smithsonian promised our country before the first brick was ever laid in the foundation of its original building site. However, despite the wonderful things this institution has always done, it must be remembered that there are finite, faulty humans behind everything it offers; therefore, "absolute truth" has historically been more of a suggestion than a mandate in its offerings.

As a quick and easy example of this that can be proven through the Smithsonian's own published documents,[44] Smithson—the founding donor who was born in Paris in 1765 and died in 1829—could not have been a day older than sixty-four years old when he passed on. Yet, visitors to the main entrance of the Smithsonian building in Washington, DC, will see a plaque in his memory ending with the words, "aged 75 years." If we can't trust the verity of the commemoration of this most celebrated founder—what some might consider the most important exhibit in the entire museum, as it bespeaks of its very own origin—how many other of the museum's displays or educational materials are untrustworthy?[45] As the *Cloudeaters* chapter goes on to show, I contacted the Smithsonian to ask this very question. The transcript of the recorded phone conversation is included in that book, but to keep it short here: Even the "information specialists" employed by the Smithsonian didn't have a clue the date on their founder's plaque was incorrect. When I first pointed this out, the specialist on the line insisted I was wrong: The inscription was accurate, because "everything at the Smithsonian is *always* accurate." When I explained that historical records, along with their very own published literature and website, conflicted with the date on display, the long silence and tripping over words on the other end of the line led to the eventual statement that this was the *only* mistake and "everything else [at the Smithsonian] is true."[46] (An interesting, unaccountable redirect, indeed...) In case you're wondering: There was no signage nearby that explained the discrepancy or corrected the date, so every person visiting the museum is greeted *in the very first room* with misinformation.

Okay, okay, but that's just a measly error. Surely, Donna, you're not suggesting that this strips the whole Smithsonian Institute of its credibility, are you?

The question remains valid, and we'll ask it again: How deep does that well truly go? If we can't even trust the people behind this organization to get their facts straight about their founder—and if this institution's own staff is unaware of what isn't accurate—how many other "facts" from their reporting or exhibits are incorrect? When can they be trusted, and when should they be challenged? Who decides which details are marginal and unimportant versus those that are critical? And why are the information specialists—a key group of employees specifically trained to have the facts nailed down—entirely unaware of mistakes in the Smithsonian's claims? (You might find it interesting to go online and search for something similar to "inaccuracies within Smithsonian literature [or "curriculum," "displays," "exhibits," and so on]" to see an overwhelming number of sources railing against the institution's numerous errors in many areas. These errors have, in the recent past, complicated their funding and forced adjustments or shutdowns of certain educational exhibits and outlets. Nevertheless, the very word "Smithsonian" still carries an air of educational authority.)

A date on a tomb might be a small issue, sure…but what about all those enormous, humanlike bones found in the ground in the Smithsonian's earlier days that, again, *the institution's* literature openly acknowledges? Imagine the possibilities if we could study those findings further. Such access could lead to unimaginable, epic discoveries of who (or *what*) shared this planet with us in ancient times, and what that means for biblical truth and evolutionary theories.

I will share an example from my *Cloudeaters* chapter using canines to highlight only one angle that would make the revision of current human evolutionary teaching not only likely, but a guaranteed reality, if the giant bones we have had access to historically were a part of our current educational curricula:

The Saluki is one of fourteen of the oldest known canine breeds, referred to as "the royal dog of Egypt" because of their association as the loyal, right-hand best friend to Egyptian pharaohs. (Their remains have been found mummified as well, suggesting that they were esteemed in high honor.) The Ibizan hound (as seen on the tomb of Tutankhamun) has a similar story, and both breeds were fit, trim, long-legged hunters. If an archeological team discovered a Saluki/Ibizan hound crossbreed buried near an ancient pyramid today, such a find *would not* shake the foundations of all we know about canine biology [and evolution]. Why? Because we know there were at least fourteen breeds of canine around the world at that time that could have procreated and produced another breed, and our modern biological science now recognizes 339 official dog breeds, according to the World Canine Organization.[47] We are already well aware that one dog can breed with another dog and create something entirely new, but the offspring is still a dog. Much funding has already backed such science, and the world is not turned on its head every time a breeder announces a new and great kind of hound for dog-lovers everywhere. Humans, also, can breed after their own kind, producing interracial offspring, and this is common knowledge. So, yes, biology has proven that when something produces *after its own kind,* then the offspring of that union is *of that kind....*

But if the remains of a gigantically proportioned, fifteen-cubit-tall, Saluki-looking dog were found near a pyramid, the measurements of which disregarded all we know of canine evolutionary development, it *would* shake the foundations of all we know about canine biology [and evolution]. Any serious biologist would consider this a possible link to a completely new biological thread—or at the very least an extreme inter-breeding tactic practiced by the ancients but unknown to our current world [as can be interpreted by Genesis 6:4]—until proven otherwise...and it should be taken very seriously.... If a discovery proves that something looks like a dog but can't be, based on known biology, then let's face it! Our biology would be determined subject to limitation, and the "dog" might not actually be a dog! Or it could be a dog that has cross-bred with some other ancient animal, testifying to a DNA-manipulation procedure carried out by an ancient unknown science. Either way, it would not be ignored by the scientific community. It might be *hidden away* if the discovery points to something scientists don't want the rest of the world to know about, but it would *not* be ignored.[48]

Proof of humanlike giants, *if the public was aware of it*, would unravel evolutionary theories about humankind (and again, especially Darwinism). Why aren't we hearing about the bones the Smithsonian team found and documented back in the day?

I'll tell you why in three words: John Powell Doctrine.

Major John Powell was to the scientific world of discovery and the Smithsonian what Archbishop James Ussher was to the development of Western theology. After Powell's explorations of the Grand Canyon propelled him into worldwide fame and marked him as a reliable voice in archeology, "his judgments on the archaeological surveys became the chief authority for everyone at the Smithsonian, as well as the listening world."[49] Early on in his career with the museum, his work was funded by massive organizations and corporations, and his name became synonymous with the mighty Smithsonian. Money poured in from excited donors everywhere who wanted to see what he would dig up in his next archeological pursuit. However, something bizarre, perhaps *dubious*, occurred before too much of his work could produce any further findings when an enormous US government grant came in:

It is not at all a secret that Powell was exceptionally bent toward rationalizing away any concepts that challenged our known evolutionary science, and although this would be the expected approach for many in his position, it is surprising to learn that his reaction to the large grant given by US Congress to the Division of Mound

Exploration was not positive [i.e., he wasn't happy about the free money he had been given from the government]....

One might take from reading Powell's writings that he wished to study only the ethnicity of aboriginal tribes and remain non-intrusive, which might explain why the grant did not result in his celebratory reaction. Others throughout the years, however, have read his statements and understandably come to the conclusion that Powell believed there were things buried in those strange mounds that he did not want the world to know about, lest everything we *think* we know about humanity's history be confronted. Why else would additional government funding be bad news? Any true investigator would tackle the mounds enthusiastically in pursuit of authentic science when backed by support of the government, not with hesitance or fear that the [current and perceived] science would be defied.

Nevertheless, Powell cooperated with the intentions of the funding, though not without a grand voicing of concern over how the resources would be employed. In 1882, the first BOE [Bureau of Ethnology] report from Powell was penned: *On Limitations to the Use of Some Anthropologic Data*. The title itself is revealing of his agenda. It does not require analysis by an achieved academic to see that before the report's first sentence graced the eyes of its readers, Powell was already placing limitations on how the data accumulated at the exploration sites were to be used.[50]

From the beginning, Powell placed limitations (calling them that literally) upon how his findings could be used in the scientific community. In no uncertain terms, within this document he prohibited his work from having any connection with research of ancient races of humans or humanlike beings that could have fit the description and size of what we would call "giants," entirely disregarding legitimate findings of that very nature reported publicly and transparently through the museum's literature for decades prior.

To share one example: Discoveries of ancient pictographs involving towering, humanlike beings with six fingers and toes and double rows of teeth were, in Powell's *Limitations* document, written off as purely imaginative drawings—a sort of creative fiction writing expressed on the stone walls of the homes of bored Native Americans thousands of years ago. Anyone fifteen minutes into research on the frescoes of Rome or Egyptian hieroglyphs (to name only two examples) would know this is an irresponsible conclusion based on assumption, not on science or dependable anthropologic examination that has historically recognized pictographs of the past to be an outright documentation of others' life experiences in this world. (Scholars use the frescoes of Rome to express what went on in the pagan temples of Christ's day. Nobody has a problem with that, but when the drawings of Native Americans attest to a giant race, its "creative writing," even in areas where the bones discovered in the burial mounds show the writing on the wall to be relevant. This is inconsistent treatment of anthropological data, and Powell was an enormous instigator of this kind of "limited use" from earlier cultures.) Likewise, this "creative writing" approach must ignore that these pictographs appeared in many locations, with huge distances between them, dated in the same or similar periods: It's impossible to imagine that an entire community of early settlers scattered across the territory now known as the United States would all face the same boredom in the same era of time, then treat that boredom by sketching images of giant beings that, by coincidence, shared intricate physical characteristics with those drawn by other Native American tribes thousands of miles away. Remember, this was before Facebook, so they couldn't "share," "like," "thumbs up," or "repost" images, or in any way know what faraway tribes were writing on their walls. How would all these people imagine the same giant-being simultaneously—and, again, in an area where inexplicably large bones were found in the burial mounds?

> Powell was correct in saying that a perfect record [of these pictures] was not made, but he was ill-informed if he assumed that anything outside his own limited worldview was the subject of fairy-tale fancy. Much to the contrary, every ancient culture we have ever studied at length have left behind their stories in wall

and rock drawings, and it is from this artistic documentation form that we have developed much modern understanding of the old world, its inhabitants, and the people groups they mingled with.

That Powell would say these images are "illegitimate…for historic purposes" [in his *Limitations* report] challenges the historical and archeological practices set in place by experts of his own field for hundreds of years.[51]

Another example is in the continuously circular logic Powell employs in *Limitations*. For instance, in considering the origin of mankind, he states: "While the doctrines [of Darwinian evolution] lead the way to new fields of discovery, the new discoveries lead again to new doctrines."[52] So, the "doctrine" of Darwinism *can* be replaced by a new knowledge base of mankind's origin as soon as the efforts of the scientific community produce new discoveries that sufficiently challenge it. For a moment, it sounds like he's open-minded.

Unfortunately, though, this moment of clarity results in a mere tease as we observe [Powell] using the very doctrines of evolution as a means to escape further study of it. Rather than to unearth and analyze the evidence that challenges evolution so our scientific database can expand, Powell states: "The truth or error of such hypothetic genealogy [referring to giant myths] in no way affects the validity of the doctrines of evolution in the minds of scientific men, but on the other hand the value of the tentative theory is brought to final judgment under the laws of evolution."[53] In other words, the theories presented by believers of the ancient giant races ultimately have to come under the final judgment of "the laws of evolution."[54]

Did you catch that? Powell first says Darwinism can be replaced by new ideologies when evidence emerges to challenge it, then he traps those ideologies from ever emerging through the Smithsonian or its researchers by saying whatever we *do* discover must be seen and evaluated through a

Darwinian lens. Again, it's circular logic that—in cheeky terminology that flaunts academic, highbrow superiority over many of his readers—champions and simultaneously stops objective, scientific progress.

Speaking of cheeky terminology, that's one area in which Powell excelled. Throughout his report, he wraps his conclusions in lengthy, wordy, straw-man arguments that a true intellect of his day could knock over with a puff of wind. But that is precisely the problem. The "true intellects" then were few and far between, as a far larger number of laypeople going about their work and trying to survive wars, depressions, etc., were either illiterate or lacked the English language skills necessary to follow the over-one's-head, complicated, anthropologic jargon of his report. He knew well that only a small minority of people would be able to follow—let alone challenge—his statements. To those who *could* understand what he was saying, he used a technique I've coined "intellectual snobbery": He applied an undertone of arrogance that indirectly insulted anyone who dared question or challenge his experience, position, education, accomplishments, or skill. It's the underlying condescending insinuation that, "If you don't agree with my conclusions, you might be pretty, but you're not very bright, Honey."

Powell's chosen words continue to imply—though carefully and politely—that anyone who would be audacious enough to demand answers from the scientific community about why there are mammoth people buried in Indian mounds across the United States belong to the unenlightened minority. The un-philosophical. The time-wasters. The resource sponges. The disrespecters of sacred Indian grounds. The meddlers. Or, in current popular parlance, "the Fake News" reporters. In the end, no matter how he veils his arguments with diplomacy, the distinguished Grand Canyon explorer is giving a nod of approval to anyone who is willing to become a member of his mature and rational club, while casting the proverbial dunce hat on anyone who isn't "intelligent" enough to dismiss the giant people as an irrelevant past quirk of regular-human biology. It's condescension at its finest, and the public has to make the choice to challenge the eminent Major Powell while the scientific community represents them as whack jobs, or be brainwashed into his reasoning. Is this not effectively the opposite of the beloved objectivity Powell treasures?

The skill Powell is using in his report is older than dirt. Take a conflict on any subject and place an articulate spokesperson at the head of one side who confidently weaves intimidating and lofty words around their claims to make their listeners feel stupid for not blindly agreeing, and it almost doesn't matter *what* the claims are, so long as the public is barraged with fancy speech that leaves them confused about why they questioned anything to begin with.....

Wouldn't it JUST. BE. EASIER. at this point to bring out the bones and talk frankly about what evolution actually *does* say on the matter? If evolution is such a pet of Powell's, why won't he let evolution address it?...

To suggest this never-ending and complicated trail of discussion [about bones] is vain and fruitless would be true if it weren't for the fact that we're still left with giant bones that nobody will answer for. Again, "giants upon the earth" [from Genesis] is no longer purely "mythology" if we have giant bones—and we do. Conspiracy is not a "theory" when there's proof. Some of the legend or lore surrounding giants might be mythological, but we won't know what is or isn't until the bones are addressed, and they can't be as long as the Powells of the world stand in the way as keeper of the keys to the mounds, canceling out the resources to dive into true science on the grounds that it would only be to prove or disprove irrational conspiracy theorist's mythological fables.

It's not about mythology.... It's about bones in the ground.

Powell refuses to appreciate this simplicity as long as his complicated lectures about largely unrelated subjects continue to herd people away from further investigation.[55]

As to how this *Limitations* report morphed into the Powell Doctrine that would forever silence further study of what might be behind Genesis 6:4 on this planet—as well as travel back in time and conceal the bones already unearthed under more red tape—much of that occurred shortly following Powell's death. Charles Doolittle Walcott, the chief executive officer of the Smithsonian, possibly saw the former explorer's untimely exit from the world as an opportunity for the public to make demands about further investigation of giant bones and took it as a threat to, or a distraction against, the path of scientific progress they were on at the time Powell died. (We honestly don't know Walcott's personal motive in championing Powell's doublespeak writings, but it is easy to see an agenda behind the decision to carry on his prohibitive stance if the excavation of bones had the potential of disrupting all then-current avenues of research.) This brings us to the "authority fortress" mentioned earlier:

Walcott hailed [Powell's *Limitations*] report with such irrefutable and mesmeric magnitude that the Smithsonian executives deemed the document the "Powell Doctrine." Powell's smarter-than-you linguistic skills naturally fed the pride of many of his followers, which by extension lent itself to further brainwashing from the top rung of the Smithsonian and down. From 1907 to this day, the now-outdated Powell Doctrine has been the final word on the issue of giant bones, as well as ancient [Native American] culture. Powell was, himself, viewed as a great authority, but he was only one man. When Walcott rallied the rest of the Smithsonian superiors to embrace the Powell report, the rest of the world embraced it as well.... As a result, then, the museum established the Powell Doctrine as a literal, official policy to exclude any and all alternative evaluations of the mounds, bones, pictographs, and human-origin hypotheses, regardless of evidence. Any perspective, no matter how scientifically sound, would be snuffed out under the suppressive abort button of the Doctrine. After 1907, it would not matter *what* was found in the ground. The policy was solid. No opinion other than Powell's would ever matter to the Smithsonian again.

And you can guess what naturally happens next [pay attention to the rest of this paragraph!]: Under this administration, *years* of the institution's time and money are placed into book collections, exhibits, staff training, and uncountable materials that support this Doctrine as truth. The fortress built cannot easily be torn down, and its influence spreads.

Tragically, because of the weight the Smithsonian's opinion holds to educational institutions across the United States, the Powell Doctrine policy of exclusion was also incorporated into the dogma of most major American universities, adding a behemoth layer of clout to Powell's appraisal. Students of reputable colleges all across the country haven't the slightest idea why they are being taught what they are, or that it all came from one man a hundred and fifty years ago. [Apply this situation to Darwinian evolution, and you can understand why that theory—which has been responsibly refuted countless times by true scientists since its conception—carries on in many educational facilities today, and why the Church Body still thinks all forms of "evolution" must mean "man came from monkeys" and therefore refuses to engage in conversations with the lost about the science that shows Earth to be old.]

Much documentation has been collected that follows an unscrupulous trajectory from various archeological digs to the Smithsonian as research teams are submitting their finds to the museum for study and/or display, and the trail goes dark at that point. The bones the Smithsonian is receiving are not making their way to the museum floor or laboratories, and nary is a word uttered that they were ever submitted after they were unearthed. [Just three nights ago at the time of this writing, I viewed a documentary showing one interview after another of folks who have found enormous bones in forests, near streams, between large rock formations, etc., and, after reporting these findings to authorities, the bones are confiscated and locked away. Nobody speaks of them once they've been turned in.] Those who contribute the bones to the museum do so in naïve trust that the Smithsonian will appeal to the government for grants and additional research funds, but because of the [Powell Doctrine], the buck stops there, and that in turn affects the budget allowance for universities to follow up with any kind of field study for tomorrow's generation of scientists. [See how *one man* with the right political connections in high places can permanently influence an entire country and culture away from absolute, transparent, scientific study? Whatever the truth is—be it in support of *or* opposition to the reality of giant races on Earth's soil in ancient times—it's hidden away and left a mystery. This is one major area where science is not dependable. For what absolute truth can be garnered from only a partial narrative?]

Despite this, well before Powell's document, the world was aware of bizarre discoveries. Not limited to bones, this also included the strange astronomical and astrological building patterns surrounding ancient structures and monolithic edifices such as those in Baalbek, as well as enormous tools, strange drawings, and prevailing legend of primitive cultures all around the globe. The Smithsonian was not always involved in every discovery reported, which is why the public does not have to search far and wide into the archives of obscurity or conspiracy to be showered with visual evidence that *something* walked the earth in the old days we can't explain away.[56]

As readers of *Cloudeaters* are aware, this in-depth examination goes on to show earlier Smithsonian literature (as well as sources outside the Smithsonian) that openly documents the discovery of many giant, humanlike bones and other artifacts that present evidence of a bizarre race alive on Earth in the past. In 1910, Dr. Ales Hrdlicka joined the Smithsonian as the first curator of the Division of Physical Anthropology, adding to and strengthening the unfortunate prohibitions of the Powell Doctrine through many aces up his sleeve. So, any chance we may have had to contest Powell's absolutist, prohibitive and, dare we say, dictatorial limitations on resources that may have otherwise debunked Darwinism were met with yet another wave of resistance. It's been a never-ending power play by authorities in or connected to the Smithsonian ever since to maintain the "man came from monkeys" curriculum (and other, similar teachings related to the origins of humanity and the cosmos) across the West.

So far, we've shown how the Smithsonian—only one of many powerful institutions dedicated to furthering knowledge in areas stemming from science to archeology, anthropology, and innumerable other areas of research while it claims to be unbiased—can place an effective ban across an entire powerful country on any educational curriculum that doesn't agree with its own agenda. Perhaps this is to save face, because any or all government funding behind it would be halted (or at least dramatically decreased) if it was proved wrong in its previous Darwinian conclusions. Maybe it's for a more controversial reason, such as the possibility that the chief executives at the Smithsonian don't want the US to return to Christian values like it might if there really is proof behind biblical claims (Genesis 6:4: "There were giants in those days…"). But whatever the cause, we've now shown that all it takes to silence legitimate investigation and direct an entire nation's attention to one restricted approach in academia is to position oneself or institution as the final authority on the topic and let the layers of tape trickle from the top powers down into society. We've also shown that this can spring from one powerful individual, if that person is in the right place at the right time to gain the support of powers in high places.

Powell and Ussher: Power Compared

The glaring difference between John Powell and James Ussher is in their perceived character and motives. Though there is an innate air of superiority behind Powell's drive to champion some avenues of discovery and silence others (as the examination on his document in *Cloudeaters* shows at greater length), Ussher was driven by a Christ-centric heart. By no means am I suggesting Ussher was a perfect saint at all times from whose head emanated rays of glory when he prayed or any other such sensational claims, but I *have* read the biographical accounts of eyewitnesses who attested to his humility and his motives. Consistently, he is remembered as a man who tried at every turn to avoid the limelight while he retreated farther and farther into his studies in hopes that his work would act as a series of Christian apologetics, reaching the lost and strengthening the faith of believers. When offered positions of power, he refused on many occasions, choosing instead to steer clear of making the game of "religio-politics" his own, because he believed it wasn't what God wanted for him. When asked to speak at grand, opulent gatherings in front of men so powerful that the lay clergy would have swooned or stood in line for hours just to shake hands with him, he looked for any way out, only accepting invitations he perceived to useful in furthering the Kingdom of God. Ussher, as far as we can tell, couldn't care less whether he was powerful. So long as he was preaching the Gospel, he was content to be as lowly as any other scholar whose modest work helped sincere seekers of God find what—and who—they were looking for. To Powell, "absolute truth" was whatever he wanted it to be as long as he kept the meddlers of the world from slowing down progress behind what was important to him at the time; to Ussher, "absolute truth" was the Word of God, and his greatest joy was revealing exactly how the Word showed true in his line of work.

In this particular aspect, these two men have nothing in common.

However, they do merit comparison in the clout their word carried among the masses, their related areas of cosmological research, and the enduring grip their conclusions had within their area of influence. Be it God or coincidental circumstances, Ussher's authority on what the Bible says was similar to Powell's authority on what science and discovery says, with one crucial difference: As hard as it is to imagine, Ussher's authority fortress was actually far more powerful than Powell's, as his audience wasn't limited to just the chief executives of a dynamic organization like the Smithsonian. Ussher was the advisor to kings, the respected champion of the people, and the voice of not only England's or Ireland's responsible theology and apologetics, but of the world's! His Young Earth sway was *global*, muting Powell's scientific influence by unimaginable margins.

Intent and motive aside, when Ussher said Earth was a mere thousands of years old via his limited approach to biblical chronology, support flew in from all over the planet and his teachings were taken to be as true as the Gospel itself. His conclusions about Earth's age were stamped in the minds and hearts of Christ's followers sank their teeth into his principles of scriptural interpretation far beyond his death, throughout the nineteenth and twentieth centuries and forward to today.

Then, sometime after Ussher went to be with Jesus, a concerning habit formed: When the sweet, well-meaning Christians, ever loyal to their predecessor's instructions, met opposition (scientific, logical, or otherwise), they and generations of believers after them adopted a response that hurt, rather than helped, their cause: They began saying "the Bible says so" when it doesn't.

Today, a similar practice continues. The hugely influential Young Earth website, Answers in Genesis, states in one of its popular articles titled "The 10 Best Evidences from Science That Confirm a Young Earth": "The earth is only a few thousand years old. That's a fact, plainly revealed in God's Word."[57] Later in the article, as an added layer of clout and offset in a giant box with green letters (so it can't be missed), we read: "When discussing the age of the earth, Christians must be ready to explain the importance of starting points. The Bible is the right starting point."[58] I agree with the latter statement, but not with its application to Young Earth as a "fact, plainly revealed" in the Bible.

It also didn't help that, as briefly stated earlier, when English Bibles were printed, Ussher Chronology was added to the margin notes of many. Though this would not (or at least *should* not) have been viewed as indicating a level of "scriptural authority," the fact that his deductions were published upon the same pages as Scripture made the "my Bible says so" phrase a reality, despite that it wasn't God's Word, but the teachings printed alongside it, claiming Earth was young.

Before long, the consensus for Christians and unbelievers alike was that it had been the Bible, itself, claiming Earth was merely thousands of years old. A proverbial "cover your ears" reaction manifested within Christian groups against any challenges of Ussher's *Annals*, as if to suggest that anyone with another idea or theory about our planet's age was a meddler, time-waster, disrespecter of God's Word, or worse, a doubting Thomas. Rejection of Ussher Chronology (and other Young Earth teachings that developed from it) became itself a shocking taboo that must be trampled underfoot and silenced. What Ussher began in humility became a thing of Powell-like arrogance for his followers—so much so that, well after James Ussher's name fell into obscurity among the commonfolk, his theories and ideas remained even while Christians had no idea who or what they were following. (This is my opinion of the Church's historical and widespread reaction. I'm not by any stretch saying Answers in Genesis or any of its staff, volunteers, or affiliate ministries are "arrogant." I don't know them personally, but I grew up with many who showed egotistical contempt in their interactions with anyone whose cosmological beliefs weren't in line with their own.) When asked which verses they got their information on Young Earth theories from, many couldn't answer, because *no verses* answer that directly. (And when they did answer, they gave the age-old "Genesis says 'day'" response we'll address in the following pages.) Oftentimes, the somewhat panicked response (as I saw in my childhood) was to flip the question on "scholars," generically, while most folks couldn't offer the first answer as to where Young Earth Creationism got its start: "Ussher who? Chronology what? I don't know, but *scholars* say…"

Long after his name had fallen out of discussion in many households, James Ussher's Chronology continued to influence Christian culture, and not surprisingly, support continued to flow in from ministries everywhere in attempts to offer proof of what was largely one person's calculations. For, without Ussher Chronology in the first place, it's likely the Christian world would never have felt the pressure to defend Young Earth so staunchly.

Let me ask an important question: Would it be so bad if Earth really *is* older? For only a moment—and while maintaining that the authority of Scripture is *not* compromised—think about that question.

Other than offering a flimsy beam of backing behind evolutionary theory that no one is forced to accept anyway, what would the harm actually *be* in admitting Earth is very old? Would it be so terrible if God, in His infinite and creative wisdom and all-powerful omniscience over every force in the universe and beyond, really did allow the science *He* designed to play a part in the origin of Earth? (Remember: "Omniscience"—an attribute irrefutably tied to God's nature—contains the very word "science"!)

Listen, readers… "Faith is confidence in what we hope for and assurance about what we do not see. This is what the ancients were commended for. By faith we understand that the universe was formed at God's command" (Hebrews 11:1–3, NIV). There is no fault in saying, "I'm not sure about Ussher Chronology or Earth being only thousands of years in age, but I *know* the universe was created by God." This is faith—based on the Word and on the assurance that what the Word says remains far more powerful than inadequate theories from a bygone era of scholarship as the irrefutable answer to questions about origins.

This leads me to another point: Perhaps there is one more area where Powell and Ussher can be compared. The Powell Doctrine, despite being massively outdated, still holds a prominent place within respected institutions viewed as being dedicated to truth. Ussher Chronology, a sort of "doctrine" in itself, *despite being massively outdated,* still holds a prominent place in the Church's teachings. This is true for both influential educational institutions (Christian universities, etc.) as well as for the lay-teaching in many local churches every Sunday morning. Yet, if we're honest, some scientific progressions since the death of our prized scholar render Ussher Chronology unlikely—perhaps even impossible.

It is well beyond time to flush from our thinking not the priceless and groundbreaking *work* of James Ussher, nor the memory his passionate trailing after Christ, but the steadfast grip we have on his outdated conclusions.

Having said all I can in favor of the person Ussher was and the value of his research at the time he lived, it pains me now to point out his errors (respectfully, of course).

Chronology Based on Assumption

It is no secret that James Ussher's biblical chronology was based entirely on assumption and basic calculations of the generations and biblical characters' life spans. Ussher's reputation among scholars is thus twofold: 1) He was an anointed man of God who gave his all to glorify his Maker; 2) he, tragically, drew many inaccurate conclusions related to biblical chronology.

Just to show a couple of examples that reflect the latter, let's focus first on a mistake he made that's *unrelated* to Genesis and the origins of Earth:

> There has long been difficulty with the chronology of this period [the era of Zechariah]. Archbishop Ussher *assumed* [note this word] an interregnum of 11 years between the death of Jeroboam II and Zechariah's accession…[but it] seems more likely that there is error in certain of the synchronisms. The year of Zechariah's accession was probably 759 BC (some put it later), and the 6 months of his reign, with that given to Shallum, may be included in the 10 years of Menahem, who followed them (2 K 15:17).[59]

I won't spend time sorting out the discrepancy just noted; I'm simply sharing this quote to show that scholars commonly acknowledge Ussher's errors. Without even having to rely only on what he said regarding the age of Earth, it's clear that he rested on "assumption" (scholars' word exactly) to calculate the eras between prophets and kings based on length of service or reign without allowing for any interim. More simply, he seamed the end of one man's service to the beginning of the next, allowing little wiggle room for overlap or gaps in the tenures on the timeline. He believed he had the exact dating, when the Bible is often silent on what specific years rulers or prophets governed. This helps us understand the mistakes he made in his calculations about the age of Young Earth. For instance:

When Ussher dated Adam at 4004 BC he *assumed* [there's that word again…] that the generations in this chapter were an unbroken chain: but the chapter neither adds its figures together nor gives the impression that the men it names overlapped each other's lives to any unusual extent (e.g. that Adam lived almost to the birth of Noah).[60]

Here, Ussher begins with the genealogy (family lineage) mentioned in Genesis (mostly chapter 5) filling in the generational years until he concludes that Adam was created by God in 4004 BC. His method was to add the twenty-one generations mentioned in the Hebrew Old Testament from Adam forward and then calculate backward to Creation. Determining the number of years in a "generation," biblically speaking, is quite complicated. Some of the Old Testament people lived to be more than nine hundred years. (To those who believe living that long would be impossible, please note: This was before the Flood of Noah's time completely altered Earth's vegetation, oxygen, photosynthesis cycles, and every natural and "good" thing God originally designed to sustain life on this planet, as outlined in the first chapter of Genesis. It was also before God's anger was riled in Genesis 6, where we read that He declared humans would never live that long again [see especially verse 3]. Add to this the fact that, even now, we're aware of nonhuman species living hundreds of years—like many marine animals [some sharks, whales, fish, urchins, etc.]—and life's sustainability under the ideal environmental circumstances [in this case, the protection of the ocean's deep waters; in the case of ancient biblical people, the protection of perfect planetary conditions], and an extremely long life span is not inconceivable.) Despite the complications of calculating life span, Ussher stitched them together as he did in the Zechariah example, arriving at 4004 BC for Adam's origin, without allowing the possibility that there could have been any gaps or overlaps in genealogy (even though "date of birth" isn't identified in Scripture for either man).

But wouldn't that make the Bible wrong? After all, it does list fathers and sons in order, doesn't it? If there are gaps or overlaps, then the Word of God didn't cover the genealogies dependably.

If we look at the text linguistically, that's not necessarily the case. In fact, the Hebrew *ab* ("father") and *ben* ("son") can also mean "ancestor" and "descendant," which means there may be lengthy sections of bloodlines involving men not directly mentioned in Scripture. In fact, some assume Matthew "whoopsed" a few names from his New Testament Gospel genealogy, as it omits a couple of names from the family line listed in the Chronicles. Luke's genealogy is also different from Matthew's. The common Jewish writer's purpose wasn't to show every single person born into a family, but to list the relationships that were righteous and honorable. If someone—such as the wicked King Ahab—turned away from God and his life was an abandonment of all God required that line would be cut off. In 2 Kings 8:18, we see that Jorab married Ahab's daughter. Ahab's line was, in fact, cut off for four generations. Instead, Jehu's sons would serve as king (2 Kings 10:30; cf. 2 Kings 10:35; 13:1, 10; 14:23; 15:8). Thus, Matthew, in his genealogy, was being obedient to Scripture *and* his culture by choosing not to mention names of people who had, by the time of the New Testament, become known as wicked, illustrating that the biblical authors emphasized the names most important to their narratives instead of centering their books on only who was born to whom and when. If that is true for Matthew, certainly there is room to consider that possibility for the genealogy in Genesis, challenging us to accept that fathers and sons whose names and life spans were not recorded may have been a part of Adam's family tree.

In April of 1890, reverend and professor at Princeton Theological Seminary, William Henry Green, wrote a strong response to Ussher Chronology, titled "Article VIII: Primeval Chronology," which appeared in the theological journal *Bibliotheca Sacra*, volume 47. Green's report is a lengthy revisiting of the aforementioned discrepancies and assumptions, and his conclusion is at the very least fascinating, and at the most, it's proof the biblical writers were never personally invested in proving any particular dates of mankind's birth and the Creation or the Flood. Early on, Green points out that the science-vs.-Bible tension was alive and well even as far back as 1890, *long* before Darwinism took the spotlight, yet he recognized even then the subject had been "long and earnestly debated"—and his "what then?" response captures my thoughts on the matter beautifully:

> The question of the possible reconciliation of the results of scientific inquiry respecting the antiquity of man and the age of the world with the Scripture chronology has been long and earnestly debated. On the one hand, scientists, deeming them irreconcilable, have been led to distrust the divine authority of the Scriptures; and, on the other hand, believers in the divine word have been led to look upon the investigations of science with an un- friendly eye, as though they were antagonistic to religious faith…. But if these recently discovered indications of the antiquity of man, over which scientific circles are now so excited, shall, when carefully inspected and thoroughly weighed, demonstrate all that any have imagined they might demonstrate, what then? They will simply show that the popular chronology is based upon a wrong interpretation…[61]

Green's succinct and well-constructed acknowledgment of the issue we're still dealing with today—alongside his calm and rational rebuttal showing a complete lack of surprise, panic, or injury to his faith at the notion that his day's leading chronology would ever be found wrong—is a good example for us to follow. If we *did* discover the Earth was quite old, as scientists say, what then? The Bible would still the infallible Word of God that breathes life into its readers, and its credibility, as well as that of its Author, is not threatened.

But Green's report goes on to say something crucial: The Bible and its authors were never motivated to establish a solid chronology in the inflexible way we expect today:

> I here repeat, the discussion of the biblical genealogies above referred to, and add some further considerations which seem to me to justify the belief that the genealogies in Genesis 5 and 11 were not intended to be used, and cannot properly be used, for the construction of a chronology….

[T]he genealogies of the Bible [are] frequently abbreviated by the omission of unimportant names. In fact, abridgment is the general rule, induced by the indisposition of the sacred writers to encumber their pages with more names than were necessary for their immediate purpose. This is so constantly the case, and the reason for it so obvious, that the occurrence of it need create no surprise anywhere....

The omissions in the genealogy of our Lord as given in Matthew 1 are familiar to all. Thus in verse 8 three names are dropped between Joram and Ozias (Uzziah), viz., Ahaziah (2 Kings 8:25), Joash (2 Kings 12:1), and Amaziah (2 Kings 14:1); and in verse 11 Jehoiakim is omitted after Josiah (2 Kings 23:34; 1 Chron. 3:16); and in verse 1 the entire genealogy is summed up in two steps, "Jesus Christ, the son of David, the son of Abraham."

Other instances abound elsewhere; we mention only a few of the most striking.[62]

Green goes on for pages addressing what he calls "only a few" discrepancies in the biblical record of important generations, including royal families. He compares Genesis 5 and 11 to 1 and 2 Chronicles, with notes from Ezra, Nehemiah, 1 and 2 Kings, Exodus, Numbers, Judges, Deuteronomy, Isaiah, and even little Ruth, among still others. Over and again, he concludes in powerful language that the biblical record absolutely can be trusted, though *it must be trusted for the purposes God had in mind when He inspired the writers* to show key links between Old Testament men and women whose roles were crucial to the continual development of Israel and their Redeemer—not to facilitate our ability to compute backward to the first man. As Green begins to wrap up his report, he summarizes:

The result of our investigations thus far is sufficient to show that it is precarious to assume that any biblical genealogy is designed to be strictly continuous.... The creation, the Flood, the call of Abraham, are great facts, which stand out distinctly in primeval sacred history. A few incidents respecting our first parents and their sons Cain and Abel are recorded. Then there is an almost total blank until the Flood, with nothing whatever to fill the gap, and nothing to suggest the length of time intervening but what is found in the genealogy stretching between these two points. And the case is substantially the same from the Flood to Abraham. So far as the biblical records go, we are left not only without adequate data, but without any data whatever, which can be brought into comparison with these genealogies for the sake of testing their continuity and completeness.[63]

He points out that, had it been the Lord's *intention* to construct a perfect genealogy, even omitting a single name would make the whole Book suspect. Then Green asks whether we should assume that intention in the first place and concludes with a resounding "no":

But are we really justified in supposing that the author of these genealogies entertained such a purpose? It is a noticeable fact that he never puts them to such a use himself. He nowhere sums these numbers, nor suggests their summation. No chronological statement is deduced from these genealogies, either by him or by any inspired writer. There is no computation anywhere in Scripture of the time that elapsed from the creation or from the deluge, as there is from the descent into Egypt to the Exodus (Ex. xii. 40), or from the Exodus to the building of the temple (I Kings vi. 1)....

The calculation which leads to such a result, must proceed upon a wrong *assumption*.

On these various grounds we conclude that the Scriptures furnish no data for a chronological computation prior to the life of Abraham; and that the Mosaic records do not fix *and were not intended to* fix the precise date either of the Flood or of the creation of the world.[64]

All things considered, Ussher's math was extremely clever and progressive for a Bible study of his day. However, rather than viewing his work as a "conclusion," it's more accurate to consider the Ussher timeline as a great platform upon which to build additional data.

Hang on, though. We're talking about the difference between thousands and billions of years. Surely, Donna, you're not suggesting this massive discrepancy is resolved by simply allowing for more generations in an early family tree, are you?

No, that's not the whole picture, either. Let me explain.

The Major Discrepancy: It's Not about Adam!

Though I—alongside many scholars—insist Ussher's timeline of the origin of man is only *assumption* and therefore cannot be viewed as the only possibility of who arrived and when, I also see the discrepancy between billions or thousands of years as a problem that can't be settled by identifying gaps in genealogy. To state that Adam was created billions of years ago (Old-Earth dating) and that only a fraction of his family line was documented appears to make Genesis 5 at least irresponsible, if not impossible. At the very least, since the lengths of these lives, as well as of their offspring, are recorded, Genesis becomes "inaccurate" if billions of years elapsed between the days of Adam and Noah. No figuring can make this short list stretch long enough to account for what transpired from the formation of the first human to the Flood if, in fact, the Flood happened anytime within the last six thousand years. This is yet another reason Young Earthers typically cannot accept the idea that the Earth is old.

But what if I were to tell you that it's not even about Adam?

Ussher made yet another assumption that overlooked perhaps the most vital piece of this giant puzzle: He linked Adam's beginning to the Earth's beginning, teaching that the two events could only have happened days apart. Therefore, if Adam originated in 4004 BC, then Earth did as well.

Yet, nowhere in any debate that I'm aware of (at least in the mainstream—and I've been investigating this research pool for the majority of my life) have studiers of God's Word allowed for the possibility that Earth was created billions of years ago...*and that* Adam came into the picture far later.

Wait just a minute, Donna. You're jumping off the deep end, here. Genesis is clear! God made the heavens and Earth, all the plants and animals upon it, and then formed man from the dust of the ground on the sixth day of Creation! That's what the Bible says...

I'm aware. But the six-day Creation narrative doesn't begin until the fifth verse, referring to the "first day." Prior to that, we have four verses, one of which describes a planet "without form, and void" (Genesis 1:2) for, well, God only knows how long. (This is referred to as the "Gap theory." We'll discuss this more later on.)

By now, you get the idea, and it's time to close the chapter on Ussher. This scholar was brilliant, but at this point we will respectfully leave his arguments—and his "authority fortress"—behind, to take a look at the list of relevant dating issues within the debate, starting with the popular discussion of whether "day" even means what we think it does, or if it could mean "age," as in an indefinite period.

Chapter 3

The Bible Says...*What?!*

"THE PLACE TO START IS IN THE BIBLE," Christians say. I agree whole-heartedly. However, finding out "what the Bible says" isn't always as easy as reading it in English, since that represents *at least two* phases of inter-pretation: 1) Scriptural translators render the biblical language (Hebrew, Greek, and a small amount of Aramaic) into a secondary language (like English); 2) Bible readers interpret what that rendering means to them in modern times. Because we're influenced by how languages and concepts are communicated in our culture, by the time we deduce what a passage means both in English and to *us*, we can, at times, be very far removed from the original Hebrew or Greek writer's intent.

Therefore, although I concur that the Bible is where we should start in researching matters of our home planet, I'm going to do something radical and pay closer attention to what was written *before* English and modern cultural influence came into the picture.

Proponents of the Old Earth view often subscribe to the "day-age" interpretation, which allows for the *order* of events from Genesis to stand, but does not force literal, twenty-four-hour periods when Genesis says something happened in or on a "day."

Why not just let the Bible speak for itself? If it says "day," it means "day," so why question this?

Because, again, it says "day" in *English*, but that isn't necessarily what is said in the original Hebrew. I admit—as one who has a college degree in biblical studies and theology and as a perpetual student of the Word—that one of the first lessons in the proper principles of biblical interpretation is that the Bible should be taken literally whenever possible, unless doing otherwise creates an absurdity. However, an absurdity is what becomes of *many* verses if literality were always the lens through which we read this precious text. We must remember that the Bible makes frequent use of figures of speech, euphemisms, hyperbole, allegory, and metaphors, among other linguistic and literary devices useful in the world of human communication, just like any language in the world today.

To Be, or Not to Be, Literal: That Is the Question

Here's an example I've used in several other books: Imagine that two thousand years ago I wrote a friend, saying, "It's raining cats and dogs outside." Today, if translated into a second language, that sentence could indicate the miraculous day Donna Howell saw canines and felines falling from the sky. Assuming it wasn't a true miracle I had intended to write about, this would be an absurdity. The only way my letter could be received with the meaning I intended is if someone fluent in that second language were to understand the familiar, cultural expression and translate it into a phrase that conveys the correct idea: "It's raining very hard outside."

This is the difference between the methods used in translating the Bible, most often referred to as "literal," "dynamic," and "free" or "liberal." A literal translation would be "felines and canines fell from the sky"; a dynamic translation would capture the author's meaning based on cultural expression and context (such as "the rain was falling hard"); and a free or liberal translation allows the translator more subjectivity, often leading to an incorrect meaning, such as if the translator were to change all New Testament references of Rome to Washington, DC, as one translation has done.

This kind of sorting process is the first step translators must consider when bringing the Good News into a second language...but it is *also* the process each reader must use in daily Bible reading, especially when something initially appears odd. Otherwise, we would have a hard time explaining why Jesus calls Himself "bread" (John 6:51) when He is clearly not a baked good; why He says we must "hate" our family members in order to be His disciples (Luke 14:26) when He elsewhere perpetually speaks of loving; how He instructed us all to eat His flesh and drink His blood for eternal life (Matthew 26:26–28; John 6:54; and others), when cannibalism is regarded as a detestable act and the symptom of a curse in His Father's Word (Leviticus 26:29; Deuteronomy 28:53–57; Jeremiah 19:9; Lamentations 2:20; 4:10; Ezekiel 5:10), and His literal body and blood are not available for all and forever (apart from the Catholic belief of miraculous transubstantiation, which I do not subscribe to); what could possibly be meant by letting the "dead bury the dead" (Matthew 8:21–22) when the deceased can't rise to carry their brothers and sisters to the grave, and so on. The list is a long one, and if literality were applied to every verse, the whole Bible—including many words from Christ, Himself—would be, as we've said, absurd.

Though it would be reckless to *assume* a passage is allegory, hyperbole, or a euphemism just because we don't immediately understand what it says otherwise, there are times when nonliteral interpretations are best. Note that the translation method behind the beloved KJV is principally literal, and that version has been enormously influential in translational endeavors since, heavily contributing to why so many English Bibles of our time prefer the literal "day" over "age."

The *question* for our purposes, then, becomes whether the writer of Genesis intended for "day" to convey a period of twenty-four hours (our current comprehension of the word) or a longer span of time. The *answer* lies in whether there is biblical, cultural, historical, and linguistic support for "day" meaning something other than twenty-four hours. Could it be that, much like our "canines and felines from the sky" analogy, the writer of Genesis used a common term that can dependably mean something other than what literal interpretations suggest?

Yes, it is possible. Some scholars believe it's even likely, though presenting evidence in favor of that doesn't always sit well with many mainstream Christian teachers. I've chosen to include this information here because of the heavy importance of the "day-age" interpretation on both Young and Old Earth sides. Let's look briefly at the word, then I'll explain why it could be interpreted either way. (By the way, though this book is so different from any others on the topic [at least that I'm aware of], I'm nowhere near the first to suggest that either interpretation could be correct. Since the popularization of the Gap theory in the early 1800s, many scholars have said this fight between Old/Young Earthers over "day vs. age" is unnecessary.)

"Day"

The English word "day" in Genesis is derived from the Hebrew *yom* (pronounced "yome"; rhymes with "Rome"). As often as it is believed to represent a twenty-four-hour period, this word is used many times throughout the Bible to refer to the passage of time in several different ways. It can certainly mean a "day," as in the period from dawn to dawn or sundown to sundown (however one wants to define the concept of a single day in relation to sunlight), but it can also mean: time generically, an indefinite period of time, a *division* of time, a year, the opposite of night, a working day, a day's journey, a lifetime, or today, yesterday, or tomorrow, based on whether the word appears in singular form and its context.

That's a lot of meanings packed into one tiny Hebrew word! This early in the discussion, it seems a little irresponsible to latch on to only one of these definitions and hold the entire cosmological-debate audience captive to that single interpretation. Don't you think that if God, Himself, allowed that word to mean more than one thing in His revelatory Word, we should at least be open to allowing it as well?

Perhaps my personal favorite is 1 Kings 1:1: "David was old and stricken in years [*yom*]." If *yom* means "a day," then David was "old" when he was a "day" old—i.e., he was a newborn. Since we know that's absurd, we must allow that *yom* here means "years." Another is Zechariah 8:4: "Thus saith the Lord of hosts; 'There shall yet old men and old women dwell in the streets of Jerusalem, and every man with his staff in his hand for very age [*yom*].'" Can you imagine the latter half of this verse with the standard "day" interpretation forced upon it?—"old men and women in the streets of Jerusalem, carrying a cane in hand on account of twenty-four hours." It's nonsensical. "Old" people carry canes due to their "age" requiring walking assistance. Nobody carries a cane at the cause of a "day."

We see many examples in the Bible of *yom* in context of an indefinite period of time, such as "the day of the Lord" from many prophets (especially Joel and Isaiah, who were obviously not talking about a great time of judgment that will occur in twenty-four hours), and other uses that read figuratively of times in the past (such as 1 Samuel 8:8; 2 Samuel 22:19). (Have you ever heard your grandpa say, "Back in *my* day," referring to an era of his life such as childhood or youth? If so, you're familiar with this concept.)

Young Earthers almost always get to this point in the conversation and say, "Yes, but the context of Genesis forces a literal day because of the language used around chapter 1, verses 3 through 5." This section of Scripture describes the creation of light and its separation from darkness, followed by God, Himself, calling the light "day" and the darkness "night." The next words are: "And there was evening and there was morning, one day." Thus, Young Earthers say, Genesis 1:3–5 clarifies the intended time span of *yom* throughout this passage, since that twenty-four-hour interval we know as a day in the Creation epic is described in such close proximity (and therefore the same context) as this description of light and darkness upon the surface of Earth. When we're looking for context, we often don't need to go any farther than the surrounding verses to see how a word or phrase applies, and, therefore, what it truly means in that passage. And whereas I would normally agree that this "close-proximity context clarification" is a good rule of thumb when attempting to find the true meaning of Scripture, we have proof in the same Word of God that this rule doesn't always apply.

For instance: We also see *yom* twice in extremely close proximity in Zechariah 3:9–10, though it can't possibly refer to twenty-four hours in both verses: "'For behold the stone that I have laid before Joshua... 'and I

will remove the iniquity of that land in one day [*yom*]. In that day [*yom*],'
saith the Lord of hosts, 'shall ye call every man his neighbour under the
vine and under the fig tree.'" The "stone…laid before Joshua" in the first
of these two verses is a reference to Jesus, the Cornerstone of the Church,
followed by a future era of blessing for God's people in the second verse.
Jesus did "remove the iniquity of that land in *one day*" (the day He died),
but the prophesied time of blessing as a result of His sacrifice is obviously
an indefinite period much longer than twenty-four hours, which means
this two-verse passage uses *yom* in both ways: 1) a single day; 2) an indefinite era. If *yom* can indicate two different time spans in such close proximity in Zechariah, could it mean two different stretches of time in similar
proximity within Genesis, too?

I'll let you be the judge of that, but know that those who insist on
Genesis 1:1–3 referring to twenty-four hours in forces a contradiction in
the next chapter. Look at Genesis 2:4: "These are the generations of the
heavens and of the earth when they were created, in the day [*yom*] that
the Lord God made the earth and the heavens." This one verse collapses
all of Creation—the entire epic, involving heavens, Earth, and all six days
plus the seventh day of rest—into a single day (*yom*). So, which is it? Was
Earth created in one single *yom* as Genesis 2:4 states, or during the six/
seven that Genesis 1:3–5 states? Again, regardless of their proximity, these
two verses refer to the same biblical event/narrative. It's a bit confusing to
those outside the Young Earth group that so many ministries go out of
their way to prove that "day" is twenty-four hours long based on Genesis
1:3–5, while they don't often acknowledge the discrepancy of the same
Hebrew word referring to at least a seven-day stretch in Genesis 2:4. It
appears that Genesis, itself, forces at least *the possibility* that *yom* indicates
to more than merely a twenty-four-hour period.

One clue in biblical interpretation that's taken into account far less
than it should be is considering how the Jews, themselves, treated certain
topics during or around the historical period described in the Bible. In this
case, the Jews didn't consider a day to be twenty-four hours. The majority
of Jews believed a day encompassed the hours when the light from the sun
was upon Earth, since God treated "light" as a synonym for "day"; many

times of the year, this would be from 6 o'clock in the morning to 6 o'clock in the evening—twelve hours, not twenty-four.

A minority of Jews took the opposite approach by considering a day to be from 6 o'clock in the evening to 6 o'clock in the morning—again, twelve hours. (This issue comes up a lot in studies regarding the exact day and time Jesus was murdered in relation to Passover. It's a long discussion involving the existence of two Jewish calendars at the time: the Judean calendar and the Galilean calendar. Since Jesus was a Galilean, He followed that calendar, having Passover Seder [the main Passover dinner] hours prior to His arrest, while the Judeans observed the Seder the following day, rectifying the discrepancy of how Jesus both a) honored the traditional Seder right on time and b) had to be taken down from the cross *before* the Passover in John 19:31. So, many observances on the earlier Jewish calendar fluctuated between the two.) Seasonal variations in the times of sunrise and sunset cause an additional problem. Because the sun doesn't come up or go down at the same times during each season, if we insist on the Young Earthers' definition of "day" being a synonym for "light," since that's the context God set as a precedent, now we have to parse out countless calculations of how the word fluctuates between seasons. A day in summer is several hours longer than a day in fall. We quickly see how arguing these distinctions would go off the rails and into irrelevant territory.

Taking this yet a step farther and applying it globally, as my thirteen-year-old pointed out just the night before I wrote this: "But, Mom, a day based only on sunlight *also* changes duration depending on where you're at in the world. Some cities in Alaska are saturated in darkness for weeks at a time!" Excellent work, kiddo. You nailed it. If we're going to argue that the Hebrew *yom* has to represent twenty-four hours in consistent relation to periods of light and darkness, then we have a lot of work to do in constructing what a day means to those in areas of the world with a different standard of God's light/darkness precedent in Genesis 1:3–5, and then determine what that would have meant during Creation week—and *from where*? Eden? Did Eden, like Alaska, have longer stretches of darkness? Or shorter?

What a can of worms!

There is yet a bigger can to sort out: None of our discussion thus far has taken into consideration that *the sun wasn't even created until the fourth day!* Without the sun to shed light on Earth during the first three days of Creation week, the entire case for this sunlight measurement context is a fallacy, since that basis of measurement wasn't established in the moment God separated light from darkness.

But, to be fair, the subject of the establishment of light and sun is also an argument for the literal translation. Readers might note that God created light on the first day of Creation week, but the *sun* was not created until the fourth day. Yet, it is the sun that provides the photosynthesis for the survival of the *plants* God had already put into place on the third day. This forces two questions: 1) If light belongs to the first day and sun belongs to the fourth, what does "light" mean if it isn't the sun?; 2) If "day" means an indefinite span of age or ages, how did the vegetational system created in age three survive without the sun of age four, especially for those who take "age" to mean millions of years? Surely the plants would have quickly died without their sunlight, which of course would have caused death to any living thing on Earth since they, too, require sunlight and food from vegetation to survive, right?

Well, that's the argument offered by many Young Earthers to prove all of Creation must have happened in the shortest fathomable time. However, it can *still* go both ways: Most scholars understand this to mean God formed light waves/particles on the first day, while He assigned them to primarily belong to the orbital body known as the sun He created on the fourth day. (The moon obviously comes in at this point as well, but because its light is reflective, it doesn't need its own breakdown.) If that's the case, then the waves/particles of light He originally formed went wherever they were needed under His guidance and nurtured the young plants for as long as necessary for them to thrive in their earliest form until the orbital space bodies became the vehicles for distributing those waves/particles. So, both "day" and "age" remain admissible, and the debate between Young and Old Earth scholars rages on…

Moreover, our concept of time is largely irrelevant anyway. Don't forget that a day to God is like a thousand years, and a thousand years is like a day (Psalm 90:4; 2 Peter 3:8). In fact, so important is this distinction that Peter specifically goes out of his way to instruct the early Church to "be not ignorant of this one thing"! That is powerful, New Testament language that brings into perspective the convicting reality that "time is not the same to God as it is to man," as one commentary put it.[65] Peter could have said any number of alternative things, but he chose to ask his readers not to be "ignorant" of the fact that God's timing is not our timing. The Spirit of God who inspired the God-breathed Bible guided both Genesis and 2 Peter with the same level of authority (2 Timothy 3:16), and, without doubt, His comprehension of hours, days, months, years, and so on is never going to be limited to what we interpret, *especially* when the Hebrew word He chose has more than one definition. This added layer of conviction—by itself!—should be enough to put the day-age interpretation in its proper place in the cosmological debate.

There is yet another contributing factor—from the scientific platform, this time. According to scientists, a day wasn't considered to be a twenty-four-hour period anywhere on the globe in the beginning, anyway. Certain experts—such as planetary scientist Takanori Sasaki of Kyoto University in Japan during the Intercontinental Academia conference in 2016—have recently calculated Earth's earliest days to potentially be just *four* hours long, though, he reports, human life had not yet inhabited this planet at that time.[66]

But Donna, I don't care what science says happened in the beginning. I don't believe in the Big Bang, and we weren't there to see the origins of the universe, so anything science says about that moment is the result of guessing games.

That argument might hold some validity if it weren't for the fact that the length of a day is even *now* fluctuating, affecting modern calculations of time as reported on satellites, cell phones, GPS navigational devices, etc., proving the speed of Earth's rotation is not steady and never has been perfectly so. It is simply an observable truth to anyone who watches the clock closely. Our atomic clocks and equipment producing "precise astronomical measurements" are showing that "a day is very rarely exactly the magic number of 86,400 seconds" (twenty-four hours); in fact, the speed of Earth's rotation had been steadily slowing since well before we had the technology to observe it "due to friction effects associated with the tides driven by the Moon."[67] However, surprisingly, since the 1960s, Earth's rotation has been speeding back up.[68]

Most scientists attest that, only thousands of years ago, a day was still very close to twenty-four hours. But if there's even a *chance* that Earth is older than thousands of years, then when God called the light "day" and the darkness "night," it was so long ago that we can't be sure how many hours we're even talking about…and none of this conjecture even touches the aforementioned *yom* discrepancy of Genesis 2:4 (which collapses all six days into one *yom*)!

After considering all the evidence and details, I feel strongly convicted to concede that *yom* can be allowed to mean "age" in Genesis (though I don't insist that must be the only possibility). From that perspective, each day of Creation was an incalculable period of time.

Now, to discuss why a number of Old Testament theologians (like Mike Heiser—discussed more in the next section) say it doesn't matter at all whether *yom* meant "day" or "age": If Earth *was* created billions of years ago and Adam came about much later, just after the planet was "without form, and void" (Genesis 1:2), then, as mentioned just before the last section, *both* day and age fit the following scenario: 1) God created Earth; 2) a crucial war between the forces of good and evil caused mass destruction *as attested in Scripture* (we're still getting to that), creating a planet that was "without form, and void"; 3) God chose—at a certain point, and for a duration of His choosing (days *or* ages) between the "void" world of Genesis 1:2 and the "good" world of Genesis 1:31—to create a better place, upon which we now live.

Would He have chosen to spend ages or days to recreate the fallen, nearly destroyed planet of the "void" era? We don't know, but if our theory is correct, then He had billions of years between "void" and "good" to get around to doing it in *His timing*, which will never conform to our own ideas of the linear progression of time, anyway. In my own humble opinion, it's not worth fighting about when yet another, more important word related to dating Creation needs to be addressed.

In the Beginning, God "Created"...

The English word "created" that appears in the Bible's first verse is the Hebrew *bara* (pronounced baw-raw). No one questions that this verb has always meant "created" or "to create," though few sources go so far as to show the varying levels at which that could be applied.

One source that has is the *Dictionary of Biblical Languages with Semantic Domains: Hebrew (Old Testament)*. The scholars behind this resource are not casual in their approach to defining words. Quite to the contrary, these linguistics experts understand the importance of etymology (studying the roots, origins, and meaning of a term at its earliest use), history (how a word or term was used in biblical and other literature and, therefore, what it means in its proper context of ancient texts), and peer review (what other experts in the Hebrew language have discovered about its early use). The result of this approach is a transparent, honest, and unbiased study of the original language of the Old Testament.

According to this group of scholars, the verb *bara* encapsulates more than one way of bringing something into existence. It can refer to making "something that has not been in existence before" (i.e., making something out of nothing), *as well as* to "form or fashion something out of elements that [already] exist"[69] (i.e., making something out of something else).

Many scholars weighing in on this issue use Isaiah 65:17–18 as an example: "For, behold, I create [*bara*] new heavens and a new earth: and the former shall not be remembered, nor come into mind. But be ye glad and rejoice for ever in that which I create [*bara*]: for, behold, I create [*bara*] Jerusalem a rejoicing, and her people a joy." This reference to the yet-to-come New Jerusalem of the end times describes a moment when God will take the rubble of Earth after the mass destruction outlined in the book of Revelation and make the New Heavens and New Earth from those formerly existing planetary and space elements. In other words, God will "create something [a beautiful New Earth] out of something else [the destroyed remains of Earth after the future apocalypse]."

In the first of these two verses, we see that the people of the New Earth will not remember their former home ("the former shall not be remembered, nor come into mind"). This passage also implies that, during this process of re-creation, there will be limited (or completely absent) "remembrance" of the former creation by the joyful souls who inhabit the latter, better home. Most scholars, theologians, and commentators acknowledge that this seeming forgetfulness is not happenstance, as if God zapped their memories for some enigmatic reason, but it's a natural side effect of being delivered into a new land so wonderful that it eclipses any memory of the former. This takes place *after* we have transcended into the eternal state with perfection of the body and mind. So, if we, even while we're perfect in the future state of eternity, cannot look back and recall what the world looks like right now…

…could the humans alive after Adam's time be equally unaware of what came before *them*, too? Of course, the context is different: In the future we will forget the past because of glory; in Adam's day, people "forgot" the former world because they hadn't existed during the "void years" that came before their time. Nevertheless, does this passage in Isaiah—perhaps even indirectly, by showing the character of God's modus operandi—give us a reason for why humanity today can't nail down what our earliest times looked like in the great "what came first" cosmological question despite all scientific advances? Could this be why there are no witness accounts or divine revelations that describe in detail what happened between the "void" and "good" worlds?

Maybe, like the future-perfect humans of the New Earth, we're *not supposed to "remember"* or know what happened to our former Earth. We're not explicitly forbidden from trying to parse it out (thus books like this), but if God's way of doing things presents the possibility that the answers to our questions regarding an old Earth aren't easy for us to sort out, then at the very least some of us should be more open-minded to alternative interpretations of Scripture in this area.

Naturally, this part of our study is purely theoretical, but the next part is not.

Because *bara* can mean both "creation" and "re-creation" (or "transformation"), it forces at least the theological possibility that Genesis 1 could be describing an initial formation of Earth *and* a re-creation of Earth at some later point from the rubble that was left after the planet became "without form, and void," regardless of whether there is a detailed record of that seemingly missing period between the two creative events.

But readers need not take only my word for it.

One of the most prolific theologians of this century—and a vast majority of today's Bible scholars agree, to the point that his opinion has widely become the litmus test of whether a new biblical theory is viable—is the late Dr. Michael Heiser. Until his journey to be with Jesus a mere three weeks before the time of this writing, Heiser consistently illustrated his expertise in many biblical languages and dialects, speaking fluent Hebrew and Greek, as well as many extinct languages/dialects from the regions of early Mesopotamia (including Sumerian, one of the first languages ever spoken that we know of and paramount to Old Testament biblical interpretation). One of the grandest positions Heiser attained was becoming the resident theologian for the enormously popular Logos Bible Software (a program dedicated to proper exegesis of Scripture, containing hundreds of thousands of books, lexicons, commentaries, interlinear word studies, and other media files all weighing in on what the Word of God says from Genesis to Revelation).

Throughout his years as a professor of Hebrew whose teachings are repeated all over the globe, Heiser frequently pointed out to his students an obvious, yet often overlooked, point concerning the original language of the Old Testament: Hebrew vowels *did not exist* in the beginning. Even the Dead Sea Scrolls—religious texts discovered in the Qumran caves, dated from the third century BC to the first century AD and involving more than 225 of the earliest copies of Old Testament writings—do not contain vowels.

To give an English example of the general idea, try reading the following "sentence" and pretend for a moment it was written by Solomon in a book like Proverbs or Ecclesiastes (I've chosen examples that are *not* in the Bible so we can consider this idea with fresh eyes): "Lt th ws mn tch th yng mn." After a bit of struggling, you may work through these consonants and conclude that Solomon wrote, "Let the wise man teach the young man." Or, say the following was written by Moses in a book like Exodus: "Nd thy jrnyd nthr frty dys dn nghts vr lnd nd wtr, fstng nd pryng fr Gd t drct thm t th lnd h prmsd." Again, after some problem-solving, you may come to understand Moses wrote, "And they journeyed another forty days and nights over land and water, fasting and praying for God to direct them to the land he promised." The unadulterated biblical Hebrew reads similarly.

If you had been a scribe alive anytime up to the era of Christ, you wouldn't have been intimidated or confused by this. You would have known from oral traditions; prior familiarity with scriptural stories, characters, writings, and sayings from your parents and elders; and scribal teaching at the weekly synagogue that vowels aren't necessary for being able to comprehend what the writers of the Old Testament intended. Although the following isn't a perfect illustration of this concept (because English *does* have vowels), think of how often we hear the phrase, "the gift that keeps on giving." Our parents said it as we were growing up; friends say it at birthday parties; commercials repeat it during the holiday season; pastors say it in reference to Christ's sacrifice; or a neighbor sarcastically says it about his car that's died for the third time in a month... Whatever our personal experience, we hear this adage so often that, if English *did not* have vowels and our eyes were adjusted to consonants-only text, we would know what "th gft tht kps n gvng" means.

After the diaspora—when the Jews were scattered all over the known world after the stoning of Stephen—they gradually took on the languages (both spoken and written) of their new cultures, and being literate in written Hebrew became far more important for younger generations forward, in order for them to understand and keep the traditions of their Jewish forefathers. The Hebrew vowel system (most often called *niqqud* or *neqqudot*) was invented sometime around the seventh or eighth century AD by the Masoretes (a group of scribes from Tiberias, Jerusalem, and Babylonia [modern Iraq]). Because they wished to take the greatest care and show the utmost respect in updating the letters to reflect intonations of a spoken language without changing the authoritative, written Word of God, they elected to keep the consonants intact and, instead of adding additional letters, they added small dots, short lines, and squiggly marks under, above, or next to each letter. Therefore, some words in the Hebrew can and do have more than one possible meaning and/or application. (By the way, we don't have to take Heiser's word for this. Google "Masoretic Hebrew" to see hundreds of articles showing this unique and clever invention by the Masoretes circa AD 600–700. I mention Heiser because he taught about this subject frequently and because what he says next in our study of *bara* is crucial.)

But I heard a presentation from [scholar/teacher so-and-so] that placed a huge emphasis on these dots and squiggles. He said they forced a specific definition over another. How can he claim this if the dots or marks didn't exist at the time the books of the Bible were written?

It's not uncommon to see a scholar responsibly show the *niqqud* system at work in modern interpretations of ancient texts for one crucial reason: The Masoretes were from the region in which and time when the traditions and sacred, scriptural teachings of the Old Testament were still being passed down orally in society, culture, and families. They were experts (literally) in what the Old Testament said, not only because of their linguistic training (although they had that in abundance), but because their parents told them what the texts meant, and their parents before that told them, and their parents before that. *Masor* means "tradition," and "Masorete" means "master of tradition," so if *they* said a word needed a dot or squiggle to produce one vowel sound over another (changing the meaning of a verse from an irresponsible to a responsible interpretation), it's definitely worth our consideration. This is the central reason many Hebrew scholars open their statements with the phrase, "According to the Masoretic Hebrew" (Many scholars assume their audience knows the history behind the term "Masoretic," but that's simply not the case. So, listeners can easily be swayed by a subsequent presentation by a scholar who pays no attention to the Masoretic text, citing conclusions to be "from [such-and-such] Hebrew word," therefore creating an interpretational fallacy that the listeners aren't trained to recognize. And then, as is the case today, there are countless possible interpretations of verses, leading people to construe the words of Scripture to say whatever they want, since "the Hebrew says…").

Relevant to this discussion is what the Masoretic text concludes about the clause structure (more on this in a moment) surrounding *bara* in Genesis 1:1–3. Young Earthers most often insist that *bara* describes God, in *the* beginning of all time (not just the beginning of a new era), creating Earth from nothing. This, combined with the "day" issue addressed in the last section, forces Earth to have been newly formed for the first time in six literal days only thousands of years ago, so it's important to see whether *bara* could have referred to a re-creation event.

First, let's review what these verses say in the most popularly read translation of the past several hundred years (KJV):

> In the beginning God created the heaven and the earth. And the earth was without form, and void; and darkness was upon the face of the deep. And the Spirit of God moved upon the face of the waters. And God said, "Let there be light": and there was light.

(Since the details regarding the water aren't related to our review of "create," for now we'll omit the latter portion of verse 2. It will come back into play later.) One of two interpretations is possible thus far:

1. In the beginning, God created the heavens and Earth out of nothing. The Earth He just created was, at first, "without form and void." So, God quickly or immediately proceeded to say, "Let there be light," and there was light (followed by the formation of everything else during Creation week).
2. When God created the heavens and Earth—Earth having already been present, though it was "without form, and void" (for an undeterminable length of time)—God said, "Let there be light," and there was light (followed by the formation of everything else on a formerly existing planet that would *no longer be* "without form, and void").

Which interpretation is more likely?

Before I give away the answer, it may help to explain clause structure, or, what Heiser refers to in his presentation on this passage as "the key to understanding *why* Genesis 1:1–3 can be taken a *variety* of ways."[70]

In Hebrew grammar, as in English, there are independent clauses and dependent clauses. An independent clause is a group of words with a subject and a verb that express a complete thought, such as Heiser's example: "Jim studied in his room for his chemistry exam."[71] Nothing else is needed for this sentence to be understood. A dependent clause is a group of words that also contains a subject and a verb, but that doesn't express a complete thought, as in Heiser's follow-up example: "When Jim studied in his room for his chemistry exam."[72] The "when" at the beginning of the sentence is a cue to expect something to be added to the beginning or end, so Heiser illustrates on-screen with underlining: "When Jim studied in his room for his chemistry exam, he was able to concentrate," or, "His brother stayed away when Jim studied in his room for his chemistry exam." In both cases, Heiser points out that we can intuitively feel whether we need more information in a sentence for the thought to be complete, even when we have no idea what a clause is.[73] He then goes on to explain that, in Genesis 1:1–3, there is a series of clauses; readers must establish which of those can stand alone—as complete thoughts—and which ones depend on the clauses around them to clarify their meaning.

Our first clause—"In the beginning, God created the heavens and the earth"—is independent; it stands alone without issue, and everyone can see it's a complete sentence. If this is where it ended, we wouldn't have an issue. The problem is introduced when we see the first English word in verse 2: "Now" in some translations (or "And" in KJV), which appears just before "the earth was without form and void."

"What is the role of verse 2?" Heiser asks. "Does it proceed from verse 1? Or does it do something else?"[74] One *could* see a linear sequence: Verse 1 happened, then verse 2 happened, then verse 3 happened; each verse is the result (and therefore follows) the former.

But is that what the writer of Genesis intended to say? Or was the writer—as a number of Hebrew scholars attest—using verse 2 to *describe* the object of creation in verse 1?

As Heiser points out, Hebrew Bible translations that stick closest to the earliest forms of Hebrew—such as the Jewish Publication Society Translation—go back to the Masoretic text…and suddenly, the clauses shift to render a sequence that looks foreign to many of us today. Genesis 1:1 becomes: "*When* God *began to* create the heavens and the earth…". As with the "Jim…studied" example, this "When" makes the first verse of the Bible a dependent clause, an incomplete thought that relies on additional details to become a complete sentence.

The difference between "In the beginning, God created" and "When God began to create" boils down to—you probably guessed it—a vowel mark that *did not exist* at the time Genesis was written. The former expression requires the addition of a vowel mark that looks like a capital *T* under the last letter of the phrase, while the latter expression requires two dots under the same letter. In its earliest form, without the vowel mark, there was no definite article, so the word "the" in the phrase "In *the* beginning" is a scholarly interpolation (an attempt to clarify something by adding words that weren't there in the original) by later translators to help us better understand it. The first syllable of *bara* in Hebrew would have either been pronounced "bah" or "beh," meaning two completely different things, as we've outlined prior: 1) God created a world that was initially void and He immediately proceeded to bring it to life further (Young Earth view); 2) *when* God *began to* create Earth, it was void *already*, and He brought *new life* to it (what Heiser calls the "Hebrew Syntax View," because "this is strict Hebrew syntax").[75]

Well, since the vowels didn't exist, it could mean either one, so I'll pick "bah," supporting Young Earth and a single Creation event, and Donna can have her "beh," supporting two Creation events—a "void" world re-created or transformed into a "good" world later on.

Not so fast. Picking and choosing biblical interpretations is what leads to a culture of embracing and justifying unthinkable acts and disregarding solid orders put in place by God, Himself.

Heiser continues:

I'm going to go to the *Biblia Hebraica Stuttgartensia* [he pulls it up on-screen]…it's *beh*… The translation, "When God began to create"…more accurately reflects the Masoretic texts…. Now, you could just as well say—and trust me, some do—"Well, it didn't have vowels to begin with, so we should put 'bah' in there and be definite: 'In THE beginning'; the first creative act!"… Yeah, you can, but there is no [scribal] tradition that supports it, and that's what we have for the Hebrew Bible; we have scribal tradition for the way it's vocalized. So, let's go back here [he pulls up the *beh/bah* comparison again]. We have two possible translations. If we opt for the "when" translation…now we have dependent clauses. We don't have a series of independent ideas. We have two full verses of clauses [verses 1 and 2] that are leading up to something, and that "something" is verse 3, and *that* is the main idea, *that* is the independent thought.[76]

On the screen behind Heiser, we see he's utilized English characters called "em dashes" (they look like this: —) as a visual aid to more responsibly and appropriately make the Hebrew flow in our language. He also bumped the middle verse over to offset it from the first and third. The first three verses of the Bible are now rendered:

[1]When God began to create the heavens and the earth—
  [2]Now the earth was without form and void…
[3]Then God said, "Let there be light," and there was light.

In this sequence, whatever appears between the em dashes is describing or qualifying the independent clause that occurs at the end of *one total, complete thought*.

This may still be complicated for readers who may not be familiar with rules of grammar (regardless of whether it's English or Hebrew, though in this case, it's both). So let me repeat this once more and simplify it by inserting what could be the Hebraic implications of *both* a former and latter Earth:

When God began to create the [current] heavens and the earth, the [former] earth was without form and void...but *then* God said, "Let there be light," and there was light.

"Now *catch* this," Heiser emphasizes regarding the first two verses:

The writer is describing conditions that already exist before God actually creates anything, before God actually speaks anything into existence. In other words, you have a situation where verses 1 and 2 lead to verse 3, and they *set it up*. The *first* creative act—the *first* thing God does—in Genesis 1, [verses] 1 through 3, in this view, is *not* verse 1, it's verse 3.... This is *strict* Hebrew syntax. Syntax is sentence structure, sentence relationships. If you're going to just go by what the Hebrew says like a zealot, strictly obeying the rules of Hebrew grammar, *that* is what you get. And that's why some English Bibles have [this wording].[77]

On a slide shortly following a profound moment when Heiser explains that Earth was "*already* formless and empty,"[78] he shows two "ramifications" of this rendering:

1. Genesis 1:1 is not the absolute beginning
2. Genesis 1:1–3 describes an ORDERING or refashioning of matter ("heavens and earth") that was ALREADY EXISTING when God got to work.[79]

To conclude the portion of this word study that involves Heiser's presentation, pay close attention to what he says about why most Hebrew scholars (including himself) say that time sequences, day-age interpretations, or talks of "millions of years" don't matter at all:

Because, if you have indefinite time going on in the first two verses...and the Creation only *starts* in verse 3...we have no time sequence *before* verse 3. You could very easily argue, "Sure! Once

Creation starts—once verse 3 starts—you got six, twenty-four-hour days, [and] you got a Sabbath Day. Great! But you got *eons* of time before that, because there was something there already." That's why they don't care.[80]

Again, although it might be interesting to ruminate over whether or not "days" mean "age," if there were millions of years between "void" Earth and "good" Earth—and since we know this was "a" beginning, but not "the" beginning, since the definite article was never present in the original manuscript and the likelier interpretation points to verse 1 starting with "When"—it could be either, and it's certainly not important enough to fight about.

But if God re-created or transformed Earth from matter that was already there, then who made the first planet before it became void? Couldn't this open a door to a heretical teaching that identifies God as only the re-Creator of Earth, while "void Earth"—and for that matter, the rest of the universe—was made by some other god or force?

It's a valid question, but the biblical answer is "no." It isn't possible in light of many other Scriptures that, in proper context for both Hebrew and Greek, still acknowledge Jehovah as the only Creator God. In Isaiah 66:2, His is the "hand" that "made *all* things" and from whom "*all* things came into being"; in Isaiah 44:24, Ephesians 3:9, Colossians 1:6, 1 Corinthians 8:6, and Revelation 4:11, He created "*all* things"; in Psalm 96:5 and Jeremiah 10:11, He is the Creator of the heavens and earth as contrasted against false gods or idols; in Isaiah 45:18, He is the One who "formed the earth and made it"; in Proverbs 3:19, it is He who "founded the earth"; and on the list goes (all emphasis added).

One can research the word "all" in both Hebrew (*kol*) and Greek (*pas*) as it comes up so many times in this list, but no matter the context of a given verse, it simply means "all." Or, as Derek and Sharon Gilbert of SkyWatch Television have said on occasion during their teachings, "'All' means *all*, and that's all 'all' means." (That one has stuck with me for years.)

Both the "void" Earth of old and "good," possibly re-created, Earth fall under God's creative work, with one crucial caveat: God may have created an Earth that *became* void, but He did not create it that way at first (as we will address in chapters 6 and 7). But perhaps the most convicting verse—so direct that it leaves no room for alternative-creator theories—is John 1:3: "All things were made by him; and without him was not any thing made that was made." To rephrase in modern English: "Every single thing was made by Him, and not a single thing that exists can be said to have been made by someone else." (Note, however, that this doesn't mean something God created cannot be destroyed, warped, manipulated, or wickedly redesigned *from* the living matter He made. That's crucial to remember in the coming pages.)

Because this is such a new idea for some just entering the discussion, I will recap the Hebrew Syntax View that sets up the rest of this book: What has frequently been interpreted as a single Creation epic is likely to have been two separate events: God 1) created heaven and Earth at some point far before Creation week; sometime later, He 2) re-created/transformed Earth (from Genesis 1:3 forward), this time bringing about the first human, Adam, from dust (1:27; 2:7).

Yet, when it comes to the subject of man, some Old Earth dating theories—especially those from my Old-Earther fellows in the Theistic Evolutionist camp—are simply not sustainable when held against the integrity of the biblical narrative. (Hey buddies, if you're reading this, we can still break bread together even if we don't agree. Promise.)

Adam from "Dust"

Adam, the first human, was made from "the dust of the earth [some translations say "ground"]" (Genesis 2:7). Theistic Evolutionists usually view this in the same manner as Natural Evolutionists. To remind readers of the basis of that idea: The "dust," they say, was merely the accumulation of ground elements of the planet that, through millions or billions of years, eventually developed into living elements, then into an ape species, and finally, into a human species. Adam was the first intelligent human, meaning that the moment this endless configuration of developing matter sprang to life in the mind of an intelligent being, this was that moment when Adam was created. In short, Theistic Evolutionists maintain that God, Himself, created the process of natural evolution and natural selection, then supernaturally guided it to fruition until it formed the first viable human mind, millions/billions of years beyond the time of the formation of plants and animals (including the primates, who preceded Adam).

Though, over the last decade of my studies, I've found this explanation to have some interesting and valid input, I find it hard to adopt in light of many biblical loopholes one must configure for this to hold. Just to name a few arguments:

1. If Adam was an intelligent descendant of an ape species, then countless apelike humans must have lived prior to him. The Fall of mankind came through Adam and Eve, and before that original sin, death was not a reality (Genesis 3; Romans 5:12; 1 Corinthians 15:22), so the ape race before Adam would have been immortal, at least partially intelligent, and morally perfect. Even for a person of extreme faith, billions of ape men with questionable intelligence and indefinite life spans who also lived constantly blameless lives is a stretch. (The argument that maintains that the forbidden fruit didn't exist prior to Adam and, therefore, the temptation couldn't have been introduced prior crumbles under the weight of additional factors, including the following.)

2. Eve came from Adam's rib, so prior to her creation, there would have been no reproduction processes. Even if we applied the same evolutionary rules to human females as male, believing that women, too, were slowly developing for billions of years from dust to ape-women to human and so on, we could not explain why suddenly *this* woman was pulled from Adam's rib. Who would have been the ape women before her, and why didn't God just use one of them to partner with Adam? Nothing about this makes sense unless humanity's mother, Eve, truly was formed at

this moment, negating the idea that a woman could have had a womb through which to produce the ape men inhabiting Earth that led to Adam and Eve.

3. Genesis 2:18 acknowledges that it is not good for man to be alone. But if Adam was a descendant of *anything or anyone else*, he would not have been alone in the Garden of Eden, because, even if they had been less intelligent, he would have had "family" there with him. The biblical account is clear that there were no forms of life resembling humanity at the time Adam was created from dust.

4. Adam was given dominion over all the animal kingdom (Genesis 1:26–28). Yet the nature and character of the rest of the biblical record shows that elders are placed in the managerial, governing chair over families and communities. The only exceptions were if elders or leaders were wicked. Again, if Adam had immortal family around him when he was formed, they would have had to have been morally perfect all the years of their lives, or else the Fall would have occurred through one of these ancestors before Adam's time. This rules out the possibility of wickedness being the reason Adam's forbearers were placed under their descendant's dominion, whether or not Adam may have been one billionth of a percentage or so more evolved in his intelligence than they were. (Also, the dominion Adam was given over the animal kingdom gets blurry and hard to define or understand if he, himself, was an animal.)

5. Genesis 1:26 records a moment when God said humans would be "made" in His image. It does *not* say humans would "eventually evolve" to some high standard that finally earns the status of His image. People were literally created through the Almighty's power to represent Him as His viceroys on Earth. Why would God need to "make" people "in His image" if a few more minutes on God's heavenly clock would have done it for Him through evolution, natural selection, or survival of the fittest?

And the list goes on and on. By now, I believe the case has been made that when the Bible describes the formation of Adam, there is no logical room for former ancestry, at least not for beings of the same make, manner, image, dominion, and intent behind God's creation of them. (If there had been any humanlike beings prior to Adam and Eve—no matter how intelligent—they would have been gone by the time Adam and Eve were in the Garden. This relates to the Pre-Adamite theory, considering the possibility of a pre-Adamic race, which we will look at soon. But relevant *here* is the acknowledgment of the difference between *pre*-Adamites and *co*-Adamites: Intelligent or semi-intelligent beings inhabiting Earth *before* Adam [pre-Adamites] is a possibility [see chapter 5, "Mystery History"]; these beings cohabiting the planet *at the same time and alongside Adam* [co-Adamites] cannot be true if the Bible remains the supreme authority for the reasons stated in the aforementioned list.)

The Gap Theory

Amidst the interpretations many scholars have long acknowledged as responsible and admissible (frequently even those who disagree with it are willing to admit it's a theologically responsible interpretation) is the well-known Gap theory. It's familiar to many but for folks who are newer to this subject, I will briefly unpack the basics.

Gap theorists concur that there is a gap in time represented between the first two verses of Genesis. In the beginning—the *very* beginning—God created space, planets, and at least some forms of life (if not yet man), as Genesis 1:1 states. But after this, and *before* verse 2, sin entered the picture through satanic rebellion, rendering Earth "without form, and void." Thus, the Creation week that follows is not the very first creative act of God, but a restorative act to bring back what He first made. This is why the Gap theory is also sometimes referred to as the Ruin-Reconstruction theory or the Restitution theory. The number of years between the first and second Creation acts (what I herein call the re-creation) is unknown, though most scholars simply allow for that time to be however long geological sciences demand. If science says Earth is billions of years old, but biblical chronology demands Adam was created circa 4004 BC, then both are correct: Earth is *old*, and the Ruin-Reconstruction or Restitution Creation week began at or around the time of Adam. (Note: Ussher Chronology may be correct with 4004 BC, but I still maintain that he was off because of his disallowance for any breaks in genealogy. As to what year Adam was *really* formed, we will never know exactly. Either way, the prior discussion of James Ussher was still necessary, as it addressed and broke down not just chronological error but the Young Earth movement—and the vast reach of its research—that stemmed from Ussher's work.)

What Earth looked like during the Gap is technically unknown, but many clues in Scripture match what science says about the history of the planet as well as the theology within Genesis. Primarily, a two-flood theory is brought into the picture, considering the Flood of Noah as the *second* time God brought a deluge on the surface of Earth in judgment. The first flood, many Gap theorists surmise, was God's response to the satanic rebellion during a time when Earth was bound in darkness (of both kinds—the physical absence of light and the spiritual presence of evil), accompanied by an Ice Age that brought death to all living things—plants, animals, and any beings of intelligence. Fossils from this period discovered by geologists in the modern age belong to this Gap in time. From this perspective, this is the "without form, and void" Earth described just prior to the Restorative Creation week.[81]

Of course, as Genesis 1:2 describes Earth covered in water or "the deep," more than chance is required for this to be true history. Some commentators show the link between this "deep" from Genesis and the "deep" of Job 38:30. If that is, in fact, the same body of water, then we see the *condition* of that early, global ocean just following God's questioning of Job about the foundations of the earth. There are, of course, many who want to view these two bodies of water as separate (meaning that the "deep" of the book of Job is just a local lake in southwestern Asia, not Earth's complete submersion as described in Genesis 1:2). However, that looks unlikely, based on the timing of the appearance of angels in the narrative. Consider the context of this verse in a slightly wider passage (brackets added for contextual reminders):

Where wast thou [Job] when I [God] laid the foundations of the earth? declare, if thou hast understanding. [This is probably when God created Earth in the very beginning, as "foundations" implies.] Who hath laid the measures thereof, if thou knowest? or who hath stretched the line upon it? [Laying measures and stretching line refers to the dimensions and capacity of the planet at its initial formation. This language technically *could* apply to a restoration, but in the context of God's questioning of Job's whereabouts when Earth was made, it's more appropriate to see that God had the youngest planet in mind.] Whereupon are the foundations thereof fastened? or who laid the corner stone thereof [a fastening or holding Earth together likewise appears to be a nod to the absolute first act of planetary formation]; When the morning stars sang together, and all the sons of God shouted for joy? [The terms "morning stars" and "sons of God" are well-known in Hebrew as a reference to the angels.[82] The fact that they are here celebrating Creation is a time stamp that points back to a time even before the angels carried out the foremost sin.] Or who shut up the sea with doors, when it brake forth, as if it had issued out of the womb? [Shutting the "doors" to the sea denotes God's majestic ability to limit Earth's waters so the planet will not fall prey to perpetual flooding. "When it brake forth" is considered by many to refer to a time Earth was flooded, and of course, most assume this to be Noah's Flood. To Gap theorists, this entire speech is a reference to an epoch more ancient than Noah; it glances back to the "deep" of Genesis 1:2.] To cause it to rain on the earth, where no man is; on the wilderness, wherein there is no man...

To satisfy the desolate and waste ground; and to cause the bud of the tender herb to spring forth? Hath the rain a father? or who hath begotten the drops of dew? [This means exactly what it sounds like: God directs the rain, including the rain of any flood. Pay close attention to what He says next:] Out of whose womb came the ice? and the hoary frost of heaven, who hath gendered

it? The waters are hid as with a stone, and the face of the deep is
frozen. (Job 38:4–8, 27–30)

Interesting… Here, we have "ice," "frost of heaven," waters somehow
hardened so they are "hid" like "stone," and the "deep" in a state of being
"frozen," *all* in very close proximity to God's first act of global creation.
The order, again, is: 1) Earth was created while the angels shouted for joy;
2) the oceans somehow, and for some reason left herein unsaid, froze.

Geologists have long proposed a theory of an early Ice Age. Coined
the "Snowball Earth theory," it is said to have taken place in the Cryoge-
nian (from Greek *kryos* ["cold"] and *genesis* ["birth"; "beginning"]) period,
approximately 720–635 million years ago, though the theory allows for
Earth's Snowball Age to have been as long ago as 2.4 billion years. During
this time, our planet was completely covered in ice, which accounts for
the bizarre paleomagnetic shifts within the sedimentary rock layers at the
equator that appear to be glacial in origin. (We'll discuss this science in lay
terms briefly in the following chapter.)

The same commentators who view this freeze-over of the "deep" in
Job to be a local lake also openly admit that, unless Earth's weather patterns were dramatically different in Job's day (and the biblical account
elsewhere does not solidify that), lakes of the Mediterranean do not freeze.
Even a thin layer of ice at the edge of a lake in those regions is rare. A popular cross-reference to this event is in the former chapter, Job 37:10: "By
the breath of God ice is given, And the broad waters are frozen" (NKJV).
"Broad waters" is unlikely a reference to a tiny lake in Job's backyard.
Therefore, scholars who do view the "deep" of Job to have been a global
phenomenon often admit that an early Ice Age could have occurred at or
around the same time angels were "shouting for joy" at God laying the
initial "foundations" of planet Earth.

At this point, the two-floods theory doesn't seem absurd, and both
geology and theology allow for God's judgment to have rendered Earth a
giant "snowball" just following this planet's birth.

Is God, in this passage of Job, regaling His righteous servant about a
day when His "breath" froze a global flood?

Well, considering that the Holy Spirit is biblically known to be the "breath" of God (compare: John 16:4–15; 20:19–23; 2 Peter 1:20–21; 2 Timothy 3:16), and He was also the One who "hovered" or "moved" upon the oceans of Earth in the beginning (Genesis 1:2), we've now thrown open the door to another possibility: Earth was flooded well before Noah's day, then it was frozen and *kept* that way by God's "breath" (Holy Spirit), and that glacial status was held together by the Spirit's "hovering" or "moving" until God deemed it time to thaw and restore Earth to what He had originally intended. From this perspective, Genesis 1:2 doesn't just bring into view the Spirit's random fluttering about water, but its sustaining a direct judgment of God upon a planet that had been deemed a "kingdom" of someone or something who messed up, big time, in the far distant past.

Of course, a judgment of that massive scale against someone's kingdom also naturally brings to mind a king and his subjects...

That Earth would have been inhabited by an intelligent race of some sort is highly controversial, for the reasons discussed in the previous section and many others. However, the Bible is clear that angels existed at the time the "foundations of the earth" were formed, and those beings of extreme intelligence "shouted for joy" at God's handiwork (Job 38:4–7; cf., Psalm 148). Some of the angels also fell with Lucifer—whose "kingdom" was, in fact, Earth—well before Adam was conceived from dust by the hand of God (we will scour the "king" and "kingdom" verses in a later chapter). So, the idea that there was a race or species of wicked life on Earth before Adam was formed might make our skin crawl, but it is nonetheless a possibility we must address and, if we reject it, we should do so for solid theological reasons rather than to fiercely cling to Christian tradition. (Therein lies a very serious problem; the proposal that intelligence existed on Earth's surface before the time of Adam and the rest of humanity is often vehemently opposed and written off as liberal interpretation or fringe theology. Yet any theory about the biblical matters, no matter how "crazy," must remain a possibility unless, and until, it's refuted *through Scripture*, not by human logic. In many cases, and from many angles, as this book will go on to address: Intelligent life on Earth prior to Adam—though not "human" in the sense of Adam and others created in the image of God—is supported by Scripture, which sharply brings into view Lucifer, his fallen fellows, and their activities from time immemorial. If a brother or sister in Christ diligently studies this topic and still maintains it is untrue or unlikely, I respect that interpretation. Those who offend me, on the other hand, are those who dismiss the possibility without honest, biblical study, simply because teachings have groomed them to cast it away without investigation. They are applying what we rebuked near the beginning of this book: "condemnation before investigation." We *must* be like the Bereans of Acts 17:11–12 who look to the Word—not people—for absolute truth. In this case, as stated, Scripture makes it clear that intelligent life through God's creation of the angels and other celestial beings *did* exist before Adam, and Lucifer's domain *is and was* Earth. Although we don't have to agree on all details, Gap-theory theology isn't as far-fetched as some powerful voices insist.)

I will close out this look at the Gap theory basics by pointing out one more popular support beam upon which theorists stand in favor of an ancient intelligent race. In Genesis 1:28, Adam and Eve were instructed by God to "replenish" Earth. This word in Hebrew, *mala*, primarily means "to fill" (as in something that is empty). Linguistic experts in support of the Gap theory see this as instructing Adam and Eve to "refill" (as in something that had been emptied or wiped out prior, as the English "replenish" indicates). If this interpretation is correct (and either could be), it intimates that a race/species of intelligence was in fact alive on Earth before Adam—the race/species Adam is now being directed to replace. In support of this connection is Genesis 9:1, where we read that God also told Noah to "replenish" Earth after the Flood had wiped out its wicked inhabitants—which, as we will discuss in chapters 5 and 7, may have no longer been human. (My view does not require the reader to accept this "replenish" interpretation, as there are so many other contributing details to the big picture of Genesis that dissention over this particular word is unnecessary. Interpret it as you will; there are much bigger fish to fry.)

Now that we've addressed what the Bible says from an angle that leaves behind Ussher Chronology but upholds the authority of the original text, let's look at one of the most heated debates between cosmological groups.

PART II

SUPPORTING EVIDENCE

PART II

SUPPORTING EVIDENCE

Chapter 4

Either All These
Scientists Are Wrong,
Or God Is "Tricky"

ONE OF THE MOST ESSENTIAL TRUTHS we need to note about the Bible relates to its *purpose*. It isn't a science manual, and it's never claimed to be one. It is unmistakably *loud* in its claim that God created Earth, but it is *silent* on how our Master Scientist utilized scientific properties and laws to do so.

Despite this, some Young Earthers state with the same straightforward conviction they impose upon their assertion that the Bible says Earth is six thousand years old that "the Bible is actually a textbook of historical science"[83] (a direct quote from an article by a leading Young-Earth teacher). Over and again, it's repeated through Young Earth literature that the Bible is *the* place to start when looking for an answer to any question. So, it seems odd that Young Earthers don't appear to have sought what the Scripture says regarding its purpose in relation to scientific study. After reading a breakdown of this approach, it's immediately clear that Young Earth adherents aren't suggesting comparing the Bible with "those [textbooks] used in public schools,"[84] which is encouraging. However, they have taken a well-known school term ("textbook") and applied it to a Book that God, Himself, wrote through the power of His Spirit to teach *morality*—not science—which is undoubtedly confusing to those who are less familiar with what the Bible, itself, says it is. (I have nothing less than the highest respect for my brothers and sisters in the Young Earth groups, and I am proud to stand alongside them in the quest to parse the Word and exegete Scripture for the edification of all mankind. But when unbelievers are watching what we say about God or His Book, we must be careful not to represent the Word as something it doesn't claim to be. Doing so is more than confusing; it's misleading. Some might hear "textbook" and, when they discover it is nothing of the sort, develop hostility against and distrust of God. We must be so, *so* careful as His soldiers on Earth never to misrepresent His self-revelation as something other than what it is just to make the Bible appear more trendy or relevant to skeptical audiences!)

What the Holy Bible *does* claim to be is the supremely authoritative and "God-breathed" tool to assist us with "doctrine" and to be used "for reproof, for correction, for instruction *in righteousness* [read: "morality"]: That the man of God may be perfect, thoroughly furnished unto all good works" (2 Timothy 3:15–17; emphasis added). The Scriptures are how we can come to "cleanse" our "way" (living in a way that pleases the Lord) by "taking heed" of their teachings (Psalm 119:9). God's Word is the testimony that invites us to believe Jesus to be the Son of God, as He claims: "And many other signs truly did Jesus in the presence of his disciples, which are not written in this book: But these are written, that ye might believe that Jesus is the Christ, the Son of God; and that believing ye might have life through his name" (John 20:30–31); "that ye may know that ye have eternal life, and that ye may believe on the name of the Son of God" (1 John 5:13). It is the moral instructions Jesus, Himself, read and observed, according to His own testimony during His trial and temptation ("it is written"; Matthew 4:4). In Hebrews we read that the Word is "quick, and powerful, and sharper than any two-edged sword, piercing even to the dividing asunder of soul and spirit, and of the joints and marrow, and is a discerner of the thoughts and intents of the heart" (Hebrews 4:12).

It is so infinitely important that we allow the Bible to speak for and position itself correctly amidst a lineup of inferior literature. Therefore, although we do plan to consider what scientists say in this chapter, it is imperative that we remember the Bible is *the* authoritative and written Word of God that never bends under the weight of humankind's science.

To that, all true Christians agree. Where we sometimes disagree is in whether to allow Scripture to be reevaluated against traditional interpretation when it appears we have it wrong—like we imprudently did in Galileo's day (discussed in chapter 1 of this book). Yet, if we agree that Scripture could have been revisited in consideration of Galileo challenging geocentricism, why is there such a resistance to revisiting it in light of what we see in science now?

One of the first moves made by many Young Earthers in seeking evidence or support for their findings of a young planet is to claim that scientific dating methods aren't trustworthy for to determining the age of a formation or object. A vast library of materials against scientific dating exists—and much of it is written *by responsible scientists* (such as the book *In Six Days: Why Fifty Scientists Choose to Believe in Creation*)—to share how and why science really cannot be trusted to have all the answers.

It may surprise some readers to know I actually agree in many cases with this statement. However, it's not "if" I agree, but "when" I agree. Let me give you a strong illustration of this principle. It may seem that we're steering off-course for a moment, but bear with me, as this will help explain what "when" means in this application.

Shroud of Turin Dating: A Terrible Fumble for Science!

My initial reaction to hearing about the Shroud of Turin (believed by many to be the authentic burial cloth of Christ) long ago was a grand shout of "Baloney!" and a good belly laugh. Radiocarbon dating tests on the fabric in 1988 asserted that the Shroud was created by a forger or an artist circa AD 1260–1390—more than twelve hundred years *after* Jesus rose from the dead—so, like many, I thought it was a hoax. I was quickly humbled when I started hearing rumors that science couldn't explain, or *reproduce*, this mysterious artifact, even with the most advanced techniques known to man.

Still a skeptic, I silenced my balking for a season of responsible research. My closed mind gradually opened when I discovered these rumors were true. For ten to fifteen straight years, any time new facts surfaced on the topic, I dove in, soaking up every word until I found myself backed into a corner called "belief." Though I still keep a respectfully open mind about the possibility that this cloth could be something the Antichrist will someday claim as his own (and therefore become a tool of dark worship in the future), I can't ignore the enormous possibility that it is exactly what it looks like: the legitimate linen placed on Christ at His burial. Present in its herringbone weave is the testimony of the moment He rose again, and as much as I wanted to write it off as an ancient fallacy planted by the Catholic Church, the evidence continued to stack in favor of it being legitimate. (Due to the uncanny association between the Shroud of Turin and Catholic history, it begs to be emphasized that I'm a Protestant.)

Then, one day, when I was talking with Josh Peck of SkyWatch TV and Defender Publishing (who has since become an award-winning documentary filmmaker), we began toying with the idea of writing a book on the transition between this life and the next. Our casual conversation quickly became the outline for our next book, which we cowrote with Allie Anderson: *Afterlife: Near Death Experiences, Neuroscience, Quantum Physics, and the Increasing Evidence for Life after Death*. Since the Shroud of Turin is possibly an ancient "photo" of the Resurrection, it fit perfectly with the theme of this project, and we agreed I would write that portion of the book since I had long been fascinated with the topic. But believing something and reporting the facts to others are two different animals; and I had to be *sure* I hadn't missed any information in years past if I was going to responsibly present the case to our readers, so I started over, repeating what had previously been years of research in a matter of months. On many occasions during that time, I honestly hoped I would find some information I had missed before that proved the Shroud to be a hoax, because the whole subject carries controversy that I didn't particularly want my name attached to. At the end of the day, however, I determined to simply report the facts from an unbiased position. In doing so, I found a strong case for its authenticity.[85] However, the many hiccups in the assignment slowed me down...the central issue being the dating of the cloth.

Skeptics (like I used to be) are quick to point to additional "evidence" against the linen unrelated to dating: The anatomy of the body isn't perfectly oriented to a human figure existing at the time of Christ (consider the unnatural posture of the shoulders); how and where the linen curled around the body showed a discrepancy of leg length between the front and back; and the cloth could have easily been painted by an artist (regardless of motive), which was further supported by such findings as antique pigments present on the fibers. Additionally, skeptics say, the image of the body on the fabric appears to have no thumbs; the number of indications of wounds doesn't match the thirty-nine lashings Christ would have received as a Jewish victim of flagellation; and so on. These arguments are unfortunately tossed out there with an air of haughtiness—a "gotcha" for the skeptic who intends to make any believer feel foolish. (Powell Doctrine, anyone?)

Not surprising, hundreds of thousands of attempts between the 1300s and today to reproduce the cloth have failed; not even those with the most advanced sciences available have been able to create a copy that produces features that are the same as (or even similar to) the Shroud's seemingly supernatural image. Tests applied include, but are not limited to:

> ...microscopy (light, polarizing, phase, fluorescent, stereo, petrographic, scanning, electron), immunochemical analysis, enzymatic chemical analysis, serological analysis, textile analysis, microchemical tests, laser microprobe Raman spectroscopy, mass spectroscopy, spectroscopy (optical, infrared), energy dispersive X-ray analysis, X-ray diffraction, micro FTIR (Fourier Transform Infrared) spectroscopy, electron microprobe analysis, Fourier analysis, VP-8 computer imaging, computer studies, pyrolysis mass spectrometry, and others.[86]

These attempts at reproduction summarily dismiss everything on the skeptic's list I just shared (and *oh so many more* rebuttals). Expounding only on what I've included above:

1. The anatomy turned out to be a flawless anatomical match to a Jewish man during Christ's era, with issues such as the "stiff, unnatural posture of the shoulders" and discrepancy of leg length supporting the rigor mortis of a victim whose arms were outstretched on a cross and whose legs were bent at the time of death. Many other details that no artist or forger of the twelfth or thirteenth century could have been expected to know were also present on the linen, like the discovery of "serum albumin retraction": blood protein "rings" or "halos" around the wounds where the blood and the serum separated just after the heart stopped beating, invisible to the naked eye and only seen after subjected to ultraviolet light. (What forger could possibly know about ultraviolet light centuries before it existed in labs, and know it well enough to "paint" that invisible effect in blood proteins…just in case someone questioned his art hundreds of years later?)

2. All pigments (such as the rod ochre discussed in many online videos and articles that attempt to debunk the Shroud as a hoax) found on the cloth were "trace amounts," nowhere near the volume needed to "paint" the image as it appears. Additionally, these pigments did not line up with the image of the man's body; they were lightly scattered all over in no particular pattern, as if they had simply floated onto the fabric from a nearby artist mixing his pigments. This is a detail easily explained by the early Catholic Church practice of painting a reproduction of the Shroud in the same room as the authentic one, and then laying it face to face on the original so it will "absorb the blessing" of the genuine article, which is a well-documented trait of Catholicism's veneration habits and a documented detail of the Shroud's history.

3. The "missing thumbs" again argue for authenticity, as that is both
   a) a natural position of thumbs at rest under the hands, as seen in

many cases of cloth-wrapped cadavers throughout time, as well as b) a possible clue that the man whose image appears on the cloth was impaled through the wrists, in the precise spot called "Destot's Space," which "snaps" the thumbs inward at the time of injury. (Such a conclusion is consistent with the New Testament *koine* Greek [the Greek language as it had developed at the time of Christ and in which the New Testament was written] word *cheir*, which refers to both the hand and the wrist. Yet, again, what early forger would know to apply this scientific and medical anomaly centuries before we knew about it, *and* at the risk of portraying a "Savior with no thumbs"?)

4. Nowhere in the Word do we read that Jesus (or any other victim of the *Romans*) would have only received thirty-nine whip marks. Though that was true for Jewish flagellation practices, Jesus was tried and sentenced as a criminal in Rome. Therefore, He was punished severely by the Romans, subject to whatever whims were birthed from their perverted justice system. Thirty-nine "stripes" thus aren't relevant to the discussion of the Shroud's authenticity in any way. What *is* relevant is that each "stripe" on the image on the Shroud leads to inconspicuous, dumbbell-shaped scourge marks, likely caused by the two or three metal pieces affixed in succession at the end of the leather thong connected to the Roman flagrum used at the time. If the Shroud was, in fact, a hoax staged sometime between AD 1260–1390, the artist/forger would have had to know precisely how a Roman flogging was conducted *around a thousand years after that practice had ceased*—in an age when, of course, the information couldn't be found on an Internet, at a local library, or from a neighbor. It was definitely *not* shown correctly in other religious artwork of that time.

So, over and over again, we can see that the very features skeptics use to tear down the Shroud's authenticity are ironically the features that build a stronger case for its validity. Other mesmerizing (and equally scientific) trails of research show that the image on the Shroud "behaves" in bizarre ways that are completely unreproducible by any technology we've ever produced when it's subjected to certain forms of testing and lab experiments. (I'm not talking about recent viral claims from a certain Italian researcher that the Shroud man "moves on his own"; that trail of evidence fell flat almost immediately and wasn't a part of my report.) For instance, under advanced 3D imaging tests that "lift" parts of a picture forward and allow us to see more dimension to study certain features, the impression on the Shroud produces many other oddities unseen by the naked eye, such as indications of swelling, bruising, and additional signs of injury that match the Gospel narratives' of Jesus' last hours of torture by the Romans (including inflammation on the shoulder blade that aligns with what would happen when a man carried a cross, as Christ did). But the buck doesn't stop there. The image also "pops" into three-dimensional contours *accurately*, which is a feat no other photo or painting has been capable of when subjected to the same experimental methods. In all other cases, something went terribly wrong: noses on faces concaved backwards into the head; mountains appeared in the foreground of a picture that originally stood miles in the background; wedding bands on fingers disappear, resulting in what looks like a severed digit; and so on. No matter how many tests were conducted, each time these methods were used on other images, the 3D features went wonky, while the Shroud showed both perfect alignment to human anatomy as well as features never seen before (like the aforementioned shoulder detail).

And we haven't even touched on the fifty-seven species of ancient pollen that were identified on the surface of the linen, most of which were from the Jerusalem area, including a group originating from the "Syrian Christ Thorn" plant (probably the one from which Christ's crown of thorns was crudely fashioned). That botanical finding adds multiple additional layers of credibility to the argument for the authenticity of the Shroud.

On and on the list goes. Hundreds and thousands of facts contributing to the miracle cloth as being genuine have been compiled in recent history...but the radiocarbon dating remains the pesky elephant in the room of faith, much like similar methods have done to Young Earthers' findings.

Yet, the dating of the Shroud *also* remains one of the worst mistakes ever made by scientists. We have very many good reasons to believe the dating methods applied to this linen were faulty. Much like the Young-versus-Old Earth debate, the arguments for and against the dating of the Shroud have established a major battleground between people of faith and people of science for centuries, as I noted in the book *Afterlife*. The details of the following are specific to the Shroud, while the overall attitude is similar to the poison currently polluting the relationships between Old and Young Earthers, as well as between unbelievers and believers when it comes to the dating of Earth:

> …vitriolic comments have been exchanged that amount to little more than immature mud-flinging, which makes each side hard to take seriously: Believers in the authenticity of the cloth make snide remarks about how the scientific community is unintelligent or silly for buying into this whole "radiocarbon dating" idea when it's clear [in their opinion] that the whole process has been historically unreliable. Too often, these jabs originate from clergy or religious people who don't have…[adequate] training in these systematic methods, attacking the principles of science and insinuating (or directly declaring) that the dating was born from a conspiracy against faith and religion. Scientists and skeptics (*especially* those personally involved with the dating of the Shroud) have encouraged believers to let go of their vice grip on faith in the authenticity of the Shroud, since fact and scientific method have irrefutably won the day over fantasy.…

That's why we chose to start with what the image on the cloth had to say for itself *before* we addressed the dating debate (backwards in order compared with the approach of many other works like this). On our end, the evidence stacked against a potential forgery—based solely on the unlikeliness of that scenario, as discussed—was so dense that it naturally drew the dating into question, not the other way around. To say this another way: We are open to the idea that the dating process was flawed because the forgery theory appears to be so, *not* because any of us wanted so much to believe in the artifact's authenticity that we would trade the integrity of truth for that age-old, blissful feeling that cohabitates with willful ignorance.[87]

The breakdown of who took what samples and when and how those samples were analyzed can be simplified by this short summary (though readers are encouraged to read the in-depth work in *Afterlife*):

1. Radiocarbon dating hasn't always been accurate, and that's never been a secret. Frequently, even many within the scientific community (like forensic analyst Frederick T. Zugibe, MD, PhD) admit that this method of identifying the age of an artifact has been off "by hundreds or even thousands of years,"[88] depending on many factors. But even if that weren't true:

2. Contamination of outside carbon or fibers on the surface of the artifact—such as the countless venerators who handled the Shroud of Turin with bare hands during sacred marches and who laid it down in many places against foreign objects or face to face against man-made artwork—can introduce younger carbon to the object and compromise the reliability of the dating methods.

3. Dating included only the less-reliable "accelerator mass spectrometry" method, and it was handled in a rush, due to the sacredness of the Shroud as a religious artifact and Turin authorities being pressed for time to return the Shroud to its resting place.

4. Portions cut from the cloth were at the linen's very edge, where contaminants were most likely to be present.

5. The dating was supposed to follow blind-study protocol (meaning samples of other, non-Shroud, linens were to be included so the researchers didn't know the Shroud from the others to ensure a nonbiased report). However, this, too, was dropped in a rush, and by the time the samples landed at the labs for testing, the scientists knew which labeled cuts were from what cloths, introducing an obvious bias behind the findings. There were also supposed to be

seven labs used in the process, and time constraints only allowed for the involvement of three.

6. The results of the dating were announced to the public immediately, without allowing time for peer review—one of the most critical steps in the scientific method.

And, most importantly:

7. In 2000, at the Sindone Worldwide Congress (Orvieto, Italy), an interesting and vital announcement was released to the public: Sixteenth-century repair patchwork had been applied to the edge of the cloth the dating sample had been taken from! Therefore, the sample cut for the 1988 dating and further divided for the three labs, experts acknowledged, was far more vulnerable to younger dating than just the typical carbon contaminations. Giovanni Riggi—the man responsible for cutting the 1988 sample—openly and transparently acknowledged that younger, foreign fibers had become mixed up in the portion he took. Other analyses by textile experts showed that the 1988 cut was *not even linen* (!!!), but was a light-yellow cotton used for historical repairs that weighed twice as much as the linen portion the image was imprinted upon.

In other words, it wasn't even the original Shroud that scientists dated, but a section of cloth that had been sewn onto it to repair damage made in the past. Despite many reports and analyses shared with the public since this major debacle, we still hear that "science dated the Shroud to AD 1260–1390" and many believe it to be true. Anyone who looks into the scientists' mistakes and chooses to believe the linen is older is branded a conspiracy theorist.

So, yes, there are absolutely times I agree that scientific dating methods for Earth and its artifacts are flawed and unreliable. If a mistake of this magnitude is possible in the research on something as famous as the Shroud, imagine how many errors could have occurred in other matters that affect our concepts of cosmology.

I don't blame Young Earthers for choosing to believe that science can't be completely trusted in matters of radiocarbon dating.

Well, to be fair, that was only one example, and it only proved those specific scientists grabbed the wrong portion of the artifact to test. Had they gotten their hands onto the correct area of the cloth, their dating methods may have been accurate, right?

It's possible (though unlikely, given the bare-hands touching that transmitted younger carbon to the Shroud's fibers). However, even when the right artifact (or portion of it) is tested, there have been bizarre and inexplicable results proving the methods, themselves, can render inaccurate reports. For instance, consider these paintings:

A contemporary artist by the name of Joan Aherns painted Indian rocks from crushed wheat during an art class sometime in the 1970s. Her paintings were stolen, swept away to South African jungles, and were found eleven years later hidden in the bushes. Oxford University—often considered an authority in scientific affairs—submitted the paintings to their radiocarbon accelerator unit…and confirmed that the paintings were 1,200 years old. For a brief stint, the museum in Natal, South Africa, celebrated these paintings as originating from an African bushman and placed them on display. Later, when the "artifacts" were credited to the original source (artist Joan Aherns in the '70s), no explanation could be found for why the wheat-based paint would have dated to such antiquity.[89]

Again, I really don't blame Young Earthers for their distrust in a system so fallible that it can date 1970s paintings to twelve hundred years ago and offer zero explanations as to how that happened.

Yet—and please get this crucial point—not every carbon dating conclusions can be disregarded as a result of lab mistakes. For every bungled linen cloth or 1970s painting, dozens more relics were handled responsibly. And carbon dating is only *one of many* methods used to date Earth (or objects upon its surface). It's not uncommon for a researcher to stumble upon the Young Earther's arguments against carbon dating. However, only a few Young Earth spokespeople or ministries attempt to take on the bulk of advanced methods (and I commend those who do!).

It's Not Just about Radiocarbon Dating

Though there are many scientific dating methods, let's look at a few and consider some of the claims regarding their reliability. But note that my goal is not to prove or disprove either Young or Old Earthers. And please remember what I said early on: This is not a college textbook, nor is it my intention to mimic that approach. Many readers very well may have read other works related to Young or Old Earth with lengthy treatments of the following subjects. I've chosen, for the sake of space and time and in the interest of the reader, not to dedicate pages and pages to a debate that's already been well covered by others in this field of study. On the other hand, some readers may be new to this subject, since materials on this topic have overwhelmingly favored Young Earth in recent history, so I cannot altogether ignore addressing the dating methods.

Therefore, this chapter is a quick, drive-by summary of these methods and an equally concise look at the Young Earther's most popular refutations of them, followed by a logical review of whether those repudiations hold water. In a conclusion to this chapter, I'll revisit the possibility that most of these dating methods could be far off base as a result of rapid geological changes during the event of Noah's Flood—a deduction that, *also*, has inherent problems (theologically speaking). I believe *some level* of truth exists in Young Earth, Old Earth, Noah's-Flood geology, and almost all fields of scientific research and discovery, as my Old Earth theory discussed in upcoming chapters permits.

Stratigraphy/Biostratigraphy

Within the layers of Earth's rock lie many small gold mines to be found by the perceptive eye. These layers are called "strata" (the singular form is "stratum"). Strata are formed as the weight of sediment and minerals atop the rock's surface compresses and hardens over time (called "deposition"), creating additional layers of rock. Many other factors such as weather, glaciers, and erosion contribute to the process before this "cementation" or "lithification" (sediment becoming solid rock) occurs.

Different layers of rock appearing in diverse colors (like the horizontal stripes on a walls of the Grand Canyon) develop within the strata, identifying variations in lithologic properties (related to the study of texture, fine-grained or course-grained composition, carbon, iron, and so on within that stratum). For instance, deep red or rust-colored strata is a result of oxidized (rusted) iron present in the minerals, while a gray rock attests to lower levels of iron, which gives geologists a clue about the air, temperature, vegetation, bacteria, and other environmental factors at the time of formation. Tilted strata indicate a disturbance (such as volcanoes, earthquakes, moving water, etc.) that led to the erosion of the rock at some point, introducing newer sediments from the environment of that time, explaining why there are occasional cross-cutting layers set in divergent directional patterns that "crack through" the earlier strata.

Since rock gradually builds additional rock upon itself in an upward pattern (called "superposition"), the "youngest" strata are at the top: The *lower* the layer, the *older* the layer, so a fossil at fifty feet down the strata will be older than a fossil at twenty feet down, and so on. Much strata stretches on for miles, showing the same layering above and below them, so if an object is wedged in a certain stratum, and another object is found wedged in the same (or nearby) layer miles away, geologists can determine that both objects are from around the same era of time.

Tephrochronology is a similar science, using volcanic rock and other materials (tephra) originating from a known historic eruption to identify the age of objects above or below the tephra; if an object is atop the tephra, it's younger than whatever year the volcano erupted, while an object *below* the volcanic rock was obviously left there sometime prior to the eruption that buried it.

Strata, as a general rule, take a long time to form; it's by no means an overnight process. The time necessary for each stratum to succumb to cementation obviously varies according to many contributing elements (wind or water carrying away fresh sediment, for example), but geologists have been able to study these elements and produce a rate of accumulation showing that many strata required millions or billions of years to stack and transform into stone.

But again, I would like to stress that this is *a general rule*.

Young Earthers believe (and often with convincing support) that many of these layers of rock stacked up quickly during the Flood of Noah's day. They point to bizarre phenomena, such as a petrified tree "growing through" strata, or a fossilized animal skeleton protruding upwards through several layers (a "polystrate fossil" in Creationist terminology). If strata take millions of years to cement, they say, the tree would have rotted away or the bones of an animal would have been carried off or swept away during that time. If the tree didn't rot and the bones didn't disappear—and the skeleton remains intact throughout the layers—it proves rapid sedimentation supporting the biblical narrative of a sudden, worldwide Flood…but not billions of years of rock layers accumulating over an animal who oddly never moved throughout that time.

Scientists frequently agree with Young Earthers that something rapid did happen at one point to cause this, though they see it as the exception in a certain area and not the rule. Depending on the type of rock, scientists say, rapid sedimentation hasn't been a mystery for going on a century and a half. Explanations often attribute these rarities to other causes, such as water-soluble sediments caused by low-salt density in the minerals—or explosive volcanic events resulting in lahars (mud-flow containing bits of debris) generating loose, discontinuous volcanic deposits like blankets—keeping the fossils in place and eventually deteriorating while the layering slowly continues. Meanwhile, the object (tree, animal skeleton, etc.) fossilizes in place. Actually, such geological phenomena are quite common in marshy or swampy areas where standing trees have died and sediment collects around them, causing the trees to fossilize (and some eventually petrify) upright through additional strata. Floods, tidal waves, harsh weather, volcanic eruptions, and other extreme environmental events can and do bury, and therefore preserve, fossils and objects that were once living organisms, and geologists have offered explanations involving completely natural and organic causes for well more than a hundred years.

Unfortunately, these causes aren't often taken into fair consideration when Young Earthers teach their beliefs.

Ocean Reefs: "Tropical Forests of the Ocean"

Why do there appear to be so many comparisons between coral reefs and trees? Why are the coral reefs called "the trees of the ocean" in much contemporary marine biology literature? What is a "tropical forest of the ocean," since we know such a thing can't literally exist?

It's widely known that if we cut down a tree and count the rings that appear across the stump from the middle to the outermost layer, we can determine its age. The bark that develops as a tree grows changes with the seasons: In spring and early summer, when rain and sunshine are plentiful, the wood is a lighter shade, reflecting rapid growth; from late summer through winter, a darker shade develops, representing a temporary cessation of growth. Therefore, each ring of color within the wood indicates one year of a tree's life, as well as points to the climate around the tree during that year.

Since trees live for a limited time before they die and rot away, we can't expect them to provide any evidence in support of either a Young or an Old Earth. Ocean reefs can, however—and by a similar dating method.

Like the aforementioned rock layers, organic materials build on the surface of coral. These materials are left behind by small fish, plants, and about a quarter of all other marine species that contribute to the ecosystem of ocean life. As coral's polyps (the "mouths," so to speak) intake nutrients, the coral secretes calcium carbonate (limestone), which, over time, develops into a compact structure, merging with other coral and creating a reef.

Coral grows in layers (referred to as "faunal succession"), like rock strata: The uppermost layer of coral is the youngest. The older layers underneath are essentially abandoned until algae, fungus, and small animals from the mollusk family (snails, oysters, mussels, squids, and others) bore into the deep skeleton and nest there, leaving the coral vulnerable to bioerosion and collapse. Just as human bones vary in thickness and density, some corals produce weaker skeletons, while others construct heartier platforms for new growth that are at a lower risk of crumbling.

For coral that produce extremely dense and durable skeletons, the layers keep climbing upwards every year atop a solid structure, changing in color and texture depending on the seasons (as we see with tree rings). Marine scientists can drill into these layered bands and measure not only the number of years the coral has been alive, but also what the salinity (salt content), water temperatures, and anthropogenic impact (human-influenced environmental changes) looked like during each season. Of course, other scientific dating methods (such as radiocarbon and uranium-thorium dating) are also applied when deciphering the age of a reef so we're not left to rely only on the testimony of the bands.

One reef that gets a lot of attention is the Chazy Reef of Isle La Motte, Vermont. Though no longer living and therefore broken in many areas (most of it is buried beneath the surface of Earth), its remaining towering fossils are said to date back to more than 450 million years.[90]

Another that's mentioned even more frequently, the Great Barrier Reef off the coast of Queensland, Australia, is still alive and well—and, according to an article released by the American Association for the Advancement of Science, researchers are shocked to discover that it is *only* between 500,000 and 1.05 million years old. "That estimate is backed up by paleomagnetic data [discussed soon], which show that this portion of the reef must have formed after Earth's magnetic poles last reversed, some 790,000 years ago."[91]

This deduction—based on the findings of seventeen researchers who supervised drilling holes in both the inner and outer shelves of the reef in June of 2001—is compared in the article to "the Pacific atolls [ring-shaped islands with coral rims] of Enewetak and Bikini, which have accumulated over more than 45 million years."[92]

If we know how a coral band is developed over the course of a year, *and we do*—and if we can drill in and count those bands to observe faunal succession that shows present and past environmental factors that coincide with the dating of ancient marine fossils between coral layers, *and we can*—then it's difficult to dismiss the legitimacy of their silent testimony to the existence of a very old planet.

River Sediments

Before we move on to paleomagnetism, take everything you've read about rock strata, tree rings, and coral reefs and apply those same ideas to lake-bed sediments.

Dried-up lakes are all over the world, and each one that has been largely undisturbed by human civilization shows layers of gathered sediment at the bottom of what used to be a body of water. These layers, too, reveal all sorts of fish fossils and underwater creatures who have lived and died at different times in the past and whose remains are wedged deep in the ground.

The sediment in these lakes was slowly deposited in very thin and fine layers when water was still present. Each is called a "varve," and each varve reflects four seasons (one year) of accumulated sediment, though the colors are flipped from those of a tree's rings: Thriving seasons of growth are reflected in dark layers, while the dryer seasons produce lighter shades.

Some of these lakes have had roads built straight through the middle of them—such as the US Route 191 that stretches through Colorado, Wyoming, and Utah, which was laid through miles of the Green River Formation. Locals of the area can hop in their cars and drive between the mountainous, looming varve walls and, if they get curious enough, they can pull over and strike the semi-fragile wall, watching as flakes of the varves chip off and fall to the ground. This particular formation's varves have been counted many times, and they attest to an unbroken chain record of six million years.

Paleomagnetism

Rocks, though inanimate, do "speak" to us about world history. One of the ways they do this is by recording the direction and force of Earth's geomagnetic field (the magnetic field that extends from the center of the planet and outward into space) during the era of their formation.

Today, a compass points north, but it wouldn't have pointed to the same place hundreds or thousands of years ago, because Earth's magnetic field changes, pulling north (normal polarity) or south (reversed polarity) at different times. Throughout history, as polarity has flipped back and forth from north to south while rocks have layered and formed, magnetic crystals embedded in the orientation of certain rocks act as silent witnesses of this shift as their magnetism points a certain direction. This is called "sedimentary magnetization."

Science shows that Earth's magnetic polarity (the fluctuation of which is being analyzed at this very moment by magnetometers all over the world) flips between normal and reversed every three hundred thousand years on average. Each time this occurs, our rocks "record" the intensity, speed, and precise direction of this alteration. According to NASA, "Paleomagnetic records tell us Earth's magnetic poles have reversed 183 times in the last 83 million years, and at least several hundred times in the past 160 million years."[93]

But if the Earth is young, as I believe the Bible says, it doesn't matter to me what scientists say happened millions of years ago. They must be wrong in their analyses.

Perhaps they are…though, if they were, we would have hefty evidence of that today.

For instance, let's say the scientists are wrong, and all the recorded magnetic shifts that the rocks indicate occurred much closer together over a period of only six thousand years (most Young Earthers' approximate age-of-Earth calculation). Crunching *only* the 183 recorded geomagnetic shifts that NASA states occurred in eighty-three million years into a six-thousand-year time frame—with the frequency of that event happening on a calculable *average* (with an even number of years between them)—we would expect to experience a shift every 32.8 years. This means we would have had approximately sixty-one magnetic, north/south flip-flops since Christ walked the Earth…and we know that's not the case, since we haven't been experiencing the incredible fallout that an event like that would cause.

The Earth's magnetic field is what guards us from extreme space radiation. Many scientific authorities believe a flip or reversal would prompt a brisk spread of cancer throughout humanity, and it would absolutely fry our power grids. Whether or not we can trace cancer back into antiquity, we *certainly* know modern technology hasn't been wiped out on a global scale in the last three decades.

More simply put: Since we're *not* currently experiencing global catastrophe every thirty or so years—and since layers of rock are *not* climbing upward rapidly at this moment with paleomagnetic records noting the magnetic shift every thirty years—we know the time span between magnetic-shift events is much longer than thirty years. This much isn't science; it's common sense. Therefore, the planet's magnetic polarity as recorded in stone points to a vast and lengthy history of Earth's continually developing surface.

I've read several articles on the Young Earthers' response to this information, and though there are good arguments for how scientists may have gotten their readings wrong, so far, I have yet to see a Young Earther explain how humanity would have survived six thousand years of extreme, intermittent radiation poisoning that would be the result of more rapidly occurring geomagnetic shifts. (I'm not saying those explanations don't exist; I'm saying they're not readily available.)

Trapped Charge Dating, Electron Spin Resonance, and Thermoluminescence

Microscopic electrons from cosmic rays and sunshine (or radioactivity) are absorbed, trapped, and stored within organic materials that are buried underground or away from sunlight at some point. (In this line of research, rocks and teeth come up a lot.) The amount of electrons can be analyzed and measured, as can the rate at which the electrons were confined within the specimen, resulting in a calculated "dose" or "dose rate": i.e., how long such material had been exposed to sunlight, how much sunlight it absorbed, and, therefore, the approximate age of the specimen prior to its burial.

If the material is exposed to extreme heat early on (such as an ancient flint tool or ceramic jar placed in the fire by a resident of an earlier civilization), the heat releases the electrons, zeroing out the "age" of the artifact. Though this may sound frustrating for those who work in this field, it's actually the opposite in many cases, as it helps in determining the date that organic material was formed into a tool (or jar, etc.) and fired (or exposed to sunlight), because the electrons are reabsorbed from that moment forward ("resetting the clock," to use a phrase many in this field have said). In other words, a tool "reset" by fire or sun five hundred thousand years ago would show five hundred thousand years of electrons trapped within it, and, thus, an approximate age reflecting that timeline.

After an object is unearthed, the electrons display "luminescence signals" that, once subjected to laboratory light waves, emit photons that can further determine how long it's been since the object was exposed to cosmic rays (how long it's been underground).

And again, since we're at this very moment still studying the relationship between organic materials and sunlight, these methods of dating do not require sticking to any previously established cosmological explanation or history of proofs on either side of the argument. It's quite simple: Electrons get trapped every day, including today, and we are able to measure the rate at which that occurs even now and sharpen our techniques of determining the age of older objects. So, dismissing these methods is not as simple as saying, "Science got that wrong, too."

Distance from Earth to the Stars

Light dims increasingly the farther away we are when it's observed. This is visible in many common-sense ways—a flashlight's beam is far brighter when the flashlight is held two inches away from a wall than it is held twenty feet from a wall. This is what science calls the "inverse square law": The name of this law of physics conveys that the intensity of light "equals the inverse of the square of the distance from the source."[94] To put this in understandable terms, imagine two people staring at the same light source, but one person is twice as far away from the source as the other.

The one who is farther away will see only one-fourth the brightness (or exposure) of the light, while the person standing closer will interpret the light as being far brighter, even though the intensity of the light source, itself, doesn't change from its point of origin.

This law applies in and throughout the universe. The farther away a star is from Earth, the dimmer it shines, and the redder its color of light appears to be to us. (As Earth rotates, these measurements become variable, since the distance is variable with a moving object like our planet.) However, because some stars (like the sun) are enormous and others are much smaller, calculating a star's emission of light and distance relies on more than just how bright the light coming from appears to us.

Let me explain: First, a "light year" is the distance light is capable of traveling in one year. Light travels at 671 million miles per hour, 186,000 miles per second. The distance of a light year is that speed multiplied by the number of hours per year. In short, one light year represents a source of light (like a star) travelling 5,878,625,370,000 miles over a year.

Second, "redshift"—the deeper reddening of color emitting from a star or space cluster—occurs when light wavelengths stretch long distances from space. Blue light wavelengths are shortest, while red light wavelengths are longest, so the farther away a star is, the more we receive "red color information" from its starlight. Through many of our telescopes (the Hubble telescope is famous for this finding), we can measure the redness of a star, the frequency of "twinkling" that may be occurring (through what is called a "variable star"), and the star's emission of light to calculate how far away that star is. (This is also in part how we can build 3D model of the universe even though, from our location, all the stars appear to the naked eye to be about the same flat distance away, despite brightness.)

Third, Earth shows through the laws of nature and physics that it's moving at a speed relevant to the objects around it in space, and that relationship is stable and irrevocable. In other words, in order for Earth to have been inhabitable in the past as well it is in the present, it has to be exactly where it is, moving just like it is, and at the precise distance it is from surrounding space objects (like the sun, which would burn us if it was closer or freeze us if it was farther away, etc.). Readers don't necessarily have to believe in the Big Bang to see the relationship Earth has with other space matter, but what we discover when we look at all this information together is this: Earth, though not inhabitable *in the beginning* (according to science), could not be a home to the humans, animals, and plants that it is *now* unless it originated—at least in some primordial form—from mutually shared governing laws of motion and gravity with other planets and stars in our solar system that developed at or around the same early time line. We also see that with the measurement of light: Earth is—right here in this very spot—receiving light information from stars that had to travel many light years to reach Earth's surface. There are billions of space objects out there in the vast universe, and as we very well know, we can't see them all from Earth. Those we *can* see have been sending us their light information for at least as long as their light-year distance away allows: closer objects would not have to be there as long for their light to reach us as those farther away, and so on.

If Earth and the universe were only six thousand years old, we would only be able to see the light from space objects six thousand light years away. In another thousand years from now, we could begin to see the light from stars *seven thousand* light years away. Or, putting it from the Old Earthers' lingo: If light reaches our planet from a star a billion light years away, that light has been traveling to Earth for at least a billion years in order for it to be seen from here.

Simply put: Since a) we know how fast light moves from a star to be visible from Earth; b) we have calculated many stars to be millions or billions of light years away from Earth, and c) we can see this light from Earth's surface...then Earth must have been around for millions or billions of years to be able to receive those traveling light waves.

Young Earthers typically explain that the stars are far closer than astronomers admit, but if that were the case, again: The governing laws of gravity and motion (along with several other natural laws) that Earth mutually shares with surrounding space objects would result in regularly occurring catastrophe when the gravitational pull of large-mass stars pulled others into them, causing epic collision and radiation explosions reaching Earth and obliterating us all…and that's only *one* of hundreds of reasons why this argument cannot stand.

A couple of other arguments arise from the Young Earthers (like the idea that the speed of light slowed way down at some point), though they, too, are dismantled. Each one of their hypotheses, when left to play out to the ultimate end of our currently known natural laws, either results in the obliteration of Earth or the lack of its formation in the past.

Stylistic/Contextual and Frequency Seriation

This category of age assignment and relative dating falls into the modern age and is thus quite different from what we've looked at up to this point (though, of all dating methods, this one relates the most to the next chapter). Archeology and anthropology have produced a vast number of relics of our past, many of which point by style or design to a certain culture or area.

For example, the technology in place to produce a VCR (video cassette recorder) was first mastered in 1956. Prior to that year, no one owned a VCR because, obviously, they weren't invented yet. Today, owning a VCR is increasingly rare, as they have already been largely rendered obsolete via the development of DVD and Blu-ray players, which are now possibly being ushered into obsolescence by digital streaming platforms (Netflix, Hulu, Amazon Prime), and so on.

If archeologists a thousand years from now were to enter a city in an abandoned area of California and see many homes with VCRs still connected to television sets, seriation would show those homes belonged to folks who likely lived there between 1956 and the early 2000s, since most VCR manufacturers discontinued making the devices between 2000–2015. Other household items—kitchen appliances or utensils dating to specific years of US patents, movie posters from films released in certain years, pharmaceuticals only prescribed within limited time windows before they were recalled by the Food and Drug Administration, products made from rubber or plastic compounds tied to a specific period of manufacturing, calculators, computers, etc.—would all contribute to the researchers' ability to hone in on dates of thriving activity within that culture.

When we apply that same logic backwards in time, we can easily see how this dating method works. A clay pot formed in the same style from materials with the same chemical composition as those produced in ancient China is likely not an artifact that originated from Egypt.

Though seriation doesn't directly date artifacts in the range of millions or billions of years, as do the other methods we've looked at, it is frequently used to describe the culture and living circumstances of people groups scientists believed were alive more than six thousand to ten thousand years ago (like the Stone Age). Seriation would not need to be the primary dating method to determine how long ago a culture thrived or survived, but it can assist in reverse: *After* deciphering how long ago the ancients occupied a certain region, we can bring in seriation to show us what they were like at that time and, in a roundabout way, support what deductions we make regarding the dating of surrounding cultures.

The "Tricky God Theory"

We've looked at several arguments from Young Earthers who believe any dating methods indicating Earth to be more than six thousand to ten thousand years old are wrong. We also looked at some of the logic behind the more popular claims of scientific inaccuracy and why the Young Earthers may be incorrect (or only partially informed) in those assessments. But one thing we haven't looked at yet is how—despite all their responsibly collected data and articulately fashioned refutations—one of their most frequently shared conclusions about the age of Earth may produce a *theological incompatibility* with the character and nature of God as He describes Himself in His very own Word.

As addressed in the first chapter of this book (in the section titled "Cosmological Views"), Young Earthers are used to being bombarded with the question, "If Earth is young, then why is there so much constant and mounting evidence that it's old?" One popular answer is that

God created Earth with "the appearance of age." Tom Horn and a dear theologian friend of Defender Publishing and SkyWatch Television, Gary Stearman, has recoined this the "Tricky God Theory," as it represents a glaring problem that your average interpretational loophole can't completely satisfy: God, in creating a young planet that *looks* old, had to have intentionally decided to trick humanity.

Let's get the quick rebuttals out of the way: Yes, God is powerful enough to have snapped a finger, blinked a planet into existence, and given it the appearance of a mature age even when it was five seconds old. Yes, such a decision would be His strict prerogative as the Almighty, and yes, technically, God *could* choose to do whatever He wants. Yes, we should accept His decisions and not beat angry fists at the sky when we disagree with something He does, because He is infinitely wiser than the collective wisdom of all humanity since the dawn of time, and He only wants the best for us.

And, for as many "yeses" as there are in this equation, there are even more "maybes":

Maybe the *universe* is billions of years old, but, six thousand years ago, God brought Earth into existence and made it bend to the same motion and gravity laws as the rest of the universe. Maybe He layered its soil and rock to make it merely appear as if there are strata dating to billions of years ago. Maybe the polarity and geomagnetism really do shift approximately every thirty years and He simply spares us from the global apocalypse such events would ignite. Maybe all the data from the Hubble telescope teams and their redshift calculations have missed a major element that would otherwise allow the speed of light and the position of Earth to be more compatible with a young planet.

But if so, why? And…*how*, when the Holy Bible is so clear that our God is not a God of deception? (Remember that, although Adam and Eve were created with the appearance of age, as well as having immediate intelligence and moral responsibility, God *told us that* in His Word, so there is no hiding anything from us on that one.) Scores of verses throughout Scripture make it immensely clear that a deception from God is not possible (see especially Numbers 23:19; Titus 1:2; Hebrews 6:18). The Bible only stands as the supreme authority if we can accept the *whole* document (all sixty-six books) together, right? Naturally, this leads to another crucial question: Is He, or is He *not*, willing for some to perish into a dark eternity separated from His presence because they bought into His own "appearance of age" deception, saw that this was "what the Bible says" (or so the Church interprets), and believed the rest of the biblical record to be untrustworthy? The Word says God is "not willing that any should perish" (2 Peter 3:9), yet the only way a soul can come to Him is through the testimony of His Word. If the Bible says Earth is young, but God, Himself, has chosen to make it look old, then doesn't that mean the Bible cannot be trusted and God has deceived us—strata, coral reefs, river sediments, geomagnetism, redshift, fossils, and all?

Donna, how can you dare even insinuate that God is a deceiver?!

I *wouldn't* dare, and that is precisely my point. Though there are Young Earthers who have given other reasons for the "appearance of age" conundrum, no matter what the response, it always comes back to the sound question: Why did God allow so much evidence of advanced age if it simply isn't true? Either *all* these scientists are wrong, or God is a trickster.

But Donna, you're assuming science to be true. The Bible doesn't bow to human observation. If there's a conflict between science and the Bible, the Bible wins!

I agree—100 percent and in every application, always, throughout the universe, and into perpetuity. There will never be an exception to this in my own mind. Yet, recall what I wrote in the introduction to this book:

> Of utmost importance…is an accurate treatment of the term "true science." By this, I refer not to what conclusions within the scientific world have arisen through exclusively human origin—as the Bible bows to no manmade investigation, discovery, laboratory result, mathematic calculation, or observation of any kind— but to genuine reality as God has ordained it.…
>
> If God personally created the world, *and He did*—and if God personally guided the writers of Scripture to faithfully pen His self-revelation to all of mankind, *and He did*—then weaving these

two threads together and seeking to find one accord between them is nothing short of a genuine act of worship.

It has never been my goal to show that human-conducted sciences are truer than the Word of God, but in seeking to praise our Master Scientist for the beautiful universe *He* has designed, I simply find that the evidence for an old planet stacks higher than it does for a young one, and the Bible absolutely allows for that interpretation. I see so many passionate Young Earthers who have given years of their lives defending our Lord and the faith, while most are seemingly unaware of the theological problem presented with the "appearance of age" ("Tricky God") theory.

A Young Earther might ask why I haven't spent more time elaborating on the geological implications of a worldwide Flood in Noah's time that may have formed many (or all) of these rock and river layers far more rapidly than scientists have reported. My response would be that it's simply not believable for every area of the world that features these gradations, once we take into account: 1) how the layers are known to form over time in relation to sunshine beating down upon them, the visual testimony of four distinct seasons, and other evidence that could not have occurred during the rain-only Flood account; 2) what fossils exist between the layers, and how they originate from different species in the animal kingdom from one layer to another (such as fossils of fish being found on a certain level, those of reptiles on another, then back to marine animals on another, land animals on yet another, and so on, which is not what a rapid "mixing" of flood damage to the planet would show); 3) the various ages they consistently appear to be—oldest on the bottom and youngest on the top—which could not have come from an overnight, global catastrophe that killed all animals living at the same time at once; 4) the fact that the layers have shown all over the world to overlap in bizarre patterns, some of which are diagonal and involve a "sea, land, sea, land" pattern with evidence of wind erosion on the land levels (showing there could not have been water on the surface of that area for a lengthy time before it became water again, explained by tectonic shifting of major land mass over millions of years); 5) the fact that, even if all else could be explained away by Noah's Flood, it still wouldn't account for the gradual growth layering of underwater ocean reefs dated millions of years old and apparently undisturbed by a deluge six thousand years ago; and so on.

But note the key words here: The Flood of Noah's day is simply not plausible as the cause for *every* spot on the globe that features such layering. This does *not* mean there is no evidence of the Flood, or that the Flood did not create some of the Young-Earth evidence we find that took place after the re-creation event.

I'm Not Dismissing the Flood

Not only are proofs of Noah's Flood in bits and pieces scattered throughout Earth, almost every culture and religion of the ancient world has legends describing a cataclysmic deluge event that matches the biblical account of the Flood either precisely or with striking similarities. In addition to written records, we have pictographs, and remember: The ancient images on walls and slabs have generally been what historians, scientists, and scholars of all sorts of conviction (secular and religious) have used to paint a picture of what humankind's earliest experiences may have looked like. We can reconstruct the past through these visual testimonies.

Following the most primitive form of writing (pictographs), early cultures recognized how tedious it was to draw or carve everything they saw and experienced, so throughout centuries they developed more innovative, time-saving forms of written communication. This led to ideographs (the combination of certain pictures to represent feelings or emotion); logographs (the combination of pictographs and ideographs); and, eventually, symbols that represented sounds uttered from the mouth (alphabets with vowels and consonants).

From records of these multiple media, we've learned much about the ancients: which deities were worshiped, by whom, and the legends that led to where, why, and how they were worshiped; what sacred beliefs were attached to specific objects, structures, substances, or medicines (gemstones, oils, herbs, spices, flowers, vegetation, altars, etc.); the relationship between people and many space objects (stars, sun, moon, planets); the experiences of people during seemingly phenomenal or spiritual occurrences (sunsets or anomalous lights in the sky, the incoming and outgoing of the tide, sudden shifts in the direction of the wind, as well as natural laws like gravity); who the leaders or royals of the locals were, what was expected of them, how they were appointed, and what some of them did to fail miserably in their duties for the people; wars, social and political subordination or rebellion, and the obliteration of entire populations (often as a result of these conflicts); what meals were eaten, what ingredients went into those dishes (barley, corn, various meats, etc.) and how they were prepared; how tools were made, and what they were used for; what common objects were useful and how (jars, baskets, head coverings, etc.); the daily routine of commonfolk; how they viewed the cycle of life and the events that contributed to them (birth, death, etc.); and many other details.

Scripture isn't the only ancient document that includes an account of the Flood. We see accounts of the global deluge coming from people from other regions, including:

- The Mesopotamians: The Epic of Gilgamesh and the story of Utnapishtim who built the "preserver of life" boat from solid timber;
- The Aztecs: The tale of a man and woman who survived a great flood because they were sealed inside a cypress tree by the deity Titlacauan (or Tezcatlipoca);
- The Greeks: Belief that a man named Deucalion, son of Titan Prometheus, was warned about a deluge sent by the god Zeus, so they built a boat, survived the flood, and landed on Mt. Parnassus, where they threw stones that turned into people who would repopulate Earth;
- The Hindus: Manu, the first man, who received word from a fish deity, Lord Vishnu, that a flood was coming, so he constructed a boat and tied it to the horn of the fish and, after the flood subsided, landed atop a mountain where he was eventually met by a

woman rising from the waters who assisted him in repopulation;

- The Chinese: A multitude of flood-story variations involving thunder gods, giant floating gourd-boats, dismembered babies becoming new men and women, etc.;
- The Norse: A folk tale about a "blood flood" that covered the earth following the murder of the giant Ymir at the hand of Odin and his brothers, though a frost giant and his wife were spared, surviving the waves of blood in an ark;
- The ancient Native Americans: A belief that the Great Spirit sent a flood and only one man, Waynaboozhoo, survived on a raft of logs…

…and this list doesn't even scratch the surface.

In short, Noah's Flood is well attested to, and additionally, we have geological evidence of it all over the world. So, by no means do I disbelieve the Flood occurred just because it doesn't *also* prove Earth is young. This leads me to an important moment in this study: I *do* think some of the evidence in favor of a Young Earth is accurate!

Could Both Young and Old-Earth Evidence Be True?

In many areas of today's world, the Flood of Noah's day certainly can account for what we see that science has a harder time explaining. One such example could be how marine fossils are found at the top of mountains scattered all over the world, suggesting that, at one point, Earth was completely covered in water. (Interestingly, Dr. Tom Horn visited the Grand Canyon a few years back, and a certain expert in his tour party presented a collection of marine fossils as "proof that the entire Grand Canyon and surrounding mountain regions were covered in water thousands of years ago." Though this individual did not expound on Noah's Flood in particular, it was clear that was a central consideration.)

And, yes, scientists *do* have an explanation for this phenomenon: Past tectonic plate shifting has raised giant areas of rock that were once buried under Earth's crust or on the ocean floor, and the fossils "hitched a ride" to the top. Global warming and rising sea levels are also factors.

Could these (and other) explanations account for some of what we find? Of course. But can we dismiss *all* mountaintop marine fossils and other evidence of Noah's Flood as naturally occurring? That is harder to accept, simply because the whole globe offers evidence of that event. Obviously, evidence in favor of the Flood as a valid event isn't limited to fossils and a few desperate findings by believing Christians. Secular sources report on Flood-related discoveries all the time. Even the Smithsonian Institution, in an article titled, "Evidence for a Flood," acknowledges that "recently scientists have started to uncover evidence that Noah's flood may have a basis in some rather astonishing events that took place around the Black Sea some 7,500 years ago," which the article links to the "last great glaciation some 20,000 years ago."[95] Another example is a report published by ABC News titled, "Evidence Noah's Biblical Flood Happened, Says Robert Ballard," which details a deep, underwater dive that "unearthed an ancient shoreline, proof to [underwater archeologist] Ballard that a catastrophic event [like Noah's Flood] did happen."[96] There is no shortage of reports on this long-ago incident, both inside and outside the Church. Yet, strangely, a great number of Flood-related findings appear to support a Young Earth. So, what do we make of the conflict?

First: If the world is very old, there would be evidence of that, and I believe there is (much more than what has been discussed regarding dating methods in this chapter). Second: If the world were created *again* six thousand years ago—over the top of, and interlaced with, the old world—we would definitely see evidence of that as well. The nature of such a seismic, global change to the planet—with fresh matter (living and non-living) of all sorts springing up from the surface of the former planet—would certainly imply a Young Earth. In fact, I not only concede that, I *expect* that. Therefore, Young Earthers wouldn't necessarily be wrong each time they interpret Flood evidence in that manner. (The error is in assuming the biblical Flood can and does account for *all* the bizarre millions of years of layering that science can otherwise explain in natural terms.)

Could massive geological damage to Earth account for the Young Earth findings that apparently defy science? Why not? Because *Earth* is old, but the re-creation from Genesis 1:3 forward through Creation week and the Flood are more recent events that left global fingerprints all over the surface of that Old Earth:

1. God created Earth millions or billions of years ago.
2. Something happened that rendered the planet "without form, and void" for an indefinite period.
3. God re-created Earth six to ten thousand years ago.

From this perspective, scientific dating methods that support millions or billions of years of history in a certain culture, region, or assortment of artifacts could point to Earth's absolute earliest days—prior to Genesis 1:3—while Young Earthers' evidence could point to what God *re*-created in six days (or ages). Earth was made, *then* it was made "formless/void," *then* it was made again.

This all throws endless possibilities into the bigger picture, some of which may account for what science has presented to be early phases of human evolution. As one example: The Bible doesn't appear to allow for any interpretation of *co*-Adamites (partly evolved ape men cohabiting Earth alongside Adam), though, from the Gap theory perspective of two Creation events, there may have been a pre-Adamic race of semi-intelligent beings science would easily see as a common ancestor of man (which is technically what Darwin said these earlier ape men were): a race or species of creatures who may or may not have appeared quite humanlike in their bipedal anatomy who occupied this planet before humanity existed and before Earth became void.

I realize that, to some, this sounds too sensational to believe, but that's likely because it's a new (or largely unheard of) idea. But consider what we're really talking about here: God is the Master Creator over all, and He has made millions of life forms that we can study and observe at this very moment. According to the Royal Entomological Society, "Over one million species of insects have been discovered and described but it is estimated that there may be as many as 10 million species on earth."[97] And that is only in reference to insects! So, if there *was* an era of Earth's history that stretched back to a time before Adam was formed, as the biblical Hebrew linguists frequently insist is a possible interpretation of Genesis, then why would it be hard to believe God's earliest creative abilities had formed all sorts of species, including something that shared visible and/ or biological traits with Adam? A dog isn't the same thing as a cat, though both grow similar coats of fur, walk on four legs, have longer tails than many other species of animals, submit to some level of domestication, interact with humanity, and share countless other similarities. So long as we don't confuse the fact that, biblically and theologically speaking, Adam was the first human, different than the rest when he was made in the image of God, I don't have a problem thinking something that looked similar to him walked Earth's surface before he did.

There is yet another possibility. What if the Darwinian ape men were something wicked developed through the detestable, blasphemous, God-usurping, fallen angels who *already illustrated their willingness and capability of manipulating the DNA of God's Creation* in Genesis 6:4 (tackled in chapter 7 of this book)?

And what about the dinosaurs? Could they be a part of that potential scenario as well?

Of course, this is hypothetical, but it sure would explain some of those "human ancestor" remains scattered about...as well as astoundingly bizarre sites that show an extreme intelligence to be alive and thriving, dated to exist well before Adam's time.

It is to that subject we'll turn now.

Chapter 5

Mystery History

APART FROM DATING METHODS that can be applied almost universally, unique discoveries stand alone as evidence of *someone* occupying this land before the Ussher-developed, Adamic timeline of humans (those made in the image of God). (Who they were, how they got here, and what they were up to is a topic that we will address in part three: "The Serpent King.")

For instance, Gobekli Tepe, an archeological site in Turkey (that we will look more deeply at in the coming pages), according to all radiocarbon dating, rock strata information, and other dating methods, appears to have been built approximately *six thousand years before* Adam's 4004 BC birthday. In this case, one of three possibilities is acceptable: 1) the dating methods are off because scientists make mistakes (or assumptions, or they conspire to hide the truth, etc.) and the site is not nearly that old; 2) Adam and his descendants were brought into the picture well before the dates posed by Ussher/Young Earth chronology, therefore these ruins and artifacts are of Adam's descendants left behind thousands of years ago; 3) someone/something was here *before* Adam, and Adam's birth marks the re-creation event when the world was restored to its former glory following the "void" era of chaos within which these ruins and artifacts originated. We'll focus on possibility number three in this chapter.

Also, because nobody knows exactly when Adam was formed, Ussher Chronology may be close in its calculations: The anomalies discovered on the apparently ancient Earth in this chapter will be compared to the 4004 BC birth-of-Adam dating. (Note that some of the research in this chapter was originally included in the 2015 Defender Publishing release, *On the Path of the Immortals: Exo-Vaticana, Project L.U.C.I.F.E.R., and the Strategic Locations Where Entities Await the Appointed Time*, by Cris Putnam and Tom Horn. As such, the reader may find certain portions of this chapter familiar.)

Before we launch, let me take a minute to explain a couple of terms.

"OOPArts": Fringe Term or True Mysteries?

The acronym OOPArts is a common abbreviation for "out-of-place artifacts." These artifacts are named "out of place," as there is no feasible explanation for their existence—when they are *real*—and this is where we land in a big mess.

To quickly close the question posed by heading of this section, OOPArts represents *both* a fringe colloquialism and true mysteries. Unfortunately, though effectively named for what they characterize, the term has gained a dubious reputation among researchers over time. Many conspiracy theorists have picked up on rumors of certain OOPArts and labeled them as things mysteriously left behind by an ancient astronaut or advanced civilization before credible analysis. Some of these folks, as well-meaning and curious as they may have been, have gone on to blast websites, television and radio programs, and other media outlets with sensational or inaccurate claims—only to eventually learn that the artifact was underwhelming and ordinary once properly examined. As a result, "OOPArts" has become somewhat of a colloquialism reserved for fringe groups and conspiracy theorists.

This, in turn, has presented another often-used term, "forbidden archeology," which refers to a) old and mysterious sites or unexplainable objects that archeologists won't touch because the discoveries have already been smeared with so much misinformation that experts write them off as nonsense without any analysis; b) the effect of studying OOPArts on the reputation of the professional archeology community; if archeologists *do* spend time on OOPArts, they're stamped "lunatics" or "religious fanatics" (since some of the findings naturally lead archeologists who are believers to draw a conclusion based on Young or Old Earth Creationism). Thus, "forbidden archeology" implies exactly what it sounds like: If well-meaning experts even so much as look at a site or object that has already been "tainted" by "conspiracists," they have engaged in the "forbidden" and have effectively ruined their careers—maybe irreparably.

This unfortunately leaves only the conspiracy theorists and layperson research groups to address the discoveries. As you can imagine, this isn't a good development.

Visitors to Amazon.com—the e-commerce company that paved the way through its Kindle self-publishing platform for e-readers that enables anyone to write a book about whatever they want and make it available to anyone else with access to the Internet—see around fifty books discussing OOPArts. Most of these are crudely self-published, resulting in a publication that not only *looks* substandard (with errors and typos), but *is* substandard. That's because much of the "research" conducted by these writers is limited to what conspiracy websites say about the artifacts, yielding conclusions that are sensational, one-sided, and incorrect. Some of these books almost entirely plagiarize unreliable sites and Wikipedia, never giving credit to the sources and exposing their writers as "cheaters" on top of everything else.

Then, often, rumors are started that touch off a ceaseless (and sometimes quite petty) mud-flinging between "conspiracists" and "professionals." The second an object is labeled an "OOPArt," professionals avoid it, so it's never subjected to proper testing methods and analysis. Conspiracists then see the OOPArt being ignored by the professionals and subsequently come up with their own conclusions about the object. They hold that their findings are the *only* valid explanations, and that scientists are avoiding it because they're secretly afraid the object threatens long-held conclusions within their field of expertise. Whether or not that is true (I believe it could be, in some cases, like John Powell of the Smithsonian refusing to allow any of his discoveries regarding a race of giants to be used to discuss, well, the possibility of *giants*), not everything is a conspiracy, as some of the OOPArts-following personalities suggest. I can imagine being a responsible and genuine archeologist sighing at yet another "ancient discovery" that my own eyes and training could immediately identify as common; therefore, I understand the frustration of being expected to waste time, money (tax dollars and other funding sources), energy, and talent explaining why a random chunk of metal in the desert may *not* have originated from a UFO, regardless of whether it has been analyzed in a lab. I can understand seeing a discovery labeled "forbidden archeology" and, with absolutely no hidden agenda of protecting scientific theory, shrugging and moving on with my life, letting others with more time on their hands sort it out. Other "valid discoveries" would need my attention. I get it.

However, despite the reputation OOPArts have gained, unexplainable artifacts *have* been found at dig sites all over the world. For example, the Antikythera mechanism—an analog computer—was found in a shipwreck from the Hellenistic period (one hundred to two hundred years before Christ). And another, the Baghdad Battery from Iraq, is what scientists believe acted as a galvanic cell (dated to around the time of Christ), possibly for use in early electrotherapy. So, if we can manage to filter out the false findings from the legitimate ones, we've landed on something worth looking at.

Since the term "OOPArts" is familiar, and still indicates objects that are "out of place," I'll keep using it in our discussion of these mysterious items. However, I'll steer clear of addressing at length OOPArts that seem less valid based on what attention they *have* received from the archeological community, as well as those that have been dated to after Adam's arrival (like the Antikythera mechanism and the Baghdad Battery).

Every true OOPArt has, like the Shroud of Turin, drawn countless theories from laypeople attempting to illuminate what ancient culture the object came from and the item's purpose. But, also like the Shroud, once many of these theories are rationally considered and weighed against the evidence, they fall flat and fail to paint a reliable picture of their origin. Since scientists largely ignore many of these findings, they remain mysteries that—conspiracy or otherwise—fall into origin classifications of the inexplicable: giant races, pre-Adamites, etc.

These objects defy the conventional chronology of human history, usually in one of two ways: 1) They are more advanced than the technology that existed at their time of origin; or 2) they are dated prior to human existence on Earth.

Pre-Adamites

I hinted at this possibility of "Pre-Adamites" earlier, but because the term will be used more often in this chapter, I'll stop here to more fully define it:

- Pre-Adamites (pre-*Adam*-ites): a hypothetical race of entities alive on Earth's surface *before* the formation of the first human, Adam. The theories relate to questions of whether this race may have shared some similarities with Adam—in some cases potentially resembling the ape men of Darwinian theories (but please see the **CRUCIAL DISCLAIMER** following these two bullets).
- Pre-Adamic (pre-*Adam*-ic): of or relating to pre-Adamites.

How I Will NOT Use These Terms

CRUCIAL DISCLAIMER: For our purposes, "pre-Adamites" will never refer to an earlier race of humans who were made in the image of God as Adam was, since that is clearly (biblically and theologically) a status reserved for Adam, Eve, and the rest of humanity from that couple forward. Though a few interpreters argue for a pre-Adamic race of people who *were* fully human—at times with the same (or similar) salvific rights and history of God's progressive redemption plan and intervention—*that is not how I am using the term in this chapter*, and that line of logic is beyond the scope of this book.

I currently find zero biblical support for the idea that a fully "human" race existed prior to Adam, because the language of Genesis (in both

Hebrew and English) is clear that humans were given dominion over the rest of earthly existence, were inherently and exclusively instilled with the *imageo dei* ("image of God") at the time of Creation, and are therefore made with a special plan and purpose unique from all of God's other created beings and entities.

Additionally, if we take what we know to be God's plan for humanity in its totality and apply it backwards in time to another, earlier "human" race, it leads to an eventual "theology" (read: "heresy") that they were either morally perfect or that Christ may have had to die for *them*, *too*, which goes against Romans 6:10: "For in that he [Jesus] died, he died unto sin *once*: but in that he liveth, he liveth unto God" (emphasis added). (Also see 1 Peter 3:18; Hebrews 7:27; 9:26–28; 10:12; Romans 5:6. All of these verses directly state that Jesus died "once," and many other passages in the New Testament say the same thing indirectly.)

Also recall that we've already dealt with (and dismissed) the concept that there would have been co-Adamites (co-*Adam*-ites)—a hypothetical race of entities alive on Earth *at the same time* as (and ancestral to) the first human, Adam (ape men, etc.). (To review why I believe this to be a theological impossibility, turn back to chapter 3, under the heading "Adam from 'Dust.'")

Now, I am aware that some of this "OOPArt" and "pre-Adamic"-type terminology is highly associated with Ancient Astronaut theories—in general, the belief that there were pre-Adamites on Earth prior to humans and that they were akin to the alien grays we see in movies—but that's not the hypothesis I'm ultimately building up to. I believe the Luciferian "void" era may have had perverted, demonic beings present on Earth, and that whatever these races may have been inspired "alien" concepts that came far later. Thus, my theory will address the possibility that *some* phenomena traditionally linked to alien visitation in the past may play a small part in the much bigger and more accurate picture of an ancient deception: a Luciferian scheme to thwart God's plans for humanity (as the enemy is recorded throughout Scripture to have tried repeatedly). With that in mind, I'm not surprised alien imagery would be linked to some of these findings, as that is partly how they later developed. However, I don't believe that bulbous-headed aliens in silver suits, devoid of any connection to God or Lucifer, are the answer to all these mysteries. If aliens, in the classic sense of the word, have anything to do with any of this, it's because they draw their origins from a time when God and Lucifer were at war. They are not intelligent life from other planets that came into being independently of God or Lucifer. This book is not about UFOs, space invaders, or any other concepts of an alien species. Thus, when I include references to something "pre-Adamic," it should not be associated with the popular topic of intergalactic trespassers...and it *most definitely should not* be linked to any speculations about aliens having been the true creators of Earth and Adam, or that humans were grown in a lab on Mars and planted here later on, or any other ideas that conflict with the clear teachings of the Word.

But could God have created angels that would later rebel and *become* the bizarre space beings described in abduction testimonies, and to whom "Creation" will be attributed by Ancient Astronaut theorists? Yes, that is possible, and yes, they would be pre-Adamic in nature since they predate Adam. But would this all be a grand deception perpetuated by the same beings who rebelled and whose *true* identity and purposes are far more nefarious than indicated by the phrase "travelers from a distant galaxy"? Absolutely.

Lastly, it is equally important to clarify that I am *not* suggesting all the strange phenomena we'll consider in this chapter that point to ancient mysteries find their explanation in a pre-Adamic race just because we have no answers at present. Many books and documentaries have made this mistake (or similar) in the past and the spokespeople behind the media suffered humiliation at the same time their work was rendered outdated and irrelevant when scientists responded with new facts. I concede—without bias or hidden agenda—that we simply *do not know* what we're looking at with many of these discoveries, and assigning their origins to a pre-Adamic race due to lack of any other leading sustainable theory is to make the same mistake I've herein criticized: deducing from assumption.

How I WILL Use These Terms

Don't make the *other* mistake I've criticized, either: "condemnation before investigation." The theory I propose near the end of this book, I hope, will not be scorned just because it might be new for some. To group these discoveries under a single question (that I acknowledge could be answered responsibly at any moment): Could these odd formations and objects point to an intelligent race on Earth before humanity entered the picture? If so, what were these pre-Adamic beings up to?

Before readers immediately think "aliens," even though I just rendered that loosely possible under strict theological circumstances (if they were to originate from an ancient war between God and Lucifer), understand that I'm referring to a *much wider* category of "beings" in general: animals *and* humanlike forms of life (which will come into a sharper focus in later chapters).

When "pre-Adamites" appears in this book from this point on, it will mean a nonhuman race of entities. From the evidence (some of which is theological, as we'll later address), there appears to be no other explanation than the possibility that intelligence was present in some form before 4004 BC and/or any other time frame near that of Adam's formation.

Certain ancient rock foundations, structures, and temples across the globe haven't ceased to baffle observers, and those who have dedicated their lives to studying these ruins have often raised more questions than they've answered. Not the least of these questions are frequently about who built these structures or left these OOPArts behind, what purposes they first served, and, most importantly, how the structures and OOPArts could have been designed when such technology didn't yet exist. For instance, the size of the monolithic stones found in these locations, as well as the archaic building technology of that period, would have made the transportation and positioning of these stones an impossibility (in some cases, that's true even for our time). Yet, these monoliths and constructs not only exist out in the open for any and all to see, but they've often been assembled with such precision that there's not even room for a needle or a human hair between the stones. These discoveries present evidence that the slaves-with-pulley-carts civilization our history books portray don't tell the whole story. These include gigantic edifices built from the largest stones ever cut and put into place, a feat that seems to indicate manufacturing skills well beyond those of what we know about primeval man.

Examples of such herculean slabs weighing hundreds of tons can be found above Lake Titicaca in Peru, with others situated in Tiahuanaco, twelve miles south of Lake Titicaca in Bolivia, South America. Even larger stones are the southern entrance of Baalbek, a city in eastern Lebanon famous for its magnificent temple ruins. These are a few of the many megalithic and mysterious structures most believe predate the great Flood of Noah's day.

Such constructs obviously didn't raise themselves thousands or millions of years ago, then mystically and autonomously carve ornate symbols on their own walls or stones. Nor could they have been fashioned by natural means. The frequent use of pagan figures and icons in many of these locations leads us to conclude we can't assume that God, Himself, raised these structures just to test or confuse us (this would be taking to an extreme the offensive "Tricky God Theory" covered in the previous chapter).

Yet, many Christians (including Old Earthers) believe Adamite humanity is only ten thousand years old at most. Why are there so many foreign bones, tools, articles of clothing or jewelry, and other artifacts that reflect flourishing (and often quite wicked) civilizations all over planet Earth right under our noses that predate human origin?

Questions like these are what drove the preliminary debates regarding human and/or other races existing in antiquity in the first place, leading to theories that now fall under the heading "pre-Adamites." Though I don't claim to have all the answers, the prophets Isaiah, Jeremiah, and Ezekiel *might* have some…

…and, if so, we have good reason to believe at least some of these structures and objects from ancient Earth were principally Luciferian in origin.

Remember this: 1) Angels were created *before* Adam; 2) all angels were beings of intelligence; 3) some of them fell, becoming evil, and when they did; 4) Earth was their home. Therefore, though I cringe at the popular term "pre-Adamites" for their association with conspiracy theories (like OOPArts), I still find it an effective label for the beings who inhabited Earth before Adam—whether they were fallen angels or some grotesque crossbreed.

But let's not get ahead of ourselves. *First*, the discoveries, *then* a review of what they may imply and how they fit with a theological and biblical worldview.

Since the objects that would fit the description of an OOPArt are often isolated discoveries unrelated to existing, complex archeological sites, we will look at a few of those first. Note that I intentionally avoided mentioning any OOPArt discovery that is only reported (in those earlier-mentioned, heavily plagiarized articles) by sites dedicated to the Ancient Astronaut theory. However, because professionals in related fields tend to run from anything the Ancient Astronaut group has latched onto, some of these have yet to be thoroughly studied and, therefore, the reports on some of the following are still early.

Ancient Nanotechnology in Russian Mountains

In 1991, a group of geologists were hunting for gold deposits in the Ural Mountains, which stretch from southern to northern Russia and create a natural border between Europe and Asia. These mountains are already linked to oddities such as incoming reports of "fireballs" and "cigar-shaped crafts" seen in the sky.[98] However, the most mind-boggling discovery there to date is what was found during the gold expedition six hundred miles north of Arkaim at the point where three rivers—Kozhim, Narada, and Balbanyu—overlap. More than thirty feet down, in a layer of soil that spans more than ten kilometers around and had been "untouched for hundreds of thousands or more years,"[99] the geologists unearthed "a scattering of tiny metal coils and springs," as reported on the History Channel.[100]

The images (available in many places online) show a number of coils/springs curling up from a metal "cap" object, but most appear to be wound around a column (like a snake slithering up a tree trunk in a circular pattern) that shows sudden, gnarled breakage at its end. Most remarkable is their size: Though the largest coils measure in at around three centimeters wide, the smallest are a mere "1/10,000 of an inch (2.5 microns—for comparison, the average hair is about 100 microns wide)."[101]

Collected samples were sent to the Russian Academy of Sciences in St. Petersburg to be analyzed against known technology in an attempt to find out what they were made of and, perhaps, what they had been used for. The results showed the tiniest coils were made of a tough metal called tungsten (used for making tools and, in the aerospace industry, "to fabricate rocket-engine nozzle throats and leading-edge reentry surfaces"[102]), as well as copper. In addition, the rare metal molybdenum was detected in some samples. Tungsten does form naturally from Earth, but never in this shape or size: In nature, tungsten's edges are ragged, with sharp protrusions jutting out in a way that's similar to a natural crystal or rock formation, while these shockingly microscopic coils being studied resembled the man-made, larger tungsten coils we would expect to see at the center of a halogen lamp. As tungsten has the highest melting point of all metals, it would have to have been melted down to temperatures of at least 3,410 degrees Celsius or 6,170 degrees Fahrenheit, then reshaped by machine to produce a coil matching the nature of the one discovered in 1991 near the Ural Mountains.

It doesn't take a genius to conclude that this discovery is not a natural formation of nature. In fact, the spirals were found to have "Golden Mean proportions,"[103] a term referencing perfection in the aesthetic proportions of an object or formation, aligning with the Fibonacci sequence in mathematics (which simply means the spirals were mathematically perfect in the way they bent and curled from the center outward, like the pattern in nautilus shells).

As for their purpose, or how they were buried beneath many layers of soil believed to be hundreds of thousands of years old, no one has a clue…but we can compare what we know about them to our own modern equipment and machinery. The result is astounding: "ancient nano-technology"—an oxymoron if I've ever heard one. A commentator from the History Channel's coverage on these mini mysteries explained:

The only way we could make them, even now, is with machine guided technology. You could not do this by hand. What we're seeing here is proof that someone had advanced technology sufficient to build the type of circuitry that we normally only see in semiconductors, computer chips, high technology equipment using metals that are not commonly known. So, these spirals are clear evidence that someone had a very advanced civilization right here on Earth.[104]

The *Epoch Times* also reported the OOPArts discovery in an article titled "Ancient Nanostructures Found Out of Place and Time," noting that these nanospirals were also sent to labs in Helsinki and Moscow: four studies in total (one location conducted two studies). Dr. Johannes Fiebag, a principal researcher on the project, passed away in 1999—just eight years after the findings—and unfortunately, the trail went cold with his death, rendering no further answer. What little we know is only supplemented by the fact that one leading theory has been ruled out: Some believed the nanospirals fell from the nearby rocket-launch site in Plesetsk, but in 1996, a report stated the spirals were buried too deep in ancient soil for the launch site to have been involved in their appearance.[105] The report from the Central Scientific Research Department of Geology and Exploitation of Precious Metals in Moscow also acknowledged that the coils "are far too old to have come from modern manufacturing…[and] despite being thousands of years old, the components are of a technological origin."[106]

Though many Ancient Astronaut websites have reported on this discovery and heavily emphasize the geological stratus the coils were found in was dated to "more than 300,000 years old," to be fair, the soil *could* be as young as only twenty thousand years old, according to the earlier, and less sensational, reports. So, rather than cling to the most impressive number, I will refrain and admit this ancient Russian nanotechnology might only predate Adam by about fourteen thousand to sixteen thousand years. And, rather than assume a UFO crashed in Russia, shattered on impact, and sent mini-coil debris flying across ten kilometers of soil,

as some have, I will also admit I have no idea what any of this means...
except that science has in its possession microscopic, mathematically perfect, machine-engineered, and unimaginably advanced technology that I
believe was dated to between Genesis 1:1 and Genesis 1:3.

One last thought before we move onto the next OOPArt: If it takes
looking in a place as unassuming as the Ural Mountains and rivers of Russia—and if what we find could be so small that it would blend in with
specks of dirt on the bottom of an explorer's shoe—then how often do we
walk over or past proof of pre-Adamic intelligence unaware?

It could be daily...and it could be all around us.

Coal, Cart Wheels, and Ruts

There is a long, *vast* historical relationship between OOPArts, coal, and
coal mines. According to the World Coal Association, naturally occurring
coal within Earth is extremely old:

> Coal is a fossil fuel, formed from vegetation, which has been con-
> solidated between other rock strata and altered by the combined
> effects of pressure and heat over millions of years to form coal
> seams. The energy we get from coal today comes from the energy
> that plants absorbed from the sun millions of years ago.[107]

This era is called the Carboniferous Age (or "Period"). We don't have
to blindly accept this dating as the last word in order to at least concede
that coal mine discoveries are worth taking a closer look at; they are unique
in the OOPArt world for being both abundant and encased in naturally
formed materials believed to be exceptionally archaic, predating humanity's relative skills and development by unfathomable stretches of time.
Explorers have stumbled upon a great number of odd items buried with
coal, including doorknobs, gears, jewelry, cooking and eating utensils,
bells, tools and building supplies, figurines, religious artifacts, "human"
bones, weapons, coins, writings (such as hieroglyphics), and stones or

metals originating from locations far away. Of course, if millions of years ago mankind was, scientists say, still part ape and only barely learning to scratch an itch, such artifacts are as "out of place" as any other OOPArt in question…and perhaps the most deserving of attention.

Though a small community of archeologists has observed the enigmatic link between coal and OOPArts and have postulated a few believable theories of their origin, their responses don't even come close to accounting for all that's been unearthed. By far, the majority of coal mine OOPArts are ignored by the scientific community, which appears to place all their resources into proving Earth is old and people came from monkeys. It's ironic at least—and infuriating for the curious. (Though, in defense of the archeologists: Some fringe communities are quick to point out that every single one of the coal-related OOPArts is ancient when there have, at times, been other explanations. This has no doubt provoked experts to believe their skills would be more appropriately channeled elsewhere.)

Wheels have been found fossilized on several occasions, and despite demands that they be analyzed, either archeologists have refused (likely related to the forbidden archeology effect discussed earlier), or access to the artifacts has been prohibited. The latter is the case for a once-wooden, now-fossilized cart wheel found embedded in the ceiling of a coal mine in Donetsk, Ukraine, in 2008. (Unlike some coal mine OOPArts, photos of this relic show that: a) the wheel is still completely surrounded by the mine's naturally occurring materials [it hasn't been excavated and messed with by modern hands]; and b) there is no way to deny it's exactly what it appears to be [in other words, it's not, say, a vague "bump" interpreted as a wheel by OOPArt hopefuls or conspiracists].) Because the Donetsk coal mine was closed in 2009 and today sits flooded in water, gaining access to the wheel for further study isn't expected to occur until someone in archeology circles with a lot of cash and a great reputation deems it necessary.

But, in 2008, coal mine explorers attempted to dislodge the wheel from the ceiling. They whittled away with pickaxes and hammers for some time until it became clear that their efforts were futile; expert extraction was needed, lest it be damaged and rendered irrelevant. When the mine owner and project director opted for the men to stop their whittling to forge ahead and clear the rest of the tunnel, they settled for photos of the artifact,[108] which is still there to this day, resting in its ceiling grave as a nod to a mysterious pastime when man—or someone/something *else*—traveled that area of our planet on a cart with wheels roughly three feet wide.

Without lab analysis, one might argue that the stratum the wheel was found in has not been, and cannot be, responsibly dated. However, the Rostov region around the city of Donetsk is sitting atop Carboniferous Period rock scientists have agreed is around three hundred million years old, and the coal mine is a part of that territory's deep, underground features. If the wheel isn't that old—and I honestly don't know—then how did it come to be lodged there? One possible explanation is that it was lost off a cart during the Carboniferous era, when it merged with the sediment layer through lithification and becoming fossilized, which appears to be its current state. That would date the wheel to about three hundred million years old. Another, less popular theory is that wood doesn't *actually* take hundreds of millions of years to petrify, and this wheel is young. Scientists have been performing studies on wood in recent years that show the process can be much faster, depending on environmental circumstances. But even if that were the case, we still don't know how a wheel got buried so deep in the middle of a Carboniferous rock region that it would eventually appear on the ceiling of a subterranean coal mine. Had it been haphazardly dropped by a roaming explorer of the recent past, it would have been on the *floor*.

The curious public will continue to apply the only logic it knows: If a fossil is wholly encased in coal or the mines that produce that coal, it's as old as the age of the coal it's buried in. Is the dating of the Carboniferous rock strata wrong? Or are the OOPArts really ancient? Or does, perhaps, another explanation just happen to keep applying to one coal OOPArt after another, after another? I find the concept of a three-hundred-million-year-old wheel hard to accept, so I'm still a little skeptical. But those pictures are *really* strange…and there's no answer for its age otherwise.

Backpacking onto the subject of the mysterious wheel of Donetsk are the cart ruts dug into the soil—now petrified stone—in many places all over Earth that likewise cannot be explained, supporting the theory that someone or something was, in fact, traveling about the "void" in these primitive "vehicles." Thankfully, unlike the wheel and other coal-related OOPArts, the ruts have stirred up quite a number of responses from the archeological world.

From the *Journal of Archeological Science*, we see this attention regularly. As one example, in an article titled "The Morphological Variability of Maltese 'Cart Ruts' and its Implications," involving considerable peer review upon some of those ruts that sprung up intermittently throughout Malta, we read:

Diverse views have been expressed on how and when the cart ruts formed, with implications for elucidating the archaeology and geomorphology of the Maltese islands. While there have been occasional suggestions that some ruts may be natural geological features (e.g. Dawkins, 1918, Sagona, 2004), the overwhelming view has been that cart ruts are the result of anthropogenic activity. The estimated age range for the ruts has included Neolithic (e.g. Zammit, 1928, Sagona, 2015, McLaughlin et al., 2018) [these names and years are references to former archeological studies linked in the journal article; I've left them in so the reader can see the vast number of studies conducted on these ruts]...

In general, the ruts have been seen as being created by vehicles, be it wheeled carts (e.g. Fenton, 1918, Weston, 2010) or other forms such as "slide cars" (e.g. Gracie, 1954, Evans, 1971). Functional interpretations have ranged from moving soil uphill to create terraced fields (e.g. Zammit, 1928, Parker and Rubenstein, 1984), the transport of quarried stone (e.g. Abela, 1647, Bonanno, 1994, Bonanno, 2007, Bonanno, 2017), and the movement of general agricultural produce (e.g. Trump, 2002).... Finally, Arnaiz-Villeina et al. (2018) suggest some ruts may have had an "astronomical/religious purpose" and were deliberately aligned as a calendar to mark things like solstices. The dominant narrative, however, sees the cart ruts as being created by, and perhaps for, vehicular transport.[109]

I would like to draw specific attention to one note in the article: "The estimated age range for the ruts has included Neolithic." This range begins in 12,000 BC and only ends in approximately 4,500 BC, according to most sources. This assessment, if correct, places these Neolithic-aged cart ruts on Earth anywhere between eight thousand and five hundred years before Adam. One thing is certain: Despite the infrequent "natural formation" argument (which this article openly refers to as "occasional suggestions" and "less common views"[110]), anyone can look at the photos of these ruts, with their sharp and precise edges veering in a smooth curve around mountains and rocks, and conclude that Earth didn't cough that phenomenon up by itself. The ruts are either man-made (indicating that the dating is off), or they're something-else-made (thus, are fingerprints of the inhabitants of Earth during the "void").

Similar cart ruts have been documented at various locations around the world, most notably in Malta, Kazakhstan, Italy, Spain, France, Ukraine, and even here in the United States.

Painting Studio of African Coast

A *hundred thousand* years ago, archeologists say, early *Homo sapiens* stumbled upon a cave on the South African coast and ground iron-rich dirt in abalone shells to form red paint. The cave was later abandoned and the painting tools were left behind. This is, as one *Live Science* article states, "the oldest evidence of humans making a complex compound, and even the oldest evidence of humans using containers."[111] The next container-related artifact of human civilization wouldn't be made for another *forty thousand* years, as far as we know.

The paint recipe—which may also have been some kind of prehistoric glue used for binding together bone or stone tool pieces—included ochre clay and charcoal. Except for the fact that "humans" cave painting or making glue a hundred thousand years ago is unbelievable, this find doesn't initially appear that exciting. But when chemistry comes into the picture, archeologists are baffled. One of the binding agents in this ancient formula was crushed bones, heated to the point that the bone marrow released its oils. Sand and chips of quartzite stone were blended in, and either water or urine was added to increase the spreadability of the pigment.[112]

Astonishingly, this recipe is nearly identical to the ones used in painting methods in Egypt circa 1000 BC, leading researchers behind this discovery—such as archeologist Christopher Henshilwood of the University of the Witwatersrand in Johannesburg—to note that these primitive cave dwellers had at least "an elementary knowledge of chemistry."[113]

Maybe you readers can explain how hunter-gatherers of this Paleolithic period—whose lifestyle involved squatting in caves and banging on stuff with bones and rocks—could develop extraordinary, successful chemical compounds approximately ninety-seven thousand years before the progressive Egyptians did...but I don't even have the beginning of a theory.

Neither do archeologists.

Puerta de Hayu Marca ("Gate of the Gods")

Just off the shores of Lake Titicaca, Peru, in a region known by the Peruvian Indians as "The City of the Gods," measuring in a perfect, twenty-three-foot square, is the *Puerta de Haya Marca* (the "Gate of the Gods"). A second name for this artifact/site is the "Doorway of the Serpent." There are a number of theories regarding the origin of this secondary name, from those indicating it refers to the shape of the entire rock (which can appear from aerial shots as a reptile slithering up through the soil) to those recalling that the early Catholics designated it as a doorway to evil (thus, "serpent," for its connections to Lucifer/Satan). And the Catholics have a good reason to deem it an evil place...

The "gate" is a strange square stamp embedded into the side of a naturally flat rock formation on the border of Bolivia. Inside the square, at the bottom center, is another recessed impression within the rock (standing around six feet high), which, from a distance, resembles a kind of keyhole. Upon closer inspection, the "keyhole" appears to be more the size of a door, and in its very center is a small, circular dent/depression in the back wall.

Local legend says the Amaru Meru (alternatively "Amaru Muru"), the Incan priest of the Temple of the Seven Rays, ran into the mountains to flee the Spanish Conquistadors who had come to rob and plunder the Incan tribes. With him, he carried a small disc, the "Key of the Gods of the Seven Rays," which had been dropped from the heavens and kept sacred by the priest. Once he reached a safe distance from the temple, the Amaru Meru conducted a ritual with his fellow priests, using the small disc to open a portal within the flat rock, through which he disappeared. Some versions of this tale claim the Amaru Meru was fleeing alongside several other priests of the Temple of the Seven Rays. Others say he fled alone, discovering the doorway while in hiding, and happened upon shamans guarding the doorway, who thereafter agreed to perform a portal ritual with him when they saw the object he held. Either way, both versions suggest the doorway was a giant image carved into the mountains *well before the priest fled the temple.* This event, the legend says, turned the solid rock into a stargate. According to local lore, this priest was the first of other "kings" who came to earth from heavenly locations specifically associated with the constellations Pleiades and Orion.

But if the Incans say the door was already there, then who carved it? And how long ago?

Other folklore offered by the Native Indians says the site is a gateway to the lands of the gods through which, in their ancient past, great heroes arrived and then departed with a key that could open the mysterious doorway. In some adaptations, these earlier men had left this world to begin life anew amidst other interdimensional heroes, occasionally returning to check up on their former kingdom.

But again, the doorway was already there…

Nobody knows who crafted this door-shaped marvel, or when. Theories abound as to its origin, and for as many archeologists who claim the site is merely an abandoned building project by the Incas, *just as many believe the site predates Incan occupancy*—and some can explain in rigorous detail how and why *the doorway carving is not typical of Incan design*. That's an important fact that means this doorway may be very old, perhaps even pre-Adamic.

Because this area is considered an ancient archeological site, and because it is protected by the Peruvian government, further excavations and dating potentially revealing its secrets and origin have not been possible. However, as of this writing, similar to the Gobekli Tepe site we will briefly discuss, there has never been any evidence of a settlement nearby that would link the Puerta de Hayu Marca to its potential builders, pre-Adamic or otherwise. This finding is literally just a door with a keyhole carved into flat-faced rock, out in the middle of *nowhere*, and linked to an amalgamation of stories that all spring from an ancient religion.

Oh yeah, and there's a *serpent*.

To this day, many report that light can often still be observed behind, or emanating through, the disc-shaped dent within the Gate of the Gods. Many of the local residents, even today, are said to have refused to go anywhere near it. Others, like those who specifically seek out paranormal pilgrimage sites, travel great distances to lay hands on the back wall or inside frame of the small door, where they report feeling energy emanating from the stone upon contact. These visitors have additionally claimed to see visions of stars on occasion, as well as hear the sounds of unusual rhythmic music.

More sensational accounts (like one I watched online by a long-haired American man) involve a spiritual seeker's disappearance for several minutes and, upon the person's return, a testimony of full-blown conversations with non-earthly beings or spirits. It is said that a great secret of unlocking the door to this portal or stargate is known among an esoteric few whose consciousness is more "open" than most: Humming or singing certain notes and tones in a specific order will bring the silica in the stone to a particular mystical vibration, awaken the energy in the wall, and transport the seeker to an internal room within the edifice where the seeker can communicate with various entities of extreme intelligence, the identity of which varies according to the testimony: aliens, long-deceased Incan ancestors, the carvers of the doorway, different gods, and so on. (Don't forget that Lucifer is thought to have been a worship leader. The prophets' words regarding his role in Heaven suggest that he had great authority over music. It's quite interesting to see that a potentially Luciferian artifact—that also happens to be a "doorway" related to a "serpent"—is unlocked or opened through a perverse musical performance by spiritual seekers… It's almost akin to a "worship song" dedicated to a satanic ruler over a location of Earth from the "void" era.) Most peculiar are the reports involving friends, family members, or casual onlookers who swear to have witnessed the person at the door glow or shimmer, then disappear, returning minutes later with quite fantastic tales of where they had been and what they had seen while they were away.

Though none of these contemporary stories of stargate travel can be substantiated, so many statements over the years have been shared that it's similar to how alien abduction is treated in conversations about paranormal activity: One has to either assume that: a) *All* of these folks are hallucinating, are on drugs at the time of their experience, or are making the stories up for attention; or b) something otherworldly takes place when an "open-minded" seeker approaches the portal. (My opinion is quite conservative: I believe most people *are* high on something at the time of the attempt, as some have openly admitted to having smoked marijuana or taken another mind-altering substance, and they are intentionally *looking for* a spiritual encounter, so they'll find what they're seeking while they're already mentally inebriated. In those rare instances when a person has legitimately experienced something mystical, whatever/whoever it is they're connecting with is *not* of God; therefore, their encounters only show that demonic activity is still active in the modern era, and deception is alive and well beyond the biblically forbidden gateways into the unseen realm [as if there was any question of that…]. If Satan can disguise himself as an angel of light [which he can and does; see 2 Corinthians 11:14], then these entities aren't going to be dumb enough to say, "Hey, brother! Welcome to the other side of the portal. We're demons. Run for your life." They'll appear friendly, supremely intelligent, and enlightened in some form of esoteric knowledge or technology unknown to mankind, etc.)

Because of the Peruvian government's protection of this gate and the surrounding territory, we may never know just how old this location is, who carved it (though it wasn't likely the Incans, because their legends say the doorway was already there, and archeologists confirm the style predates them), or whether some aspect of the doorway involves ancient technology that would explain the site's unearthly episodes. As such, it wouldn't typically qualify as an OOPArt (we don't know if it's out of place or in any way technological).

The reason this "Doorway of the *Serpent*" is mentioned briefly here is because, apart from potentially dating to the pre-Adamic age, it may be yet another link to the goings-on upon Earth during the serpentine "void" era, as the following chapters will show.

Stone Forest of Markawasi

The mysterious Gate of the Gods discussed in the previous section is near the Stone Forest of the Markawasi (or Marcahuasi) plateau in the Andes Mountains. The Stone Forest is home to a wealth of oddities, including gigantic stones that strongly resemble human faces and heads (as well as many animals), many of which could easily be interpreted to represent various ancient world cultures.

One sculpture mirrors many features and contours of the "face on Mars." Another, the "Monument to Humanity," is so named for the "four distinct races of humanity which can be found on this 85-foot-high monument."[114] It is especially fascinating that the images of the faces of four races of people might be sculpted from the same rock so near the Gate of the Gods that legendarily became the portal for ancient heroes who had access to seeing whatever races of humanity they wished—all at once. There don't seem to be many theories to explain how an ancient civilization would be so familiar with faraway races, or why that civilization would consider those foreign races important enough to memorialize in giant stones—all within the same time frame and location.

The human "faces" appearing in the Stone Forest *could have* originated naturally as a result of weathering over many years. However, anthropologists thus far can't account for how there appears to be such a significant cluster of them; one or two faces appearing to jut from a cliff in a mountainous region isn't necessarily any more sensational than recognizable shapes appearing in the formations of clouds, but toss a few more "faces"—on the same rocky canvas—and the likeliness of natural causes dwindles.

Could it be that the entities behind the wall of the Puerta de Hayu Marca, who have historically responded to the "open mind" of spiritual-experience seekers, also "visit" the ancients at this nearby location? Or, had the Stone Forest visitors already been to the serpent doorway, and then came here to carve something they were told to? If so, did the voices behind the wall tell the wanderers about the heroes whose faces are depicted in the monument?

Was this fascinating cluster of stones naturally sculpted by millions of years of weathering? Or are the images of "faces" coincidence? At present, we simply don't know.

Tiahuanaco and the Gate of the Sun

The archway of Tiahuanaco (or Tiwanaku) near La Paz, Bolivia, is a puzzling discovery on many counts. To begin, this arch—placed in what appears to be a worship temple courtyard a stone's throw from palace ruins and a short jaunt to the nearby Acapana Pyramid—raises the same questions as the upcoming Baalbek and Gobekli Tepe sites regarding its megalithic size and expert composition. The gate is 9.8 feet tall, 13 feet wide, and weighs approximately 10 tons (20,000 pounds).

Though the gate was found in the early 1900s resting on its side and having been split into two at some point in history, it was originally constructed from a single, enormous stone. The gate's age varies greatly, depending on the source. Though some postulate that the Gate of the Sun was designed by Tiahuanacans as late as the first century AD, many other sources date the stone to around 12,000 BC,[115] in part due to the this structure's similarities to other strange archeoastronomical findings. (Archeoastronomy is the study of how the ancients understood the sky and space bodies.) All over the world, antediluvian (pre-Flood) structures have been found that are positioned in precise alignment with the stars, planets, and constellations; most feature carvings of symbols outlining what could be cultural beliefs regarding mystical, spiritual events that occurred at different times of the year in relation to sunrises, sunsets, and other manifestations of the relationship between Earth and sky. (You may recall that archeologists believed the lithified cart ruts were potentially linked to an "'astronomical/religious purpose' and were deliberately aligned as a calendar to mark things like solstices."[116] This would be one example similar to this Gate of the Sun.) Various features in and around Tiahuanaco show parallel alignment.

But the mysteries yet to be unlocked by the experts involve more than just the answer to a "when" question, *possibly* qualifying the Gate of the Sun as an OOPArt due to the out-of-place (and time) knowledge these ancients illustrate.

At almost thirteen thousand feet in elevation, the land is deprived of the level of oxygen needed for long-term human occupancy. The human body, when exposed to altitudes this high for more than a few days, is known to suffer all sorts of health concerns, some of which can be fatal (pulmonary or cerebral edema). Yet the ruins of Tiahuanaco heavily suggest that a population remained there for at least half a century. How did they survive that long?

The iconic Gate of the Sun piece is not by any stretch the largest stone moved at the apparently inhospitable site, a location known for housing *two-hundred-ton monoliths* (twenty times the size of the large gate) in the structures some *ten miles* away from the quarry.

These ruins, too, are unique in their cutting-edge geometric design, which could only be accomplished with techniques that involve expert drilling, the flawless, interlocking placement of modular blocks, the development of early "staples" holding walls together, and other high-level practices only acquired within the last hundred years by modern-day builders. It's a mystery how the stones, and the symbols they display, were cut, tooled, and carved. Even more puzzling is how rocks weighing hundreds of thousands of pounds were transported ten miles across awkward terrain *and* bodies of water…by a likely hyperventilating community of ancient Andeans whose most impressive method of transportation were tiny river canoes made of reeds.

Unlike some of the other sites up we've looked at, there ample evidence at this one of settlement, resources, intelligence, and planning. That all makes the question of "who" even more interesting, when we consider what this early population knew of the stars. Whereas we might wonder how Neolithic, nomadic, wandering wheat-plowers could possibly comprehend the Gobekli Tepe structures we'll discuss later in this chapter, at the Tiahuanaco site we find ourselves asking how a race of humans that proves to be in some ways more intelligent than we are today could possibly have lived as long ago as they did—whether in the first century AD or, as the archeologists from the 1940s who link the site to astrological anomalies estimate, ten thousand to sixteen thousand years before Christ (yes, you read that correctly: archeologists at one point dated this site to 10000–16000 BC). Although archeologists and historians agree this settlement was built by Tiahuanacans, there is no easy explanation for what kind of people—or race—they were, exactly. Set apart from other ancient civilizations as a result of their advanced intelligence, it is no surprise that many individuals label them as some pre-Adamic race we can't know anything about. In fact, proponents of the Ancient Astronaut theories view Tiahuanaco as a possible extraterrestrial habitation because, as illustrated by the Gate of the Sun and surrounding artifacts, the Tiahuanacans had an extraordinary comprehension of space and mathematics.

And what's up with these ancient cultures and their gates, doors, and keyholes? Is it possible that there's actually something to this? Just perhaps, did some serpentine hero of old spring up to all these early sites and communicate to the folks there what they needed for their religion and communication with the divine? Or, if not, is there any explanation for the obsession the ancients had with serpents and the gateways/stargates that led to communication with them? Why do documents and pictographs originate from all over the planet that attest to a very old form of snake worship? And why were these cultures so far advanced?

In 1956, researchers Hans Schindler Bellamy and Peter Allan teamed up to compile an investigative book on this site, titled, *The Calendar of Tiahuanaco: A Disquisition on the Time Measuring System of the Oldest Civilization in the World.* As the title suggests, Bellamy and Allan viewed the Gate of the Sun and other "documents" at the site as an early calendar. Though the time measurements recorded don't match the modern, Gregorian concept of days, weeks, months, or seasons, leading some today to write off the carvings as abstract art, a deeper look reveals an articulate and meticulous understanding of what the heavens may have looked like long ago. Throughout this four-hundred-plus-page report of the site, the authors repeatedly demonstrate the Tiahuanacans' knowledge of: a spherical Earth (not the "flat Earth" most ancient cultures conceptualized!); details involving astrological phenomena in relation to equinoxes and solstices; the latitudinal position of the civilization as it would have appeared on a GPS system at the time (approximately 10 degrees); the obliquity of the ecliptic (aka, the axial tilt: the alignments and angles between Earth's rotational axis and its orbital axis); and complex mathematics, including the correct ratio of pi (22/7), square roots, the degree angles (30, 60, 90) and their practical, trigonometrical uses in construction and astronomy— just to name a few—all documented in stone.[117]

Because of the propensity of the conspiracy crowd to brand every fascinating object an OOPArt, I will refrain from selling the idea that this gate would qualify. However, it definitely appears that such extreme intelligence encoded within a stone archway slapped in the middle of Nowheresville, Bolivia, is an out-of-place object.

But despite the speechlessness that such irrefutable brainpower hidden away in the hills of the sun would cause, the yearning within human nature to solve the unsolvable inspires many to speculate about various building methods. Many experts on ancient architecture have attempted in the recent past to reconstruct the structures of Tiahuanaco to try to identify the astoundingly progressive methods used by these early inhabitants...an endeavor that has been to no avail. One article, written in 2000 by J. P. Protzen in the *Journal of the Society of Architectural Historians*, dedicates around fifteen long pages to reimagining ingenuity. Though the writer shared a diverse collection of ideas, many of which are far more plausible than earlier theories, he finds the Tiahuanacan structure is in "sharp contrast to...Incan architecture,"[118] which places doubt on some archeologists' conclusions that Tiahuanaco was just another Incan city dating to that era. In his conclusion, Protzen admits that "in spite of our findings to date, we are not even close to comprehending Tiwanaku [Tiahuanaco] in architecture."[119]

And, of course, there's the bizarre "overnight" factor. Regardless of the methods used for building, there is no evidence that this culture had experimented on or near this locale for generations, starting with the construction of simple homes and gradually demonstrating increased architectural knowledge up to the level these ruins exhibit. It's as if they knew by instinct exactly how to construct the building from their very first attempt; in other words, there's no evidence of any evolutionary phases of skill levels.

Not surprisingly, the Tiahuanacans' ability to survive and maintain food/plant resources—in a climate hostile to vegetation—has the world baffled. When the ancient settlement was finally discovered, it proved to be a cleverer feat than what many farming communities could organize today. Canals were dug into the soil at the correct depth in grids around the plants: When the sun bore down on the canals, the water would heat to the point that, after dark, the water would cool slowly overnight, dissipating heat in a steam or mist that wrapped the plants like a blanket. Thus, the surrounding air never dipped to the below-freezing temperatures that would have ravaged them. And, as if this strategy in and of itself wasn't sophisticated enough, the canals also doubled as an irrigation system!

As a point of further intrigue, the site tells excellent stories and displays impressive religious imagery within its artwork. The deity at the center and top of the Gate of the Sun has been identified by some historians and archeologists as Viracocha, Incan god of the sun and storms. Upon his head is a crown made of sun rays, from his eyes fall tears of rain, and in each of his hands are tightly clasped thunderbolts. This god, according to legend, created the race of giants, among other accomplishments, such as: creating the sun, moon, stars, and all light of the universe; forming mankind by breathing life into stones; sending a flood to destroy the giant race that angered him; disguising himself as a beggar and educating his prized human race on the basics of civilizational development; and performing all sorts of miracles and wonders. (Some details of these stories are carved on the surface of the Gate of the Sun.) It's not difficult to see how the tale of Viracocha plagiarizes characteristics first attributed to the God of Genesis.

It's not hard to imagine that, if Tiahuanaco was home to a pre-Adamic race *prior* to the arrival of the Incans, the Incans may have subsequently embraced Viracochan legends and religion into their culture, adopting this god as their own. Might this have occurred because they stumbled onto an area exhibiting advanced building technology, exceptionally high levels of mathematical aptitude, keen resourcefulness in farming and irrigation practices, and an understanding of precise astronomical/astrological alignments between Tiahuanaco and the broad universe? Might the Incans, in their human imaginations, have attributed such dexterity to some transcendent race of gods, godlike people, or people who intermingled *with* the gods? Would the Incans scan the area upon arrival for signs of previous settlements and, after finding none, conclude that this godlike race came out of nowhere, overnight, with esoteric and mystical technologies that baffle the minds of regular, unexceptional humans?

Do we, today, look upon this peculiar site and maybe—just *maybe*— see signals in stone of a malicious and deceptive spirit who wanted to be viewed as, and worshiped like, the Almighty God of Genesis? If so, it would certainly make sense for this presence to prop himself up as Viracocha, the god with Jehovah-like attributes. But who could that presence have been? And if he wasn't alone, who were the otherworldly builders who accompanied him?

Interesting guy, that Viracocha. Peruvian civilization shows long historical links between this god and serpentine iconography. In fact, in many cases, Viracocha's actions and legends identify him by other names: Quetzalcoatl to the Aztecs and Kukulkan, Q'uq'umatz, and Tohil among various regions of Mayan lore. Each of these entities was, at one point in legend, a white, bearded man dressed in robes who ventured across the sea to give wisdom to the ancients. This entity, known by different names, was the Feathered Serpent, worshiped in early Mesoamerican religion, and, as Viracocha, he kept a condor snake as his pet. In some effigies, he is depicted as holding a snake in each hand.

While we're on the subject of Tiahuanaco, let's turn to another mystery nearby…

Geoglyphs of Tiahuanaco

David Flynn—author of best-sellers *Cydonia* and *Temple at the Center of Time*, two works that made waves a couple decades back for their astounding discoveries related to ancient cultures—wrote an article on February 24, 2008, called "Discovery of Vast, Prehistoric Works Built by Giants?: The Geoglyphs of Tiahuanaco."

Tom Horn wrote of this article:

> The size and scope of David Flynn's Tiahuanaco discovery simply surpasses comprehension. Mammoth traces of intelligence carved in stone and covering hundreds of square miles. For those who understand what they are seeing here for the first time, this could indeed be the strongest evidence ever found of prehistoric engineering by those who were known and feared throughout the ancient world as gods.[120]

The rest of this section, until the next header ("Gobekli Tepe"), is, at Tom's humble request for its inclusion in this book, Flynn's original article in its entirety and as it first appeared (including his original citations). (Much of the relevant information involved in this article requires reading the image captions, so don't skip those.)

This satellite image (above) is a portion of the Andean foothills surrounding Lake Titicaca in Bolivia, South America. It is a small sample of a vast network of patterns that surround the lake and extend for more than one hundred miles south into the Bolivian desert. The patterns display geometric repetition and intelligent design. There are interlocking rectangular cells and mounds, perfectly straight lines, and tree-like arrays that are uncharacteristic with natural erosion. These cover every topographical feature of the high plateau surrounding the lake and over flood plains, hills, cliffs, and mountains. Although these geoglyphs are remarkable in their obvious strangeness, what is more astounding is that they have remained in obscurity until now. In the same way modern archeologists recently found the ruins of hidden Mayan temples in the Guatemalan jungle by using earth-orbiting satellites, we have discovered what could be one of the greatest finds of our time.

Directly South of Lake Titicaca, the foothills are embossed with mound and rope arrangements of earth and rock. These form a contiguous "geomantic" and "circuit-like" network visible only from the air.

The "dendrite" forms above seem to be the most extensive patterns on the Bolivian Altiplano (the 226-foot "747" airplane is inserted for scale). When viewed from above, the terrain appears disconcertingly "alien" and surreal.

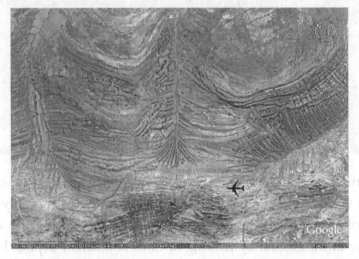

The combined mass of the walls on these mountains easily rivals Hadrian's seventy-three-mile-long wall in England.

Perfectly straight lines and repeated sharp-angle turns such as pictured do not occur through natural erosion. One hundred and twenty miles south of Lake Titicaca, near Chata, Bolivia, lines and geometric shapes were set in the ground by removal of earth at different depths, leaving various colors of strata underneath exposed. The effect is like a Zen garden covering the entire desert.

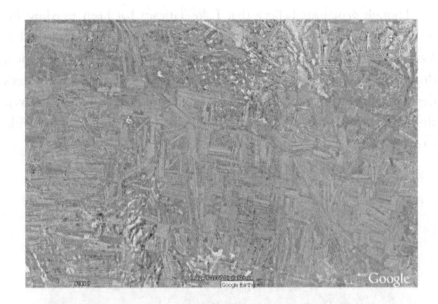

Amazing patterns (above) on the Bolivian desert cover approximately ten square miles.

Close-up of the same area in the Bolivian desert, approximately one square mile

Though geologists believe that Lake Titicaca has been receding for nearly thirteen thousand years, having been formed at the end of the last Ice Age, patterns of stripes are evident under the lake's shoreline for a distance of at least nearly two miles before being obscured by the water's depths. At first glance the stripes appear to be cultivation plots. However, they are extremely narrow in relation to their length…some five feet wide to several thousand feet long.

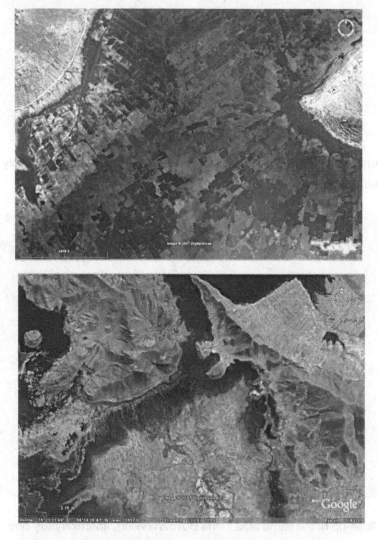

Linear features of the South shore of Lake Titicaca from the altitude of 10 miles

Above is a ground view of the linear features as they extend
from the shore of the lake. They appear to have been scored into
the ground. No explanation of their purpose is recorded by the
local Indians, only that they are remnants of the civilization of
Vircocha, the Inca god of creation.

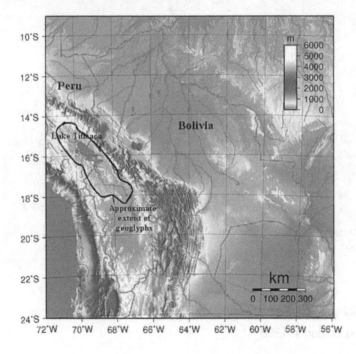

Twelve miles south of Lake Titicaca, located within the center of the array of geoglyphs, lies the megalithic ruins of Tiahuanaco. Known as the "American Stonehenge" or the "Baalbek of the New World," its architecture exhibits technological skill that exceeds modern feats of building. At Tiahuanaco, immense stone works were joined with modular fittings and complex breach-locking levels that have never been seen in any other ancient culture. Many of the blocks were joined together with T-shaped metal clamps that were poured into place by a portable forge. According to engineers, one of the largest single stones ever to be moved and put into building anywhere on earth (about four hundred tons) was transported to Tiahuanaco from a quarry over two hundred miles away. This feat is more incredible when one realizes the route of transport was through a mountain range up to fifteen thousand feet.

Conventional historians assign the age of buildings of Tiahuanaco at around 600 BC, believing that a pre-Inca civilization, without benefit of the wheel, modern tools, or even a written language, constructed these architectural marvels.

Tiahuanaco, Boliva: Image from Hermanos French-American expedition in 1903

The historian, Arthur Posnansky, studied the area for over fifty years and observed that sediment had been deposited over the site to the depth of six feet. Within this overburden, produced by a massive flood of water sometime around the Pleistocene age (thirteen thousand years ago) fossilized human skulls were unearthed together with seashells and remnants of tropical plants.[121] The skulls have nearly **three times the cranial capacity of modern man** and are displayed in the La Paz museum in Bolivia.[122]

An ancient shoreline was etched into the hills surrounding Tiahuanaco that had been lifted out of the horizontal plane. Additionally, there were lime deposits on the surface of the exposed megaliths, indicating that they had been submerged in water. Posnansky wrote:

> The climate is dry, the foliage is scanty, the weather is cold, the neighboring people wretchedly poor and few in number. The top soil of the plateau is a two-foot dry deposit, now soft stone. Below it stands the lignite of charred tropical plants. Next come a layer of ash deposited amidst rainfall, and then appears an alluvial deposit. In such a place, one would normally expect merely a scanty soil, windswept, on rocky ground.[123]

The geoglyphs in this area are found extant in all three layers of stratum, described by Posnansky, some of the most complex and ancient were carved into bedrock. In places, the rock was hewn into intricate mazes, rectilinear cells, mounds, and other geometry. These can be seen protruding from the valley floor of Ice Age sediment.

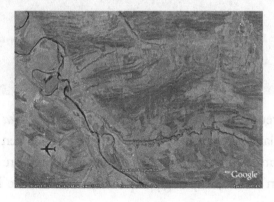

At the outskirts of the Bolivian village of Viacha, entire hills were excised in this manner. Other examples can be seen near the village of Batallas and Ancocahua, and on the foothills around Pucarani and Machacamarca. The geologically younger stratum around these patterns is easy to discern in satellite images.

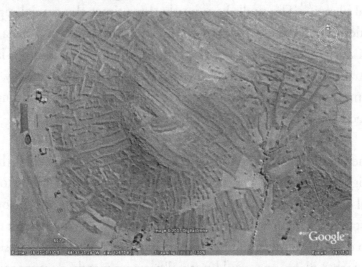

Though remnants of ancient farming, known as *suka kollus* in the local Aymara language (artificially raised fields), can be seen among these geoglyphic features, these are found in the valleys and are easily distinguishable from the majority of glyph patterns around Lake Titicaca.

The raised farming fields (viewed above) are distinctly labyrinthine in design and, though extensive, constitute a small portion of the patterns that appear more "ritualistic" in design. However, because these features are so ancient and no longer used for farming due to the poor climate, they are termed "fossilized *suka kollus*" by archaeologists.

The horizontal terracing seen on many hills around the lake seem to have been designed to collect and hold rainwater to create additional farming land. However, the vertical features that are far more extensive on the Altiplano are composed of rock piles and, in some places, they are hewn into the bedrock itself. Vertical walls of earth and rock cannot have been built to hold water. Some areas exhibit rectangular cells, others, perfect circles.

The geoglyphic pattern above is found twelve miles to the northeast of Lake Titicaca and is thirteen thousand five hundred feet above sea level. Its function is not consistent with any Inca farming technique.

The Inca civilization was relatively short-lived, lasting only one hundred years. Their culture inherited most its technology and legend from civilization stretching far into antiquity. It is known that the Inca and their predecessors possessed no written language. Instead, they used an arrangement of knotted ropes that communicated extremely complex information. This system, called *quipus*, was only understood by the highly trained Inca elite. The Spanish explorers recorded that the *quipus* was capable of recording not only census and crop records but lineage of kings and narratives of history. Examples of *quipus* from the pre-Inca cultures have recently been discovered in excavations in Peru dating to c. 3000 BC.[124] More significantly, the knotted and colored patterns of ropes that formed the *quipus* seems to be represented in stone among some of the more ancient geoglyphs on the Altiplano.

These are examples of *quipus* knot-writing of the Inca.

The similarities of the *quipus* type rock glyphs and examples of Inca *quipus* rope are compellingly similar. The monumental work required to carve these geoglyphs suggest the importance of the message they conveyed. It is also remarkable that the knotted configurations of *quipus* seem to have been carved into the bedrock of hills rising above sediment that was deposited over the bedrock itself. This suggests that the age of these features is in excess of many thousands of years.

As in the case of the Nazca lines of Peru, the Tiahuanaco geoglyphs represent hundreds of years in construction and communal effort of thousands. However, unlike Nazca that was constructed in low altitude, the more extensive Tiahuanaco geoglyphs lie in a region that cannot support a population capable of producing such vast works, existing on a plain twelve thousand five hundred feet above sea level and higher. Nevertheless, they saturate the countryside for hundreds of square miles, a fact that presents enormous architectural difficulties. Modern-day visitors to the region are advised to limit activity due to the danger of altitude sickness. In fact, hotels in La Paz actually provide supplementary oxygen for their guests.

This image, from the Sintich Hermanos French-American expedition in 1903, shows a megalith detached from the major complex of Tiahuanaco. Its surface is etched by a massive flow of water that also deposited the sediment around it. The geology of this area is characteristic of the glacial flooding associated with the end of the Pleistocene era, thirteen thousand years ago.

When the first Spanish chroniclers arrived with the conquistador Pizaro, the Inca explained that Tiahuanaco had been constructed by a race of giants, called *Huaris*, before *Chamak-pacha*, the "period of darkness," and was already in ruins before their civilization began. The giants had been created by Viracocha, the god who came from the heavens.

He [Viracocha] created animals and a race of giants. These beings enraged the Lord, and he turned them into stone. Then he flooded the earth till all was under water, and all life extinguished. This flood was called *uñu pachacuti*, by the Inca which means "water that overturns the land." They say that it rained 60 days and nights, that it drowned all created things, and that there alone remained some vestiges of those who were turned into stones. Viracocha rose from the bosom of Lake Titicaca, and presided over the erection of those wondrous cities whose ruins still dot its islands and western shores, and whose history is totally lost in the night of time.[125]

Less than a mile from Tiahuanaco, at a place named Puma Punko, immense stone ashlars, some in the two-hundred-ton range, were scattered and tossed like a child's building blocks in an episode of unparalleled seismic violence. Posnansky believed that it was more ancient than Tiahuanaco, and modern researchers have suggested that both sites may have been built over previous cultures with antiquity stretching back tens of thousands of years.

A recent excavation of the ruins near Tiahuanaco:
Note the six-foot layer of water-born sediment at the
altitude of 12,500 feet.

Posnansky also suggested that the Kalasasaya temple of Tiahuanaco had been aligned with the angle that the sun and planets passed overhead. This "obliqueness of the ecliptic" at Kalasasaya indicated that nearly seventeen thousand years had passed since the Tiahuanaco had been constructed.[126]

The broken, hundred-ton megaliths of Puma Punku

Modern claims of destroyed, lost civilizations of earth, underground cities, giants, and alien beings from the heavens are fertile subjects for ridicule. However, all these topics are found concentrated in the founding myths of the Inca and their predecessors.

The Peruvian historian Montesinos, in *Memories Antiguas, Histories, Politicas del Peru* wrote:

> Cusco and the city of ruins, Tiwanaku are connected by a gigantic subterranean road. The Incas do not know who built it. They know nothing about the inhabitants of Tiwanaku. In their opinion it was built by a very ancient people who later on retreated into the jungle of the Amazon.

The Tiahuanaco researcher, H. S. Bellamy, believed that the Tiahuanacan civilization had been destroyed by a small moon that decayed in its orbit and crashed into the earth. His findings were based on the hieroglyphs of the gateway of the sun in the main temple of Tiahuanaco. Additionally, Bellamy wrote that the cataclysm was only one of a series produced by several captured moons. Tiahuanaco and Puma Punko were the last remaining edifices to cultures that existed in extreme antiquity... up to hundreds of thousands of years old.[127]

This assertion seems to be verified in the extreme erosion of the geo-glyphs in a margin around Lake Titicaca above fourteen thousand feet. At this altitude, the surface features show the effects of prolonged rain and wind. Below fourteen thousand feet, the geoglyphs remain much more intact due to being submerged in the post-glacial extent of Lake Titicaca...at its largest volume circa thirteen thousand years ago.

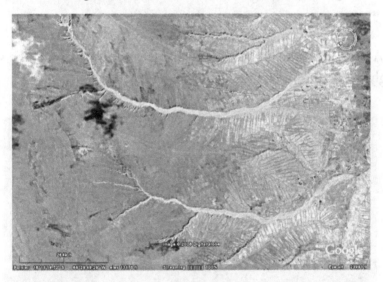

The margin of erosion can be seen above. The rectangular features on the right are intact below fourteen thousand feet at the ancient shore line of Titicaca. This indicates that the majority of the Tiahuanaco geoglyphs were constructed before Lake Titicaca grew to its post-glacial depth.

A further example of the Pleistocene age of the geoglyphs is seen below on a hill to the north of Lake Titicaca at a fourteen-thousand-foot margin. Near the center of the image is an alluvial fan, created by sediment-bear-ing runoff meeting standing water.

A close-up of the hill reveals the highly eroded shadows of the same geoglyphic features seen throughout the area.

The patterns carved in the bedrock (seen in the next image) were covered with Ice-Age sediment. Over time, wind and rain have removed the glacial deposits to reveal the geoglyphs underneath.

Inca civilization founding myths of giants and world deluge agree with similar legends from the Maya, Olmec, and Aztec cultures of Mexico. These are also consistent with Sumerian and Hebrew accounts of the Flood and of giants.

> And when the sons of men had multiplied, in those days, beautiful and comely daughters were born to them: and the Watchers, the sons of heaven saw them and desired them. And they said to one another, "come let us choose for ourselves wives from the daughters of men, and let us beget for ourselves, children"... Then said the Most High, "go to Noah and tell him that a deluge is about to come upon the whole earth, to heal the earth which the angels have corrupted, that all the children of men may not perish through all the secret things that the Watchers have disclosed." (1 Enoch 6:1–7, 10)

The Greeks also believed that the giants were responsible for the creation of megalithic structures that have been discovered over the entire earth. Islamic folklore also describes the "building" activity of a race of super beings called the "Jinn": "The Jinn were before Adam: They built huge cities whose ruins still stand in forgotten places" (Qur'an, Surah 89: 9–15, 27).

In Egypt, the Edfu temple texts, believed to predate the Egyptians themselves, explain: "The most ancient of earth's temples and monuments were built to bring about the resurrection of the destroyed world of the gods."

The impression that the Tiahuanaco geoglyphs leave is of both complexity and symbolism. Their extreme age and vastness conveys purpose beyond the realm of modern thought. If a creation of art, their purpose may have been to merge human culture with the processes of nature. However, within the Inca religious paradigm, the oldest record of the Andean region available to us, they are the vestiges of a lost civilization that knew its destiny…to be destroyed by world cataclysm. In this regard, the geoglyphs would serve not only as a memorial of an ancient existence, but also as a warning for future humanity of the return of a destructive epoch.

The geoglyphs seem to be physical evidence that support the Middle and South American myths of world deluge and giants. Their discovery in modern times fits Inca and Mayan prophecies of an "awakening" to knowledge of the ancient past, of the "builder gods" and of their return. It is perhaps testament to the accuracy of these prophecies that the date, December 21, 2012, is known so widely in modern times…the end of the Mayan calendar.

End of excerpt from *The David Flynn Collection*

Gobekli Tepe

Perhaps one of the most debated locations on earth today is the Gobekli Tepe structures in Turkey, just north of the Syrian border. However, it should be noted that with as much discussion as this site inspires, it has so far provided few plausible human-hands theories.

Gobekli Tepe is unique from other archeological sites in that the oldest and deepest layer of the structure excavated dates to Pre-Pottery Neolithic (or "PPN"; 10000–6500 BC; though radiocarbon dating suggests this first layer could be as old as 9600 BC). Though the math on this is simple, it's so unbelievable that it begs to be clarified in even more straightforward terms: Gobekli Tepe was inhabited by its first builders *more than eleven thousand years ago*. Yet it is home to almost two hundred *T*-shaped pillars (according to geophysical surveys; not all of them have been excavated as of this writing), standing up to twenty feet (six meters) high and weighing up to twenty tons (forty thousand pounds). Most of these are between seven and ten tons. Note also that one stone in the nearby quarry weighs an estimated fifty tons, posed as if it was the next stone to be erected as a pillar when the construction suddenly stopped.

These are the oldest known megaliths in the world. Only this far into our discussion of this location, we're already scratching our heads as to how humans of this time—who hadn't yet perfected the process of crafting pottery over or within high-temperature heat sources (thus the "pre-pottery" designation of the Neolithic Age label)—could have quarried, lifted, transported, and erected towers this heavy, standing this high, and involving this level of artistry.

Many of the pillars feature ornate carvings involving animals—both docile and predatory, reptiles, birds, etc.—but not surprisingly in relation with Neolithic cave paintings and very few humanoid shapes. Interestingly, but I suppose not surprisingly, archeologists report in "The Snakes of Gobekli Tepe: An Ethological Consideration": "The animal most frequently depicted is the snake, most likely the *Macrovipera lebetina* [the venomous, "blunt-nosed" viper]," which some archeologists consider to be "evidence for a [biblical] theology that featured supernatural *watch-ers*,"[128] a term for the fallen angels of Luciferian origin. Many areas of the ruins also connect serpentine iconography to the male reproductive organ, which is telling. If the Watchers, as these fallen angels are known in Eno-chian literature, were in fact serpentine in their appearance—and if they did actually crossbreed with human females, as both Genesis 6:4 and the Book of Enoch describe (which we will address later)—it may account for why the world of archeology now identifies within the edifices of Gobekli Tepe "groups of male snakes...pursuing a female with the intention of mating."[129] Either way, "the snakes do in some sense represent something sexual (and perhaps the [male reproductive organ], metaphorically)."[130]

The largest pillars stand in the center of mysterious circles made up of smaller pillars and stones. The contrast of such magnificent stones being dated to within the PPN era draws serious attention from archeologists and historians because of the implications this combination has upon everything we know of early human-civilization development, which is what links this site to its fame. Though these professionals would abso-lutely avoid using the term OOPArt in association with any artifact of Gobekli Tepe, for reasons stated earlier, nearly everything in the Gobekli Tepe site is strange, "out of place," and most certainly outside the correct epoch of humanity's level of advancement.

Prior to modern farming settlements, which created the blank grounds we see today, this area would have been an ideal plant/animal source for the nomadic hunters/gatherers of the Pre-Pottery eras. Chief German archeologist Klaus Schmidt, the original excavator of Gobekli Tepe who devoted twenty years of his life to its mysteries between 1994 and his death in 2014, was able to rule out that the summit, itself, was ever a permanent residence to any early inhabitants. That would suggest, to Schmidt, that this location—*said to predate Stonehenge by more than six thousand years*—was a place of worship; the "first human-built holy place";[131] "humanity's first 'cathedral on a hill.'"[132]

Seriously, what's the deal with these sites and sacred god snakes?

One leading theory as to the purpose of Gobekli Tepe proposes that the pillars and circles were intended as a pilgrimage site, and to welcome the deceased as a final resting place. This is supported by the carvings, primarily of predatory animals; some suggest these were made to drive away evil spirits from tampering with the bodies of lost loved ones. Because vultures—as well as chipped human bone fragments found in the area—appear often amongst the ancient artwork. This points to the possibility of early sky burials in which travelers would have left their loved ones' remains behind at the pillars for the carrion birds to scatter. Butchered animal bones were also discovered, despite the lack of houses or cooking constructs, which suggests that the congregants would share a brief meal (prepared elsewhere or aboveground outside the circles) before their departure from the hill and the trek back home. That seems like a logical answer to "why," but what remains unanswered is "how," when these people lacked the resources, housing, time, and intelligence to do so.

Because only approximately 5 percent of the site (about one acre) is currently unearthed, many secrets may yet remain beneath the soil. (The focus for archeologists shifted in 2018 when Gobekli Tepe was designated a UNESCO World Heritage Site. That same year, Schmidt's widow observed what she felt was harsh treatment of the area. Since then, uncovering mysteries through further digging has taken a back seat to maintaining careful preservation of what has already been unearthed, so we have little reason to believe new layers of Gobekli Tepe will be excavated in the very near future.) However, despite the minimal unveiling that has been accomplished as of this moment, there is good reason for such global attention being paid to this hill.

According to *Smithsonian Magazine*, "Scholars have long believed that only *after* people learned to farm and live in settled communities did they have the time, organization, and resources to construct temples and support complicated social structures."[133] But with no evidence of settlement ("no cooking hearths, houses or trash pits, and none of the clay fertility figurines that litter nearby sites of about the same age,"[134] among other items), the only human explanation for these monumental complexes would attribute the building, stacking, lifting, shaping, and conceptualization of these pillars to *travelers* of that time. Because the site is dated to PPN, we are left to believe it was established by people without even the "time, organization, and resources" to construct a clay pot. Not to mention, as the constantly moving/relocating/survival lifestyle of these pre-sedentary-society nomads suggests, they would have had to accomplish this task overnight, so this theory isn't even taken seriously by most archeologists. Schmidt, no doubt sharing the opinion of his peers, recognized the absurdity of this theory, saying these monuments absolutely were *not* put together by "ragged bands of hunter-gatherers." He notes that crafting, assembling, and setting up stone pillars weighing an average of seven tons (though some are heavier) would have involved "hundreds of workers, all needing to be fed and housed."[135]

As one example: Pillar 27 from Enclosure C, Layer III (the oldest and deepest of the three layers) features a predatory animal elaborately carved in the likeness of a short-mouthed crocodile or large-breed feline with teeth bared and tail swerving at an extreme angle. Of all the pillars in Gobekli Tepe, this pillar has drawn the most attention, since it is carved "in the round" (meaning it's rendered in three dimensions and is viewable in "pop-up" form from any direction). It's hard to imagine the sort of artistic training it would take to achieve this high level of skill in carving; that these hunter-gatherers would be able to undergo that training would be shocking considering that we can assume they were simultaneously trying to survive—and apparently without food or housing. Even today, if an artist had a lifetime of experience, making him the fastest in the business, as well as access to the most impressive catalog of sculpting tools and high-tech machinery, creating something similar to the carving of the predator on Pillar 27 could easily take months or years if the craftsman were also required to feed himself on the harvest of his own land and, as we've shown, there was no land to live off of anywhere near the site.

Could it be that these ancients, too, were visited by the strange, white, long-bearded god-man, Viracocha or Quetzalcoatl, also known as the Feathered Serpent, who apparently had the capability of wandering anywhere on Earth in places possibly dating to a "void" era to teach early nomadic wanderers the tricks behind advanced civilization? Was the god of the Gobekli-Tepe builders also the god of snakes? Or was he, himself, a snake entity of some form? And did he, too, like the "watchers" of

Enoch, instill within these pre-pottery-era nomads an understanding of some sketchy interbreeding between snake heroes and human women? The ruins appear to suggest as much…

Layer II, consisting of structures in, on, and around Layer III, is dated to the latter half of the PPN Age and involves the installation of small, windowless rooms and smaller *T*-shaped pillars. Layer I is the youngest of the layers, located at the topmost portion of the hill (ground level prior to excavation) and only offers loosened sediments from erosion gathered since the hill had been intentionally backfilled (ca. 8000 BC, the Stone Age, as per carbon dating; reason for the deliberate backfill is unknown), as well as other small stone tools and limestone fragments from the refuse that was used as the filler. An article in *National Geographic* explains the layers in a way that is, perhaps, easier to understand, though it simultaneously presents more questions than answers: "Bewilderingly, the people at Gobekli Tepe got steadily *worse* at temple building. The earliest [and deepest] rings [of Layer III] are the biggest and most sophisticated, technically and artistically."[136] This article goes on to say that, as time passed, pillars in Layer II were "smaller, simpler," and erected with "less care," until the whole community effort "petered out altogether" when the site was backfilled. The conclusion made by the *National Geographic* piece is that the community of Gobekli Tepe—whoever they were; early humans, pre-Adamites, who knows—was "all fall and no rise."[137]

Wait…what? They got worse instead of better at building over time? How? That defies logic. Why wouldn't the future generations of this people group be able to replicate their forefathers' knowledge and develop the intelligence it takes to make even more advanced pillars in the later layers of the site?

Trust me, I would love to have the answer, but no one does. I theorize that whatever person, "god," or traveling being who taught the earliest builders had left them to their own devices at some early point. Their descendants could never quite recapture the technology of their ancestors. But an even more important question is this: How were multiple generations of society able to survive in this place long enough to carve *anything* in stone—no matter how meticulously—if they didn't have a settlement nearby to keep them alive and healthy? Keep trekking with me a bit and you'll see this question come back again and again. It's as if most historians and other experts acknowledge everything *up to* that question with various workable theories, then the debate drops off.

A whisper among some involved in the debate suggests this may have been one of the world's first farming initiatives, originating from desperation, as opposed to ingenuity and planning. If this were true, the story, as hypothesized by archeologists, would unfold like this: Neolithic hunters/gatherers set out to create a holy place. They found a quarry and began digging up multi-ton megaliths with flint flakes (sharp-edged, palm-sized stones used by early settlers for varying uses, often appearing similar to obsidian arrowheads or the like, except much lighter in color). Quickly, their resources ran out as they realized their building undertaking would take much longer than planned, so they began to gather wheat from surrounding fields to survive. The result was eventually the first domesticated wheat farm. As they continued to dig up stones and build their holy site, they learned about planting and harvesting; the knowledge they gained was based more on happenstance and the sheer will to survive than by planning. They continued to apply their intelligence to achieving the goal of remaining in one place, their dedication to the holy site forcing them into a new way of life, so the hunters/gatherers eventually became the earliest farmers/settlers.[138]

Another version of this postulation was conceived by Schmidt, as noted in an interview between him and German physicist and Doctor of Human Sciences Klaus-Dieter Linsmeier:

> Such scholars suggest that the Neolithic revolution, i.e., the beginnings of grain cultivation, took place here. Schmidt believed, as others do, that mobile groups in the area were compelled to cooperate with each other to protect early concentrations of wild cereals from wild animals (herds of gazelles and wild donkeys). Wild cereals may have been used for sustenance more intensively than before and were perhaps deliberately cultivated. This would have led to early social organization of various groups in the area of Gobekli Tepe. Thus, according to Schmidt, the Neolithic did

not begin on a small scale in the form of individual instances of garden cultivation, but developed rapidly in the form of "a large-scale social organization."[139]

We know that human domestication had to have happened at some point in history, so why not there and then? Again, the theory could make sense, and has even been supported by recent DNA analysis linking the modern domestic wheat strands with the wild wheat strands of Mount Karaca Dag, only twenty miles from Gobekli Tepe, which is evidence that today's wheat likely could have originated from wheat domestication experiments just like the one in Schmidt's theory.[140] Yet, the farther we get into this story, *again*, the more questions surface. How could there have been an early farming initiative without a nearby settlement? The neighboring towns weren't built until centuries later. These ten- to fifty-ton stones are estimated to have required five hundred men to pull them from the quarry a quarter mile to the pillars and circles. Even *Archaeology Magazine* acknowledges this as a well-known puzzle: "How did Stone Age people achieve the level of organization necessary to do this?... [Some archeologists speculate] an elite class of religious leaders supervised the work and later controlled the rituals that took place at the site."[141]

An elite class of supervisory religious leaders...hmm. Now, *that* is interesting. Who were these religious leaders, what religion did they observe, and were they *human*?

Were they some form of *snake*?

Possible Link to Activities of Ancient Jericho?

Some folks have taken all of this Gobekli Tepe information into account from a biblical perspective and see a connection to the giants of Genesis 6:4. That opens up a whole new world of possibilities if it can be counted as true, especially in light of the fact that these so called Pre-Pottery Neolithic hunter-gatherers were within migrating distance from the ancient town of Jericho, and at approximately the same time this massive building project was underway. (The fall of Jericho in the book of Joshua occurred just when the Bible says: within a few years of 1400 BC, approximately 6,600 years after Jericho had been erected by the former ancients; see this endnote for a quick breakdown of the debate.[142])

The culture at the famous biblical site of Jericho dated to 8000 BC started something in haste that could be telling. The hunter-gatherers there who had been living in mud huts and tents and following the seasons wherever they led, suddenly stopped migrating and started a massive building project of their own—and it was purely defensive. Very quickly, a people who until then would have simply run away from any superior army abruptly reacted as if they perceived something they could not outrun. If we piece together what the books don't directly state, we see their need to surround their settlement with a massive wall that was ten feet thick and nearly a half mile long around the inner city. As part of the wall, they also erected a gigantic stone lookout tower thirty-three feet in diameter and about that high. The wall was surrounded by a moat, of sorts, which was cut out from solid bedrock and filled with mud. It was approximately nine feet deep and twenty-seven feet wide, with another wall outside that perimeter. The purpose of the moat was to restrict an enemy's ability to get to the wall with scaling gear (or, some say, to stop something such as giants from jumping over the wall). Of course, I'm theorizing, but clearly something was suddenly confronting the inhabitants of what would become the city of Jericho. The apocryphal Book of Enoch records serpentine immortals—fallen angels; Watchers—who descended in the later days of Jared and created mutant life forms called Nephilim. (We will discuss Nephilim a little later.) Because these entities were offspring of fallen angels whose wickedness led to the Flood of Noah's day, which Young Earthers and Ussher date to *after* Adam's birth in 4004 BC, could there have been a pre-Adamic precursor species of mutations alive as far back as 8000 BC, when Jericho was first built? Were there some "void"-era beings whose warped DNA matched (or resembled) those of the later Nephilim?

We don't know. What we *do* know is this: While Jericho ancients were erecting the wall that would crumble thousands of years later in Joshua's day, over at Gobekli Tepe, the people rushed to bury the archaic construction site of their ancestors under tons and tons of earth-fill for reasons that remain unclear. Was it so this site could be uncovered in the future, just after the Flood, as many Bible scholars believe? Or is there something in Turkey yet to be discovered that might explain why it was abruptly abandoned: something that might even be used by the enemy for some part of the great deception of the end times?

Even more so perhaps than Baalbek, Gobekli Tepe remains a mystery. We can't say for sure who, how, or for what purpose it was built; nor can we know for sure why it was ever ordered to be backfilled (unless *someone* wanted their religion to survive a great destructive event on Earth and resurface later on), or why each generation of builders became *less* proficient and impressive than the previous, instead of the other way around, which is what natural evolutionary intelligence would suggest. But, if Gobekli Tepe *was* the result of human hands, then, at the very least, it erases everything we *thought* we knew about early human development, agricultural efficiency of nomadic persons, and settlement domestication.

Oh yeah, one more thing: It also bungles up the proposed historical timeline of human evolution for both Young Earthers and scientists alike, making a few less-trod paths of Old Earth thought regarding the "void" era more plausible. Then such OOPArts as the pillars of Gobekli Tepe—though experts may squirm at that inference—make "crazy" ideas like mine and Tom Horn's (theories that would "start a war" amidst theologians and Bible scholars as several of our companions have warned) look a little less crazy.

Karahan Tepe to Reset the Game?

Just under thirty miles to the East is Gobekli Tepe's sister site, Karahan Tepe. Archeologists have only barely begun to tap into the mysteries of this secondary location (only 1 percent of it has been excavated), but at this early point, we see that much of its features are strikingly similar to those of Gobekli Tepe. Some experts believe it is even *older*.[143] (The details we know about this second site are so similar to those of Gobekli Tepe that this section will be refreshingly short.)

Right away, we see the remains of serpents everywhere in stone.

At the top of the third chamber is the image of a long, slithering viper, which mysteriously matches to startling detail the same shape of the black Great Rift in the middle of the Milky Way (i.e., "the heavens"… note that for later). The "tail" of the Great Rift connects to another, *different* constellation, known as Serpens Cauda (literally "Snake Tail"). The astrological links are certainly fascinating, especially in light of their serpentine nature.

However, the central draw of Karahan Tepe—for both tourists and archeologists—is the "phallus room," where it is believed that the builders gathered for spiritual rituals or prayer. In Structure AB, eleven stone "phalluses" (male reproductive organs) appear to be growing upward from the stone floor, standing in a cluster with little room between them, each measuring about six feet tall. Overlooking these structures is a peculiar stone character, whose head is around two or three times larger than that of a human. A website put together last January by one of the site's excavators describes this menacing face in an article called, "Strange Phallic Pillars at Karahan Tepe," under the section titled, "The bearded head with a serpent's body at Karahan Tepe." This source states the carving is of a "human head, [with] a beard and a snake-like body that extends toward the right, parallel to the ground." This head, the author goes on to say, "becomes illuminated during the winter solstice. *The sun shines through the [doorway] to Structure AD and lights up the face.*"[144]

The pattern of snakes, gods, and astrological phenomena is increasing. But who might this character be?

Hugh Newman—video producer, author of books on ancient-Earth mysteries, worldwide explorer, frequent guest on History Channel programs, and researcher of giants, giant legends, and their links to megaliths—in a video he created representing his theory regarding the identity of the bearded snake man, says it's likely to be:

> Enki, the great Sumerian god…of virility, god of water, also the
> god of wisdom as well, [who was believed to have] given virility to
> everything: the water, the lands, the farms, the people, abundance

in every possible way...and Enki is related to the serpent. His symbol is the serpent rising up a caduceus [staff], much like the rising serpent here [in Karahan Tepe].[145]

Enki was a well-known Anunnaki—a god of great strength mentioned in the Epic of Gilgamesh (the earlier-referenced ancient Sumer-Babylonian account of the great deluge that the Bible refers to as the Flood of Noah's day). As readers of our past books are well aware, "Anunnaki" is another name for the offspring of fallen angels and human women called Nephilim in the Bible. Could this theory be correct? Could this bearded snake god—here depicted as supervising, surveying, protecting, drawing sacred attention to, or "watching" the phalluses of Karahan Tepe's ritual cult room—be the Watcher known as Enki? Is there some connection between this serpentine figure and the bearded man in robes who visits other ancient cultures and teaches esoteric wisdoms and technology, like those worshiping Feathered Serpent gods Viracocha and Quetzecotl?

And what was that about Enki being the god of water? Does "water" link to "serpent" in some way? Hmmm...wasn't there something about a water serpent in the Bible? (Some of you see where this is going. For those who may not, the answer comes in chapter 8: "Lucifer's Fall and the Extinct Animals of the 'Void.'")

In any case, just about the time archeologists began believing we had answers for Gobekli Tepe—as insufficient as those answers may have been—the excavation of Karahan Tepe has reset the whole game and forced us to travel backwards yet again.

Back to the old, serpentine drawing board...

Really, I can't blame some of these OOPArt researchers who keep going back to the Ancient Astronaut theories. Though I don't agree with their "astronauts-created-mankind" conclusions in the slightest, mysteries *can* be explained away by an imaginary, superior race of beings who can float in on UFOs and deliver an all-you-can-eat buffet to their workers from faraway lands. Sure, it's ridiculous to many, but at least it answers the otherwise unanswerable questions...

But what if there was *another* answer that didn't need to rely on aliens?

Boncuklu Tarla to Reset the Game *Again*?

Just under two hundred miles to the east of Gobekli Tepe is *yet another* excavation site in Turkey that is home to *T*-shaped pillars like those found in its sister predecessors, Gobekli Tepe and Karahan Tepe. Its name, Boncuklu Tarla, means "field of beads," which is a fitting label considering the surprising number (currently more than a 150,000 and climbing) of handmade jewelry pieces unearthed in this third relative site up to this point. As yet, the endeavors of the archeologists since this location's discovery in 2008 have resulted in only an estimated 5 percent excavation (the digging officially began in 2012).

Unlike the others, our fascination with Boncuklu Tarla is not about serpents (although the earliest jewelry discovered here does involve a number of pieces that are serpentine); it's the dating of the location that has people buzzing: Archeologists are reporting that Boncuklu Tarla is older than Gobekli Tepe by *one thousand years.*

According to a Turkey news source, *Anadolu Ajansi* ("Anatolia Agency"), this place is "one of the first settled areas of humanity and shows that the first people settling here were believers." Believers in *what*, we're not sure, but there is no doubt—Ibrahim Ozcosar, rector of nearby Artuklu University, says—the inhabitants were religious.[146] From the same article, we read that Ergul Kodas, prized archeologist of Artuklu University and the excavation's chief supervisor, agrees with other professionals in his field when he says Boncuklu Tarla is "around 12,000-years old," a conclusion supported by the dating of revealed "temples, religious places," and "a 26-inch...long human statue dating back 12,000 years."[147]

Regarding evidence of intelligence, Boncuklu Tarla has a functional, "11,800-year-old sewer system," as well as "eight-story historical buildings reaching up to seven meters in height,"[148] though little information on these details has been released to the public at this time. Kodas told *Anadolu Ajansi* that his team was "only able to unearth a certain portion of the sewer system,"[149] so we can imagine there will be forthcoming reports in the near future regarding how a Pre-Neolithic cluster of hunter-gatherers could manage a feat of ingenuity that, until now, we believed to be a very recent development of humanity's history. When those details do surface, I wonder if there will be an explanation regarding the ancients' apparent obsession with bull heads and horns delicately set up in a similar worship fashion as those in the forthcoming discussion on the location of Catalhoyuk, and if Boncuklu Tarla's archeology team will link that in some way to a religion behind the snake beads of the inhabitants' jewelry.

But in any case, if Karahan Tepe forces experts to expand their philosophical approaches to early hunter-gatherer travelers in this area of the world, then so, too, do the discoveries of this much older, and incredible, site.

It resets the game...*again*.

Baalbek

Since 1956, Baalbek (often spelled "Baalbeck" or "Baalbec") has been home to "the oldest and most prestigious cultural event in the Middle East,"[150] known simply as the "Baalbeck International Festival." Although this annual summer event suffered great decline, followed by temporary cessation, between 2006 and 2007 as a result of political instability, by 2008, it had "regained its place in the line of the most prestigious international festivals with varied and excellent [Lebanese] cultural quality programs performed by great artists inside the magnificent Baalbeck Acropolis."[151] A curious outsider traveling major Roman historical sites for the first time will find the attention-grabbing sights, sounds, celebrations, and almost explosive energies bursting from the seams of this small location—spanning less than three square miles. It's a tourism force to be reckoned with. Among the appearances of and performances by internationally acclaimed stars of the music, television, and film industries, as well as many celebrated stage performers, one might struggle to find time to breathe, let alone rest, in this town that never sleeps every June through August.[152]

However, when September rolls around, the tent stakes are pulled and the droves of vacationers return home from the lively festival. Even then, and despite how deserted and forgotten the area looks in pictures of crumbling temple ruins, Baalbek continues to welcome an almost never-ending stream of spectators all year round. Scholars, historians, architects, and archeologists continue to name Baalbek one of the greatest mysteries in world history for its monumentally scaled temple ruins and enigmatic findings at the nearby quarry.

Known by early inhabitants (ca. 334 BC after Alexander the Great's victory in the Near East) as "Heliopolis"—which translates to "City of the Sun" from the Greek *helios* ("sun") and *polis* ("city")—Baalbek was one of the most prevalent sanctuaries in the Roman Empire, and its structures are some of the most well-preserved standing today. Much discussion has centered around theories that the town may have been an ancient settlement predating Roman rule by centuries at least, and recent pottery fragment finds along the trench channeling the Jupiter temple now date the site to between the Pre-Pottery Neolithic B Age (or PPNB, representing the latter stages of the Stone Age before mankind could craft pottery, approximately 8000 BP [Before Present] and 6000 BCE) and the Iron Age (approximately 1200 BC–AD 550).[153] Several skeletons and some pottery from Persia were discovered under the Roman flagstones, indicating additional settlement evidence dating to around 550 BC.[154]

The largest confirmed ancient stone building block on Earth at the time of this writing (but see note about Mount Shoria later in this chapter) was found in Baalbek by German archeologists in the middle of 2014 at the quarry of a building site at which gigantic stones had been used for the podium of the enormous Temple of Jupiter (built later on by the Romans atop the original mound construction, Tel Baalbek). This unfathomable monolith measures in at 64 feet (19.6 meters) in length, 19.6 feet (6 meters) wide, and 18 feet (5.5 meters) high, and it's estimated to weigh 1,650 tons (3,300,000 million pounds).[155]

Prior to the unearthing of this giant rock in 2014, one of the largest quarried stones on Earth had been the Stone of the Pregnant Woman (*Hajjar al-Hibla*), also located in Baalbek, which protrudes from the ground at a sloping angle directly alongside the even larger stone. There are several stories and claims behind the name of this rock. One tells of a pregnant woman who duped the Baalbek inhabitants into believing she held the secret behind lifting and moving the rock in one piece. In trade for her secret, they would feed her and the baby in her womb and take care of all her prenatal needs, but after her child was born, no hidden truths emerged, and the stone has remained tilted out of the ground ever since.[156] Another story suggests that jinn—the Arabian and Islamic mythical beings made of smokeless, yet corporeal, fire—assigned their pregnant women to move the stones, and when one such jinn heard the news that Solomon had died, she excitedly dropped it to the ground where it still lies.[157] Yet another rumor lingers around the locale that the name originated from the stone's ability to increase the fertility of any woman who touches it.[158] Whatever the true origin of its name, the Stone of the Pregnant Woman (weighing just over 1,000 tons [approximately 2,205,000 pounds]) is estimated to have required more than forty thousand laborers to move it,[159] though the sources that suggest this number seldom seem to provide a convincing answer as to *how* that would have been accomplished with the building technology of the time regardless of the number of available work hands. It is so close to its newly found and massive counterpart that a fascinated voyager to Baalbek can reach out and touch two of the largest stones on earth at the same time. (Note that there is a third stone across the road from these, more vast than the Stone of the Pregnant Woman, but not as enormous as the most recent find by the Germans in 2014.)

In photographer Daniel B. Shepp's *The Holy Land Photographed* from 1894, we read that the Stone of the Pregnant Woman has been a mystery for hundreds of years already:

> Taken as a whole, the ruins of Baalbec are among the grandest in the world. Nowhere is there evidence of more exquisite workmanship. To an antiquarian they are the study of a lifetime.... Before us is one lying in the quarry, whence it had been hewn. It measures sixty-nine feet in length, thirteen feet in breadth and thirteen feet three inches in thickness.... It is accurately squared and trimmed on three sides, showing that it was the custom of the

people to dress the stones while quarrying them. There has been much speculation as to how stones like this were quarried and moved into their positions, but no satisfactory theory has been advanced. There is a peculiar absence of inscriptions in connection with all these massive ruins, hence we are left in much doubt and darkness.[160]

Dear Daniel Shepp, we are still, almost 130 years later, "left in doubt and darkness."

There are many theories, sometimes heatedly debated, regarding who carved the monoliths of Baalbek (both those left at the quarry and the base stones of the Temple of Jupiter known as the "trilithon"), when they were created, for what purpose, and how they were transported. Because we know the Romans responsible for building the uppermost portions of the Temple of Jupiter (as well as the *Heliopolis* temples of Bacchus and Venus in the Baalbek temple complex over two centuries) based on biographical Roman engineering documentation ordered during the Roman Empire, it seems, for many, quite rational to assume the Romans were responsible for the larger stones in this area as well.

Visiting that possibility, and focusing only on the Temple of Jupiter, we will start at the top and work our way down. In order to understand my take on the Romans' involvement with the monoliths, some knowledge is needed of their usual building practices.

Columns and Cornerstones

Fifty-four columns were raised in the original Temple of Jupiter structure, involving blocks weighing up to sixty tons each (120,000 pounds). Each cornerstone weighed more than 100 tons (200,000 pounds), and they were hoisted to 62.34 feet (19 meters) above ground surface.[161] The method used for the top of the temple construction could *in part* be attributed to the Greco-Roman man-operated treadwheel pulleys (*pentaspastos* or *polyspastos*, depending on the number of men required to operate them), the tools and techniques of which were well documented by engineers Vitruvius (*De Architectura* 10.2, 1–10) and Heron of Alexandria (*Mechanica* 3.2–5).

The maximum weight these early cranes could lift and carry when operated to the maximum capacity of their design, and with a full crew, did not usually exceed 6,000 kilograms (13,228 pounds).[162] Mathematically, this would mean that the machinery—when used alone—fell shy of the capability of lifting a single cornerstone of the temple by a little under a staggering 200,000 pounds.

The most likely explanation for the additional weight lifting and maneuvering for the top of the Tower of Jupiter—often mentioned by historians and architects today (and discussed in historical accounts associated with the raising of the Lateranense obelisk of the Circus Maximus [*Ammianus Marcellinus* 17.4.15] ca. AD 357)—points to the installation of lifting towers (*Mechanica* 3.5), used in tandem with early capstans (horizontal rotators) fixed upon the ground around the lifting tower. The capstans each contributed less weight-lifting efficiency than did the treadwheel pulleys, but they required fewer men (or animals) to function, and more of them could be placed upon the ground when needed, offering increased leverage overall than the pulleys alone. If more weight was required to lift an individual stone, more capstans would be installed on the ground around a lifting tower, and so on.

The average capacity of the joined capstans in tandem with a lifting tower of this era has been estimated at 7.5 tons per capstan,[163] and the method of lifting by capstan was via attachment to lewis iron holes in each stone. For example: a 60-ton architrave block (one of the stones placed near the top of the Roman columns) from the Tower of Jupiter, discovered with eight lewis iron holes, delivers this equation: 8 capstans x 7.5 tons per capstan = 60 tons capacity. The architrave blocks in the Jupiter tower weighed *up to* 60 tons, so the capstan/lifting tower combination theory is certainly feasible for the tower stones when inflated for more weight, even for the over-100-ton cornerstones.

With enough capstan and lifting-tower installations scattered about, and with the assistance from treadwheel pulleys on the lighter stones, the placement of the Tower of Jupiter columns above the original and far more ancient foundation stones could be explained and easily attributed to Roman ingenuity.

Below the columns, however, is the trilithon (three extremely large and heavy monoliths, resting between the Tower of Jupiter and the Tel Baalbek mound). This is where we first begin to run into the heated debate regarding the whos and hows of this so-called Roman architecture.

Trilithon

The first theory (most often associated with Arabian lore involving the "magician" works of Solomon, and therefore taken less seriously than theories involving Roman origin) can be seen in another image caption from Daniel B. Shepp's *The Holy Land Photographed*. In regard to the trilithon, Shepp says:

> Even more wonderful to many than the ornate ruins of the temples, is the masonry of the outer walls of Baalbec. Here are the three largest stones ever used in architecture…. One of these is sixty-four feet long, another sixty-three feet eight inches, and the third sixty-three feet. Each is thirteen feet high and thirteen feet thick. To these dimensions must be added the fact, that they have been built into the wall fully twenty feet above the ground [note that Shepp is referring to the measurement from the stones to the ground as it lay in 1894, prior to further depth revealed in archeological digs, which increased that measurement later], and the further fact that the quarry from which they were taken is fully a mile distant. Those who identify Solomon with the buildings of Baalbec, connect these stones with the narrative in I Kings VII [1 Kings 7:10]: "And the foundation was of costly stones, EVEN GREAT STONES, stones of ten cubits, and stones of eight cubits." The Arabs believe that Solomon was a magician, and by a magic word, moved these giant slabs.[164]

Yet, it goes without saying that most great minds that approach the mystery of the trilithon will disregard the idea that Solomon transported the stones by magic.

Considering other mainstream theories, we almost immediately land on the arguments put forth by French archeologist Jean-Pierre Adam, author of the 1977 scholarly article, *A Propos du Trilithon de Baalbek. Let transport et la miseen oeuvre des megaliths* ("Concerning the Trilithon of Baalbek: Transportation and the Implementation of the Megaliths").[165] Adam's approach to the mystery involves a look at the Thunder Stone, a giant boulder (one and a half times the weight of the trilithon blocks of Baalbek [1,250,000 kilograms; 2,755,778 pounds])[166] that makes up the base of the "Bronze Horseman" (*aka* the Statue of Peter the Great) in Saint Petersburg, Russia.

The composition of the Bronze Horseman statue was ordered by Catherine the Great in an attempt to inflate her position as Peter the Great's rightful heir. Beginning the planning for the statue in 1766, the Thunder Stone was found in the deep marshlands of Lakhta, just a few miles from the Gulf of Finland, in 1768. Greek engineer Marinos Carburis agreed to oversee the moving of the stone and began the intimidating trek as soon as manpower resources were in place.

The stone was transported approximately four miles (six kilometers) within two years over both land and water. Most land transportation took place during a nine-month period by four hundred men using ingenious roller tracks and capstans; water transportation required a gigantic barge built specifically for carrying the Thunder Stone, with a warship on each side of the barge for additional support. The capstans were put into motion using only human hands; no oxen or cattle of any kind were used for the moving project. The operation was observed by thousands of witnesses in the company of Catherine the Great, herself, while the boulder sat atop the ball-bearings-like roller tracks designed by Carburis. The tracks would be assembled in front of the stone, the stone would be pulled by the crews at the capstans to the front of the tracks, and simultaneously the tracks at the back would be disassembled and carried to the front, where they were reassembled for further transport—one centimeter at a time.

Because the distance between Lakhta and the Senate Square of St. Petersburg is about four miles, and the distance from the trilithon to the quarry in Baalbek is only about 800 meters (2,600 feet)—and because the Thunder Stone is larger than the trilithon stones—Jean-Pierre Adam finds moving the trilithon stones an even lesser feat than moving the Thunder Stone when hypothetically applying the same or similar transportation methods.

Understandably, this comparison inspires that "aha" moment for many researchers and is considered a feasible explanation for the potentially applied physics of the brightest minds in ancient Roman engineering. Jean-Pierre Adam presents an interesting theory, for sure, and one that has gained immense following as a result of the Temple Mount structure ordered by Roman client King Herod the Great in Jerusalem, Israel, which is home to base stones weighing close to the same weight as those of the trilithon at Baalbek. The Temple Mount stones (the largest of which is 630 tons) remain unchallenged as having Roman origin, so many suggest with good reason that the stones of Baalbek would have only required a slight increase in construction efforts to accomplish. Further, many assume the three monoliths left at the nearby quarries represent a point at which the Romans bit off more than they could chew, so to speak, cutting and shaping stones that ended up later to be more than their machinery could move. This would explain not only why the stones were abandoned at the quarries, but also why the monolith across the road from the Stone of the Pregnant Woman shows deep, squared cuts on one end, as if the Romans acknowledged their inability to move the stone and therefore decided to cut it into smaller stones until it was of manageable moving size. (Note, however, that the stone with the rivets cut on one end also has imperfections, so for just as many people as there are who assert that the Romans cut it down to a size they could lift, an equal number claim the stone was merely being cut to preserve quality and avoid the evident risk of cracks quickly appearing in a foundation stone.)

Left wanting in this "aha" theory, however, is any documentation whatsoever by the Romans that they would have used this Thunder Stone method of transportation for the trilithon stones when all other building practices were so well documented during their heyday...

The Romans were a proud and brilliant people who left our world with many records of what they accomplished and, in many cases, of how they accomplished those feats. The records have been thoroughly researched and studied for hundreds of years. And, sure, a Roman building that followed known patterns of the day may not have revolutionized the world, so the masterminds behind it may not have felt the need to keep track of *everything* they built. But had Roman architects accomplished something as grand as moving the trilithon stones at Baalbek, it seems likely they would have made absolutely sure that the rest of the world knew about their achievement. We cannot attribute this stone-moving method (as well as the other methods mentioned by Adam in his study) to their book of tricks without also asking why they wouldn't have been intelligent enough to record such an accomplishment.

And, of course, as an even more important argument against Roman origin, as stated earlier in this chapter: There have been discoveries from the Pre-Pottery Neolithic era within the soil along the channels of the Temple of Jupiter that point to this site *predating the Romans by centuries*. At this point, the completely absent entry of proud Roman architects who would have had every reason to revel in their triumph—alongside scientific dating showing the trilithon was situated where it stands hundreds of years before the Romans entered the picture—is a final nail in the coffin of all conjecture involving Roman resourcefulness as the means by which the trilithon was assembled.

On the tail of the prevailing theories of Roman attribution come thoughts perpetuated by archeologists that the trilithon stones were of Greek origin for use as a retaining wall in soil-erosion circumstances. Again, we have no record of this, but we also have no reason to believe the Greeks—despite their impressive ingenuity that we see evident in their amphitheaters and other structures—would be capable of achieving more than the Romans in relation to moving stones that weigh hundreds and hundreds of tons. If it's hard enough for us to believe the builders of

Gobekli Tepe became worse—not better—at raising pillars over time, why would we rule out Romans for the trilithon at Baalbek and then accept the Greek explanation when we know that nearly everything the Greeks accomplished was passed down to, and exceeded by, Roman culture?

Other ideas have surfaced throughout the decades. Some are sensational and even altogether incredible. For instance, there's one proposition that says the Romans would have built a Nile-like river that carried the trilithon stones by boat when there doesn't seem to be enough solid evidence that a river of that magnitude ever existed that close to these structures. On and on the Roman-origin explanations seem to arrive, each one supported by its own list of professionals, and each one eventually challenged by just as many or more well-respected archeologists. Skeptics chastise those who attribute the monoliths to ancient extraterrestrial activity or the giants of Genesis, saying that just because we can't find origin in human life, we turn all too quickly to the supernatural for explanation. Sometimes these comments are delivered with extreme sarcasm, flowing to the tune of: "We can't understand how ancient humans could have done it, so, yeah, why not? Let's just say the aliens did it." Believers in the supernatural chastise the skeptics in turn, questioning their outright denial of the possibility of supernatural activity or a pre-Adamic race when there remain to be found any other solid explanations as to how ancient humans could have accomplished more than our historical records have *ever* indicated.

But whatever the theory, the fact remains that the origins of the trilithon and quarry stones at Baalbek remain unknown and have baffled researchers and archeologists for centuries. Without documentation by a race or people as to the materials and methods used, as well as the purpose behind the structures in Baalbek, the answers may always be obscured, and speculation may always engender even further mystery.

Note, however, that there is one historical document we have yet to visit in this chapter, which seems to give just as likely an explanation as the speculated "ancient humans." The Bible is respected, even by many nonbelievers, as a historical document, and one that has proven time and time again to connect the dots where other sources have failed. This was the source reflected in the 1860 diary of the Scottish diplomat and writer David Urquhart, whose mind was "paralyzed" by "the impossibility of any solution" involving how, why, and who engineered the original construction at Baalbek. Urquhart's only conclusion was that the temple had to have been built by those megalithic masterminds of the days of Noah:

> There was here, therefore, not one of the elements combined at Memphis, Babylon, Nineveh, or any of the seats of empire, of the ancient or modern world [but] ruins, surpassing in their indications and evidences of greatness anything to be found in those ancient capitals, to an extent which defies all calculation, leaving the imagination itself stranded on a bank of mud.
>
> On the top of this comes a third riddle; how these works were interrupted. They are not merely not concluded, but they are stopped at the very beginning....
>
> Was it a foreign invasion? Was it an irruption of savages? Was it a "confusion of tongues?" What could it have been?...
>
> My first exclamation, on looking down into the quarry, had been "There were giants in the earth in those days."...
>
> The builders of Baalbeck must have been a people who had attained to the highest pinnacle of power and science; and this region must have been the centre of their dominion. We are perfectly acquainted with the nations who have flourished here or around, and their works; they are the Assyrians, Chaldeans, Medes, Persians, Egyptians, Canaanites, and Jews. These complete the catalogue of ancient empires, and this work is none of theirs....
>
> It was only on my way back, and when the tomb of Noah was pointed out to me by the wayside, that it occurred to me that there might be something in Emir Hangar's story, and that the stones of Baalbeck had to be considered as some of "those sturdy fellows that the Deluge could not sweep away." This, then, was a remnant of that pride and presumption, which had brought the waters over the face of the earth.[167]

Could there be something to Urquhart's train of thought that actually provides more answers than it poses further inquiry? Is it even possible that there would be "sturdy fellows" that the Flood of Noah's time "could not sweep away"? Is that what the passages in the Bible mean that say there were giants upon Earth in the generations following Adam "and also after that" (Genesis 6:4)? Were there giants who went down with, and then reemerged after, the Flood? And if so, could they, or something similar, have existed before Adam? Could we be looking at an even more ancient race from the "void" era before the first human was formed in the image of God?

As some of the pottery fragments *predate* humanity's pottery days, at the very least we know this site was visited by some race of beings circa 8000 BC—*before both Adam and the Flood of Noah*—which likely means the builders of the Trilithon were pre-Adamic, intelligent, technologically advanced in construction methods, and extremely strong!

Russian Megaliths of Mount Shoria

Lastly, supposing the mysteries of Baalbek were finally cracked, attributing the movement of the trilithon stones and the existence of the quarry stones to human hands, a more recent discovery could potentially erase all of that decryption progress and render it largely irrelevant in comparison to the latest thrill: As mentioned prior, the largest stone in the world—*confirmed for the purposes of building*—at the time of this writing currently rests in the quarry of Baalbek, weighing an estimated 1,650 tons. However, just a few years ago, stones estimated to weigh *an astounding 3,000–4,000 tons* have been discovered on Mount Shoria in Siberia. At this present time, the site is such a young find that little is known about these stones, so theories have only just begun to surface. Before this dig officially launches all the who-and-how questions that we've attempted for centuries to answer about Baalbek, further study on the megaliths of Mount Shoria must rule that the stones were, in fact, dressed by hand, and therefore are not a product of natural formation. That said, pictures of the stones can be viewed online, and archeologists are already buzzing about the proof that the stones are much more than that:

> This site consists of huge blocks of stone…**with flat surfaces, right angles, and sharp corners.** The blocks appear to be stacked, almost in the manner of cyclopean masonry, and well…they're enormous!…
>
> The site at Shoria is unique in that, if it's man-made, the blocks used are undoubtedly **the largest ever worked by human hands.**[168] (Emphasis in original)

Archeologist John Jenson also notes that "these megaliths are much larger (as much as 2 to 3 times larger) than the largest known megaliths in the world. (Example: The Pregnant Woman Stone of Baalbek, Lebanon…). These [Mt. Shoria] megaliths could easily weigh upwards of 3,000 to 4,000 tons."[169]

Folks, that is between six and eight *million* pounds…

In his characteristic sarcastic, Southern tone, Tom Horn, when these stones were first found, said, "Ain't no pulley-carts gonna account for *them* rocks!" (Seriously, look this up online. The naked eye is all that is needed for the curious Internet surfer to see these stones and know that rain and weathering have never formed anything so precise anywhere on Earth.)

Thus far, no expert analysis exists for these stones, as we're still waiting for this project to be funded and prioritized. However, that hasn't stopped folks from talking about some of the strange or mystical occurrences linked to this location's earliest (and unofficial) examinations, such as one oddity noted in an article by a Russian news website. During an expedition to the area back in autumn of 2013:

> The compasses of the geologists behaved very strangely, for some unknown reason their arrows were deviating from the megaliths.… All that was clear was that they came across an inexplicable phenomenon of the negative geomagnetic field. Could this be a remnant of ancient antigravity technologies?[170]

Needless to say, Mount Shoria is about to become the source of much news. Should these square, stacked stones prove to be dressed by tools and not by weather conditions—which is a true "LOL-meets-facepalm" suggestion, considering the stones' masterful shaping, *including* sections wherein perfect doorways have been hewn from the middle of them—Baalbek will no longer hold the heavyweight title as the world's greatest archeological monolith mystery.

Catalhoyuk

The Neolithic-age Catalhoyuk, situated in south central Turkey near the modern-day city Konya, was inhabited "9000 years ago by up to 8000 people,"[171] predating the dust-formation birth of Adam by about three thousand years. The site is most known for being a record of "one of man's most important transformations: from nomad to settler,"[172] as well as the home of what some archeologists are calling the "world's oldest map" depicting an erupting volcano.[173] Like some of the other locations we've looked at, its inhabitants here lived during a time when humanity wasn't sophisticated, yet they were advanced farmers who knew how to survive in one place for thousands of years without ever having to expand outward for new lands.

Depending on the community one belongs to, however, the true fascination with this location is not just showing that pre-Adamic settlers lived three thousand years before God's first human beings bit into the forbidden fruit in the Garden of Eden and that they cultivated the land, but also the bizarre way they lived. For instance: The houses are squashed together, separated only by walls, and the residents went from home to home by walking across the rooftops and entering their neighbors' homes by ladder; when an inhabitant passed on, the body was buried under the floor of the home—and each time this took place, more symbolism was painted on the walls (the artwork on the walls of some dwellings indicates as many as sixty-two bodies were buried in the floor); as the settlement grew in size, additional housing was provided by building atop existing homes, to result in structures that eventually reached more than twenty meters (sixty-five feet) high; symbols and art on the walls and other places humanoid shapes, with heads missing, and, as the original archeologists back in the 1960s identified, carnivorous vultures (or other birds of prey known for picking the flesh off the bones off the decaying deceased), along with bears, leopards, and bulls, were scattered among the artistic frescoes as well.

Today, we have no way of knowing *why*, but occasionally, body parts (such as the head) of a deceased person would be removed from a body, kept for a long time, plastered back together if damage or crumbling occurred, and then buried with another loved one upon their subsequent death. (Some comment that this was an endearing or loving practice— a "lay Sarah to rest with Judy" sort of idea—and that is supported by the position of the skeletal remains at discovery [such as the arms of one dearly grasping onto the head of another, and so on]. Personally, I see the pictures and just find it creepy.)

Ian Hodder, an archeologist at the site, weighs in by sharing a strange habit the locals apparently adopted in this regard: "But we also have other examples where the head [of one deceased body] is present, but the legs and arms are missing. So, again, we think that part of the body is buried, but the legs and the arms circulated around the village. So, if you [traveled there] nine thousand years ago, you would meet real people, alive, but you would also meet parts of bodies [displayed about the home]."[174]

One kind of building Hodder is most fascinated with is what he has coined "history houses"—places offering abundant evidence of rituals carried out "to protect the dead in some way," and where the "religious elite" or "ritual specialists" maintained and "cared for the symbols" associated with the culture.[175] (Shrines are common in Catalhoyuk.) Hodder goes on to explain that, unlike many ancient cultures, these religious leaders did not appear to have any particular privileges, at least from what can be gleaned from their modest housing; evidence of such luxuries as extra space, storage rooms, ornate surroundings, or economic power or benefits of any kind above those of their fellows has not been found.[176]

This is extremely unusual. Any archeologist, historian, or anthropologist worth their weight in pennies will tell you that the vast majority of the ancient world is rife with evidence that the religious leaders were given some social or environmental privileges, as seen in various ways throughout ruins (pictographs, idols, housing accommodations, etc.). And although I haven't yet run across any expert who has stated this possibility outright in regard to *this* settlement, the lack of this treatment of the religious elite *may* indicate that the inhabitants of Catalhoyuk were devotees of a religious ruler or group who did not live directly within their midst.

One might expect to read all about the serpents at this site, but actually, this culture was fascinated with something else...something that might link directly to the biblical cherubim. First, though, we have to get the "Mother Goddess" thing out of the way, as it is evidently irrelevant.

Many of the figurines found in the upper levels of housing represent older, nude women, quite obese, with sagging breasts, stomachs, and buttocks, which has led to Mother Goddess cult speculation. However, had that been the religious motive of this settlement's occupants, it then raises the question of why these "idols" are "found most frequently in garbage pits, but also in oven walls, house walls, floors and left in abandoned structures, [and] show evidence of having been poked, scratched or broken."[177] If their central deity was some kind of revered Mother Goddess, why is dear Mother Goddess treated so casually? Elsewhere, like in one article titled "New Techniques Undermine 'Mother Goddess' Role in Ancient Community" from the *Irish Times*, Hodder is known for stating that Catalhoyuk "is perhaps best known for the idea of the mother goddess. But our work more recently has tended to show that in fact there is very little evidence of a mother goddess."[178]

I therefore side with those who alternatively suggest that this group allowed women to be equal figures of leadership in their community, and the fact that they are nude, but not sexualized (as many ancient female idols tended to be in the old world, like the many-breasted idols of Artemis/Diana), suggests women were revered for their unique ability to carry male seed into new life (and then rear them into full participation in communal productivity and survival). This is further supported by the fact that the deceased youths of this settlement were "the only bodies which were treated differently," adorned in beads and red ochre, with special paintings archeologists noted on the walls adjacent to their remains.[179] Adult males were also at times buried with red ochre stripes on the front of their skulls, which was likewise unique to *them*. So, far from a Mother Goddess-worship scenario, it looks as though these inhabitants had a specific way of remembering and honoring each member of their tribe or clan, and statuettes of plump, older women were the go-to for matriarchs. (Sadly, as is often the way with archeological discoveries, this Mother Goddess has become so tightly knit to stories of Catalhoyuk civilization that, even when experts like Hodder shoot down the connections, the narrative clings on, and may continue to for decades until enough voices challenge it into permanent dismissal.)

The images of bulls' heads all over the walls bring us much closer to identifying this community's form of worship, and of all symbolic and sacred relics and images at the site, bulls outnumber all other objects and imagery by far.

Interestingly, the bull god idea connects to the earliest concept of the appearance of a holy cherub in Sumerian, and later Akkadian, religious texts, which bled into world culture through the first widespread religions.

Did the inhabitants of Catalhoyuk receive a visit from a holy leader who descended from the heavens and who also had the capacity of appearing as a bull-headed god? If so, is there a link between the pre-Adamic "void" era and the relics of bull worship in Catalhoyuk that show the folks there were subservient to a god or "shining one" that chose to lead them but also chose not to live amidst them?

It's only a theory, but it would explain why the religious elites weren't given the same special treatment in this settlement that they were apparently given in almost every other ancient community we've looked at.

But to the secular-minded, the greatest mystery of Catalhoyuk is not the inhabitants' gods or religion. The biggest missing puzzle piece is how in the world the nomadic hunter-gatherers of the Neolithic Age could have developed such an advanced farming community and stay-put survivability—along with carrying out creative and economic pursuits like making statues and beads, repairing and building functional homes, implementing expert agricultural practices, domesticating wild animals, crafting pottery and obsidian tools, and achieving other major accomplishments at least more than five hundred miles away from any nearby towns or settlements (and therefore receiving no help from the outside world). Interesting.

Mehgarh, Pakistan

In 1974, French archeologists Jean-Francois Jarrige and his wife, Catherine, happened upon six giant mounds in the province of Balochistan, Pakistan, and began a twelve-year excavation that would generate a second dig between 1974 and 1986. More than thirty thousand artifacts have been unearthed from this location, and some are quite a mystery. Results from inquiries into the etymology of the site's name, Mehgarh, are frustratingly diverse and tend to be explanations based on conjecture about whether it derives from French, the native Balochi language, or neither, or a blend of the two, or some other language entirely. It *could* mean "Fort of God" or "God's Fort," though "Heaven[s] of Love" is the more popularly referenced possibility.

Mehgarh is dated to 7000 BC—three thousand years before Adam's Ussher-conceived birthday—though its occupants inhabited the site off and on until around 2000 BC. Eight periods of occupation break down the site's artifacts into subcategories. The earliest period, aceramic-Neolithic (meaning that the inhabitants were of the Neolithic age but they *had not yet developed pottery*) is linked to the widely known discovery of proto-dentistry. From the teeth of nine ancients are eleven permanent crowns that had been fixed upon their teeth while they lived.

Several scientific methods were applied to the study of these teeth, including microtomography (a type of x-ray), scanning electron microscopy (or SEM: a microscope that uses electrons rather than light to form images), and light microscopy. These scans showed that the teeth had been drilled where cavities had been, and the subsequent wear of the enamel around the cavity proves the recipients of the dental work were still alive and continued to chew food for some time following the installation of their crowns. Around this layer of Mehgarh, drill heads made of flint were lithified and scattered about the debris, no doubt belonging to these prolific, early dentists who, archeologists say, were capable of making a hole in a human tooth via this method in less than a minute. The abstract from a *Nature Magazine* journal article related to these findings states: "Prehistoric evidence for the drilling of human teeth *in vivo* [in living patients] has so far been limited to isolated cases from less than six millennia ago. Here we describe eleven drilled molar crowns from nine adults discovered in a Neolithic graveyard in Pakistan that dates from 7,500 to 9,000 years ago."[180]

"Human beings," not yet advanced enough to make a pot and who lived in mud-brick houses, were practicing dentists?

Yep. And they were making impressive jewelry.

Amidst many religious artifacts is the strange Mehgarh Amulet, a small, six-thousand-year-old, wheel-shaped amulet made from unalloyed copper that was carefully studied with photoluminescence technology. Results show this discovery is now the oldest-known example of the "lost-wax casting" technique: 1) wax or a soft, oil-based clay is formed into a model shape, like a pendant, face, figurine, etc.; 2) the shape is then covered with a more rigid clay or substance with an exit point for the first materials to leave the mold in step three; 3) the mold is then baked, allowing the heated substances on the inside to pour out; 4) molten metal is poured into the mold through the opening; 5) once cooled, the mold outside of the model is intentionally broken away to reveal the final piece of artwork within.

The mixture and handling of materials involved in this process show the workmanship of Mehgarh occupants to have been quite advanced for their time. A researcher looking into lost-wax casting will discover quickly that, although Mehgarh is the oldest example, this art wasn't uncommon in civilizations all over the world at around this time. Artifacts at Bulgaria's Varna Necropolis, Judean deserts near the Dead Sea (especially those from the Nahal Mishmar area) in Israel, Mesopotamia, and later Europe show this technique in use around the beginning of Adam's era. Though skeptics may assume this finding isn't a great example of human or pre-Adamite technology, I will remind the readers that, according to known history of this time, folks were still learning how to grow crops of wheat and hunt for food to survive. Expertise in metallurgy to this degree as attested by the Mehgarh excavations has been, archeologists admit, a mystery. The fact that this is not an isolated finding (but it *is* the oldest) shows that there were, indeed, more advanced civilizations in operation around Earth earlier than our university and academic textbooks claim.

More could be stated of the Mehgarh inhabitants' ingenuity (including the discovery of cotton fibers around the site, which some believe had no business being there). I believe, by now, the point of looking back on these mind-bending mysteries of the old world has been accomplished. I'm eager to move onto the next part of the book.

A Quick Thought on the Endless Barrage

By no stretch of the imagination is this short study of these objects and sites exhaustive. In my library, I have a number of books—some with page counts that creep upwards of seven hundred—presenting more and more astonishing and extraordinary mysteries of Earth. But, in conclusion to all of this "mystery history," which I'll now wrap up, just remember that an abundance of bizarre and unexplainable artifacts and locations support the idea that Earth was inhabited by intelligent beings prior to Adam, *or* that Adam was created far earlier than Ussher Chronology demands (a true possibility, as discussed earlier in chapter 2). And, if these beings of intelligence weren't truly human in the sense of the God's-image-bearing Adam, then they were something *else*…and I have a theory that traces their origin to Genesis 1:2—a time of a great war between good and evil, as the language of the Word and the visions of God's prophets confirm.

Let's visit a biblical possibility that doesn't rely on Ancient Astronaut and equivalent theories: Lucifer falls, takes many angels with him, and destroys the Earth that God created in *the very* beginning (millions/billions of years ago). He doesn't have the same creative power as God, so Earth becomes "without form, and void"—a completely wrecked version of the paradise God originally envisioned. Then, sometime while Earth is still void, Lucifer does the best he can in his limited power to create *his own* race of beings that will follow him—which is in perfect alignment with what we know of Lucifer's nature and plan to exalt himself as the Most High. His perverted "creations" are not really creations as much as they are a manipulation of the DNA of living creatures on Earth, as we know him to be capable of (Genesis 6). Then, we get to the *nachash* (serpent) of the Garden, which is not the slithering snake cartoons depict. His presence in Eden proves that even after God's re-creation of Earth, there was evil and temptation on the planet's surface in some form. However, some time *prior to* the Flood, Lucifer led wicked beings (perhaps bipedal, humanlike entities) to worship Lucifer, himself, even if indirectly through pagan, pantheonic religions. This they did at such sites as Gobekli Tepe (which *may* have been backfilled because Lucifer and/or his "gods" [the fallen angels the Bible says followed him] saw that his time of glory was coming to an end under the Almighty God and wanted to save their sacred site to be unearthed at a later time for a pagan revival, end-times worship, or something else).

Is all of this possible? Is it even theologically admissible?

Let's look at supporting scriptural evidence.

PART III

THE SERPENT KING

Chapter 6

Earth between "Void" and "Good"

UP TO THIS POINT, we've talked about the inerrancy of Scripture—a doctrine I hold to unequivocally—as well as Ussher Chronology, admissible Old-Earth interpretations of terms in Genesis, what science has to say about Earth's age, and the evidence of a very ancient intelligence. We have flirted with the possibilities of a pre-Adamic race and the OOPArts they left behind, hinted at a possible link to a "void" era of Earth's history that might explain an enormous gap in time within God's Creation epic, and promised to address what I believe the Bible might be saying about it all. Finally, we are at that promised point.

Some readers might be wondering why I tackled only part of Genesis' terminology in the first couple of chapters, then broke off that topic to explore science and mysterious locations, and am only just now returning to take on the rest of the words in Genesis. In short, this was because I wanted to build the case that the Bible allows for an Old-Earth interpretation (covering issues that consistently arise early on in the debate), followed by evidence of Old Earth being true—all *before* diving into what may have actually occurred between the initial formation of the planet and its later re-creation beginning in Genesis 1:3. By now, readers should have a general feel for why what we are about to delve into is not only possible, but also happens to connect the wayward, detached dots in a way no other interpretations have done. For the rest of this chapter and the next, we'll take a look at a powerful cherub of God's design; the self-inflating decision he made; what the prophets also saw in their visions related to this cherub; and what disastrous conditions that may have thrust upon Earth, its surface, its earliest inhabitants, and even dinosaurs.

The first item on this list is a "Who got there first?" question some may have regarding the earliest religion on Earth. I'll address that briefly.

The Doctrine of Original Revelation

In a study reviewing the most ancient sites and objects on Earth that also appear to be man-made, it's crucial to get one thing established before anything else: The very first, and therefore *original*, revelation of all things spiritual came from God. If Adam was, in fact, born around 4004 BC—and if, in fact, someone or something was walking Earth before him—then it would be easy to think the first true, image-bearing human beings merely copied spiritual concepts from the surrounding cultures that pre-dated them. In other words, one might say, Christianity is not the fore-most or final Word on the spiritual realm, as it is younger than whatever was going on during the "void."

This could not be farther from the truth, as God was still first. He is eternal, so He is always the First and the Last (Isaiah 44:6–8).

A doctrine sometimes referred to as the "Doctrine of *Original* Revelation" (a term that originated with Tom Horn years ago and is not to be confused with the "Doctrine of Revelation" [which says the Bible is God's trustworthy self-revelation to mankind]), that goes like this: Adam was the first human being who walked in the Garden of Eden alongside God. The two spoke with one another and discussed an unimaginable number of deep, spiritual topics, as can be gleaned from Genesis 3:8. The Fall of mankind was what initially drove a wedge between God and man, but Adam and Eve felt remorse for their rebellion and attempted to mend their ways—in part, by rearing children who were trained in the spiri-tual matters of the original teachings God gave Earth's first parents. This model of training up children in the ways of the Lord would also be passed down to biblical writers (cf., Proverbs 22:6). As the population multiplied and pagan nations arose, they hijacked the original revelation of God to Adam and twisted it to attempt to make their gods look more powerful than Jehovah/Yahweh. Heavenly concepts that were at first unblemished, beautiful, and wholly good became warped as evil, ugly, and overbearing, while what was intrinsically wicked came to be viewed by the pagans as the right way: the way to true liberty of the soul, mind, body, and spirit. Though history records many complicated religious shifts within early human cultures, this is how we came to have, as one example, the many gods of Egypt, Babylon, etc., most of which can be linked to some aspect of God's character or His control over His Creation.

The central point is that God was first, and every other god or religion was a pathetic imitation giving allowance for sin: The Doctrine of Original Revelation states that Adam had it right and everyone *after* Adam who developed pagan ideas from his stories and ran with them had it wrong. Obviously, if Adam got here first, then his testimony of who God is, what happened in Eden, and all other details passed down through generations—eventually reaching Noah, then Moses, then the Israelites, then the Jews, and so on until the authoritative canon of Scripture was established—are the first, and therefore original, spiritual truths drawn from God's revelation to man (and recorded in the Word).

But what happens when someone suggests that there was life on Earth *prior* to Adam, such as a pre-Adamic race? Does the Doctrine of Original Revelation go out the window? Can it no longer be trusted if someone *else* got here first?

Not at all. But in that case, we need to bring into view a different relationship that may even make more sense in the perspective of Original Revelation: God and *Lucifer*.

The Scriptures make it infinitely clear that way before Adam was formed from dust, the angels were observing God at work during this planet's Creation (this can be gleaned from a number of biblical passages, though Job 38:4–7 states it outright). Lucifer was an angel—a cherub, to be more specific—who rebelled against God and fell from Heaven to his kingdom, Earth. Before he fell, Lucifer would have had privileges similar to Adam's in the Garden, understanding the ways of God as he had communed with God in His very presence in Heaven. Since God's plan for mankind doesn't come into the biblical narrative until the re-creation, the "void" era belongs to Lucifer, the angels that fell with him, and whatever pre-Adamic beings may have walked Earth prior to Adam millions and billions of years ago, nearer to when science acknowledges humanity's "ancestors" to be (though that's not what I think they were).

Then God, having heaved His righteous judgment on the "void" planet, brought what He first created back to perfection as recorded in Genesis 1:3 and following, and Adam was the pinnacle of that Creation, as well as the initial human recipient of the divine revelation.

Again, so readers don't misunderstand: If beings of some kind were living on Earth before Adam, they would have been under Lucifer's influence. Their religions would have ignited a worldwide catastrophe of satanic implications, evidences of which were possibly preserved in some or all of the sites we looked at in the last chapter. (However, there are Gap theorists who do believe that there was a pre-Adamic, humanlike creation *made by God* [but not necessarily in His image] who joined Lucifer in his fall and were then destroyed in the chaos battle between God and the fallen beings. This theory acknowledges that Noah's Flood was a repeat case of God's judgment, and that it will happen again to those who join Lucifer following the Great Tribulation, and yet again during the thousand-year Millennial Reign of Christ. I find this theory possible, but unlikely, due to the explicit and special nature of God's salvific plan for humanity.)

If this *is* possible, then the Doctrine of *Original* Revelation still stands—God imparting Adam knowledge as they walked together in the beginning and eventually becoming what we know of the Word. Lucifer lying to a *lot* of people in history doesn't change that.

Regardless of what Lucifer knew of God before he fell to Earth, we know he has been mimicking God any way he can in an attempt to deceive, warp, and destroy what God had made, throughout the "void" era, into the Garden where a "serpent" was waiting to deceive Adam and Eve.

Either way, I will repeat, and build on, something I said just paragraphs ago: The very first, and therefore *original*, revelation of all things spiritual came from God and was carried by His Spirit onto the pages we now know as the Bible…which can be trusted. (As many Bible readers are aware, it will always be Lucifer's grandest trick to make humankind believe that *his* ways are the true ways and God is a capricious and overbearing rule-maker. He brought this trick into the Garden of Eden and that's what heavily contributed to the separation between God and man. Jesus reversed and repaired this horrendous mistake. In the end, through the satanic seed of the serpent, Antichrist, Satan will once again claim to be the True God [2 Thessalonians 2:4]. We must always trust the Word that God, Himself, wrote [2 Timothy 3:16; 2 Peter 1:20–21; 1 Corinthians 2:4–16].)

Now let's dig in…

"Without Form, and Void": Era of the Fossils

"And the earth was without form, and void; and darkness was upon the face of the deep. And the Spirit of God moved upon the face of the waters" (Genesis 1:2). The words "without form, and void" come from the rhyming Hebrew words *tohu* and *bohu*. Because these are in immediate proximity and appear to be somewhat synonymous (in both English and Hebrew), we'll look at them together to see what they are truly describing. (Note that in all cases but one [these the endnotes], italics were in the original sources.)

Although "without form" isn't an inaccurate or irresponsible translation of *tohu*, we are so far removed from the original implications of this word to the original Jewish readers that we don't get the full picture of what an Earth "without form" would have meant at the time. The first readers of Moses' day would have gotten it, though.

The first source I'd like us to consider is *The Abridged Brown-Driver-Briggs Hebrew-English Lexicon of the Old Testament: From A Hebrew and English Lexicon of the Old Testament by Francis Brown, S.R. Driver and Charles Briggs, Based on the Lexicon of Wilhelm Gesenius*. As the (rather long) title implies, this lexicon wasn't just a compilation of some guy's opinion; it was the result of years and years of reflection, study, deep digging, and peer review by some of the most prolific Hebrew linguists in history who have made it their lifelong duty to dissect the etymology of terms and bring back a full understanding of what the writers of the Bible intended to communicate. The most basic meaning of *tohu*, these masters say, is "formlessness, confusion, unreality, [and] emptiness—1. *formlessness*, of primaeval earth, of land reduced to primaeval chaos [as in Isaiah 24:10; 34:11; 45:18]…*nothingness, empty space*; of empty, trackless *waste* [as in Deuteronomy 32:10; Job 6:18]."[181]

Land "reduced to" a chaotic state—*not* land "formed that way in the beginning."

The second definition of the same word relates to its figurative use: as a reference to something "*empty, unreal*, as idols (coll. [collective] of idolmakers), groundless arguments or considerations, moral unreality or falsehood; = *a thing of nought, worthlessness*; as adv. [adverb] acc. [accusative] I said not…seek me *emptily, to no purpose*."[182]

So far, "without form" means far more than just a harmlessly "formless" area God had not yet perfected because it was still being worked on. It means something that had been "reduced to chaos and trackless waste."

Pay attention to this part, because this is a key to opening the door of my later conclusions: *In order for the planet to have been "reduced to" anything, it had to have been something else before.*

The phrasal verb "reduce to," according to the *Cambridge Dictionary*, when referring to an object (and not a person), means "to cause something, especially a large structure, to be destroyed and broken into pieces." Like Earth, perhaps? The example they give of this is: "Allied bombing reduced the city to ruins/rubble."[183] Interesting. So, if the grammarians behind our choice Hebrew lexicon say the chief definition of *tohu* relates in any way to the English words "reduced to," and all that phrase implies, then we have one source (so far) supporting the idea that, after God created Earth, something happened to the planet's surface that *caused it to become* "chaos" and/or "waste." Again, "without form" is not inaccurate, but it doesn't convey the whole picture.

As for the figurative meaning of *tohu*, it's eminently clear that the term was used at this time to denote idolatrous, depraved immorality that amounts to "worthlessness" and/or "falsehood" in the eyes of God.

But is the figurative meaning of a word even relevant in this discussion regarding a "literal" act of God?

To those who understand how a root word takes on deviations throughout time and history—to those who comprehend how etymology works—yes, it's relevant. Over time, words take on figurative (figure of speech, often metaphorical) applications associated with the nuances of meaning they gained in their earlier use. One example of this idea in English would be the word "allergy." We know this *literally* refers to the human body's adverse immune response to a food or other substance (like pollen) that a person's DNA is hypersensitive to. Yet, it is common to hear this word used figuratively in our culture to represent a feeling of extreme dislike or aversion to someone or something: "Don't let Sarah's reaction to this conversation bother you. She's allergic to politics." If those who first heard the word *tohu* knew it meant a chaotic formlessness that had come from something evil, it's not hard to see how the figurative application would link to idolatry, worthlessness, or deceit, etc. At some point in the development of Hebraic figures of speech, *tohu* became so associated with the idea of malevolence and chaos (wonder where they got that idea?— could it have been from the "void" era?) that they began using the word to identify or describe other people, places, or things they believed had an innate element of iniquity. As the world during the "void" is considered by a growing number of scholars to be a time when evil was rampant upon our planet's surface, this is telling.

Flipping to the *Brown-Driver-Briggs* lexicon's page on *bohu* ("void"), the central definition for Genesis 1:2 is: "emptiness [of] primaeval earth; of earth under judgment." These scholars mention the appearance of *bohu* in Isaiah 34:11, which alludes to "the line of wasteness and the stones of emptiness." These "stones," as conjoined with *bohu*, are "not as usual for building, but [as a reference to] destroying walls."[184] In other words, there is an inherent component of devastation behind *bohu*.

Thus far, still having only visited a single expert source on the topic, *tohu* and *bohu* transparently speak of a destructive evil that reduced Earth to chaos and brought the planet "under judgment"—*all* of this well before God ever said anything about Earth being "good." (Remember, we're only on verse 2 of Genesis.)

Then why aren't Bible teachers talking about this? Why does my pastor skip straight past this? How come I never learned about this in seminary?

Well, I have a few theories on this.

First, this topic is not an essential doctrine for salvation, and before science started producing discoveries that "prove the Bible wrong" today (or so they think), scholars didn't see this as the utmost priority as long as the dying world needed a Savior. (However, because the dying world *still* needs a Savior in an era when science is the reason some people may not accept Christ—a true concern today that will only become more alarming in years to come—we are starting to see a growing number of scholars prioritize this subject. I hope we're not too late to skyrocket this truth to the forefront! It's still a tedious topic in the opinion of many well-intended Christians, unfortunately. It's like they don't see all the precious souls out there who are struggling to believe in a God whose existence and activities "science has refuted." And when scholars do step up to gently defend the faith in light of science and what the Hebrew honestly communicates about Earth's age, they receive a tremendous amount of backlash for trying to force the Bible to agree with science *when it already does.* It's that age-old, inaccurate concept that science is opposed to, or separate from, God, and interpreting the Bible in light of it is heresy. But that will never be the case for "true science" as I have defined it in this book [i.e., what God *actually* did and what is *actually* around us—not merely what mankind observes in finite fields of study]. Even I, earlier in this very book, made sure to note that the Bible is not a science manual. But studying science and the Scriptures side by side is, as I also said, nothing less than a form of worship if it leads to praising God for His Creation. I pray we can more and more clearly see that God is the Master Scientist and, therefore, bringing the study of His Word into harmony with His Creation *is* an act of worship. But I digress...)

Second, when Ussher Chronology became the leading influence on determining Earth's age, the true meaning of Hebrew words was back-burnered and considered largely inconsequential since most of the Church had adopted Young Earth interpretation.

Third, English translations around Ussher's time rendered *tohu* and *bohu* "without form, and void," which appear synonymous to "as yet incomplete" instead of "became destroyed."

And fourth, only a measly 13 percent of professing Christians in the West—the part of the world where most of our theological studies come from—read the Bible regularly,[185] meaning that the vast majority of Christians are waiting for someone else to figure it out and tell them what it means, so the scholarly pool is overwhelmed.

However, though it's been a tragically marginalized teaching, this interpretation of Genesis 1:2 is nothing new. It wasn't thought up yesterday; it has been known by Christian scholars, Jewish sages, Hebrew linguists, historians, and even the first readers of Moses' writings since literally the beginning of (human) time. (By no means am I suggesting that this is the *only* way Genesis 1:2 can be interpreted and that anyone who doesn't agree is less educated or uninformed. I simply hope to leave you with the true impression that this is as valid an interpretation of this verse as any other, and when you see how this theory compares with other Scripture passages, you may, like me, believe it's the likeliest to be true.)

But, of course, I don't want you to take the word of just one source.

In the *Dictionary of Biblical Languages with Semantic Domains: Hebrew (Old Testament)*, we see how *tohu* is used throughout Scripture, and the references are revealing (pay special attention to the cross-references from Jeremiah and Isaiah, as some will be crucial in our later discussion):

> **formlessness**, emptiness, i.e., a state of empty space and so noth-ingness, so not having a shape, implied to be a state prior to order and form (Ge 1:2; Job 26:7; Isa 45:18; Jer 4:23+)... **wasteland**, i.e., what is barren and void of use, as tracts of unpopulated land (Dt 32:10; Job 6:18; 12:24; Ps 107:40+)... **idol**, i.e., an object which are worshiped, with a special focus on the uselessness and worthlessness of the fashioned object (1Sa 12:21+)... **ruination**,

destruction, i.e., what has been destroyed and in chaos and confusion (Isa 24:10; 34:11+).[186]

Now, of course, not all of these definitions are linked to the context of Genesis 1:2 (as the excerpt shows), but they still help us drill into the general spirit of the word *tohu* ("without form"). As for *bohu* ("void"), this source offers the following meaning:

> **emptiness**, the void, i.e., an emptiness that shows lack of order (Ge 1:2; Jer 4:23+)... note: some interp[ret] this as *a void from a prior creation*... [or] total chaos, i.e., a physical state of total lack of order (Ge 1:2; Jer 4:23+).[187]

James Strong—the scholar most known for the ever-popular *Strong's Concordance*—provides a sharp look at *tohu* in his *Concise Dictionary of the Words in the Greek Testament and The Hebrew Bible*, saying it means "to lie *waste*; a *desolation* (of surface),"[188] while *bohu* is "an unused root (mean. to *be empty*); a *vacuity* [a "nothingness"], i.e....an undistinguishable *ruin*."[189] Then there's the *Gesenius' Hebrew-Chaldee Lexicon*, which is acknowledged by Logos Bible Software to have been "among the most trusted and definitive resources for students of Hebrew for over a hundred years."[190] In this source, German Bible professor William Gesenius sees *tohu* as "*that which is wasted, laid waste*, Genesis 1:2"[191] and *bohu* simply as "*emptiness, voidness*."[192]

The question we must ask at this point is: Would God, Himself, create something so associated in the language of His people (the Jews and their Hebrew) with destruction, waste, desolation, chaos, confusion, worthlessness, and moral depravity?

The answer is, of course, an emphatic and resounding "no." Especially when we consider that this same language elsewhere in the Old Testament says God's works are "perfect" (Deuteronomy 32:4) and "glorious" (Psalm 111:3), to name only two of countless other biblical references that acknowledge His handiwork to be exactly what He calls it throughout Genesis after He restored it: "good." And in 1 Corinthians 14:33, we specifically read that God is *not* the "author of confusion," meaning He wouldn't have purposefully designed a planet *tohu/bohu*. But if God is not personally accountable for this state of Earth—if He did not set out to make a paradise for His creatures that would ever be described in this way as so many other Old Testament verses show—then we're left to fill in the blanks as to what may have occurred between "void" and "good" Earth, and what being(s) took part in that destructive event.

Lexicons are useful for isolating words for deep studies, especially when there is an interpretational discrepancy. But obviously, taking a word or two out of the verse that surrounds it can result in abandoning its first context, which is an interpretational fallacy none of us should want to be guilty of. Therefore, in addition to looking at these two words in lexicons, let's look at what commentaries have to say about what these words are describing in *the whole verse*.

I will start with one of my all-time favorite commentary teams: Robert Jamieson, Andrew Robert Fausset, and David Brown. For many students of God's Word, these men are already familiar, household names. It's difficult to go very far in the exegesis of Scripture without running into their work. (And that's for good reason: Jamieson was awarded his doctorate of divinity by Glasgow University, Scotland, in 1848, and went on to become moderator of the General Assembly of the Church of Scotland [the highest leadership position in the Scottish Church] by 1872. Fausset, after receiving a mountain of prestigious scholarships and awards for excellence in biblical studies, was also awarded his doctorate in divinity from Trinity College in Dublin in 1886, maintaining his position as rector of St. Cuthbert's Church in York, England, from 1859 to the day he died in 1910. Brown's doctorate of divinity was awarded in 1821 from Scotland's Aberdeen University, where Brown chose to stay for a length of time as a professor of theology. All three of these men specialized in Hebrew, Greek, and biblical history, and their expertise in the linguistic and historical implications of Scripture has been celebrated and their writings analyzed for more than a 150 years by top scholars all over the globe.)

This trio first penned the *Commentary Critical and Explanatory on the Whole Bible* (often abbreviated as *Jamieson-Fausset-Brown*, or *JFB*) in

1871, and it has produced many derived works, including abridgements, volumes, and appraisals by later scholars. Of *tohu* and *bohu* in Genesis 1:2, they conclude: "This globe, at some undescribed period, having been convulsed and broken up, was a dark and watery waste for ages perhaps, till out of this chaotic state, the present fabric of the world was made [by God] to arise."[193]

They aren't the only team of scholars to arrive at this reasoning.

Although Allen P. Ross of *The Bible Knowledge Commentary* ultimately comes to a different conclusion than I do about what might have occurred between "void" and "good" Earth, he does admit that the Hebrew terms *tohu* and *bohu* describe the early planet as "a chaos of wasteness, emptiness, and darkness." He immediately goes on to say: "Such conditions would not result from God's creative work (*bara*); rather, in the Bible they are symptomatic of sin and are coordinate with judgment."[194] Cyrus Ingerson Scofield of the best-selling, highly acclaimed, and fundamentalist *Scofield Reference Bible* takes Jeremiah and Isaiah into account to further deconstruct this "without form, and void" conundrum. His study notes of Genesis 1:2 opens by cross-referencing Jeremiah 4:23–26 and Isaiah 24:1 and 45:18, which, he says, "clearly indicate that the earth had undergone a cataclysmic change as the result of a divine judgment. The face of the earth bears everywhere the marks of such a catastrophe."[195] And in truncated, staccato form, Ethelbert, W. Bullinger—of *The Companion Bible: Being the Authorized Version of 1611 with the Structures and Notes, Critical, Explanatory and Suggestive and with 198 Appendixes*—looks at more than just *tohu* and *bohu*. He zeroes in on what happens just before these terms to when Genesis 1:2 states Earth "was" (Hebrew *haya*) *tohu* and *bohu*, and compares what "was" means in relation to *tohu* and *bohu* throughout the rest of Scripture:

> **was** = *became.* See Gen. 2:7; 4:3; 9:15; 19:26; Ex. 32:1; Deut.
> 27:9; 2 Sam. 7:24, &c. Also rendered *came to pass*, Gen. 4:14;
> 22:1; 23:1; 27:1; Josh. 4:1; 5:1; 1 Kings 13:32; Isa. 14:24, &c....
> Hence, Ex. 3:1, kept = *became* keeper, quit = *become* men, &c.
> [The bottom line here is that "was" is better rendered "became."]

without form = *waste.* Heb. *tohu va bohu.…* Not created *tohu* (Isa. 45:18), but became *tohu* (Gen. 1:2; 2 Pet. 3:5, 6). "An enemy hath done this" (Matt. 13:25, 28, 39. Cp. 1 Cor. 14:33).[196]

Wait a second…what was that? The Hebrew allows "the earth became" instead of "the earth was"?

Actually, yes.

The Hebrew word *haya* often conveys "became" over its "was" alternative; it's surprising how many English Bibles prefer "was" in this location, when it's clear that God would not have created an Earth that "was" a place of pure chaos. Recall that the diacritical marks in Hebrew didn't exist at the time Genesis was written, so we cannot rely on any help in that area. If we take the base root word back to its foundational concept, as *The Abridged Brown-Driver-Briggs Hebrew-English Lexicon* has done, we see the following:

> [*haya*] vb [verb]. **fall out, come to pass, become, be** — Qal I. 1. **a.** *fall out, happen.* **b.** *occur, take place, come about, come to pass.* 2. esp. & very oft., *come about, come to pass* sq. substantive (subj.) cl. almost alw. + modifying (usu. temporal) cl. or phr.: **a.** (1)…*and it came to pass* that[197]

It isn't that *haya* must mean "become"/"became"; it's it *can* mean "become"/"became," and once we look at all the evidence—especially considering God's nature, character, and creative power throughout the rest of the Creation epic—that's the more reasonable interpretation of the word.

Consider this example from Genesis 19:26: "But his [Lot's] wife looked back from behind him, and she became [*haya*] a pillar of salt."

The respected Blue Letter Bible Online—well known for its "Outline of Biblical Usage" section that, as the title implies, gives a general understanding of how certain words are used in the Bible—shows that "become"/"became" is actually the first definition of *haya*: "Outline of Biblical Usage: I. to be, become, come to pass, exist, happen, fall out."[198]

Just under that, the *Brown-Driver-Briggs Lexicon* agrees: "fall out, come to pass, become, be."[199] In Bullinger's aforementioned treatment of "without form," the last thing he does before moving on to another word is link the concept of "became" to the working of an enemy: "'An enemy hath done this' (Matt. 13:25, 28, 39. Cp. 1 Cor. 14:33)."[200]

An "enemy," huh? That's a fascinating cross-reference for this study, indeed. It implies that when Earth "became" (or "was reduced to") this chaotic state, it was because of the workings of an enemy of God.

But just before Bullinger says this, he states something quite telling about what else was on Earth in those days as a result of this enemy. The first words of the entire *Companion Bible* work—in relation to Genesis 1:1 and the ancient state of our planet—are: "1: 'The world that then was' (2 Pet. 3:5, 6).... Creation in eternity past, to which all Fossils and 'Remains' belong."[201] To restructure Bullinger's point in an order I find easier to follow: The "fossils" and "remains" of a civilization—including bones of humanity's common ancestor (to use the Darwinian turn of phrase) and other animals (which have now become extinct, as we will address in the following pages)—Bullinger says, "belong" to a "world that then was." This quote from 2 Peter 3:5–6 is often assumed to be a reference to the Flood of Noah's day, but I'm not surprised to see some scholars take it farther back and accept it as a reference to pre-Adamic times.

First, consider Peter's words as they appear in English, and note the italics I've added: "For this they willingly are ignorant of, that by the word of God the *heavens were of old*, and *the earth* standing *out of the water and in the water*. Whereby *the world that then was*, being overflowed with water, *perished*." (The use of both "out of water" and "in the water" is confusing, and this description has often been a matter of much debate. After consulting many sources, I found this can be interpreted one of three ways: 1) Earth was made out of water and was also covered with it entirely at this time; 2) Earth had two sources of water, the heavens [rain] and the springs that came up from within Earth in Genesis 2:6; or 3) vast regions of land appeared and came up from of the water on the third day of Creation, as Genesis 1:9–10 describes. Our study of this passage doesn't rely on a solid solution to this debate, as none of these interpretations are critical to our emphasis on a "perished" Earth.) Not wishing to be sensational, I cannot guarantee that this is a reference to the "void," as Peter could very well be viewing the Flood event. However, in the previous chapter, Peter talks about the fallen angels under Lucifer's leadership *and* the Flood together in a single sentence, though they are two separate events:

> God spared not the angels that sinned, but cast them down to hell, and delivered them into chains of darkness, to be reserved unto judgment; And spared not the old world, but saved Noah the eighth person, a preacher of righteousness, bringing in the flood upon the world of the ungodly. (2 Peter 2:4–5)

Similar to the prophets' words (tackled next), Peter is clearly amplifying a link between the day the "angels...sinned" and "the flood upon the world" in a dualistic linguistic pattern: They are two different things, but he sees them sharing the element of God's judgment. So, when we happen upon his words in 2 Peter 3:5–6, we cannot insist he's referring *only* to the Flood. The late Marvin Richardson Vincent—New Testament word-study expert, professor of New Testament exegesis and criticism at Union Theological Seminary in New York City, and author of the *Word Studies* series—acknowledges Peter's mention of "the world that then was... perished" could be a "reference to the original liquid condition of the earth—*without form and void*."[202] Since Genesis 1:2 also describes a world that is covered with liquid (water), it appears to fit. Thus, the "void" era shows that, obviously following God's corrective response to what Earth had "become," the planet was covered in water...from time immemorial *before* Adam was ever formed.

What's interesting about Peter's glance into the past here is that he says the "world...perished." The Greek for "perished" is *apollymi*, which means "destroyed." This is derivative of Apollyon ("destroyer") who comes up out of the bottomless pit to incarnate within Antichrist, son of Satan, perhaps showing another connection to the reptilian spirit linked with chaos, destruction, and the usurpation of God. Though the word for "world" is *kosmos* (from which we derive our English "cosmos"—i.e., the universe), the immediate context dismisses the idea that he's referring to all of space. However, the dramatic phrase expresses an emphasis on the widespread destruction of this watery judgment of God. When the Flood occurred in Noah's day, there is no doubt it had a permanent effect upon Earth: every living thing (except the inhabitants of the ark) died. Absolutely, that can be considered a "perished world." What once was a place of life was rendered a planet-wide grave. However, scholars who have counted the number of days mentioned in the Flood narrative (Genesis 6–8) have calculated that 370 days elapsed between the beginning of the rain and Noah's departure from the ark. That's only five days over the duration of a year. Then, the vessel's inhabitants (both human and animal) went forth into the devastated planet, multiplied, and repopulated. In other words: Yes, the "world" was destroyed, but only a year later, it was in a state of reparation. Genesis 1:2, if any variation of the Gap theory is correct, represents a state of God's wrath, followed by a watery-grave destruction for an unknown time, possibly millions or billions of years.

Perhaps Peter, while recalling the "heavens" that were "of old" (Greek *ekpalai*, "of a long time [ago]"; i.e., an ancient subject), had not the Flood in mind, but the watery, "without form, and void" Earth that: 1) science has deemed to be millions/billions of years old; and 2) God brought judgment down upon in pre-Adamic times. His choice words—"the world… perished"—appears to describe such a thing. That Bullinger (and others) connect this era to fossils and remains of Earth's earliest and most ancient inhabitants is a possible arrow likewise pointing to pre-Adamic species/ races.

With this in mind, let's look at what else Jamison, Fausset, and Brown had to say about not only *tohu* and *bohu* in Genesis, but about their relation to Isaiah, Jeremiah, and the issue we just raised in relation to "was." They say *tohu* and *bohu*, "in passages where they occur conjointly (Isa. 34:11, and Jer. 4:23 [in context of the Babylonian exile])" are:

> …used to describe the desolations which were to overspread Idumea and Palestine respectively, and by which those countries would be reduced from the settled and flourishing condition which they

exhibited at the time of the predictions into universal disorder and ruin. The analogous use [in Genesis 1:2], therefore, of this rare and peculiar phraseology in the verse before us may imply…that the world, which had formerly been a scene of material beauty and order, was by some great convulsion plunged into a state of chaos or widespread disorder and desolation. Hence some eminent critics, who take this view, render the clause thus:—"But (or afterwards) the earth *became* waste and desolate."… Dr. M'Caul has shown that the verb [*haya*] "was," is, in some twenty places in this chapter, used as equivalent to "became."[203]

Did you happen to catch the bottom line? "Eminent critics" (renowned, important, prominent, distinguished men, celebrated in the scholarly world for their skills in exegesis) render Genesis 1:2 to say: "But (or afterwards [after a yet-undisclosed event]) the earth became waste and desolate."

Why do they start the verse with "But" instead of "And"?

Well, unlike in English, the Hebrew conjunction—a single character that looks like a shepherd's hook—cannot stand alone as a word. In our language, we have "and" *and* "but," each easily standing alone and with certain distinctions. In Hebrew, this tiny word must be joined like a prefix to another word for its meaning to be identified—and it can mean either "and" or "but" based on the context. In this case, the context could go either way, so we can only assume which was intended. Should it be a conjunctive conjunction that joins two separate ideas/words/statements ("and") or a contrastive conjunction that contrasts two separate ideas/words/statements ("but")? We don't know, but when the "void" Earth interpretation is applied, the contrastive conjunction fits and is a perfectly permissible interpretation. (We do know this single-character prefix is elsewhere translated "but," like in Genesis 6:8: "But Noah found grace in the eyes of the Lord.") If this is the correct approach, the "but" at the start of Genesis 1:2 indicates contrast between the original planetary state in verse 1 to its later "without form, and void" condition.

After looking at a few of hundreds of commentaries that point to the same conclusion, I'll ask the question of the day once more: Would God, in His infinite creative ability and scientific mastery, ever make a planet of chaos on purpose?

Here are a couple more questions to ponder: Would He do so on accident? Does the Master of the universe not think ahead? Does He accidentally create things that weren't good, as He originally intended, so He has to fix His own flubs? Couldn't He have made a planet beautifully perfect the first time around? Did He have to fix all of creation, starting in verse 3, when He looked at his handiwork and realized in hindsight that it was a desolate place unworthy of His best? Is He, or isn't He as powerful as the *entire Word of God* says He is?

If *tohu* and *bohu* mean what these Hebrew linguistics experts say, then I have a hard time believing God is the reason behind the "void" Earth.

If I wanted to belabor the point, I could list another thirty examples from trusted resources…but instead, I find myself wishing there was just one verse somewhere in the sixty-six books of the scriptural canon that would clarify all of this so we wouldn't have to rely on interpretations.

Oh…

Hang on a sec…

Found one.

There *is* a verse that brings direct clarity to the subject!

This evidence I've pointed to that is heavily quoted by Old Earth scholars is not even the most important factor in all of this. Over in Isaiah 45:18, we're expressly told that God did *not* create Earth this way: "God himself that formed the earth and made it; he hath established it, he created it not in vain, he formed it to be inhabited: I am the Lord; and there is none else."

In English, this sounds like it's describing the concept that God's plans were not fruitless—that the Almighty (eventually) carried out Creation successfully and powerfully, establishing it as a place where His people would inhabit it happily—but once we bring the original language of Hebrew into the mix, something suddenly pops. The English word "vain" here is from the Hebrew *tohu*. This verse literally says that "God himself formed the earth…[and] created it *not* in *tohu*."

The Bible says God did not create Earth "without form." In fact, in

Psalm 104:30, we read of God: "Thou sendest forth thy spirit, they are created: and thou renewest the face of the earth."

God "renewed the face of Earth"! In other words, the "surface" ("face") of Earth was restored after something else had happened to it.

English theologian George Hawkins Pember was evidently riled by the translator's decision to render *tohu* "in vain" in this location, believing that conclusion could have only been born from inadequate cross-referencing to the point of neglect in the translational process:

> We have a direct and positive assertion to that effect in the forty-fifth chapter of Isaiah: for we are there told that God did not create the earth a *tohu*. This word, therefore, whatever meaning be assigned to it, cannot at least be descriptive of the earliest condition of earth. But our translators have obscured the fact by rendering *tohu* "in vain": they can hardly have compared the passages in which it occurs, or they would surely have seen the propriety of translating it in Isaiah's manifest reference to creation by the same word as in Genesis.[204]

Many choose to see this verse in Isaiah with an emphasis on God's *intention* ("he formed it to [eventually] be inhabited"), meaning that He did, in fact, create the Earth "void," but He mended that state right away as it was mid-Creation (it was "void," but He just wasn't finished yet), and we can see the fruits of His handiwork from "Let there be light" forward. Many ministers and teachers consider this a valid approach to this verse; however, with 100 percent respect to my Christian fellows, that's not what the verse *says*. If we were to study all hard-to-understand verses in light of what we think is implied instead of what is *said*, the Bible would very quickly become a subjective experience instead of an authoritative directive from God to humanity. In the direct language of this verse, we are told by God's prophet, Isaiah, that *it was not God* who should own the "without form" era or status of Earth. Yet Genesis 1:2 acknowledges that was the state of the planet at some time…which means someone or something else caused this cataclysmic condition.

When Eve fell into the trap of the serpent in the Garden of Eden, Gary Stearman of *Prophecy Watchers* observes, the spirit world around her was in a fallen state *already*.[205]

Who could have rendered Earth to such a condition?

It appears a few of the Lord's prophets—who personally experienced God-given visions that later became canonized as Scripture—had the answer.

The Obvious Perpetrator

In this section, we'll look at the "who" behind the "void" era. However, as obvious as his identity has probably been up to this point, the ultimate conclusion I've drawn about the fall of Lucifer is not one that's received much coverage in the scholarly world. That said, though the "who" is likely obvious to many, the answers to the "when," "how," and "what" questions are those that make this book differ from all others that I know of. Readers should not assume they know where all this is going just because the culprit behind much of this is being postured as Lucifer.

As in all my books, however, I never want to assume *all* readers know how I arrive at any conclusion, even if it's one Bible-reading folks often already know, like the "who" behind the "void." For this reason, I'll briefly explain how scholars conclude that Lucifer was the guilty party and Earth was his kingdom before I move on to look at the prophets' words about this being and details surrounding his fall. (I'm only partly covering Lucifer here as he relates to what the prophets saw. Later, in chapter 8, I'll return to the subject of the perpetrator and take it a bit deeper.)

Scripture makes it very clear that the central enemy of God is the "ruler of this world," as well as "the god of this age" (John 14:30; 2 Corinthians 4:4). He is the "prince of the power of the air," still "work[ing] in the sons of disobedience," who become "children of [God's] wrath" (Ephesians 2:2–3). In the account of Christ's temptation, we read that Lucifer (Satan) had authority over all the kingdoms upon Earth (Luke 4:5–6). This makes Earth Lucifer's past and current kingdom (at least from his fall forward; as we arrive at Ezekiel's words in the next few pages, you will see why I conclude that Earth was Lucifer's kingdom from the moment of his creation). He began as an "anointed cherub" who was "perfect in beauty"; covered in precious gemstones; residing "upon the mountain of God"; and "perfect in [his] ways from the day that [he] was created," until "iniquity was found" within him (Ezekiel 28:12–15). Then, he attempted to "exalt [his] throne above…God" (Isaiah 14:13), fell "like lightning from heaven" (Luke 10:18) taking a third of the heavenly angels with him (Revelation 12:3–4) whose "first estate" wasn't good enough for them and whose ultimate fate is thus "everlasting chains under darkness unto the judgment of the great day" (Jude 6). (The words "first estate," if it is a location, could mean either Heaven or Earth. Much of this depends on the interpreter's insistence that Earth had *already been* Lucifer's assigned domain from the beginning. If this planet was, in fact, his, then he and the angels left Earth to storm Heaven; if their first estate was Heaven, then their revolt against God was the event that led them to leaving their home to be bound upon Earth. However, there is yet a third possibility: "First estate" has been translated to suggest their "first position" or "first principality," as in not a location at all, but possibly a prestigious rank or status they held in the beginning. According to this interpretation, the angels' arrogance, following Lucifer's example, led to their goal of being promoted to a higher level of authority—a goal that they obviously did not achieve. The fact that the next words in Jude 6 regards them leaving their "own habitation" suggests that it is a location that Jude had in mind. Some help for this again comes from 2 Peter 2:4: "For if God spared not the angels that sinned, but cast them down to hell, and delivered them into chains of darkness, to be reserved unto judgment." The Greek word for "hell" here is *tartaroo*, which refers to the Greeks' infernal underworld, which was, in fact, a part of Earth in their mythology.)

In Isaiah 14:12, what we read in English about Lucifer being "cut down to the ground" (KJV) is too generic a reference to help us comprehend the full picture. However, "ground" is the Hebrew *eres*, meaning "earth," and, in joint context with other Scriptures (those just mentioned) identifying planet Earth as his domain, we can definitely know that Earth is Lucifer's "kingdom." (No scholars I know of have ever reached a conclusion other than that Earth is Lucifer's territory.)

Let's look at Lucifer through the eyes of the prophets.

Isaiah Knew Who the Culprit Was

First consider the context of the book of Isaiah. Judah, also referred to as the Southern Kingdom of Israel (within which was the great city of Jerusalem), had fallen into the hands of Babylon as a result of the Jewish-Babylonian War. King Nebuchadnezzar conquered Judah and exiled the Jews to Babylon, far away from their beloved, sacred home, and, as Bible-readers are aware, the Jews spent a long time dreaming about returning. Isaiah was a prophet alive at that time who saw the former abominable, meaningless sacrifices of the Jews in Jerusalem, as well as their deplorable pagan behavior against God, as the cause for being taken away from their home.

What does that have to do with the era of Earth between "void" and "good"?

If you immediately thought to ask this question, you may be missing a key link. The simple math Isaiah's words rest on is rendered thus: going against God + ignoring His laws and warnings = judgment upon the homeland and its occupants. As we've been talking about the "void" Earth being "under judgment," this prophetic word from Isaiah is relevant...especially when he turns his focus to a mysterious character whose role in the earliest ages of Earth led to massive, global destruction.

In Isaiah chapter 14, we run across a collection of verses that, at first (and in English), appear to be unrelated to the exile (or generally anything else in the surrounding text). In the KJV, Isaiah 14:12–15 reads:

How art thou fallen from heaven, O Lucifer, son of the morning! how art thou cut down to the ground, which didst weaken the nations! For thou hast said in thine heart, "I will ascend into heaven, I will exalt my throne above the stars of God: I will sit also upon the mount of the congregation, in the sides of the north: I will ascend above the heights of the clouds; I will be like the most High." Yet thou shalt be brought down to hell, to the sides of the pit.

Scholars are quick to point out that this passage is Isaiah's way of speaking to the Jews in exile about the spirit behind Nebuchadnezzar—the "bad guy" in this section of the Word—and the sentence he will eventually face for his arrogant stance against God's people (if he does not come to God and repent, obviously, which is a matter of debate because of his praise to God in Daniel 2 and 3 and the contrast of his words in 4:8: "Belteshazzar…my god"). As true as that is, however, that spirit behind Nebuchadnezzar did not originate with him or any other human king, but with a far more ancient enemy of God (Lucifer) who was alive and well at the time Earth was initially formed. By using the fall of Lucifer to describe the essence behind the Babylonian nature, Isaiah *is* talking about Nebuchadnezzar, but he is *also* talking about Lucifer, whose "spirit" or "self-idolizing power" has been active on Earth in the past and present, and will continue to be so into future end times. This is called a "dual prophecy," and it occurs often in the words of the prophets. The *JFB* commentary, in reference to this character portrayal in Isaiah 14, states:

> The fall of *Babylon* as a self-idolizing power, the type of *mystical Babylon* in the Apocalypse (Rev. 17:4, 5), before the providence of God, is described in language drawn from the fall of *Satan* [Lucifer] himself, the spirit that [first] energized the heathen world-power, and now energizes the apostate Church, and shall hereafter energize the last secular Antichrist.[206]

This Luciferian spirit may have led to an *imitational* fall of Judah to Babylon, but Isaiah is here clearly recalling the original fall of the entity known as Lucifer. Since a) Lucifer fell well before humans were created, b) his influence on the Earth continued through humanity (as seen in the narrative involving the serpent of Eden), and c) this was the true origin of all earthly sin from Adam forward: Lucifer's fall could very well be the catalyst for Earth becoming a *tohu/bohu* wasteland of chaos. The timing fits; the interpretation is admissible per both Genesis' and Isaiah's related passages.

But Isaiah wasn't the only one who knew who caused Earth's "void" era.

Ezekiel Knew Who the Culprit Was

In the same way Isaiah was recognizing Lucifer as the spirit behind Nebuchadnezzar, Ezekiel detects a Luciferian spirit behind the king of Tyre in Ezekiel 28:12–19. Ezekiel, like Isaiah, was speaking to Israel during the Babylonian exile. Tyre was a territory known for its greedy trades and never-ending line of exploitative merchants. Let's read those verses in their entirety before we pick them apart:

> Son of man, take up a lamentation upon the king of Tyrus, and say unto him, "Thus saith the Lord God; 'Thou sealest up the sum, full of wisdom, and perfect in beauty. Thou hast been in Eden the garden of God; every precious stone was thy covering, the sardius, topaz, and the diamond, the beryl, the onyx, and the jasper, the sapphire, the emerald, and the carbuncle, and gold: the workmanship of thy tabrets and of thy pipes was prepared in thee in the day that thou wast created. Thou art the anointed cherub that covereth; and I have set thee so: thou wast upon the holy mountain of God; thou hast walked up and down in the midst of the stones of fire. Thou wast perfect in thy ways from the day that thou wast created, till iniquity was found in thee. By the multitude of thy merchandise they have filled the midst of thee with violence, and thou hast sinned: therefore I will cast thee as profane out of the mountain of God: and I will destroy thee, O covering cherub, from the midst of the stones of fire. Thine heart was lifted up because of thy beauty, thou hast corrupted thy wisdom by reason of thy brightness: I will cast thee to the ground, I will lay thee before kings, that they may behold thee. Thou hast defiled thy sanctuaries by the multitude of thine iniquities, by the

iniquity of thy traffick; therefore will I bring forth a fire from the midst of thee, it shall devour thee, and I will bring thee to ashes upon the earth in the sight of all them that behold thee. All they that know thee among the people shall be astonished at thee: thou shalt be a terror, and never shalt thou be any more.'"

The historical king of Tyre was a real human being; however, things are spoken of in this passage that cannot apply to this ruler, proving once again that he is being compared to (some would say "possessed by") the spirit of Lucifer in Ezekiel's dual prophecy. For instance, we know the historical king of Tyre was never in the Garden of Eden; he wasn't "perfect" at any point in his life; he never resided on the holy mountain of God; and he is most certainly not "the anointed cherub that covereth." These attributes are well known references to Lucifer.

Cherubs—*cherubim* in Hebrew—are important to God and Israel's history. Thanks to the art of the Renaissance Period and stretching back to the days of the Byzantine Iconoclasm (an era when all religious artwork was destroyed and, when it became legalized again, depictions of Trinity Persons, saints, and angels became merged with Greco-Roman pantheonic imagery), the word "cherub" brings to mind a cute baby angel. But this could not be farther from the truth. Cherubim were fierce. Recall that, whenever an angel appears to a human throughout the narrative of Scripture, they most often look like grown men and are so frightening in appearance that they have to comfort the person they're appearing to with the words, "Fear not." From this, we gain a picture of a highly authoritative and powerful presence, one so intimidating that we must be told there is no reason to be afraid. Yet cherubim outranked angels, so we can only imagine that seeing one of those magnificent beings in person would probably inspire intense and reverent awe and fear surpassing that sparked by the appearance of any angel. The Old Testament shows that: Cherubim guarded the Garden of Eden after the Fall (Genesis 3:24); their images were embroidered into the veil of the Holy of Holies (Ezekiel 26:1, 31); their likenesses were crafted in gold atop the Mercy Seat of the Ark of the Covenant where God's presence came to speak to His people (Exodus 25:22; Numbers 7:89); they are the entities whom God, Himself, "dwells between" as He sits upon His throne (Isaiah 37:16; 2 Kings 19:15; Psalm 99:1; and others); and, thus, they are the top-ranking of all celestial beings God made.

Lucifer was the "anointed cherub that covereth," giving him the highest rank of all God's created beings. If "anointed" is to be taken literally (as most scholars suggest), then Lucifer had, at or near the time of his creation, ceremoniously received the anointing oil over the head that consecrates one to follow the Lord and lead others to do so, just as the kings of the Old Testament were anointed.[207] As a head cherub and all that implies, we can view Lucifer as the one most closely associated to the presence of God. He was the Lord's "right-hand king-servant," so to speak, and "kings" have "subjects" they rule over.

Lucifer was a king? Are you sure you're not taking this too far, Donna?

Not even a little bit. But let's not get ahead of ourselves. I want to stay focused on the vision of the prophets for now. Lucifer as king of a race of some form of pre-Adamic beings—and how that fits theologically, etymologically, and symbolically—will be addressed in the next two chapters.

As many scholars interpret from "tabret" (a tambourine or drum player) and "pipes" (a reference to the holes in flutes) in Ezekiel 28:13, Lucifer was made specifically to be a worship leader. (Recall that "Doorway of the Serpent"—aka Puerta de Hayu Marca—that "opens" to spiritual pilgrims in Peru? It is through humming or singing certain notes in a specific order that the entities behind the wall respond. It's not a leap to imagine that, when Lucifer fell, he perverted music as well. Might this also be at least a partial explanation for why so much of what the music industry is offering today—especially what's marketed to teens—is so blatantly wicked? Many scholars have argued in favor of that conclusion.) Before his fall, he was adorned in the precious gemstones reserved only for the breastplates of the high priests of the Temple (Exodus 28:17–20; Ezekiel 28:13). He was "perfect in beauty" (Ezekiel 28:12), meaning his appearance was aesthetically stunning; perhaps he was even the handsomest and most beautiful entity God ever made. This being was *very* close to God in the beginning, extremely influential, and everything we know of him (and of cherubim) positions him as a big man on the heavenly campus...

...until iniquity was found within him, and he was cast to the "ground" (*eres*; Earth; Ezekiel 28:17).

Yet, being cast to the ground does *not* mean Lucifer had never inhabited this planet before, as Ezekiel 28:13 states he "hast been" (past tense) in the Garden of Eden. More accurately, he was cast out of Heaven.

Lucifer's First Location and Final Destination

At this point, the object of our focus is on this fact: Because Isaiah 14:12–15 recounts the moment this very first sin occurred through Lucifer, we can dive into his words and get a unique view not only of the circumstances of Lucifer's wickedness, but the physical state of *his own kingdom, Earth*, when it became "without form, and void." Note the locational references in the following verses:

> How art thou fallen from heaven, O Lucifer, son of the morning! how art thou cut down to the ground, which didst weaken the nations! (Isaiah 14:12)

We've covered the fact that "ground" means Earth. This is further supported by Job 1:7: "And the Lord said unto Satan, 'Whence comest thou?' Then Satan answered the Lord, and said, 'From going to and fro in the earth, and from walking up and down in it.'" Here, in Isaiah's account of Lucifer's fall, we see the mighty cherub descending "from heaven," which is a downward motion—from God's presence amidst the other angels and celestial entities to a planet as his prison. However, in Ezekiel 28, we read that Lucifer was present in Eden even before his fall, suggesting that he was already on Earth at some point and, as countless scholars believe, Earth was supposed to have been his special dwelling place from the very beginning. Therefore, we cannot assume Lucifer's fall from Heaven was his first visit to our planet. Likewise, after his pride led him to turn his back on God, he is still seen in cameo appearances in the heavenlies as an accuser of human men (Job 1:6–12; Zechariah

3:1–2). Therefore, we likewise cannot assume that his fall locked him out of Heaven permanently (although will be his ultimate fate as we read in the book of Revelation). What we *can* make of this is that Earth may have been given to Lucifer as a kingdom before his fall, but his wickedness limited his occupancy in Heaven to a prosecutor-visitor only, in the Court of God. He was no longer welcome in the heavenlies to accompany fellow worshipers of God and participate in the joys of God's presence and love. Earth—despite the occasional return to Heaven to point an accusatory finger at humans—became his territory, and the result of that was a weakening of the nations of Earth.

This also opens up the possibility that there were nations on the Earth before Lucifer's fall...*if* there is more to this reference than Babylon and Nebuchadnezzar, etc. Could this be an allusion to the idea that there was some pre-Adamic race inhabiting our planet before Adam was created? If not, what "nations" were weakened on the surface of our planet at that time?

> For thou [Lucifer] hast said in thine heart, "I will ascend into heaven, I will exalt my throne above the stars of God: I will sit also upon the mount of the congregation, in the sides of the north." (Isaiah 14:13)

At the time of Lucifer's fall, he fantasized about an ascension (upward motion) back into heaven, where he will take over God's rule and establish his throne higher than that of God. Again, locationally, this is most logically Earth. (Scholars don't all agree about what is meant by the "mount of the congregation." Because Isaiah 14:12–15 is a dual passage, covering both Lucifer's fall and the kingdom of Babylon, interpretations range anywhere from it being a reference to Zion [literally or figuratively], to Mt. Hermon [the landing mountain for the fallen angels, according to Enoch], to the meeting place of God and His angels [supported by a deep interpretational dig into 2 Corinthians 2:12 and Nehemiah 9:6 that some scholars show to mean various "layers" of Heaven—Lucifer hoped to take over the highest layer], and beyond. A "meeting place" where God would conduct business with His angels or cherubim makes the most sense in light of our lead cherub, Lucifer.)

I will ascend above the heights of the clouds; I will be like the most High. (Isaiah 14:14)

Again, this verse shows that Lucifer, after his fall, was fantasizing about ascending to someplace *above clouds*; i.e., a planet-like Earth with clouds in its atmosphere. It also notes the reason for his descent in the first place: because he aspired to be like (or more than) God. This is a well-known characterization of Lucifer, but it is also crucially important in the "void" era, as it transparently shows Lucifer's grandest dream and goal of being powerful enough to carry out the same acts as God: If Lucifer could *truly* be like the Most High, then he would be able to create species of life on Earth, right? Yet, without the real power of God, those creations would be abominations. We see this kind of perverted creative power in Genesis 6:4.

At the time of Adam, Lucifer the cherub had *long since* fallen already, though he kept Earth as his kingdom. When the Earth was "without form, and void," Lucifer was still bound to the limitations of this planet, and we see the serpent (Hebrew *nachash*, which doesn't mean "snake," as we will tackle in the following pages) in Eden, alive and well, after the formation of Adam from dust. Ezekiel specifically says he was "in Eden, the garden of God" (28:13). He is still present on this planet, working in the "sons of disobedience" (Ephesians 2:2–3). Evidently, he has always been here, and this place has always been his home—before, during, and after the chaos state of Earth's earliest ages. Nobody knows how long that state endured, but there is no doubt in my mind that it could be the millions or billions of years science decrees, while "nations" were being "weakened" through Lucifer's reign until the day God re-created it all...approximately six thousand years ago, just like Young Earthers' evidence has shown.

Chapter 7

The State of the "Void"

NOT SURPRISINGLY, the prophets aren't quite finished weighing in on this era of Earth. Primarily, we gain insight on the conditions of our planet from Isaiah and Jeremiah.

However, to more thoroughly understand some of their visions, we'll now briefly examine one event straight from the biblical narrative so we have something against which to compare the "void" era.

Giants' Bones in Native American Burial Mounds

In the second chapter of this book, we compared the weight of Ussher Chronology to that of the Powell Doctrine to show how influential one man's word can be to the society of his day. However, I intentionally left out the findings of the Smithsonian Institution until this point, as these undated bones may link to the "void" era. (They may also link to the giants of Noah's day.) Let's consider the bones of giants from my previous *Cloudeaters* research.

Well before Powell's *Limitations* document (the Powell Doctrine), the world, including the Smithsonian, was aware of bizarre sites and objects on Earth's surface. Not limited to bones, these also included strange astronomical and astrological building patterns surrounding ancient structures and monolithic edifices such as those in Baalbek, as well as enormous

267

tools, strange drawings, and prevailing legend of primitive cultures around the globe. The Smithsonian was not always involved in every discovery reported, which is why the public doesn't have to search far into archives of obscurity or conspiracy to find abundant visual evidence that *something* walked the earth in the old days we can't explain away, despite the Smithsonian's attempts to squash them into obscurity.

Note that many of the following accounts refer to skeletons that measure more than seven feet tall (although some are far taller). André René Roussimoff (popularly known as "André the Giant") was seven feet, four inches tall, and Robert Pershing Wadlow (the "Giant of Illinois") stood eight feet, eleven inches. (Tom Horn's grandfather had gigantism and stood right at seven feet tall.) So, we do know that through a rare malfunction in the human growth hormone, a regular human can grow extremely tall. However, before we can consider that as proof that all of the giant bones were simply cases of growth-hormone glitches, remember that many of these discoveries involve mounds that hold many giants all in one place; further, some of the skeletons have six fingers and toes on each hand and foot, as well as two rows of teeth. If this was an issue of rare biological conditions, we wouldn't discover huge groupings of these specimens in one mound.

In 1882, the same year as Powell's published report, Powell appointed Cyrus Thomas to supervise the Division of Mound Exploration. Thomas was originally more than open-minded about the legends regarding an ancient and lost race of giants, as he had paid close attention to the reports concerning gigantic human skeletons unearthed in and around enormous structures involving complex mathematics and astronomical alignment. But because he didn't go around advertising his theories, Powell may not have known Thomas was progressive in this "mythological" area when he chose him to oversee the mysterious burial mounds. Thus, Thomas would—at least initially—lead teams to document the discovery of impressive skeletons (though he steered clear of speaking of them himself).

The following is a brief list of documented findings, all recorded in the *Annual Report of the Board of Regents of the Smithsonian Institution*

Showing the Operations, Expenditures, and Condition of the Institution for the Year [...] series (each book title ends with the year the discovery was made):

- One skull measuring "36 inches in circumference."[208] Anna, Illinois, 1873. (The average circumference measurement for the human skull is between twenty-one and twenty-three inches, depending on varying factors such as sex, ethnicity, etc.)
- One full skeleton with double rows of teeth, buried alongside a gigantic axe, referred to in the report as a "gigantic savage."[209] The skeleton—with a colossal skull—fell apart after exhumation, so an exact height/head circumference was not reported, but the record states that "its height must have been quite [meaning "at least"] seven feet." Amelia Island, Florida, 1875.
- Giant axes and "skinning stones."[210] One weighed over fifteen pounds, had an ornately carved handle, and was of such great mass that it was documented: "Only a giant could have wielded this." Kishwaukee Mounds, Illinois, 1877.
- One jawbone that easily slipped around the entire face of a large man on the research team; one thigh bone measuring "four inches longer than that of a man six feet two inches high"; one "huge skeleton, much taller than the current race of men."[211] Kishwaukee Mounds, Illinois, 1877.

According to the *Fifth Annual Report of the Bureau of Ethnology to the Secretary of the Smithsonian Institution 1883–1884*, shortly following the discoveries in the above list, the Smithsonian team found ten more skeletons in mounds and burial sites in Wisconsin, Illinois, West Virginia, North Carolina, and Georgia. Not every one was measured for height, but each was documented as being much larger than the skeletons of our current race; those that were measured ranged between seven to seven and a half feet long.[212] Similarly, in the *Twelfth Annual Report of the Bureau of Ethnology to the Secretary of the Smithsonian Institution 1894*, two enormous skulls, several baffling femur bones, and seventeen full skeletons also measuring between seven to seven and a half feet long (one in East Dubuque, Illinois, measured almost eight feet) were unearthed in Illinois, Mississippi, Georgia, North Carolina, Tennessee, Ohio, Pennsylvania, and West Virginia.[213] The West Virginia dig report contains an additional claim of finding "many large skeletons," generically.[214] These reports list the discovery of more than forty thousand artifacts, including weapons, tools, jewelry, and various utensils that couldn't feasibly have been used by average-sized humans.

There has been some indication, based on later writings of Cyrus Thomas, that he eventually did cave in to Powell's way of thinking, likely due in part to pressure from the Smithsonian, which contributed to the extreme acceptance of the Powell Doctrine in 1907. Following this, as mentioned prior, all theories, reports, or evidence that led to any discussion in opposition to the doctrine were silenced.

Outside news reports involving the Smithsonian's knowledge of giant bones include:

- One skeleton of "a gigantic Indian" was discovered by the Smithsonian BAE's own John W. Emmert. Bristol, Tennessee. Reported by *The Weekly Democratic Statesman,* 1883.[215]
- One seven-foot, two-inch, giant skeleton with a copper crown on its head, "jet black" hair to the waist, possibly a royal leader, was buried in a mound in a secure vault with undecipherable inscriptions carved into the outside. The relics were "examined by a committee of scientists sent out from the Smithsonian Institute," then "carefully packed and forwarded to the Smithsonian." Gastonville, Pennsylvania. Reported by *American Antiquarian,* 1885.[216] (Note that another giant with possible links to royalty was found by H. R. Hazelton in Cartersville, Georgia, reported the previous year, on July 23, 1884, by *The North Otago Times.* Though that discovery did not mention any links to Smithsonian involvement, it's interesting to see that we have at least two possible "king" giants. The giant of Cartersville, Georgia, was nine

feet, two inches, had hair to his waist, wore a copper crown, and was surrounded by seven skeletons belonging to children, buried in a vault under flagstones [both the vault and the flagstones were deeply etched with undecipherable inscriptions], and resting on a bed of dry grass and animal skins. Some have suggested that the giants of Pennsylvania and Georgia were the same discovery due to their similar descriptions, and that the *American Antiquarian* simply reported the same skeleton later, listed fewer details, and stated the wrong date, location, and skeletal height. This is a possibility, but it's just as likely there were two separate discoveries, one with the involvement of the Smithsonian, and one without, because of how dissimilar the reports were.)

- Water recession from the Tumlin Mound field revealed "acres of skulls and bones," one of which was so massive, an article titled "Monster Skulls and Bones" states that "their owner must have stood 14 feet high." In the final sentence, we read, "A representative of the Smithsonian Institution is here investigating the curious relics." Cartersville, Georgia. Reported by *The New York Times*, 1886.[217] (Note this is the same city as one of our "king" giants noted in the preceding bullet. This "monster" was discovered two years later due to water recession [not an intentional uncovering of a mound] and was reported to be much taller than the "king" [taller than fourteen feet high].)

- One eight-foot-two giant was discovered to be well preserved and measuring at two feet, two inches across the pelvic bone. "About six miles" away from this find, "at the mouth of the Sioux Coulec," a Smithsonian representative (referred to only as a Smithsonian agent or employee) "exhumed the remains of another skeleton the size of which was calculated to be about 9 feet in length." Crawford, Minnesota. Reported by *American Antiquarian*, 1887.[218]

- Many giant artifacts, eleven full skeletons, one with an enormous jawbone "twice the ordinary size," were discovered "by Warren K. Moorehead of the Smithsonian Institution." Romney, West

Virginia. Reported by *The Baltimore Sun*, 1889.[219] (Warren
Moorehead was not a direct employee of the Smithsonian, but he
most often reported his archeological findings to them.)

• At least fifteen, and possibly as many as twenty, full skeletons
"more than seven feet tall" were discovered by "members of the
Smithsonian Institution." Natchez, Louisiana. Discovery in 1891.
Reported by *The Spokane Daily Chronicle* years later.[220]

In *Cloudeaters*, we explained in greater detail how these findings were
disregarded by powerful men who—despite *years* of transparent discovery
documentation from their own research and education teams—sought to
bury and erase all evidence that didn't align with the Darwinian paradigm,
which would account for 1) why we don't hear much about them today,
and b) why there hasn't been responsible, peer-reviewed analysis of the
bones involving confirmed dating. And don't forget that even the Bible,
itself, acknowledges such bizarre occurrences as giants with six fingers and
toes (for instance, see 2 Samuel 21:20), linking directly to the findings in
these lists.

In case you're wondering, these giants cannot be explained by current branches of evolutionary theory. Neanderthals were, as evolutionary science has shown, shorter than today's human species. Consider the
classroom and textbook charts showing the man evolving from crouched
monkey to upright human. Some charts show the Neanderthal man in
the middle, others toward the end, depending on the physical phases featured in each chart. Scientists say this *hominin* species was one of the final
phases of man before transforming into today's *Homo sapiens*, and that
they lived amongst the *Homo sapiens* as recently as thirty thousand to
forty thousand years ago (though some scientists say they aren't quite that
recent). One interesting tidbit science has shared with the rest of the world
regarding this species is that the average male height was around five and
a half feet tall when standing upright, supporting the idea that humans
began smaller and have grown—not decreased in size—as they've evolved.
(According to Rudolph Zallinger's "March of Progress" chart of 1965, the
first sequence of man had dawned from the now-extinct *Pliopithecus* ape,

which stood at an average height of three feet. Though this chart, too, has been updated, the fact remains that evolution shows man has increased in size over time from the mysterious arrival of the very first *Homo* species—supposedly our earliest human form.)

Regardless of the missing scientific dating methods applied to these bones (that the Church only takes so seriously, anyway), due to the lack of priority these bones have been given since their discovery, one could put all other known data in a blender and conclude that these bones are a remnant of the giants, Nephilim, or the Watchers of Genesis 6. *If so*, the bones have little or no connection to a pre-Adamic race, since Adam came first in the chronology. (Of course, if they do eventually receive dating proving them to be far older than Adam, they very well may be evidence of a pre-Adamic race. We simply won't know until they are further studied.) What the remains of these giants *can* certainly attest to, however, is the Luciferian nature to pervert humanity as it had been warped in Genesis 6, possibly even as an attempt to create life the way God had done in the beginning. And if we know that's a part of Lucifer's nature—if we know this was what he was up to *after* Adam—it's not a stretch to see this may have been a strategy he applied *prior* to Adam as well, during the "void" era.

Nephilim: Successors to a Similar Pre-Adamic Race?

For those who may not be familiar with the subject of the Nephilim, I will *briefly* explain the trail, starting with the biblical identification of this bizarre race in Genesis 6:4: "There were giants [Hebrew: *napil* or *Nephilim*] in the earth in those days; and also after that, when the sons of God came in unto the daughters of men, and they bare children to them, the same became mighty men which were of old, men of renown."

"Sons of God," according to Hebrew expert Dr. Heiser, is "a term for the divine members of God's divine family-entourage"; i.e., angels.[221] This is important, considering how many Bible teachers today claim this term simply refers to the sons of Seth (meaning ordinary and good men in the assembly of the Israelites). But, "sons of God" *cannot* mean regular, human "descendants of Seth" in Genesis 6:4, because that renders the context nonsensical: This verse describes a race of giants who were the offspring of a union with "the daughters of men," meaning natural, human females. These offspring became "mighty men…men of renown," or famously known for sensational feats (above those a human could be expected to carry out). If mere human males were copulating with mere human females, then why would the writer of Genesis feel the need to note this totally ordinary relationship at this point in the biblical narrative, just before the Flood? If God's "good guys" were around at this time, going about their daily lives, procreating, being fruitful and multiplying, and pleasing the Lord, the Flood wouldn't have been a necessary cleansing of evil upon Earth.

The reason this clear teaching is so frequently refuted in the Church is large in part because Matthew 22:30 explains angels "of heaven" do not marry (or copulate; the terms are synonymous throughout the Bible) and Psalm 103:20 explicitly states that angels obey God. If that were true of *all* angels, then Lucifer—one of God's most amazing cherubim—would have never fallen. The key here is to remember that we're not talking about obedient angels "of *heaven*," as referenced in the aforementioned verse in Matthew, but of wicked angels who turned their backs on God and left their heavenly position and "first estate," as we know Lucifer and his fallen-angel army did (Jude 6). After having fallen, they were no longer "of heaven"! In Job 1:6 and 2:1, we see these same "sons of God" (often translated "angels") arriving with Satan in their midst specifically to accuse the upright man of God. Are they good guys there, too?

Also, the Hebrew word for "Nephilim" is derived from the Hebrew root *naphal*, which means "fallen ones." It is extremely difficult to configure how "fallen ones" would ever describe godly sons of Seth.

Proceeding with the proper treatment of the Hebrew "Nephilim" in mind, and knowing that their activities led to God's anger and the subsequent Flood, we understand the Nephilim to be offspring of *wicked* "sons of God" (fallen angels) and "the daughters of men" (human women). The Book of Enoch was read, studied, and quoted by the Jews, including the apostles of Christ, one of whom quoted Enoch in his epistle (look up the context of Jude 14–15). If the very apostles of Christ took Enochian literature so seriously, then it is relevant to the subject of fallen angels today, despite its exclusion from the canon of Scripture. Enoch 6:1–2, 7:1–5, and 10:1–3 expand on Genesis 6:4. Here are those verses, in that order:

> And it came to pass when the children of men had multiplied that in those days were born unto them beautiful and comely daughters. And the angels, the children of the heaven, saw and lusted after them [again, holy angels would not "lust after" anyone or anything, so these are fallen angels], and said to one another: "Come, let us choose us wives from among the children of men and beget us children."

> And all the others together with them took unto themselves wives, and each chose for himself one, and they began to go into them and defile themselves with them, and they taught them charms and enchantments, and the cutting of roots, and made them acquainted with plants. And they became pregnant, and they bare great giants [the Nephilim], whose height was three thousand ells: Who consumed all the acquisitions of men. And when men could no longer sustain them, the giants turned against them and devoured mankind.

> Then said the Most High, the Holy and Great one spake, and sent Uriel to the son of Lamech, and said to him: "Go to Noah and tell him in my name 'Hide thyself!' and reveal to him the end that is approaching: that the whole earth will be destroyed, and a deluge is about to come upon the whole earth, and will destroy all that is on it. And now instruct him that he may escape and his seed may be preserved for all the generations of the world."

Noah was "perfect [Hebrew: *tamim*] in his generations" (Genesis 6:9). At first, this appears to describe moral perfection, but other than Christ, no human has ever been morally perfect, which has led Hebrew scholars to view the Hebrew *tamim* in context of other writings of this time. Just like the "*yom*/day/age" issue we dealt with earlier, *tamim* can mean "perfect," but it also denotes "pure" and "undefiled." Since moral perfection is likely not the best rendering of this term, we are encouraged to assign the "undefiled" meaning to the writer's intent here. Noah and his family were the only humans left whose DNA was pure and undefiled (not corrupted by the Nephilim or "giants'" seed). So, God told Noah to build an ark to save his family and two of every animal (as well as additional pairs of "clean" animals for sacrifice [Genesis 7:2]) so they would be protected from and preserved through the Flood (Genesis 6:14–22). (By the way, if you've wondered all your life how any boat in the world could have been large enough to carry two of every animal, remember this was before any form of select breeding. Noah wouldn't have had to carry two black Labradors, two Chihuahuas, two German shepherds, two bulldogs, two poodles, etc.; he would have boarded two *canines* of the earliest parent breed, two felines of the absolute earliest parent breed, and so on. Also, the animals were more likely puppies, kittens, etc., not massive, clumsy, kibble-devouring monster-animals. The ark of Noah is not that far-fetched when we consider the small number of land-animal breeds he would have needed just to preserve the bloodlines of Earth's earliest species that would *later* breed into the vast variety we see today.)

Not only does this satisfy the mysteries presented in Genesis 6:4, it explains why, when humanity was new to Earth around the time of the Fertile Crescent, stories from almost every culture produced tales of human/god-hybrid "giant" offspring:

> In the ancient world, stories were often told of sexual intercourse between the gods and human beings; and the semi-divine offspring of such unions were held to have abnormal energy and other powers. In Mesopotamia and Canaan, divine-human marriage was celebrated in the sacred marriage rites that took place in the temples.[222]

Gordon Fee, a beloved scholar well-known for his strict adherence to proper principles of biblical interpretation and exegesis (who was also the writer of, or his work was highly praised in, many of my college textbooks), writes in his book, *Eerdmans Companion to the Bible*:

Verses 1–8 of [Genesis] chapter 6 tell of spirit-beings (or angels; Job 1:6; 2:1) marrying human women, and these women bore them children who became "mighty men" (Nephilim, v. 4). This account parallels other ancient Near Eastern stories of divine-human marriages that produced superhuman progeny and implies the practice of sacred prostitution for the purpose of ensuring fertility (both of the soil in farming and in normal human marriages). But this grieves God greatly, and because humankind seems bent on pursuing wickedness, God resolves to destroy not only humans [in the Flood] but also all other creatures that inhabit the earth and sky. As the extent of sin intensifies, so does the degree of God's judgment.[223]

There is also another way to interpret Genesis 6:2: "The sons of God saw the daughters of men that they were fair." The word "fair" (Hebrew *tob*) may not be the whole picture, as it likewise means "agreeable" or "accommodating." Don't misunderstand: It might not mean that the women, themselves, were agreeably accommodating to the fallen angels' schemes to procreate, but that, to the angels, the genetic makeup and biology of the human female body could accommodate the fallen angels' plan. What appears in English to be a synonym of "beautiful" is misleading. This is why some brilliant scholars, like our dear, late friend, David Flynn, have found this a better rendering: "the daughters…were fit extensions." In other words, the fallen angels wanted to "incarnate themselves into the material world," and female bodies were suitable for the job.[224]

Some readers, if this is the first time they've heard this take on Genesis 6:4, might be reeling with the implications of this teaching. But I assure you, for the majority of those who have read the books that we (Defender

Publishing) have released, the Nephilim topic is nothing new, so in the interest of those individuals, I will get back to the central subject. (For further reading on this subject through our company, I highly recommend directing your Internet browsers to SkyWatchTVstore.com. Tons of materials are available in our store regarding this subject.)

As I said earlier: Because Adam was formed *prior to* the Flood event that the existence of the human/fallen-angel hybrid Nephilim-offspring contributed to, the giants of Genesis 6 are *not* related to a pre-Adamic race alive on Earth during the "void" era. But, we don't know yet whether the giant bones mentioned previously are before or after Adam's time. All we know is this: Lucifer, in his fallen, wicked state, along with a third of the angels who left their "first estate" alongside him, were not above attempting to "create" as did the Most High. The unfortunate offspring generated by the fallen angels' unions with human females may not have been Lucifer and his minions' first attempt to launch their own, warped "creation." The "void" era may very well have had all sorts of genetically modified abominations walking around, since we know this was something Lucifer would "do *again*" in Genesis 6.

As to his motive in designing this Genesis 6 perversion, almost all the scholars who teach on this subject postulate one answer: Lucifer had been with God when Earth was first formed, so he knew God's ultimate plan for His Creation. When Lucifer saw that his pitiable takeover attempt would not stop God, he tried to pollute humanity so the Messiah could never be born through a pure bloodline, and salvation through sacrifice and the concurrent reconciliation of man to God would never take place. God sent the Flood to save Noah's "perfect" (read: "undefiled") DNA and preserve humanity so Jesus could be brought forth from an ancestry untouched by the giants.

If there *was* a pre-Adamic race of Luciferian breeding, would it have been something similar to the giants of Genesis 6?

For that matter, when the Bible says there were giants on Earth "in those days; and also after that," what "days" are being referred to specifically, and what era is represented by "also after that"? Scholars have been confused about this for a long time, calling the "also after that" era the "second incursion." Occasionally, we see scholars come to terrifying conclusions about the second incursion, even going as far as to say that the demonic DNA still exists today within some races of humanity (a proposal I don't find viable because it refutes our status as humans with access to the very salvation Christ offered humanity).

Others have taken an alternative approach, asking: What if the real answer wasn't that sensational? What if "in those days" is a reference to a pre-Adamic race of the "void" era, and "also after that" is a reference to what happened in Noah's day? Genesis scholar Derek Kidner, in his *Genesis: An Introduction and Commentary*, states: "It is worth noting that the giants are not said to have sprung solely from this [Genesis 6:4] origin: if some arose in this way (*also after that*), others existed already (*in those days*)."[225] The chronology of this would be:

1. *First* incursion: "in those days"; after God made Earth the first time, after Lucifer's fall, and during the "void" era, but *prior to* the re-creation beginning in Genesis 1:3
2. *Second* incursion: "and also after that"; after the re-creation beginning in Genesis 1:3, noted in Genesis 6:4

If—and I admit it's only an "if"—the Nephilim were on Earth way before Adam's time, then obviously the genetic manipulation in Genesis 6:4 wasn't the first time Lucifer attempted such a thing, and a pre-Adamic race of some sort is real.

As long as we know Lucifer had the goal of creating his own perverted race of beings in mind around the time of the Flood, then a pre-Adamic race is a possibility anyway…and the more science discovers bones, Gobekli-Tepe-like buildings, structures that humans don't appear to have originated, OOPArts, etc., the more likely that scenario appears to be.

Now that we have a potential foundation for what destructive "creation" Lucifer may have been up to during the "void" era, let's look at what the prophets said about the condition of the planet at that time.

Isaiah Saw the "Void"

In the verses following Isaiah's identification of Lucifer as the one whose fall created the "without form, and void" era of Earth, we see that very era described in further detail:

They that see thee shall narrowly look upon thee, and consider thee, saying, "Is this the man that made the earth to tremble, that did shake kingdoms; That made the world as a wilderness, and destroyed the cities thereof; that opened not the house of his prisoners?" (Isaiah 14:16–17)

Again, scholars are often quick to point out that this is a continuation of the taunt directed at Nebuchadnezzar, and, again, I will remind the reader that it is *both*, as the prophetic utterance is dual purpose: Isaiah was describing Nebuchadnezzar as possessed by, or driven by, the ancient Luciferian spirit of self-aggrandizement, and therefore, the fall of Lucifer is here described in cautionary fashion. It is said, at times, that verses 12–15 describe Lucifer, while verses 16 and 17 switch back to Nebuchadnezzar; in other words, by the time we reach verses 16–17, Lucifer is out of the picture and we're back to looking at a human king. The same scholars, however, only rarely explain *how* verses so widely acknowledged by theologians to have been a description of Lucifer (vv. 12–15) suddenly shift back to the human king, and why it's irresponsible to see verses 16 and 17 as a continuation of Lucifer's fall narrative. (When they do explain this, their answers are based on each scholar's own interpretational logic and is, therefore, not binding.)

Well, I mean, it sounds like it's a human in reference. After all, it says "the man," right? Lucifer was not a "man."

No, he wasn't, but he *was* "male," and that's what the Hebrew word (*is*) in this instance means: "Is this the [non-female being] that made the earth to tremble…?"

Many other Bible scholars naturally view certain portrayals in these verses—such as making the whole Earth a "wilderness"—and conclude that this could not be done by a human king. Nebuchadnezzar, as powerful as he may have been, wasn't capable of wielding such a widespread influence on the planet. Thus, Lucifer may still be in the prophet's mind here. If this is so, we have a description (albeit a small one) of the Earth during its "void" era: "*They that see* thee [Lucifer]" is from the Hebrew primitive root verb *ra'a*, meaning "to see," as opposed to any kind of identified people groups or species, so there is no way of knowing who is currently observing the enemy's actions. The door is left ajar for this to be a pre-Adamic race of some sort (those who also watched as Lucifer "weaken[ed] the nations" in verse 12), or possibly the fallen angels who followed Lucifer in his fall, now clearly disappointed in the trembling of Earth and the shaking of kingdoms they first believed would thrive under their God-usurping leadership. (And why couldn't it be both? If archeologists have discovered non-human bones—or bones that evolutionists claim to have been the common ancestor to humanity [like a Darwinian man-ape species the biblical narrative doesn't support]—it shows that some kind of beings inhabited Earth prior to Adam's formation approximately six thousand years ago. Were these a primordial, but not image-bearing, creation of the Lord's who were also affected by the fall of Lucifer like humanity would be later on? Were they some earthly form of fallen angels? Were they—as some theologians entrenched in the study of the giants or Nephilim of Genesis 6:1–4 believe—a demonic hybrid of a natural pre-Adamic race *and* fallen angels, together? Considering the wide variety of bones that have been unearthed and reach back to the pre-human, pre-Adam era, it could be any number of theories, related to these or otherwise.) But regardless of who is doing the "seeing" here—and again from the perspective that Lucifer is still the subject of Isaiah 14:16–17—the object of their observation is the state of Earth following Lucifer's fall: the devastation of cities and kingdoms, the whole planet taken captive (everyone made "prisoners"), and a vast "wilderness" of nothingness to live upon.

Later in his prophecy, Isaiah says: "He [God] shall stretch out upon it the line of confusion, and the stones of emptiness" (34:11). These words may not be directly linked to Lucifer, but the indirect implication is related to how precisely God's wrath will pour out, as George H. Pember identifies in his 1876 work, *Earth's Earliest Ages*:

> In a prophecy of Isaiah, after a fearful description of the fall of Idumea in the day of vengeance, we find the expression, "He shall stretch out upon it the line of confusion, and the stones—or, as it should be translated, the plummet—of emptiness." Now "confusion" and "emptiness" are, in the Hebrew, the same words as those rendered "without form, and void" [*tohu/bohu*]. And the sense is, that just as the architect makes careful use of line and plummet in order to raise the building in perfection, so will the Lord to make the ruin complete.[226]

More simply put: God's perfect wrath is like the architect's perfect building patterns—both are executed with precision. When Lucifer took his kingdom, Earth, and made it a place of degenerate, deviant fallen-angel worship, God, Himself, executed ruination upon the planet to bring down his regime.

Jeremiah Saw the "Void"

Jeremiah 4:23–27 is a unique passage. The prophet Jeremiah was, like Isaiah and Ezekiel, active during the days of the exile; he came later than Isaiah but earlier than Ezekiel. Along the same lines as those other two prophets, he recalls a time when Earth was *tohu* and *bohu*:

> I beheld the earth, and, lo, it was without form, and void; and the heavens, and they had no light. I beheld the mountains, and, lo, they trembled, and all the hills moved lightly. I beheld, and, lo, there was no man, and all the birds of the heavens were fled. I beheld, and, lo, the fruitful place was a wilderness, and all the cities thereof were broken down at the presence of the Lord, and

by his fierce anger. For thus hath the Lord said, "The whole land shall be desolate...."

I will share a few commentaries on this passage before making any comments of my own. First, from Tyndale's Old Testament Commentaries series, volume 21, *Jeremiah and Lamentations* by R. K. Harrison, we read:

So devastating is the judgment upon Judah (23–28) that Jeremiah instinctively thinks of the state of primeval chaos (Gen. 1:2), except that what then became "good" [the re-creation in the time of Adam] will now [in the time of exile] be turned to desolation at the divine presence. This description is one of the most dramatic of its kind in the entire Old Testament. The heedless destruction consequent upon apostasy has brought ruin upon the land, and the skies are darkened in mourning (cf. Isa. 24:10; 34:11). The imagery is that of the judgment day (cf. Isa. 13:10; Joel 2:10; 3:15; Amos 8:9, etc.) which had now arrived in all its terror, eclipsing the celestial luminaries and making the earth return to its primitive barrenness before the creative word emerged (cf. 2 Pet. 3:10).

Cosmic disturbances are matched by terrestrial upheaval. *The mountains*, symbols of stability and strength, are trembling for very weakness at the majesty of the divine visitation. People have fled from the scene, and even *the birds*, the most widely distributed of the animal species, have themselves long departed.[227]

According to this source, it's clear that Jeremiah is using the former period of "primeval chaos" described in Genesis 1:2 as a "dramatic" description of what happens to Earth's surface upon "divine visitation." To say this another way: When God's judgment falls upon a land filled with apostasy and pagan practices, we may expect to experience the same (or similar) "chaos" upon Earth as that awful *tohu* and *bohu* state described in Genesis 1:2. However, though this conclusion isn't based on not rocket science, it indirectly illustrates that, although God didn't create the *tohu/bohu* Earth, His judgment further broke down the planet with its nations and inhabitants.

Another Jeremiah commentary by Elmer Martens of the Baker Reference Library also sees that Jeremiah is here looking back on the state of the "void" and the corresponding, relentless judgment of God at that time upon Earth:

> The earth becomes chaotic, formless, and empty as before the creation (Gen. 1:2). There are four references to nonlife (earth, heaven, mountain, hill) and four mentions of life (man, birds, fruitful land, cities). Behind that army is God's wrath. God is fully committed to this action of judgment and will not be dissuaded.[228]

God's judgment will pour out on those who mock His laws and Creation in the manner the Israelites did, which led to their exile. Applying this to the "void" era, it's *also* clear that it was God's judgment upon Lucifer's actions (whether or not that involves genetic manipulation) that caused the *tohu/bohu* Earth. Obviously, Lucifer was up to something terrible—a direct assault to God's Creation—when he was meddling about prior to Adam.

Generally speaking, because of the references to *tohu* and *bohu* in Jeremiah's words, scholars largely agree that Jeremiah is viewing some sort of pre-Creation or "void"-era chaos as he compares it to the state of Israel during exile. But, peculiarly, Jeremiah's vision involving the "void" era also shows a time when light, birds, and even humanity are completely absent:

> Jeremiah 4:23 utilizes the words of Gen. 1:2, "formless and void," to express the resurgence of chaos and disorder that is experienced by the poet at every dimension of life. Then in quick succession [in the following verses] the poet characterizes the loss of "light" (sun, moon, stars), the failure of even mountains and hills to embody stability, the disappearance of humanity and the absence

of birds, and finally the end of fertile land and functioning city. Wholesale dismantling follows massive disobedience. The power of chaos is so dominant, it is as though creation never happened. This sad turn of events is the result of Yahweh's action, for Yahweh's patience has finally been exhausted.[229]

Jeremiah is clearly seeing a time when birds, light, and people were *expected to be present* on the planet—yet they were gone, and this was alarming to him. God's Creation was "good," and even God, Himself, said so throughout the Creation week we read in Genesis. Now, specific aspects of Creation are destroyed or absent, which is *not* "good." It's "void" (as well as chaotic, and all those other adjectives listed in the previous chapter). Whatever God made prior to the re-Creation in Genesis 1:3 was *also* good, until Lucifer ruined it.

As far as what sin Lucifer and the fallen ones participated in that would have kindled God's fury, it's so obvious that it does not necessitate a lengthy explanation: They failed to care for God's initial creation, and if they *did* engage in days-of-Noah perversion prior to Adam, they were "creating" other beings (perhaps like the Nephilim) who would have followed Lucifer and forsaken God. This, alone, is worthy of God's greatest wrath, even without the contribution of bringing humanity's pure DNA to extinction and, thereby, cutting off a potential bloodline through which Christ would eventually hail from.

Since we can jump to Genesis 6:4 to retrieve an outline of Lucifer's corrupt attempt to manipulate creation nature (using sexual intercourse between fallen angels and human women to create a new hybrid offspring "better than" what God had made up to that point, or so Lucifer may have hoped) and apply it farther backward to the chaos of the "void," I believe there was some form of nonhuman, pre-Adamic "something" alive between Genesis 1:1 and 1:3 that Lucifer and his minions "fathered." For what would be more fitting of a Luciferian agenda than to dismantle God's Creation by forming abominations? If science and archeology hadn't found so many bizarre discoveries linked to this time, I wouldn't insist so staunchly upon this biblical interpretation.

But, as readers are no doubt aware, alongside giant bones and ancient, megalithic structures are the discoveries of bones of animals now extinct—primarily dinosaurs. The biblical record acknowledges that God created every living thing that creeps upon our current, re-created Earth, but since dinosaurs are dated to millions or billions of years before that time, might they have been another of Lucifer's sickening "creations"? Since they, too, suffered the blow of God's wrath and judgment upon the "void" era and every one of them died—*but they were not a part of the re-Creation that God called "good" in any way*—could this point to the possibility that God intentionally left them out in the phases of His restoration of Earth as they were never a part of the perfect Creation He intended in the first place?

Chapter 8

Lucifer's Fall and Extinct Animals of the "Void"

AS *EARTH'S EARLIEST AGES* author George H. Pember so obviously concludes regarding Earth's chaos-age, "Sin was the cause of the preadamite
destruction." Thankfully, this is not all he has to say. He immediately goes
on to share his own interpretation of the state of the "void," followed by
the natural link to "fossil remains" of pre-Adamic races/species and how
they link to a fallen state for more than just humanity:

> We see, then, that God created the heavens and the earth perfect
> and beautiful in their beginning, and that at some subsequent
> period, how remote we cannot tell, the earth had passed into a
> state of utter desolation, and was void of all life. Not merely had
> its fruitful places become a wilderness, and all its cities been bro-
> ken down; but the very light of its sun had been withdrawn; all
> the moisture of its atmosphere had sunk upon its surface; and the
> vast deep, to which God has set bounds that are never transgressed
> save when wrath has gone forth from Him, had burst those limits;
> so that the ruined planet, covered above its very mountain tops
> with the black floods of destruction, was rolling through space in
> a horror of great darkness....

The fossil remains indicate preadamite ages of sin: for they may be proved to be the relics, not [of] the Six Days [of re-Creation—Pember calls this period the Restoration], but of far earlier creations.

For, as the fossil remains clearly show, not only were disease and death—inseparable companions of Sin—then prevalent among the living creatures of the earth, but even ferocity and slaughter....

On the Sixth Day God pronounced every thing which He had made to be very good, a declaration which would seem altogether inconsistent with the present condition of the animal as well as the vegetable kingdom. Again; He gave the green herb alone for food "to every beast of the field, and to every fowl of the air, and to every thing that creepeth upon the earth" [Genesis 1:30]. There were, therefore, no carnivora in the sinless world.

Lastly; in a great prophecy of the times of restitution we read: "The wolf also shall dwell with the lamb, and the leopard shall lie down with the kid; and the calf and the young lion and the fatling together; and a little child shall lead them. And the cow and the bear shall feed; their young ones shall lie down together; and the lion shall eat straw like the ox. And the sucking child shall play upon the hole of the asp, and the weaned child shall put his hand on the cockatrice's den. They shall not hurt nor destroy in all My holy mountain: for the earth shall be full of the knowledge of the Lord, as the waters cover the sea" [Isaiah 11:6–9]. That is, that, when sin has been suppressed by the return of the second Adam [Jesus], the curse shall lose its power, the savage nature of the beasts of the field shall disappear, the carnivora shall become graminivora, the poisonous shall lay aside their venom; all shall be restored to their first condition, and be again as when God pronounced the primal blessing.

Since, then, the fossil remains are those of creatures anterior to [or before] Adam, and yet show evident tokens of disease, death, and mutual destruction, they must have belonged to another world, and have a sin-stained history of their own, a history which ended in the ruin of themselves and their habitation.…

And since a lord and vicegerent [Adam] was set over the animal kingdom of our world, through whose fall deterioration, disease and death obtained irresistible power over every living creature, so we should naturally conclude that superior beings [pre-Adamites] inhabited and ruled that former world, and, like Adam, transgressed the laws of their Creator.[230]

In short, Pember's final remark from this excerpt recognizes the following, naturally formed logic: Fossils of both humanlike and animal origin exist dating to well before six thousand years ago. Since we know what the Fall in Adam's time created through the entrance of sin on Earth, we can apply it to fossils originating from earlier in time to the "void" era and bring into view not only a fallen race of "superior beings" (Luciferian in their nature, no doubt, as Pember's entire book goes on to support), but an animal race as well.

Were Dinosaurs the "Subjects" of "King Lucifer"?

To answer this question, let's look at how dinosaurs link to Lucifer chronologically, representatively, theologically, etymologically, historically, scientifically, and geologically. Note that we will not visit the probability that this Luciferian-dinosaurs theory also connects to the aforementioned two-floods or Snowball Earth theories (inherent in many Gap theory outlines) since dinosaur fossils have been connected to so many Ice Age and glacial layers that it goes without saying.

(As for Behemoth and Leviathan—the possible references to dinosaurs [or dinosaur-like animals] spoken of in Job 40–41, Isaiah 21:1, Psalm 74, 104:26, and others—scholars are still divided about these creatures. When we compare the biblical descriptions of these beasts to what we know of the animal kingdom today, the closest match to Behemoth is a rhinoceros or a large hippopotamus [both can be extremely dangerous and quite fierce to look upon], and Leviathan resembles a giant crocodile [among a few other guesses]. We cannot study the active behaviors of the dinosaurs today, but we can look at their fossilized anatomy and compare them to the details we find in the biblical narrative to eliminate almost all dinosaurs as a match to these characters. But apart from that angle, a vast number of scholars believe both Behemoth and Leviathan were personifications of something spiritual—metaphors used by God to further instruct and warn His people. Of course, this would account for the bizarre details that don't match any real, historical animal. Leviathan, for instance, is a "dragon" described as a "piercing...crooked serpent" with multiple "heads" [Isaiah 27:1; Psalm 74:13–14]. Let me go ahead and give you a spoiler here, so you can keep it in the back of your mind as you read on: The "dragon" language associated with Leviathan puts me in the same pool as most other scholars who view that cunning sea beast as *both* a metaphor for, and a variant reference to, Lucifer/Satan, who later appears in the book of Revelation as a dragon, also sporting multiple heads. Whether Behemoth or Leviathan were literal members of the historical, earthly dinosaur family is speculation.)

Right away, I'd like to draw attention to something stated in an article in the May 2023 issue of *Prophecy Watcher Magazine*, written by well-known and respected Bible scholar and prophecy expert, Gary Stearman. First, he explains that Lucifer is known by four other names throughout the Word: "Satan," meaning "accuser"; "the devil," meaning "slanderer"; "a dragon," which is a "physical description of Satan in his original glory"; and "the serpent," which refers to his "reptilian physical shape." Stearman goes on to explain that, when Lucifer was the dragon, he was "beautiful, wise and powerful," but when he fell, he *became* the "serpent."[231] It hasn't escaped Stearman that *all four* of Lucifer's other names are grouped in one verse, Revelation 12:9, referring to only *one* evil character: "And the great *dragon* was cast out, that old *serpent*, called the *Devil*, and *Satan*, which deceiveth the whole world: he was cast out into the earth, and his angels were cast out with him" (emphasis added). Biblically, then, there is no way around admitting that these terms, in the context of a figurehead of evil, all refer to one individual who was, as the Bible says, both a dragon and a serpent. Whether we should take that figuratively or literally—and how important it is that we stick to one or the other of those conclusions— is, *for this book*, not a deal-breaker (though I believe the literality of the applied terms are clear, as I will show in the coming pages). If Satan, also known as Lucifer, is a *representative* reptile, serpent, dragon, etc., the argument for his link to dinosaurs still stands. "He *is* a reptile," Stearman says, "in fact, *king* of the reptiles," who, as a result of his role in humanity's Fall, was "transformed into a repulsive serpent" after Adam and Eve took a bite of that which God had forbidden.[232]

Interesting...

Chronologically, It Fits

Since: 1) God, in His "good" Creation, formed only animals that ate greenery and cohabitated Earth peacefully; 2) sin was the condition that altered the state of the animal kingdom to involve carnivores; and 3) the future Second Coming of the "Second Adam" (Jesus; cf. 1 Corinthians 15:45–49) is that Almighty Power that removes the curse of "the savage nature of the beasts of the field" and the predatory, carnivorous nature of the present animal kingdom, restoring it to its perfect state wherein the "wolf also shall dwell with the lamb" and so forth—then we know that what God originally intended for animals to be is *not* reflected in what we know dinosaurs to have been (savage, carnivorous, etc.).

Now, revisiting all we possibly can regarding the chronology of their existence, we can't assign the dinosaurs' extinction to the Fall during Adam's time...because they are millions of years older than Adam, scientists say. According to the United States Geological Survey website, dinosaurs had roamed Earth for 165 million years before their demise more than 60 million years ago.[233] One who accepts the scientific dating methods of these monsters must also accept that they were not here during Noah's day, either, as he came after Adam, so they may *not* have been victims of the Flood (despite Young Earthers' insistence that they were). In view of the age of their bones and fossils scattered about Earth and in museums today, biblically, they would be dated to the "void" era, linking them to a sin condition of that time under Lucifer and the fallen ones that stretched over *at least 165 million years*, giving the evil one plenty of time to devise the strange schemes he had planned for them that we will look at in this chapter.

So far, the chronology supports this theory, placing the origin of dinosaurs to the epoch of Luciferian rule between the very first state of Earth and the latter re-Creation. Thankfully, we do not have to rely solely on how the timing of this fits. There is more to the picture.

Representatively, Theologically, and Etymologically, It Fits

Recall what we covered in chapter 6 regarding Lucifer's pre-fall status. He was an anointed cherub adorned with the precious gemstones of the high priests of the Temple whose dwelling place was the Garden of Eden (Ezekiel 28:13). The fact that Lucifer had a "kingdom" (Earth) means he was king over some brand of "subjects," be they angelic, pre-Adamic (but not "human" in the sense of Adam), animal, or a combination of all the above. So far, we have in view a king-priest and ruler of the highest biblical ranking. (A cherub who "covereth" would be even higher status than the human kings or priests of the Old Testament. The only exception to this would be if Melchizedek was, in fact, an appearance of the preincarnate Christ [a Christophany], as many scholars believe.)

I'd like to turn back for a moment to research shared in my last book series, *The Mystery of Jesus from Genesis to Revelation* (showing that Jesus was all three—King, Judge, and Prophet—over all of Israel in Old Testament foreshadowings). This will assist help us understand not only who Lucifer was (as that was partly covered), but just how powerful he could have been had he not wasted his calling on self-aggrandizement, and what that God-assigned power may have overseen.

The Hebrew term *hammashiach*, or, *mashiach YHWH* (the lengthier version of the term involving the tetragrammaton, the unspeakable name of God), means "Yahweh's Anointed." (It is from the truncated appearance of this term, *mashiach*, that we derive "messiah.") After the anointing of Israel's first king, Saul, *hammashiach* gained an added layer of meaning.

Though there were certainly evil kings—and though Israel most definitely served other gods—*hammashiach* was the moniker for any reigning king of Israel.

When the Hebrew Bible was translated into Greek (the translation known today as the Septuagint), the term *hammashiach* became the Greek *christos*, which simply means "anointed." Though the Greek *christos* is the term from which we would later derive "Christ," it did not originally have anything to do with the risen Jesus of Nazareth…at least not in human history (God was not surprised). It would not be until after the New Testament writers reflected on Israel's back story and considered Jesus in that framework that He would be called "the Anointed."

More simply, the Greek *christos* meant "God's Anointed One," and this term was a title for the king over all of Israel.

In a literal sense, to be anointed for a special office or duty of God meant that one knelt and received a pouring out of the sacred oil, which was carefully brewed with four fragrant substances. The first time we read of an anointing in Scripture is in Exodus 30:30–32, when Aaron, Moses' brother, became Israel's first priest:

> And thou shalt anoint Aaron and his sons, and consecrate them, that they may minister unto me in the priest's office. And thou shalt speak unto the children of Israel, saying, "This shall be an holy anointing oil unto me throughout your generations. Upon man's flesh shall it not be poured, neither shall ye make any other like it, after the composition of it: it is holy, and it shall be holy unto you."

Initially, it seems odd that God just told the Israelites to pour the oil on Aaron and his sons, and then said *not* to pour it on them ("Upon man's flesh shall it not be poured"), but this faux discrepancy is easily explained: The word "man" in this passage is the Hebrew *adam*, which, outside the context of the first man in the Garden of Eden whose proper name was Adam, *adam* simply meant "man," generically. Although priests, prophets, and kings were also "man" in the sense of "mankind" or "human," in

the Hebrew context, "man" was a broad word referring to "men" generally. Think in our own terms, and you might see "guy" or "chap" in its
place. In other words, and meaning no disrespect to Scripture (just putting together a simplified word picture), God basically said, "This sacred
oil is *not to* be poured onto the flesh of regular guys." The ESV (English
Standard Version) translation renders this: "It shall not be poured on the
body of an ordinary person." This oil was reserved only for the anointing
of those whom God had justified and approved to be his utmost trusted
leaders over all His people, acknowledged by all as the holder of the holiest
of positions. They were consecrated, which, understandably, means to be
declared before all as "sacred."

This act of anointing marked the official beginning of service for
priests and kings always, and for prophets sometimes. Therefore, Israel's
leaders received an anointing as opposed to a coronation with crowns and
scepters or whatever other imagery comes to mind when we think of the
beginning of a historical king's reign. The symbolism of the act represented
the indwelling of the Spirit of God. We can see this in Psalm 89:19b–21:

> I have exalted one chosen out of the people. I have found David
> my servant; with my holy oil have I anointed him: With whom
> my hand shall be established: mine arm also shall strengthen him.

Some may naturally note that not every king was indwelt with the
Spirit of God, both because there were wicked kings and, though it wasn't
God's plan, the throne was passed to sons who inherited the throne by
birthright, not because they had been chosen by God. However, when
David became king, as this passage shows, he was "chosen out of the people," which had been God's ideal in the first place before the demands of
the people messed it up. (It's little wonder, when God was no longer doing
the choosing, that Israel produced many terrible leaders.) God's model,
therefore, is that a man whom "His hand has established" as king would
have God's "arm also" to strengthen his kingship; i.e., God would be
"with" and "in" the king (so to speak), and that king would be "indwelt"
with the Spirit of God.

This is why, as stated a few paragraphs ago, *hammashiach* (or "messiah"), and therefore the Greek *christos*, gained an added layer of meaning when kings entered Israel's history. The word "anointed" (*hammashiach/christos*) didn't just mean "one appointed by Yahweh to lead His people"; it also meant "king" to Israel (the original recipients of the Word).

Lucifer, before his arrogance and pride contributed to the most epic of all failed efforts in the history of the cosmos, was an anointed priest-king; established by the hand of God; adorned in the gemstones found on the breastplates of the high priests of the Temple (Exodus 28:17–20; Ezekiel 28:13); ruled over all Earth as his kingdom (some scholars believe that what Lucifer "covered" in references to the cherub who "covereth" was the surface of Earth, though it may also have been a figure of speech denoting his place at the throne of God, since the cherubim are associated to "covering" the place where God dwells [for example, the Mercy Seat of the Ark of the Covenant]); inhabited the Garden of Eden (likely as the location of his throne; see Ezekiel 28:13); and, if scholars are correct about Ezekiel's vision of Lucifer's musical abilities, he possibly even led the first worship service in the heavenlies when the morning stars and sons of God shouted for joy at the Creation of the universe.

What a being he originally was!

(Crucial warning: Though it's one of the most heretical teachings I've ever heard, the parallels between Lucifer and Jesus are the foundation of the Mormon concepts that assert Lucifer was Jesus' brother. There are so many holes in this "theology" that cancels it out—especially the claim that both Christ and Lucifer were created beings, since we know Jesus shares His Father's eternality—so if you find yourself taking in those teachings, be aware that they embrace countless fallacies. When comparing Hebrew terms in relation to Christ and Lucifer, Mormon teachings attempt to prove their "sibling rivalry" from the beginning of time. At most, Lucifer may be seen as a "type" or "figure" foreshadowing the coming Messiah before he fell, like many other Old Testament characters, but in no way can they have ever been born from the same hypostatic union [God's "substance," addressed in the early Church councils], because Lucifer was a created being and Christ was/is eternal. Christ and Lucifer were not "brothers." Period.)

As to who may have been his royal subjects prior to his fall (and the possible Snowball Earth Ice Age that occurred simultaneous to the "void" era, addressed in chapter 3), we know: 1) he had a congregation of angels that followed him; 2) we can view his perverted "creation" from Genesis 6 as a potential *successor to* an earlier "without form, and void"-era race of inhuman, pre-Adamic beings; and 3) we likewise have reason to believe dinosaurs—whose characteristics do not match the animals God called "good" during Creation week—could have been this musically talented lizard-king's prized pets.

Hold up a sec. What was that about a "lizard king"?

Etymologically, "dinosaur" comes from two Greek terms: *deinos*, meaning "fearfully [or "terribly"] great," and *sauros*, meaning "lizard." Thus, the English "dinosaur" is literally translated from "fearfully great lizard" or "terrifyingly great lizard." But the emphasis here is *not* just upon the etymological history of a young English word. In order to connect Lucifer to lizards, we would have to see if the Word of God identifies this king in reptilian terminology…and it does so in spades.

Earth has, to this point, experienced two Creations: the initial epic recorded in Genesis 1:1 and the latter re-Creation from Genesis 1:3 through Creation Week. There is yet a *third* Earth—called the "New Earth"—that will be established in the future. It's written about in John's book of visions called Revelation (chapter 21). This New Earth is re-created yet again out of preexisting matter (from our current Earth) because it will have "passed away" by that point. The inauguration of our brand-new and restored planet of the latter days shortly follows the introduction of a wicked character named "Satan," also identified as a "serpent" and a "dragon" (Revelation 12:9; 20:2).

Are you seeing a pattern? I hope so, because that's pretty crucial to where we're going: Every time Lucifer/Satan shows up to wreck Earth, God brings judgment and re-creates it. He did so in Genesis 1:3–31 when Lucifer made Earth "without form, and void"; He did so again by Flood in Genesis 6:9–9:17 when Lucifer's band of fallen angels created Nephilim offspring with the daughters of men to cut off the messianic bloodline; and He will do so again in the end times of Revelation when Lucifer fuels his satanically inspired son, Antichrist, to mislead many of Earth's inhabitants to follow the deceiver and all Hell breaks loose on Earth (literally) through God's judgments. If we can look at what happened in the past that led to God's wrath, we should be able to see similar movements coming in the future and delay that awful Revelation judgment. Keep that in mind as we proceed.

Now that we're getting a bit deeper into the study of what Lucifer is responsible for, we must address a conundrum.

Scholars, for millennia, have debated whether Lucifer and Satan are the same entity, which flows into all sorts of variations regarding what or who was in the Garden of Eden the day Adam and Eve gave into the enemy's temptation. For our purposes in viewing Old Earth, its judgments, and the link between Lucifer and dinosaurs (our present effort), it isn't necessary to establish a solid conclusion. Why? Because if it wasn't Lucifer, himself, the tempter in Eden would have been one who followed in Lucifer's footsteps (his servant, perhaps): Theologically, there were no enemies of God prior to Lucifer, and when he fell and took a third of the angels with him, this band was the "bad guys" in the scenario of the "void." When we arrive at the point in the biblical narrative that Earth is re-created the first time and the Garden of Eden is occupied by Adam, Eve, and the animals, the evil, tempting "serpent"—a being represented by reptilian terminology—is already there. So, the serpent may have been Lucifer, himself, or one of his fallen sidekicks, but the spirit of iniquity is the same.

However, throughout history, many scholars have chosen to view Satan and Lucifer as the same being primarily for the following reasons: 1) Jesus saw "Satan" fall from Heaven (Luke 10:18); Lucifer also fell from Heaven (Isaiah 14:12); 2) "Satan" can transform into an "angel of light" (2 Corinthians 11:14); Lucifer, a cherub angel, is literally named after light (as I will show in a moment), and there is no doubt that he appears as one of the good guys to anyone willing to lend him an ear.

Then why is it even a question whether they are separate entities?

Apart from being a name, "Satan," the Hebrew word *satan* also means generically "adversary" or "accuser." But not every "adversary" in the Hebrew Bible was evil. For instance, when studying Old Testament Christophanies, Numbers 22:22 (the story of Balaam's donkey) comes into the picture quite regularly. The text, in English, states: "And God's anger was kindled because he went: and the Angel of the Lord stood in the way for an adversary against him." This Angel of the Lord is, many scholars teach, Jesus, Himself, in His eternal nature prior to the Incarnation. In close proximity, even the English makes it clear that this being is sent by the Father to intervene upon an act of evil. Therefore, this character cannot be the same "Satan" that appears as the enemy of God in the New Testament. However, the "adversary" in Numbers 22:22 is, in fact, the Hebrew word *satan*. This angel may have been an "enemy" or "adversary" in his opposition to Balaam or his donkey, but his purpose was to accomplish a righteous task God had sent him to do, negating the idea that every time *satan* appears in Hebrew, it's one of the bad guys. So, let's take a look at a word that is more relevant to reptiles.

The word "serpent" in the narrative of Eden is from the Hebrew *nachash*. As a noun, it is translated "serpent" or "snake." Its verb use, however, means "deceiver," "diviner with divine knowledge," or "to practice divination," and the adjective use translates "shining one." Angels and divine beings are often described as shining or luminescent in the Bible, and the proper name of the fallen cherub, "Lucifer" (Hebrew *Helel ben-Shachar*), literally translates "Shining One, son of the Dawn." Many of the studies therefore consider Lucifer to be a shining, serpentine deceiver associated with the Divine Council mentioned in the Old Testament that God pronounces judgement upon (Psalm 82:1; 1 Kings 22:19; all of Job).

Genesis 3:14 ("upon thy belly shalt thou [now] go") has many times been the proof-text of choice for why all snakes today don't have arms and legs, and the assumption is that the all the animals in the Garden of Eden prior to the Fall of man were able to speak and Lucifer, or a *satan* ("adversary"), simply possessed one of them or appeared to her as one of them. Nowhere in Scripture does it suggest that talking animals were the norm in the Garden of Eden or anywhere else before or after the Fall. (Balaam's donkey is, of course, an exception to that norm, with highlighting the animal's miraculous ability to talk.) And if the curse upon the serpent was merely to render all snakes armless and legless, this punishment doesn't appear to have accomplished anything since they still thrive to this day in that form—and yes, they can still climb trees. Also, if the curse in Genesis 3:15 says there will be "enmity…between thy seed [the serpent's offspring] and her seed [human beings]," why isn't there enmity between snakes and humans today? Sure, snakes are territorial, but so is an enormous chunk of the animal kingdom. For the most part, unless they feel provoked or threatened, they usually mind their own business—and not every human hates or fears snakes. This doesn't sound like enmity. Likewise, we all know that snakes don't survive on eating dirt, even though the curse said, "and dust shalt thou eat all the days of thy life."

From Derek Gilbert's *The Great Inception* articles, we read of Eden's "serpent":

Was it a talking snake?

In a word, no.

So who or what was the serpent? Most of us assume it was Satan, but maybe not. The serpent isn't named in the book of Genesis. In fact, Satan wasn't even a personal name in the Old Testament.

Satan means "accuser," written *ha-shaitan* in the [Old Testament]. It's a title, *the* satan, so it really means "the accuser." Think of it as a job title, like prosecuting attorney.

The adversary in the Garden is the *nachash*, which is the word translated into English as "serpent." It's based on an adjective that means bright or brazen, like shiny brass. The noun *nachash* can mean snake, but it also means "one who practices divination."

In Hebrew, it's not uncommon for an adjective to be converted into a noun—the term is "substantivized." If that's the case here, *nachash* could mean "shining one." And that's consistent with other descriptions of the satan figure in the Old Testament.…

The bottom line is this: What Adam and Eve saw in the Garden wasn't a talking snake, but a *nachash*—a radiant, divine entity, very likely of serpentine appearance.…

For centuries, well-meaning Christians have pointed to Genesis 3:14 as the moment in history when snakes lost their legs.
That misses the mark entirely by desupernaturalizing the story.
God didn't amputate the legs of snakes; He was describing the
punishment the *nachash* would suffer in figurative language. Even
casual observers of the animal kingdom know that snakes don't
eat dust….

The main takeaway of this article is this: Eden was a lush, well-
watered garden "on the holy mountain of God," which was where
Yahweh presided over His divine council. The council included
the first humans. They walked and talked with the supernatural
"sons of God" [angels] who, based on clues scattered throughout
the Bible, were beautiful, radiant beings. At least some of them
were serpentine in appearance.[234]

Suffice it to say this entity most likely was *not* a walking or talking
snake, but a bright (perhaps luminescent), intelligent master of deception
with all arms and legs intact. This thing was a being of extreme power and
persuasion, most likely a "professional" accuser within the Divine Council, and he had a major agenda to reverse the beauty of what God had
created. And again, if this being was not Lucifer, himself, it was a straggler
of his fall. Either way, the Luciferian spirit that perpetuated the original
sin (before Adam, and through to Adam's Eden residency) is personified
in both names: "Lucifer" and "Satan." Whether it is the same entity or
not, Lucifer's fall prompted a serpentine wave of rebellion headed by him
and his fallen-angel companions. (This is why, though scholars are correct when they say "Lucifer" and "Satan" are not always interchangeable
names for the same entity, I believe the *wicked* accuser in both Testaments
points back to the event of Lucifer's fall, original sin, and, therefore, his
leadership of iniquity against God. The same spirit of rebellion inhabits
both.)

One key verse envisioning Christ's victory over Lucifer/Satan on the
cross well before it happened is Psalm 91:13: "Thou shalt tread upon
the lion and adder [a venomous snake]: the young lion and the dragon

shalt thou trample under feet." The Latin Vulgate translation renders this: "The asp and the basilisk you will trample under foot; you will tread on the lion and the dragon." This is particularly fascinating reptilian language associated with our formerly anointed cherub. The asp is a venomous snake in the Nile region of Egypt, while the basilisk is a *serpent-king* (!!!) known for his legendary ability to kill any person through eye contact, alone. As for the lion in this verse, that causes some confusion, since Jesus is the Lion of the Tribe of Judah. First, the deceiver who appears as an angel of light (Lucifer/Satan) will always mimic Christ any way he can (and that mimicry climaxes during the end times when Antichrist will position himself as the Son of God and lead many astray as a result). So, it's not particularly unusual to see lion imagery associated with Jesus' grandest enemy's impersonation. Second, the lion, as a beast of the field, carries a natural threat. Saint Augustine expounded upon this verse in this way:

> Ye know who the serpent is [Lucifer/Satan], and how the Church, treadeth upon him, as she is not conquered, because she is on her guard against his cunning. And after what manner he is a lion and a dragon, I believe you know also, beloved. *The lion openly rages*, the dragon lies secretly in covert: the devil hath each of these forces and powers. *When the Martyrs were being slain, it was the raging lion*: when heretics are plotting, it is the dragon creeping beneath us. *Thou hast conquered the lion*; conquer also the dragon: *the lion hath not crushed thee*, let not the dragon deceive thee.[235]

So, it is not the majestic king of the jungle in mind here, but a ferocious beast of destruction. At least that's how the early Church interpreted it. The identity of the serpent in this verse is so clear that Augustine evidently didn't feel the need to elaborate.

In any case, it doesn't take a lot of digging to see the nearly countless ways King Lucifer was a reptilian king (i.e., the king of reptiles). We hear that today and think, *Why would God create such an outstandingly beautiful being and anoint him for special service, yet cause him to resemble such a fierce, frightening, and evil-looking animal species?* (Maybe, for some, the villain Lord Voldemort of the Harry Potter film series comes to mind: pale or bluish skin, slits where nostrils should be, no eyebrows, thin lips, and so on.) But this question is canceled out by the fact that God did not originally intend *any* of His precious animals to be that way. What God made was "good," and at the time He designed them, they weren't dangerous or threatening. Had Lucifer never fed his pride and fallen—had he never been found with iniquity in his heart and became the ultimate icon of evil in every way—we may never have landed on the concept that snakes, reptiles, dinosaurs, etc., were anything other than beautiful, magnificent, and loving creatures playing a part alongside their fellow animals and humans as participants in, and caretakers of, God's creation. To visit this idea from another angle: Imagine that, instead of resembling serpents or dragons, Lucifer had been bovine in his appearance. Today, because of the evil long linked to Lucifer, snakes would be far less terrifying than common cows in the field. We would read articles like Gilbert's above, and instead of referencing "serpentine angels," they would speak of "bovine angels" and bring to mind—to our horror—cows with pointy wings and sharp, gnashing teeth. (Actually, the idea of Lucifer as a cow or bull is not terribly uncommon anyway. When we get to the upcoming look at the word "cherub" and its Akkadian equivalent, *karibu*, you can imagine how Lucifer as a bull materialized early on. For this reason, and a few others, some scholars believe Lucifer had bovine qualities in his external appearance at some point.)

Lucifer's fall is what made reptilian imagery scary in the first place. So, in the beginning, as Gilbert acknowledges, a bright and shining angel of light, though also resembling a serpentine quality, could very well be the image of beauty as God designed it. Gary Stearman's aforementioned article recognizes that Lucifer, prior to his fall, was not the "loathsome" snake we have in mind, but a beautiful divine dragon, which even the "ancient pagan histories" view to be "the wisest and most beautiful of all creatures." Stearman then points out that, even today, the dragon is "highly revered in the country of the orient," so, when he appears to Eve in the Garden of Eden for the first time, "he presented an attractive image of glory and wisdom, not a repugnant snake."[236]

I dunno, Donna. This "snake angel" thing is weird...

I know, I know...but it also happens to be biblical. Remember: The Hebrew word *nachash* can mean "snake" or "serpent," but it is based on an adjective that means "brazen" or "bright," and can describe a being who practices divination. How can one small word mean such a variety of otherwise unrelated things? Moses and the Israelites would have known the Hebrew word for "snake" could be used interchangeably with "shiny brass" or "shining one" because that described the *being known as nachash* who was present in the Garden of Eden at the time of the world's first human. The *concept* predates the language, so the concept defines the latter words, not the other way around.

Gilbert and his wife, Sharon, coauthored a book titled, *Giants, Gods & Dragons: Exposing the Fallen Realm and the Plot to Ignite the Final War of the Ages*. In this work, after showing how the original Hebrew allows for the likely translation of *nachash* into "shining one," which is "consistent with other descriptions of the Satan figure in the Old Testament" (such as the example of the angel who battled the prince of Persia in Daniel 10:5–6: "his face like the appearance of lightning, his eyes like flaming torches, his arms and legs like the gleam of burnished bronze"[237]), these authors immediately go on to say:

> Another example occurred about nine hundred years before Daniel, when the Israelites began to complain (and complain and complain) on their way out of Egypt. In response, God sent *saraph nachash* ("fiery serpents") to torment them. *Saraph* is the root word of *seraphim*, which roughly means "burning ones." The Hebrew words *saraph* and *nachash* are used interchangeably, so rather than "fiery serpents," the actual translation should read "*saraph* serpents."
>
> Deuteronomy 8:15 praises Yahweh for bringing Israel through "the great and terrifying wilderness, with its fiery serpents," reinforcing the interchangeability of *saraph* and *nachash*.
>
> Now, if the mental image of flaming snakes isn't weird enough, the prophet Isaiah twice referred to *flying* serpents (*saraph `uwph*,

in Isaiah 14:29 and 30:6). And in his famous throne-room vision, Isaiah saw:

> ...the Lord sitting upon a throne, high and lifted up; and the train of his robe filled the temple. Above him stood the seraphim. Each had six wings: with two he covered his face, and with two he covered his feet, and with two he flew. (Isaiah 6:1–2)

Again, the root word of "seraphim" is *saraph*, the same word translated "serpent" in Numbers and Deuteronomy. In fact, aside from the Isaiah 6 passage above, every single mention of "seraphim" in the Old Testament refers to serpentine beings![238]

So, even apart from Lucifer—the bright, shining, anointed cherub/priest-king enthroned in Eden—the celestial, angel-like beings called *seraphim* who guard the throne of God in Heaven were serpentine in their appearance as well, according to Isaiah and many of the linguistic experts that interpret him, including my favorite late Hebrew master, Dr. Michael S. Heiser:

> As I noted in *The Unseen Realm*, "It is more likely that seraphim derives from the Hebrew noun *sarap* ("serpent"), which in turn is drawn from Egyptian throne guardian terminology and conceptions." As recent research demonstrates, the Egyptian Uraeus serpent, drawn from two species of Egyptian cobras, fits all the elements of the supernatural seraphim who attend Yahweh's holy presence in Isaiah 6. The relevant cobra species spit "burning" venom, can expand wide flanges of skin on either side of their bodies—considered "wings" in antiquity—when threatened, and are (obviously) serpentine. As Joines notes, the protective nature of the uraeus cobra is evident: "A function of the uraeus is to protect the pharaoh and sacred objects by breathing out fire on his enemies."[239]

Thus, shiny, "serpentine or snakelike angels" is not only an admissible translation, it's the direct description of the beings God created to have the highest level of authority just under the Godhead—and they stand in His very throne room! Gilbert also points out that "the cherubim Ezekiel saw [in Ezekiel 1:5–14] looked like something from a nightmare," showing in Scripture that "they sparkled like burnished bronze" and "darted to and fro, like the appearance of a flash of lightning."[240]

Rewind to the Garden of Eden... The "snake" Adam and Eve spoke to, instead of being a talking animal (which now appears to be a preposterous idea, despite the hold this concept has on Christian cartoons for kids), was a divinely created, authoritative, shining being, serpent-like in appearance. The fact that this former servant of God turned Adam and Eve away from God through pride and deceit—and the fact that he was in Eden already by the time Adam and Eve were formed—shows that he was an occupant of Eden during the fallen, "void" era of Earth: either Lucifer, himself (the most likely), or, at the least, a lead "accuser" and "adversary" (a non-proper-noun *satan*) who jumped on board the ludicrous insurrection plan. And, as you've likely pieced together by now, this whole movement against God brought unfathomable imagery links between Lucifer and reptiles.

Lucifer was the representative of Earth's "lizards." (The angels who fell with him may have been, also.) It's the only explanation that makes sense (at least to me and at least ten theologians from SkyWatch TV circles who speak on this matter). The dinosaurs were the greatest of all the lizard family, *and* they posed the greatest threat to the humans God made to carry on His plan for Creation and redemption through His Son.

One may wonder why, if Lucifer's fall caused the global wipeout of all dinosaurs, other lesser reptiles were allowed to remain on Earth through the re-Creation and up to today—after all, there *are* reptiles in our current animal kingdom. If our theory is correct, the answer is in the question: God *intended* for the lesser serpents to exist and cohabitate on Earth alongside man. If Adam and Eve hadn't fallen, the whole snake family may not have ever been a threat to man (as Pember explained in the excerpt at the beginning of this chapter), but if God had created the dinosaurs from the very beginning—millions of years ago—why did He choose not to include them in the Creation beginning in Genesis 1:3 that so many believe occurred around six thousand years ago? Why haven't archeologists found dinosaur fossils dated to around the time of Adam or Noah, or after the Flood?

Could it be that our not-so-beloved King Lucifer pulled a Josef-Mengele-of-Auschwitz scheme, and the dinosaurs were the aftermath of that "creation"?

Josef Mengele was a Nazi surgeon called the "Angel of Death" who mercilessly performed gruesome and gristly experiments on human subjects at Auschwitz during Adolf Hitler's regime. For such undertakings as sewing twin children together back to back in an attempt to play God and "create" conjoined twins (and many other examples too disturbing to mention), Mengele is an archetypal Lucifer—a demonic "creator" in his own mind. Obviously, his crude surgeries and "medical" practices never rendered his desired results; those who survived were sent to the gas chambers when Mengele's trials only made them sick, and the remains of those who died were thrown in the furnace or sent to Austria for further study.

Lucifer, on the other hand, wouldn't only have surpassed Mengele's human knowledge of the sciences and medicines—as he witnessed God's very first Creation and "shouted for joy" on that day alongside God and all the angels (Job 38:4–7)—but he has *already illustrated his capability of "creating" monsters* through unorthodox, spurious, counterfeit-Creator-breeding methods! The Nephilim of the Old Testament are proof of that.

Interestingly, ancient apocryphal literature usually grouped with Enoch also acknowledges that early Luciferian "sciences" of Genesis 6 were applied to animals. In Jubilees 5:2, we read:

> And injustice increased upon the earth, and all flesh corrupted its way; man and cattle and beasts and birds and everything which walks on the earth. And they all corrupted their way and their ordinances, and they began to eat one another. And injustice grew upon the earth and every imagination of the thoughts of all mankind was thus continually evil. (Jubilees 5:2; cf. 7:21–25)[241]

Our early Church Father, Eusebius, also spoke of Luciferian mutations that occurred during this epoch…and he, too, recognized the evil
was carried out in such a way that it involved animals (and note the last
line):

> And they begat human beings, with two wings; and then others
> with four wings and two faces and one body and two heads…
> still others with horses' hooves, and others in the shape of a horse
> at the rear and a human shape at the front…they also made bulls
> with human heads and horses with dogs' heads as well as other
> monsters with horses heads and human bodies…*then all kinds of
> dragon-like monstrous beings.*[242]

Tom Horn and Cris Putnam, in their book, *Exo-Vaticana*, noted the
following regarding Eusebius' observations:

> Of the "winged humans" and "dragon-like monsters," prophecy
> expert, J. R. Church, once made an interesting point that since
> this activity was satanic in nature, it refers to the "seed of the ser-
> pent" that was at enmity with Christ. "The concept of a reptil-
> ian race continues throughout the Bible as a metaphoric symbol
> of the devil," Church wrote in *Prophecy in the News* magazine,
> February 2009. "Later Scriptures add the term 'dragon,' with the
> implication that these otherworldly creatures were designed with
> the DNA code of a reptilian race." Church went on to state that
> some of these satanic creatures were depicted as "bat-like gar-
> goyles, or winged dragons" in ancient art, and that we should not
> be surprised that "a humanoid-type reptilian race could cohabit
> with human women and produce a race of giants." In what could
> be historical support of Dr. Church's premise, a document frag-
> ment found in Cave 4 among the Dead Sea Scrolls contains an
> admonition by Amram, the father of Moses, to his children. In a
> badly damaged segment of the text, Amram sees the chief angel of
> darkness, a Watcher [fallen angel] named Melkiresha in the form

of a *reptilian* (bracketed suspension points represent scroll damage/irretrievable text):

> I saw Watchers in my vision, a dream vision, and behold
> two (of them) argued about me and said [...] and they
> were engaged in a great quarrel concerning me. I asked
> them: "You, what are you [...] thus [...] about me?" They
> answered and said to me: "We have been made masters
> and rule over all the sons of men." And they said to me:
> "Which of us do you choose [...]
>
> I raised my eyes and saw one of them. His looks were
> frightening like those of a viper, and his garments were
> multi-coloured and he was extremely dark [...]
>
> And afterwards I looked and behold [...] by his
> appearance and his face was like that of an adder [a venomous snake], and he was covered with [...] together, and
> his eyes [...]."[243]

A fallen-angel Watcher described in the Dead Sea Scrolls as a reptilian with the face of an adder… It's getting harder and harder to dismiss these serpentine links.

It was also during Tom Horn's trip to meet Dr. Don Mose—a third-generation Navajo medicine man, retired academic who authored many of the Native American nation's textbooks and cultural programs throughout the Four Corners area, and a proficient oral-traditions historian well known to the local tribes—that our Defender Publishing and SkyWatch Television team learned one the oldest historic traditions among Native Americans regarding the time of Creation. In this account, there was a "good God" who created all things "good." These praiseworthy formations of Earth were later spoiled when a reptilian entity appeared and misled humanity. The early Anasazi tribe—rumored in the *sanctioned* legends of the area to have migrated and mingled with the Pueblo tribes—actually "disappeared," Mose said, after they came under the mind control of a reptile with a halo, a carnivorous creature suspiciously similar to what Cris Putnam describes in *On the Path of the Immortals* as:

> ..."fiery seraphim" (Hebrew: *saraph*, "fiery serpent," also corresponding with many other testaments around the ancient world, including Sanskrit *sarpa, sarpin*—"reptile"—whether with legs like the lizard or legless like the snake).[244]

Human-angel hybrids are more familiar to the Nephilim crowd, whereas dinosaurs originating from satanic, biological-manipulation methods are harder to imagine, since we don't have an equivalent Genesis 6:4 account of their origin. But if even human beings, through completely natural means, can take the first canines and breed everything from a toy-breed, yapping, lap Chihuahua that would greet an intruder with kisses to an enormous and fiercely protective St. Bernard whose bite can flatten a basketball, what could God's most intelligent cherub accomplish after being an eyewitness of God's creative ability and having had millions of years to play God and mess with unnatural DNA modifications after his fall?

Were the first dinosaurs of God's own design? Perhaps a better question is this: Could an argument be made for how the prehistoric beasts *changed into something else* at some early period of their earthly existence?

Surprisingly, yes. Science acknowledges this as well, and the details are only just now surfacing. The Smithsonian Institution, of all sources, concedes to this in a May 2023 article titled, "The Rise of Meat-Eating Dinosaurs Is More Complicated Than We Thought: Paleontologists Are Searching for How Carnivorous Dinosaurs Went from Pipsqueaks to Titans." Riley Black, Smithsonian's science correspondent, begins his trek on the "titan" end, listing three frightening examples of bipedal lizard-monsters we now know to have been "latecomers" to the scenario: tyrannosaurus, torvosaurus, and giganotosaurus. Towering carnivores such as these "weren't around," Black says, and in their earliest days, they were no bigger than a large dog (he lists the German Shepherd as an example). After explaining that all meat-eating dinosaurs came from theropods (a hollow-boned, three-toed, and clawed species), Black goes on to say: "Up until now, paleontologists thought theropods remained generally small and on the ecological sidelines from about 235 through 201 million years ago. It was only...at the end of the Triassic [Period]...that carnivorous dinosaurs started to get big."[245] *Science Daily* also sees a change in the size and behaviors of these creatures at one point. Their information derives from bone studies first published in the scientific journal *Science Advances*, concluding that "*something must have happened* in the Triassic that allowed dinosaurs to endure the Triassic-Jurassic mass extinction and adapt in its aftermath, *becoming* the dominant group for the rest of the Mesozoic."[246] And *LiveScience*, after stating that dinosaurs were "mostly dog- and horse-size creatures" in the beginning, likewise documents their transition "into the most enormous beasts that ever existed on land." But of equal interest to our study is this journal's admission that this group of terrifying creatures had "unique anatomy [that] set them apart from other animal groups."[247] It appears clear: "Something" happened that took dinosaurs from their original form to...*something else.* Therefore, we either a) subscribe to scientific theory of random evolution (which, as Chuck Missler illustrated at the beginning of this book, is ludicrous), or b) admit that there may be another explanation, perhaps involving a lizard king.

Of course, aside from my Auschwitz-Lucifer "gristly experiments" theory or breeding, there's also the witchcraft angle: Satan's son, Antichrist, will perform true miracles in the sight of all during the end times (2 Thessalonians 2:9; Revelation 13:30; 19:20). The Bible tells us so. Since this ancient spirit alive in the future Antichrist is the same spirit born in and through the iniquity of Lucifer, the "false creator" *may not* have even needed sciences, surgeries, or breeding if he set out to divine his own servant beings through sorcery. The Wicked Witch's flying monkey-servants in *The Wizard of Oz* are similar: wicked entities were somehow "magicked" into existence to serve the king of reptiles. (But one important detail about this angle needs to be stated: Witchcraft or the redesigning of any life form through sorcery is still not "creation," even if the change is brought about through invisible or spiritual methods. Lucifer has never had, nor will ever have, the power of creation as God does. Lucifer would have still had to take something *God had already made* and warped it.) From this angle, not all of them would have had to be carnivorous people-eaters for Lucifer to utilize them in his own schemes, so, for those who have been wondering how I was going to separate the "evil" dinosaurs from the "peaceful herbivores," I don't think an "innocent" dinosaur requires an explanation. It's about who they were serving and following, not what we can glean from their anatomical functions and behaviors based on fossils. Nor do I believe all extinct forms of life have to correspond to the dinosaurs. Lucifer could have made all sorts of weird things... (Darwinian ape men, anyone?)

So, I ask again: Were dinosaurs bred or designed intentionally by Lucifer/Satan or his Auschwitz-style doctors to dominate Earth? Did these ancient monstrosities originate through the evil one's plan to, say, thwart God's creation and introduce an uninhabitable planet where no human could ever survive long enough to produce the Messiah through a pure bloodline? Why not? He did so after Adam...

Or, perhaps, were dinosaurs: 1) *included* in God's very first Earth Creation event; 2) made by God to be peaceful, harmonious, and "good" as God intended all animals to be; 3) fell with Lucifer at the onset of the "void" (in the same way the animal kingdom would later fall with Adam and Eve); and 4) excluded from the re-Creation of Earth at the time of Adam because they resembled their reptilian king in some way (maybe spiritually?) that God deemed unworthy of re-creating?

Either way, whether the "great lizards" of old were the perverted creation of Lucifer or beasts that God deliberately excluded from the "good" world, there is yet another link between King Lizard and his savage darlings we have to visit before we move on to the historical "fit" in this big picture. The cherub *may* have even been one of the original five "living creatures" in Heaven, and if he was, the absence of dinosaurs could explain the missing link of these Creation representatives.

Wait... "Five" living creatures? Don't you mean to say "four"?

No. I mean five...

Understand that this is only a theory, but it's one I find fascinating in light of the idea that reptiles, snakes, dragons, etc., weren't originally

associated with evil. Yet, free from imagery of sin or wickedness as they
may have initially been, they appear to be *completely missing* in the roster
of representatives in the throne of God. We see these bizarre, but frighten-
ingly authoritative and holy, beings described in Ezekiel 1:10-11:

> As for the likeness of their faces, they four had the face of a
> man, and the face of a lion, on the right side: and they four had
> the face of an ox on the left side; they four also had the face of
> an eagle. Thus were their faces: and their wings were stretched
> upward; two wings of every one were joined one to another, and
> two covered their bodies.

First, note the four faces of each of these beings: man, lion, ox, and
eagle. Now, note the similarity of these four living creatures and the celestial "beasts" of Revelation 4:6–11:

> And before the throne there was a sea of glass like unto crystal:
> and in the midst of the throne, and round about the throne, were
> four beasts full of eyes before and behind. And the first beast was
> like a *lion*, and the second beast like a *calf*, and the third beast had
> a face as a *man*, and the fourth beast was like a flying *eagle*. [So
> far, the same animals are represented here.] And the four beasts
> had each of them six wings about him; and they were full of eyes
> within: and they rest not day and night, saying, "Holy, holy,
> holy, Lord God Almighty, which was, and is, and is to come."
> And when those beasts give glory and honour and thanks to him
> that sat on the throne, who liveth for ever and ever, The four and
> twenty elders fall down before him that sat on the throne, and
> worship him that liveth for ever and ever, and cast their crowns
> before the throne, saying, "Thou art worthy, O Lord, to receive
> glory and honour and power: for *thou hast created all things, and
> for thy pleasure they are and were created.*" (Emphasis added)

The last line of this passage makes clear not only that God is being worshiped, but it states what He is being worshiped *for*—the things He created. Thus, a number of scholars have, long linked the beasts/creatures to beings representative of Creation. Before we proceed, though, we should look at precisely what these beings are. Ezekiel chapter 10 (especially verses 6–9) makes it clear that these beings or creatures are cherubim—just like the cherub king. Though we've seen what Ezekiel 1 describes, let us—for the sake of edifying repetition and academic comparison in a theory I imagine most readers have never heard—be sure we know what he saw just after calling them "cherubim" several times in chapter 10:

> And every one had four faces: the first face was the face of a cherub, and the second face was the face of a man, and the third the face of a lion, and the fourth the face of an eagle. And the cherubims were lifted up. This is the living creature that I saw by the river of Chebar. (Ezekiel 10:14–15)

You may have noticed the four faces are slightly different here: the "face of an ox" has been replaced by "the face of a cherub." However, the likeness, according to historians and anthropologists, might be the same. First, note that in Genesis 10:8–10, we read: "And Cush begat *Nimrod*: he began to be a mighty one in the earth.… And the beginning of his kingdom was Babel, and Erech, and *Akkad*, and Calneh, in the land of Shinar" (emphasis added). (By the way, this verse is widely accepted as referring to Nimrod's "mighty one" [Hebrew *gibor*] status which traces him back to Nephilim DNA. The words "mighty men" in Genesis 6:4—the verse that describes the fallen angels taking human females to produce giants—is *gibborim*.) Akkad was an early Mesopotamian city that, at the latest, would have established its cultural language and imagery when the Akkadian Empire rose in Nimrod's day, sometime circa 2335–2155 BC. However, as the language and mythology of the Akkadians had migrated from Sumer, their myths regarding gods and celestial beings (like the cherubim) were far more ancient, tracing back to the early generations of Adam and Eve's offspring. Thus, the Hebrew word "cherub" very likely links etymologically to the Akkadian *karibu*. Derek and Sharon Gilbert, commenting on Ezekiel 10:14, make this connection as well. Anticipating their readers' confusion, they ask:

> *Wait—why a cherub instead of an ox for the fourth face? Is there some*
> *connection between the cherub and the ox?*
>
> Actually, yes.

The word "cherub" probably comes from the Akkadian *karibu* (the "ch" [in "cherub"] should be a hard "k" sound). It means "intercessor" or "one who prays." The *karibu* were usually portrayed as winged bulls with human faces, and huge statues of the *karibu* were set up as divine guardians at the entrances of palaces and temples. This is the role of the cherubim "at the east of the garden of Eden...to guard the way to the tree of life [Genesis 3:24]."[248]

The Gilberts aren't the only scholars to discover this etymological trail. Charles H. Dyer, a commentator who collaborated on the study of Ezekiel in *The Bible Knowledge Commentary: An Exposition of the Scriptures*, points out that, from this view, "the face of an ox was, in fact, the normal understanding of the face of a cherub. In Akkadian literature the *kuribu* (cognate of 'cherub') appear to have nonhuman faces."[249] The *Lexham Bible Dictionary* relates the etymological history of the Hebrew "cherub," and concurs that it "is probably related to the Akkadian word *kuribu*, referring to a divine being associated with a sanctuary.... The related Akkadian verb form *karabu* means 'bless'.... In Akkadian literature, the *kuribu* were not associated with any single deity, but they symbolized divine presence and protection."[250] This conclusion is shared by the *Lexham Theological Wordbook* as well.[251] Michael Heiser also finds the Akkadian *kuribu/karabu* origin of "cherub" admissible, as well as "bovine" characteristics, in his book, *Angels: What the Bible Really Says about God's Heavenly Host.*[252] (By the way, as a crucial reminder: It is dangerous to assume that Christianity or its precursor, Judaism, borrowed ideas from the surrounding pagan lands and conformed their languages or culture to match what came earlier. Keep in mind—always—that the God who formed the heavens and Earth was the *original* revelator of the supernatural, and those who first observed reality on Earth and in the heavens were the angels. So, even if a word in Hebrew draws its etymological roots from Sumerian or Akkadian, it only proves that they mingled early on and found more accurate ways of describing their spiritual beliefs. As one example: Old, Anglo-Saxon English existed for centuries before the language called "Old French." Yet the English word "fiancé" ["to be betrothed"] came from French and is still used in English today. That doesn't mean the French had the *idea* first, as betrothal is as ancient as the earliest beings on Earth. It merely shows that English speakers found a word from a foreign neighbor that more accurately expressed an unconsummated betrothal relationship [engagement].)

Thus, if the bull face of the Akkadian being is, like these scholars attest, similar to the face of the guardian cherubim of God, then there is no discrepancy. We're still looking at four representative faces of God's Creation, as the "face of a cherub" in Ezekiel 10:14 is synonymous to the "face of an ox" in the earlier part of his vision. (Recall the settlement in Catalhoyuk we looked at a few chapters back. Their obsession with bull heads on the walls of their homes and all over their shrines is more fascinating in light of this concept of the bull-cherub. From what we know, Catalhoyuk predates even Sumer by about a thousand years and maybe far longer. Also recall that we have a hard time identifying their form of worship based on remains, alone. The only lead we have is the Mother Goddess idea, which we found reason to dismiss [the "idols," if that's what they were, were cast into the garbage pits and nonchalantly left behind]. Could it be that these pre-Adamite "people"—which scientists say are human but who arrived on Earth a millennium before Adam—received a bright and shining visitor, resembling some sort of cow-Satan, who instructed them how to live, worship, and cultivate land to survive…and who also explained their origins had been given through a bull-headed cherub? Lucifer can appear as an angel of light, so we know he's capable of changing his form. But even if he didn't, one of the angels that fell alongside him may have resembled an Akkadian-like *karibu* cherub.)

Now that we know we're talking about the cherubim Lucifer was amidst before he fell, we can look at these representative beings and consider how they characterize four distinct categories of God's creatures:

1. Mankind ("face of a man" in both Ezekiel and Revelation);
2. Wild, undomesticated animals of the land, forests, and fields (face/beast like a lion);
3. Domestic animals that can be made to serve humanity ("ox" in Ezekiel 1, "cherub"/*karibu* in Ezekiel 10, and baby ox ["calf"] in Revelation);
4. Animals of the air (face/beast like an eagle).

If the living creatures—cherubim—both a) represent God's creation and b) praise Him for it, then why are the reptilian and aquatic species left out of these categories?

Remember that Leviathan is a "dragon" described as a "piercing... crooked serpent" with multiple "heads" (Isaiah 27:1; Psalm 74:13–14). He also just happens to live in the *sea*. Far from being a now-extinct dinosaur, as some scholars claim, I believe it's infinitely clear that the dragon named "Satan" that has multiple heads as described in Revelation 12:3 is a picture of Lucifer as a giant, twisting reptile, *and* as an aquatic animal: Both serpents and sea creatures are captured in Leviathan, that Luciferian entity of the end days.

From the *Faithlife Study Bible*, we see a clue to yet another incredible link: "Biblical references to Leviathan are often symbolic references for chaos *itself*."[253]

Did you catch that? Leviathan is chaos, itself?! Leviathan "is"—not "looks like," not "shares similarities with"; he *is*—*tohu/bohu*?

In this same source, in reference to Isaiah 27:1, we read:

While the apocalyptic imagery in [Isaiah] ch. 25 alluded to the watery chaos of the flood and victory as swallowing death (25:8), here Yahweh's ultimate victory is represented as an assault on the serpent—invoking an ancient theme of gods bringing order by subduing the chaos monster....
The battle with the dragon appears in Rev 12:3–9, where he

is identified with Satan himself. In the OT [Old Testament] references, God brings order to the universe by slaying a primeval dragon symbolizing chaos (compare Isa 51:9; Pss 74:14; 89:11; Job 9:13; 26:12; 40:24). The motif of divine combat with a serpent or dragon was found in Mesopotamian and Canaanite mythology. The biblical theme inspired apocalyptic writers in Jewish and Christian literature, especially the books of 1 Enoch and Revelation.[254]

Many sources attest to this thread, including the following from the *Lexham Bible Dictionary*: "**DRAGON AND SEA:** Figurative representatives of chaos in the Bible,"[255] and, "chaos could be represented as a great sea serpent or dragon...known as Leviathan."[256] *Holman Illustrated Bible Dictionary* states that "Leviathan...represented chaos in a personified manner."[257] From *The NET Bible First Edition Notes* by Biblical Studies Press, in a commentary on Job 3:8: "Job employs here the mythological figure Leviathan, the monster of the deep or chaos."[258] According to the *New Bible Commentary*, both Leviathan and Behemoth are "symbol[s] of chaos."[259] From the *Dictionary of the Old Testament: Prophets*: "The 'crushing of the head' of the chaos monster, Leviathan (as in Ps 74:12–14), means that the Lord establishes cosmic order and justice."[260]

Order and justice. That's a far cry from "without form, and void"—statuses that now appear to be embodied in the chaos monster, Lucifer-Satan-Leviathan. Even Dr. Heiser states in one of his books that Leviathan is the pure "image of chaos...common throughout the ancient world."[261] In his famous, groundbreaking, and critically acclaimed *Unseen Realm*, Heiser points out an incredible (and far too often overlooked) link between the ancient sea-serpent and the purpose Christ had when He walked on water:

In the ancient world the sea was a thing of dread. It was unpredictable and untamable. It was a place upon which humans couldn't live. Consequently, the sea was often used as a metaphor for chaos, destruction, and death. The power and chaotic unruliness of the sea was symbolized in both the Old Testament and a wide range of ancient Near Eastern literatures with a dragon or sea monster, variously known as Leviathan and Rahab (e.g., Pss 74:14; 89:10).

Sea imagery conveys these ideas from the very beginning of the Bible. The waters of the primeval deep (Gen 1:2) must be calmed and restrained by God. The defeat of the gods of Egypt happens when the sea obeys its Maker (Exod 14). Jesus walks on the sea and instantly brings it into submission. To the ancient mind these incidents symbolized power over chaos and everything that might bring harm and death to humanity. Absence of chaos meant that everything was in perfect, divine order and calm.

This is why Revelation ends as it does, with God's return to permanently dwell with his family on a new earth. When [the future] Eden comes, there is no more sea.[262]

When Jesus walked on water, He was not only "calming" it; He was illustrating His authority over the chaos-dragon, the serpent under His feet!

I have probably another two hundred books in the lineup that say the name "Leviathan" is synonymous to, and interchangeable with, "Chaos," as this sea-serpent is the personification of it (just like Lady Wisdom is capitalized as wisdom personified in the Old Testament), but I will spare you from having to read through all of them. Suffice it to say that when God made Earth, it was *not* a *tohu/bohu* world, but Lucifer—also known as Leviathan, also known as Chaos—fell, and Earth *became* the home of King Chaos. Suddenly, around that same time, due to a judgment of God, all dinosaurs became extinct…

…And we do *not* have a holy cherub among the *possible five* living creatures identified in the Bible as the Creation representative of aquatic and reptilian animals.

Could Lucifer, in his pre-fallen state, have been the fifth cherub of these pictures?

Gary Stearman of *Prophecy Watchers* believes so. In one article, he reminds readers that the four "beasts" are the cherubim, "each assigned to watch over an animal kingdom." If Lucifer hadn't fallen, Stearman says, a fifth Creation cherub "would" stand amidst the others and "watch over the kingdom of the reptiles…[and] dinosaurs." Since Lucifer *did* fall, this "great dragon" became "a dust-eating serpent" (as Genesis 3:14 acknowledges). Stearman relates that "long before [Lucifer] came into the earthly Garden of Eden":

> The [dino]saurian kingdom was on its way out. Yet, though no longer co-regent at God's throne, apparently he still retained some of his former glory. That is, until he had finished his work with Eve. At that point, he and his breed were reduced to the state in which we see them today.[263]

I believe this is becoming more than a theory. Although I cannot (and will not) call it "fact," the evidence stacks so highly in favor of the dinosaurs' extinction being a casualty of Lucifer's fall that I'm frankly shocked more scholars haven't already written about this.

So far, we have a "fit" for chronology, symbolism, representation, theology, and etymology supporting this king-of-dinosaurs theory. Just a couple final links remain…

Historically, Scientifically, and Geologically, It Fits

Scientists widely attribute the extinction of dinosaurs to a comet or asteroid called Chicxulub that crashed to Earth about sixty-six million years ago (at or near the end of the Cretaceous Period; most dinosaur fossils died in the strata layers of this time), just off the northern coast of what is now Mexico's Yucatan Peninsula. The *Harvard Gazette* reports that this colliding space body left a crater "that spans 93 miles and goes 12 miles deep."[264] But dinosaurs weren't the only casualties. When we think of the day the dinos died, images of a roaring T-Rex or leaf-eating "long-necks" come to mind, but that's not the whole picture. This mass extinction event also brought an end to "almost three-quarters of the plant and animal species then living on Earth."[265] From what we just learned about Lucifer being a representative of both land and sea serpentine animals, it shouldn't surprise us to learn that among those that died off were…

...a great number of large marine reptiles!

Think about that for just a moment. The most prevalent scientific explanation for why these larger creatures didn't survive impact was that the asteroid wiped out almost everything over a certain weight. (Estimates of this weight range from more than fifty pounds to more than a hundred pounds; however, it's all conjecture based on decent supporting evidence.) That very well may be true, but if it must apply to both water and land, then it demands an answer for why certain large marine animals were allowed to survive (whales, giant sharks, etc.). I don't have a problem admitting that every single living thing at and around the site of impact was obliterated, and that all of life even on the other side of Earth would have been affected in some devastating way, leading to far more than just the extinction of large marine reptiles. Nothing about that is surprising. But why, of all life forms that went extinct at the time of the Chicxulub, and amidst all other marine animals that survived, do *reptiles* appear to be the species in the animal kingdom that took the biggest hit?

The evidence just keeps stacking up...

But the takeaway from the asteroid/comet Chicxulub is its ties to Lucifer/Satan. Chicxulub is a Mayan term meaning "the devil's tail." (I am aware the crater was named after a local community of the same name, not for a particular religious connotation. Still, I find the link astounding, poetic, and even ironic, as it connects to my theory. It's perhaps one of those moments when a finite, human mind assigned a name to something God had named before the beginning of time.)

Lucifer was a "morning star" described as a "shining one," and in the New Testament, Jesus, Himself, says in Luke 10:18: "I beheld Satan as lightning fall from heaven." By the time of Christ, the Chicxulub asteroid was distant history.

Can you imagine a scene in Heaven wherein God, fed up with Lucifer's pride, hurls the fallen serpent-cherub like a bolt of lightning to Earth, as Jesus "beheld"?

Reader's Digest journalist Meghan Jones reminds her readers of what Earth would have looked like just after the dinosaur-extinction event: "Dust and debris would have blocked out the sun, hurting life-giving processes like photosynthesis. The Earth's temperature also would have surged dangerously because of all of the greenhouse gases in the atmosphere. [This is] backed up by significant scientific discoveries."[266] The impact of Chicxulub expelled what many scientists believe to be upwards of hundreds of billions of tons of sulfur into Earth's atmosphere. This, in turn, rendered a global blackout lasting years, blocking light from our planet's surface and creating freezing temperatures, though "there is also evidence of substantial fires from that point in history."[267]

Fire is not a big leap from Luciferian terminology in the Word, but sulfur—translated "brimstone" in many translations—is also associated with Lucifer/Satan *and* events of God's wrath (Revelation 9:13–19; 14:9–11; 21:8; Genesis 19:24–25; Deuteronomy 29:23; Psalm 11:5–6; Isaiah 30:31–33; Ezekiel 38:21–23; and many others). In fact, God's wrath frequently appears in Scripture as "sulfur" (or "brimstone") falling from the sky, as seen in Luke 17:28–29 (as well as several verses just referenced): "Likewise also as it was in the days of Lot; they did eat, they drank, they bought, they sold, they planted, they builded; But the same day that Lot went out of Sodom it rained fire and brimstone [sulfur] from heaven, and destroyed them all." In Isaiah 30:33, the "breath" of the Lord (the Holy Spirit) is "like a torrent of brimstone." And God not only supplies and creates light, He *is* light (1 John 1:5; many others), so the darkness over Earth's surface in Genesis 1:2 might mean more than just the absence of illumination; it might mean a certain level of restriction of God's presence from the planet of sin as well.

We know from this same verse that the Holy Spirit was "hovering" over the "deep." Thus, we can be sure that, at the very least, God was guarding Earth in some regard, perhaps against the spread of evil. Many theories related to the Chaos legends propose that this "deep" may have been a personified, cosmic "waters of chaos" idea relating to a number of ancient aquatic monsters. In other words, it might have been Tiamat or some other sea monster of Sumerian, Akkadian, or Babylonian derivation. If there is any truth to that—and I think there might be—then all of these tales again trek back to the *first* and *original* story of our own cherub-sea-monster, Chaos-Leviathan, an enemy of Yahweh and one of the known formations of Lucifer. In turn, however, if God was "hovering" to keep something imprisoned on Earth so it could not travel outward (for another insurrection?), then, again, God's presence was *here*, but more in capacity to safeguarding (as opposed to God's Spirit joyfully fluttering over waters from which the first Earth was about to be formed).

Whatever the state of Earth the day Lucifer fell, it appears clear that the absence of light, freezing temperatures with intermittent fires, sulfur all around, and a possible Chaos-Leviathan trapped in the "deep" all fit the "without form, and void" status as it has been herein determined. It's not a stretch that an event involving God's judgment against Lucifer and the fallen ones would be the largest sulfur expulsion in the history of Earth—on the same day the dinosaurs died, light was temporarily removed, and something treacherous slithered in the murky depths of the oceans, still alive in serpentine form…until it could emerge again in the Garden of Eden.

Then, humanity would be made for the first time in the image of God.

Does that perhaps point to a new understanding of the image of Him we mirror? If all of these pre-Adamic beings or fallen angels whose remains and fossils we've discovered were so easily influenced by Lucifer, maybe—*just maybe*—the image of God instilled within us isn't just creativity, a moral attribute, or an intelligence, but an intrinsic moral intelligence: an innate and Holy-Spirit-guided gut feeling about what is right or wrong that the beings of the distant past didn't have. If so, that would explain why humans, unlike whatever the pre-Adamic ancients were, had at least one man among us (Noah) who recognized the evil for what it was and maintained his righteous standing in the midst of the Genesis-6:4-Nephilim-and-"void"-era *chaos*. It's just a theory, but it also explains why pre-Adamic discoveries look very human, but Adamites are special.

That brings us back to Genesis 1:3: the *re*-Creation, restoration, restitution, and redemption of Earth.

Our home.

The "War" I've Started

It *Is* Worth It in the End!

"YOU'RE GOING TO START A WAR," the theologian said. "If you write this book you're planning, you *will* start a war. What you are saying—your approach to cosmology in light of all parties currently involved in the debate—is not one the world is ready to hear. And it doesn't matter what your reasons are. As driven as you are to reach the lost through this message, if you write what you're planning to write, you are literally begging for an unfathomably deep pool of argumentative agitators to surface from out of the woodwork on all sides and argue with you. Are you prepared to respond to *all* of them?"

This book began with these words, and it will end by addressing the same words from a perspective some readers may not have seen coming.

The question of whether I—or Tom Horn, or both of us, or any other scholar who makes the same conclusions we have in this book—want to "start a war" relies on identifying what that actually infers. If the goal is to "win" and then "rub elbows" with those who agree with my theory, while treating with intellectual snobbery and condescension those who don't, then no.

Let me say it again: Big. Fat. No.

I don't have time to spend even a moment engaging in certain kinds of banter that have become intrinsic in the dissension within today's Body of Christ. But the truth is a war has already begun, and it has been going on since before the beginning of time. It is this war between God and Lucifer that led to the very Fall of humanity and ushered in this temporary confusion of cosmological details. As I said at the beginning of this book, there is "truth" from the eyes of man—flawed, finite, imperfect, and rightly called "theory"—and the *truth* of the universe as it really is, which we are still trying to parse out with our limited observation. As a follower of Messiah, I chose long ago to participate in a war for the lost: to become the apologist God wants me to be, and to represent "true truth" as much as I can in my fallen form. At this juncture in my life, I felt led to tackle the subjects this book covers in that interest. Could I have made a mistake somewhere in this book? Despite my grandest efforts *not* to, yes. That's always a possibility, because, like all other people on Earth, I'm a post-Adam's-Fall being, sharing the humanity the Fall event weakened.

Of course, there's no pressure to agree with any of the material this book presents. And, if this explanation of Lucifer's role in cosmology has inspired someone to dig into the Word of God—whether their motive is to argue *or* to study all these topics for themselves and carry what they learn into our dying world—the biblical information they put into their gray matter as a result can only be edifying, always (2 Timothy 3:16–17). If even one reader grows closer to the Savior after learning the Bible *does* allow for Earth to be ancient—if *just one reader* comes to know that the God of the Bible is relevant in a scientific world and that He is, in fact, the Master Scientist to whom all the universe belongs—then I have accomplished what I set out to do. I wrote this book to reach two types of people: 1) the lost, who believe being a Christian means you can't also appreciate, follow, believe in, or give ear to scientific theory, fact, or discovery—or that, if you do, you can only accept *parts* of the Bible but discard the others involving Earth's origin; and 2) the saved, those who struggle with reconciling their faith in God and their belief in science.

Every follower of Christ is an enduring soldier of *a* war. The Bible says: "Thou therefore endure hardness, as a good soldier of Jesus Christ. No man that warreth entangleth himself with the affairs of this life; that he may please him who hath chosen him to be a soldier" (2 Timothy 2:3–4).

In other words, the "affairs of this life" are not the basis of any war we should ever want to engage in. Whatever war we decide to enlist for, we must keep in mind pleasing the One who chose us as His soldiers in the first place. And, if that is kept at the forefront of our actions, decisions, and work, then we're doing what has been asked of us by the Father, even while "enduring hardness"—which can sometimes come in the form of opposition from others who don't agree with our work (as the Gospel is simply becoming less popular with the world).

In the recently released film, *Jesus Revolution*, Pastor Chuck Smith (portrayed by *Frasier* star Kelsey Grammer) is initially offended by the actions and appearances of young teens belonging to the counterculture movement in the era of the Jesus People Movement, despite their focus upon the same Jesus Smith teaches about every Sunday. Though his character is based on a real person, his attitude at the beginning of the film is representative of many real-life ministers of that era. When we think back, we can almost hear their disdain reverberating through time: "Get a job—and a haircut—ya bum hippie!"

Not long into the film, Smith's daughter brings home a ragged straggler she met on the roadside by the name of Lonnie Frisbee (also a historical figure of that day). After a conversation at their dining room table that challenges Smith's rote, ritualistic, and frankly *dead* religion (reflected in his church's abysmal attendance), an unlikely friendship between Smith and Frisbee brings a revival to his church...along with a huge congregation of barefoot, long-haired, bell-bottoms-wearing teens. Smith, now open-minded to ministering to these beautiful and sincere people, is challenged by his church's leadership, who make it clear these new guests are unwelcome. One goes as far as to mention that the rush of bare feet each Sunday is staining the carpet of the sanctuary. Smith, bearing a soul-searching expression, eventually replies sarcastically that, yeah, it's a good idea in light of the kids' souls to worry about saving the *carpet*. Unfazed, the church leader confirms that the hippies are making the former congregation uncomfortable, and then he exits.

I nearly cried when I saw the next scene. Smith responded to a "Christian" church member's remarks about the incoming barrage of hippies with one of the most Christlike examples of behavior I've seen, and he did it without engaging in any "war" between himself and his co-ministers: He set up a foot-washing bowl at the entrance to the church, and every barefoot hippie who came to the service was treated to a personal foot bath by Smith—an act of service that made the unshod congregants feel loved and the religious-spirited congregants desist in expressing their concerns about a clean floor. Smith never made it about arguing with the leadership. He never made it about the carpet, which could have humiliated the new attendees. He made the whole squabble go away by practicing the Savior's example:

> Now before the feast of the passover, when Jesus knew that his hour was come that he should depart out of this world unto the Father, having loved his own which were in the world.... He riseth from supper, and laid aside his garments; and took a towel, and girded himself. After that he poureth water into a bason, and began to wash the disciples' feet, and to wipe them with the towel wherewith he was girded. (John 13:1, 4–5)

Over and over again, when Smith was threatened with the possibility of being ostracized from his church and flock, he continued to embrace "weird" for the sake of the lost while the stuffy, nose-up leaders around him wouldn't hear of it. In this way, he participated in "war," but it was that which is invisible...and he won.

The rest of the film is a record of this man's ministry which, alongside Frisbee, launched an incredible (and otherwise unlikely) spiritual awakening. There's a lot to learn from this.

When we see the messages in these types of movies, we cheer. But then, on Monday morning, do we go back to our judgmental, unwelcoming, elitist, and discriminatory interactions with those who are different from us? Do we participate in war with humans or the war of the invisible? If the "human war," we lose *no matter what we win* in the interim, because souls are hurt.

Recall that, in the first chapter of this book, I expressed that "we aren't required to believe the testimony of the Bible, but that doesn't mean we are free from having to put our faith in something unseen and unprovable." I went on to say: "Though the Bible cannot be irrefutably proven via empirical data or the scientific method, when it comes to cosmology, science can't, either…[And] in my opinion…it takes *more* faith for mature and rational thinkers to believe in the randomness of evolution than it does to believe in Intelligent Design." I shared Chandra Wickramasinghe's famous quote comparing the likeliness of random evolution to a typhoon whirling through a junkyard and the pieces coincidentally falling together to construct one of the most impressive airliners mankind has made to date. Earlier on, I quoted Chuck Missler's example of random evolution in comparison to his accidentally placing a pile of black and white beads on a string and spelling out Genesis 1:1 in Morse code. I referred back to his explanations of the extremely complicated hemoglobin and how the most basic rules of mathematics in science and physics rule out development by mere natural occurrence, calling it "absurd," and followed it with many other of his comments regarding the implausibility of evolution being the sole source behind the entire animal kingdom—let alone humanity. There's no way around it: Though nothing is wrong with following, studying, and appreciating the discoveries of science—as even I have done herein—what I said before remains true: "One can remove God from the picture and disassociate their scientific creeds from all labels resembling 'religion,' but….: Both religion and science, when it comes to the great cosmological debate, *require believing in something we cannot see.*"

Today, "hippies" are not the problem. Secularists are the problem…

…and their god goes by the name "science."

How many secularists find themselves entertaining the possibility of a God "out there somewhere" when their lives take a turn that provides such a reflective occasion? Is there something to that "God-shaped vacuum/hole" that French philosopher and theologian Blaise Pascal talked about so long ago? Does the Spirit call out to the unsaved—constantly but gently—reminding them that there is something or Someone bigger than they are, whom they long to know?

Well, yes. The Bible tells us so (John 16:7–11).

Will Christian soldiers be willing to engage in this invisible but very real war for the souls of the lost, *even when* that is uncomfortable? Even when that requires us to say, do, or write things that might be less popular among other leaders of the Church who would rather hobnob among like-minded folks every Sunday morning and shake hands about having "figured it all out" like the leadership of Chuck Smith in *Jesus Revolution*? Even when that means we have to embrace "weird"? Even if doing so might ostracize us from certain circles of critical people?

I ask this because I truly believe God personally revealed something to me several years ago from the balcony of a hotel in Arizona. The longer story is included in my previous book series, *The Mystery of Jesus: From Genesis to Revelation*, but instead of reiterating the whole testimony here, I'll give you the bottom line (and you can read it there if you're inclined). I was standing there completely flustered by a conversation with a member of our production team regarding an upcoming release. Out of the *wild* blue, He interrupted my human grumbling and gave me a download. As suddenly as the human brain can be interrupted, as the third volume of my *Mystery* series attests:

> I saw riots in the news, buildings on fire, folks huddling under-ground in hiding. I felt the palpable hatred of brother against brother, smelled the sickening stench of human deception, and tasted the bile of the bloodshed of the innocent. Crosses were taken down from churches. Bibles were burning. Pastors were sleeping at the pulpits while their people were screaming. Grand-parents were praying in tears and on their knees while their young grandchildren were porn addicts. White powders and needles were casually lying in dumpsters in the alley and nobody cared. Disease and pandemic was spreading like a brushfire and nobody was immune while women of the night continued to sell them-selves for a meal. Busses and other public transportation vehi-cles were floating slowly downstream in a dirty flood filled with uprooted, dead plants. Military troops fired guns at will. Earth-quakes destroyed immense buildings and monuments. Weather

maladies of all kinds rained down on vulnerable humanity. Chaos, anarchy, disorder, and confusion were the norm, while hands in high places were shaking on foreign deals from every platform in government.

...And all of this flickered through my head before the year 2020 brought even a fraction of this picture to fruition.[268]

In bizarre juxtaposition to all this darkness, I distinctly heard the voice of the Lord: "The Great Awakening has already begun. It's in the beginning phases. Only those with eyes to see and ears to hear will see it and hear it. It's starting with My people, My *true* people, while a good portion of the Church and the world around it are asleep and unaware."

Another Great Awakening isn't coming "despite" today's demoralization; it's coming "because of" today's demoralization. From the ashes of pure, unadulterated *chaos*, God brings order...and *revival*.

Sound familiar? It should. It's what this whole book has been about. God did it before, when this planet called "Earth" was despairing in a *tohu-bohu* state of desolation. He did it again with the Great Awakenings of recent Western history. He did it with the "hippies" of the Jesus People Movement through the people whose first response was to shun what was weird and cordially uninvite them from their midst.

And He's doing it again right now. At this very second.

Please listen: God is taking the current secularists—those "weirdos" we would rather shun and ostracize than "waste time on" or minister to—and breathing new life into their old bones (cf., Ezekiel 37:5–10). From within their circles of veiled but very real science worship, He is calling and equipping leaders who will stop at nothing and slow down for no one while they preach the Gospel with a roar that will break down demonic walls and usher in a fire we haven't seen since the outpouring of the Spirit at Pentecost in Acts 2. Some of today's staunchest adherents to the secular sciences are going to be tomorrow's leaders of what could be—and God, I pray it is—*the grandest display of "Jesus revolution" this Old Earth has ever seen.*

But sadly, *some* of these potential ministers will question the Spirit's calling and voice because, at some point, a well-meaning Christian will have told them that "the Bible says" Earth cannot be what we observe it to be and, therefore, the God of the Bible is less relevant to their life than whatever headline appears on tomorrow's science journals. But remember, fellow brothers and sisters in Christ, those headlines tell a bleak story: one that begins when "nothing" exploded billions of years ago and ends in the return to nothingness. Anyone who *truly* believes in that is, even if deep down, open to a different Story—one that gives their life purpose. They may resist and deny, they may even curse, flail, agitate, roll eyes, scoff, and laugh in your face, among a thousand other fathomable reactions to your Good News. But at the end of the day, when they are alone and made to fearfully face the end of their own existence and consciousness as the god called "science" narrates—which is nothingness in the beginning and nothingness in the end—the depths of their spirit, even from their subconscious minds, will cry out for something more substantial, gratifying, and purposeful.

There *is* a movement of the Savior coming…and it's gonna be messy. Instead of bell-bottoms and long hair, we're going to be confronted with young people who are sneering about our God while the labs are their god. If the two—God and science—could ever harmonize, can you imagine the harvest?!

Believers *must* be willing to engage in the conversation that merges science with the Master Scientist and what He spoke in His Word…and this book is *one way* to do that.

So, have I "started a war" by writing this book?

Well, if the "war" in question is between me and other Christians who want to argue their positions while the world is dying all around them, then I'm sorry. Forgive me in advance when I ignore the angry phone calls and emails. But if the "war" is between Christian soldiers and the forces of darkness who would keep these young, precious, scientifically minded souls—each one a creation of the Creator—captive forever under the weight of the enemy's grandest deception that God and science are unrelated…then I have my answer: By God, I hope so.

USE THE QR-CODE BELOW TO ACCESS MANY
SPECIAL DEALS AND PROMOTIONS ON BOOKS
AND FILMS BY THESE AUTHORS FEATURING
DISCOVERY, PROPHECY, AND THE SUPERNATURAL!

Notes

1. Missler, Chuck, "Genesis: Session 4: 3rd Day: Chapter 1:9–13," fourth video from "Genesis: An Expositional Commentary," *Koinonia House*; this story was told in the first eight minutes, alongside the discussion of relevant math. This series, along with the study book, can be purchased from Missler's personal ministry website at the following link: https://store.khouse.org/products/genesis-an-expositional-commentary; permission to quote granted to Tom Horn for all his projects prior to death; emphasis only added where vocal emphasis was applied in the original presentation.

2. Ibid.

3. Ibid.

4. Ibid.

5. Ibid.

6. Ibid.

7. Missler, Chuck, "Genesis: Session 6: 5th Day: Chapter 1:20–23," sixth video from "Genesis: An Expositional Commentary," *Koinonia House*, 41:38–45:10. This series, along with the study book, can be purchased from Missler's personal ministry website at the following link: https://store.khouse.org/products/genesis-an-expositional-commentary.

8. Missler, Chuck, "Genesis: Session 7: 6th Day: Chapter 1:24–28," seventh video from "Genesis: An Expositional Commentary," *Koinonia House*, 34:00–35:36. This series, along with the study book, can be purchased from Missler's personal ministry website at the following link: https://store.khouse.org/products/genesis-an-expositional-commentary.

9. Strobel, Lee, *The Case for Christ: A Journalist's Personal Investigation of the Evidence for Jesus* (Zondervan. Kindle Edition), Kindle locations 3024–3025.

10. Ibid., locations 3030–3032.

11. Ibid.

12. Wickramasinghe, Chandra, "Threats On Life of Controversial Astronomer," *New Scientist Magazine*, January 21, 1982, 140.

13. Aquinas, Thomas, *On Faith and Reason* (Indianapolis/Cambridge: Hackett Publishing Company; 1999), 126.

14. Lewis, C. S., *Mere Christianity*, book one, "Right and Wrong as a Clue to the Meaning of the Universe." In: *The Complete C. S. Lewis Signature Classics* (New York: HarperCollins Publishers; 2002), 28.

15. Harrison, T. Mark, & Lovera, Oscar, M, "The Multi-diffusion Domain Model: Past, Present, and Future," *Department of Earth and Space Sciences*, University of California, Los Angeles, last accessed May 3, 2023, https://sims. ess.ucla.edu/argonlab/Research/GS_Ar_book_final.pdf.

16. Dumin, Yurri, V., "The Faint Young Sun Paradox in the Context of Modern Cosmology," May 2015, Lomonosov Moscow State University; retrieved from *Research Gate* on May 3, 2023, https://www.researchgate.net/ publication/276296220_The_Faint_Young_Sun_Paradox_in_the_Context_ of_Modern_Cosmology.

17. Faulkner, Danny R., "The Young Faint Sun Paradox and the Age of the Solar System," June 1, 1998, *Institute for Creation Research*, last accessed May 3, 2023, https://www.icr.org/article/young-faint-sun-paradox-age-solar-system/.

18. Faulkner, Danny R., "The Young Faint Sun Paradox and the Age of the Solar System," August 1, 2001, *Answers In Genesis*, last accessed May 3, 2023, https://answersingenesis.org/astronomy/sun/the-young-faint-sun-paradox-and-the-age-of-the-solar-system/. Originally published in *Journal of Creation* vol. 15, no. 2, (August 2001): 3–4.

19. Humphreys PhD, Russell, "Young Helium Diffusion Age of Zircons Supports Accelerated Nuclear Decay," *Institute for Creation Research*, last accessed May 3, 2023, https://www.icr.org/i/pdf/technical/Young-Helium-Diffusion-Age-of-Zircons.pdf.

20. Ibid.

21. "Radioactive Decay," *United States Environmental Protection Agency*, last accessed May 3, 2023, https://www.epa.gov/radiation/radioactive-

decay#:~:text=Radioactive%20decay%20is%20the%20emission,emitted%20
can%20include%20alpha%20particles.

22. Humphreys PhD, Russell, "Young Helium Diffusion…"

23. Ibid.

24. Ibid.

25. Loechelt, Gary H., "A Response to the RATE Team Regarding Helium
Diffusion in Zircon," *American Scientific Affiliation*, last accessed May 3, 2023,
https://www.asa3.org/ASA/education/origins/helium-gl4.pdf.

26. Harrison, T. Mark, & Lovera, Oscar, M, "The Multi-diffusion Domain
Model…"

27. Lochelt, Gary H., "Critics of Helium Evidence for a Young World Now
Seem Silent?" *Creation Ministries International*, last accessed May 3, 2023,
https://creation.com/images/pdfs/tj/j24_3/j24_3_34-39.pdf, 34.

28. Lochelt, Gary H., "Fenton Hill Revisited: The Retention of Helium in
Zircons and the Case for Accelerated Nuclear Decay," *American Scientific
Affiliation*, last accessed May 3, 2023, https://www.asa3.org/ASA/education/
origins/helium-gl3.pdf.

29. Loechelt, Gary H., "A Response to the RATE Team…"

30. Loechelt, Gary H., "Accelerated Nuclear Decay in the Light of New
Experimental Data," *American Science Affiliation*, last accessed May 3, 2023,
https://www.asa3.org/ASA/PSCF/2020/PSCF3-20Loechelt.pdf.

31. Jackson, Brittney, Defender Publishing assistant and *SkyWatch TV
Magazine* guest journalist, May 1, 2023, from a report attached in a personal
email between Jackson and Donna Howell.

32. Arnold, B. T., *Encountering the Book of Genesis: A Study of Its Content
and Issues.* (W. A. Elwell & E. H. Merrill, Eds.; Grand Rapids, MI: Baker
Academic; 1998), 27.

33. Easton, M. G. In *Illustrated Bible Dictionary and Treasury of Biblical History,
Biography, Geography, Doctrine, and Literature* (New York: Harper & Brothers;
1893), 144; emphasis added.

34. Erlington, Charles, "The Life of James Ussher, D.D., Archbishop of
Armagh." In *The Whole Works of the Most Rev. James Ussher, D.D.: Volume 1*
(Dublin: Hodges, Smith, and Co.; 1864), 5.

35. Ibid., 11.

36. Ibid., 26.

37. Ibid.

38. Ibid., 29–30.

39. Ibid., 5–8.

40. Ibid., 10.

41. Ibid., 8.

42. Quayle, Stephen, and Dr. Thomas R. Horn, *Unearthing the Lost World of the Cloudeaters: Compelling Evidence of the Incursion of Giants, Their Extraordinary Technology, and Imminent Return* (Crane, MO: Defender Publishing; 2017), 278.

43. Ibid., 278–279.

44. As merely one example, see: Cyrus Adler, *An Account of the Smithsonian Institution: Its Origin, History, Objects, and Achievements* (Smithsonian Press, 1904), 5.

45. Quayle and Horn, *Unearthing...Cloudeaters*, 271.

46. Ibid., 274.

47. Stanley Coren, PhD, "How Many Breeds of Dogs Are There in the World?" May 23, 2013, *Psychology Today: Canine Corner*, last accessed December 15, 2022, https://www.psychologytoday.com/blog/canine-corner/201305/how-many-breeds-dogs-are-there-in-the-world.

48. Quayle and Horn, *Unearthing...Cloudeaters*, 284–285.

49. Ibid., 280.

50. Ibid., 280–281.

51. Ibid., 289–290.

52. John Wesley Powell, *On Limitations to the Use of Some Anthropologic Data* (Public domain; Amazon Digital Services LLC, Kindle Edition: 2012), Kindle locations 90–91.

53. Ibid., Kindle locations 86–88.

54. Quayle and Horn, *Unearthing...Cloudeaters*, 290.

55. Ibid., 291–294.

56. Ibid., 294–295.

57. "The 10 Best Evidences from Science That Confirm a Young Earth," October 1, 2012, *Answers in Genesis*, as featured in *Answers*

Magazine, last accessed January 6, 2023, https://answersingenesis.org/evidence-for-creation/10-best-evidences-young-earth/.

58. Ibid.

59. Caldecott, W. S. "Zechariah." In J. Orr, J. L. Nuelsen, E. Y. Mullins, & M. O. Evans (Eds.), *The International Standard Bible Encyclopaedia Volumes 1–5* (Chicago: The Howard-Severance Company; 1915), 3136; emphasis added.

60. Kidner, D. *Genesis: An Introduction and Commentary: Volume 1* (Downers Grove, IL: InterVarsity Press; 1967), 88; emphasis added.

61. Green, William Henry, "Article VIII: Primeval Chronology," *Bibliotheca Sacra: Volume 47*, 285–303. Viewable online here: https://biblicalelearning.org/wp-content/uploads/2022/01/Green-PrimevalChron-BibSac.pdf.

62. Ibid.

63. Ibid.

64. Ibid.; emphasis added.

65. Green, Michael, *2 Peter and Jude: An Introduction and Commentary: Volume 18* (Tyndale New Testament Commentaries; Downers Grove, IL; InterVarsity Press; 1987), 157.

66. "When a Day Lasted Only Four Hours," March 2016, *Intercontinental Academia*, last accessed February 27, 2023, http://intercontinental-academia.ubias.net/nagoya/news/when-a-day-lasted-only-4-hours.

67. King, Matt, and Christopher Watson, "The Length of Earth's Days has Been Mysteriously Increasing, and Scientists Don't Know Why," August 5, 2022, *The Conversation*, last accessed February 27, 2023, https://theconversation.com/the-length-of-earths-days-has-been-mysteriously-increasing-and-scientists-dont-know-why-188147.

68. There is no single, authoritative source to attribute to this. Simply Googling "Earth rotation speeding up in modern times" (or something equivalent) will lead a researcher to a plethora of online science journals noting this change and offering up countless reasons for why Earth has apparently increased rotational speed since the 1960s.

69. Swanson, James, *Dictionary of Biblical Languages with Semantic Domains: Hebrew (Old Testament)* (Oak Harbor: Logos Research Systems, Inc., 1997), entry 1343, ברא "bara."

70. Heiser PhD, Michael, "Genesis 1 1 3 Michael Heiser PhD NEW,"

YouTube video, uploaded by Naked Bible on January 26, 2016, last accessed March 13, 2023, https://www.youtube.com/watch?v=diEzuGvDjU0 8:29–8:57; emphasis added only on words that were emphasized in Heiser's own verbal presentation; open and limitless permission to quote granted by Heiser to Tom Horn prior to Heiser's death.

71. Ibid., 10:11–10:27.

72. Ibid., 10:48–11:00.

73. Ibid., 11:55–12:48.

74. Ibid., 16:30–16:42.

75. Ibid., 26:41–26:50.

76. Ibid., 23:05–25:15.

77. Ibid., 25:54–27:12; emphasis added only on words that were emphasized in Heiser's own verbal presentation.

78. Ibid., 28:27–28:29; emphasis added only on words that were emphasized in Heiser's own verbal presentation.

79. Ibid., 28:43–29:12; all-caps in original.

80. Ibid., 47:17–48:16; emphasis added only on words that were emphasized in Heiser's own verbal presentation.

81. Ryrie, Charles Caldwell, *Basic Theology: A Popular Systematic Guide to Understanding Biblical Truth* (Chicago, IL: Moody Press, 1999), 209.

82. Heiser, PhD, Michael S., *Angels: What the Bible Really Says About God's Heavenly Host* (Bellingham, WA: Lexham Press; 2018; Kindle Edition), Kindle location 401–411.

83. Hamm, Ken, "Is the Bible a Science Textbook?" December 18, 2016, *Answers In Genesis*, last accessed March 30, 2023, https://answersingenesis.org/blogs/ken-ham/2016/12/18/is-the-bible-a-science-textbook/.

84. Ibid.

85. In the following pages, portions of the text I wrote for *Afterlife* may look familiar as I have copied over a few spots verbatim. Note that this was done with permission from both coauthors and the publisher.

86. Zugibe, MD, PhD, Frederick T., *The Crucifixion of Jesus: A Forensic Inquiry* (New York, NY: M. Evans and Company, Inc.; Kindle edition, 2005), location 3779.

87. Howell, Donna, Allie Anderson-Henson, and Josh Peck, *Afterlife: Near Death Experiences, Neuroscience, Quantum Physics, and the Increasing Evidence for Life After Death* (Crane, MO: Defender Publishing; 2019), 186, 188.

88. Zugibe, MD, PhD, Frederick T., *The Crucifixion of Jesus: A Forensic Inquiry*, location 2711.

89. Howell, Donna, Allie Anderson-Henson, and Josh Peck, *Afterlife*, 195–196; this example (though reworded by Howell) is originally from: Zugibe, Frederick T., *The Crucifixion of Jesus*, location 5062–5071.

90. "Chazy Reef at Isle laMotte," *Department of Environmental Conservation*, last accessed May 4, 2023, https://dec.vermont.gov/geological-survey/vermont-geology/Chazy#:~:text=The%20significance%20of%20recognizing%20 reefs,Vermont%20460%20million%20years%20ago. The top of the article says this information was "Condensed from text by Dr. Charlotte Mehrtens, Vermont Geological Society Summer Field Trip, 1998."

91. Harder, Ben, "Great Barrier Reef Surprisingly Young: New Geological Data Point to Age of Less Than a Million Years," June 1, 2001, *American Association for the Advancement of Science (AAAS)*, last accessed March 15, 2023, https://www.science.org/content/article/great-barrier-reef-surprisingly-young.

92. Ibid.

93. Buis, Alan, "Flip Flop: Why Variations in Earth's Magnetic Field Aren't Causing Today's Climate Change," August 3, 2021, *Ask NASA Climate*, last accessed March 9, 2023, https://climate.nasa.gov/ask-nasa-climate/3104/flip-flop-why-variations-in-earths-magnetic-field-arent-causing-todays-climate-change/.

94. "Inverse Square Law," *Energy Education*, last accessed March 14, 2023, https://energyeducation.ca/encyclopedia/Inverse_square_law.

95. Trefil, James, "Evidence for a Flood," April 1, 2000, *Smithsonian Magazine*, last accessed May 4, 2023, https://www.smithsonianmag.com/science-nature/evidence-for-a-flood-102813115/.

96. Millman, Jenna, Bryan Taylor, and Lauren Effron, "Evidence Noah's Biblical Flood Happened, Says Robert Ballard," December 5, 2012, *ABC News*, last accessed May 4, 2023, https://abcnews.go.com/Technology/evidence-suggests-biblical-great-flood-noahs-time-happened/story?id=17884533.

97. "Understanding Insects: Facts and Figures—Did You Know?" *Royal Entomological Society*, last accessed March 17, 2023, https://www.royensoc. co.uk/understanding-insects/facts-and-figures/.

98. "Ancient Nanostructures (Season 11): History," YouTube video, uploaded by HISTORY on March 4, 2019, last accessed April 27, 2023, https://www. youtube.com/watch?v=EcoaDllsiic; 0:32–0:37.

99. Ibid., 1:15–1:20.

100. Ibid., 1:04–1:12.

101. Daniel, Samuel, "Ancient Nanostructures Found in the Mountains of Russia Raise Questions about Humanity's Level of Development," Jun 13, 2022, *Science Info*, last accessed April 28, 2023, https://scienceinfo.net/ancient-nanostructures-found-in-the-mountains-of-russia-raise-questions-about-humanitys-level-of-development.html.

102. "tungsten," *Encyclopaedia Britannica*, last accessed April 28, 2023, https:// www.britannica.com/science/tungsten-chemical-element.

103. Vintini, Leonardo, "Ancient Nanostructures Found Out of Place and Time," November 6, 2014, *Epoch Times*, last accessed April 28, 2023, https:// www.theepochtimes.com/ancient-nanostructures-found-out-of-place-and-time_1058362.html.

104. "Ancient Nanostructures…" https://www.youtube.com/ watch?v=EcoaDllsiic; 2:32–3:12.

105. Ibid.

106. Ibid.

107. "What Is Coal & Where Is it Found?" *World Coal Association*, last accessed April 29, 2023, https://www.worldcoal.org/coal-facts/ what-is-coal-where-is-it-found/.

108. This is the official story floated over and over again online. One can easily locate the images, and this story, by Googling "Donetsk coalmine wheel." As explained, there has been no official research or analysis of this OOPArt (and many others). This is the reason why I handled the wheel of Donetsk briefly.

109. Groucutt, Huw S., "The Morphological Variability of Maltese 'Cart Ruts' and its Implications," *Journal of Archeological Science: Reports: Volume 41*, February 2022, 103287. Including contributions from: Extreme Events Research Group, Max Planck Institutes for Chemical Ecology, The Science of

Human History, and Biogeochemistry, Jena 07745, Germany, Department
of Archaeology, Max Planck Institute for the Science of Human History,
Jena, Germany, Institute of Prehistoric Archaeology, University of Cologne,
Cologne, Germany. Received August 7, 2021; revised November 24, 2021;
accepted November 25, 2021; available online December 7, 2021; Version
of Record December 7, 2021. Last accessed April 29, 2023, https://www.
sciencedirect.com/science/article/pii/S2352409X21004995?via%3Dihub.
Quoting from this scientific article is open-access, "distributed under the terms
of the Creative Commons CC-BY license, which permits unrestricted use,
distribution, and reproduction in any medium, provided the original work is
properly cited." As such, I am "not required to obtain permission to reuse this
article," according to the statement at the following related link: https://s100.
copyright.com/AppDispatchServlet?publisherName=ELS&contentID=S2352
409X21004995&orderBeanReset=true.

110. Ibid.

111. Pappas, Stephanie, "Oldest Human Paint-Making Studio Discovered
in Cave," October 13, 2011, *Live Science*, last accessed May 1, 2023, https://
www.livescience.com/16538-oldest-human-paint-studio.html.

112. Ibid.

113. Ibid.

114. New documentary release announcement, "The Mysterious Stone
Monuments of Markawasi, Peru," as seen on "The Documentary Channel,"
BBC Video, last accessed March 23, 2023, http://www.bcvideo.com/
markawasi.html.

115. Though we can't buy into every claim that floats around in fringe
archeological circles, the Gate of the Sun is referenced as "14,000 years old" or
"14000 BP" regularly. As examples: Dan Eden, "The Amazing Engineering
Designs of Tiahuanaco: Gateway to the Gods," *ViewZone*, last accessed March
23, 2023, http://www.viewzone.com/tiax.html. (See the breakdown of the site-
dating and its controversy under the heading "How old is this site?") Further
reading includes: Stone-Miller, Rebecca, *Art of the Andes: From Chavin to Inca*
(Thames & Hudson, New York: 1996); Fagan, Brian M., *The Seventy Great
Mysteries of the Ancient World: Unlocking the Secrets of Past Civilizations* (Thames
& Hudson, New York: 2001).

116. Groucutt, Huw S., "The Morphological Variability of Maltese 'Cart Ruts'…"

117. Bellamy, Hans Schindler and Peter Allan, *The Calendar of Tiahuanaco: A Disquisition on the Time Measuring System of the Oldest Civilization in the World* (London: Faber & Faber; 1956). There is no specific page number to point to for this information as these findings were repetitiously discussed throughout the entire 400-plus-page investigation.

118. Protzen, J. P., and S. E. Nair, 2000, "On Reconstructing Tiwanaku Architecture," *The Journal of the Society of Architectural Historians: Volume 59* (September, 2000, no., 3), 370.

119. Ibid.

120. Horn, Thomas, as quoted in: Flynn, David, *The David Flynn Collection* (Crane, MO: Defender Publishing; 2012), 487.

121. Posnansky, Arthur, "Tiahuanacu" (New York: J.J. Augustin; 1946).

122. Childress, David Hatcher, "The Coneheads of Peru," *World Explorer Magazine* (Kempton, Il: World Explorers Club, Vol. 3, No. 4).

123. Posnansky, Arthur, *Tiahuanaco: The Cradle of American Man* (4 vol.; New York: J. J. Augustin, 1958).

124. http://www.encyclopedia.com/doc/1G1-134180707.html

125. Acosta, Hint, of the New World, bk. y. chap. 4, bk. vi. chap. 19, Erif. trans., 1701, "History of the Incas" by Pedro Sarmiento De Gamboa, translated by Clements Markham (Cambridge: The Hakluyt Society 1907), 28–58.

126. Posnansky, Arthur, *Tiahuanaco: The Cradle of American Man.*

127. C.f.: Bellamy, H. S., and P. Allan, *The Calendar of Tiahuanaco* (1959); and *The Great Idol of Tiahuanaco*; both published by Faber and Faber, London.

128. Henley, Tracy B., and Lani P. Lyman-Henley, "The Snakes of Gobekli Tepe: An Ethological Consideration," December 2019, *Research Gate*, last accessed May 5, 2023, https://www.researchgate.net/publication/337914981_The_Snakes_of_Gobekli_Tepe_An_Ethological_Consideration; emphasis added.

129. Ibid.

130. Ibid.

131. Curry, Andrew "Gobekli Tepe: The World's First Temple?: Predating Stonehenge by 6,000 Years, Turkey's Stunning Gobekli Tepe Upends the Conventional View of the Rise of Civilization," November 2008, *Smithsonian*, last accessed March 27, 2023, http://www.smithsonianmag.com/history/gobekli-tepe-the-worlds-first-temple-83613665/?no-ist.

132. Ibid.

133. Ibid., emphasis added.

134. Ibid.

135. Ibid., emphasis added.

136. Mann, Charles C., "The Birth of Religion," June 11, 2011, *National Geographic Magazine*, last accessed March 27, 2023, https://www.nationalgeographic.com/magazine/article/gobeki-tepe; emphasis added.

137. Ibid.

138. This theory appears in many places throughout research. For further reading, consider: "Which Came First, Monumental Building Projects Or Farming?" December 18, 2008, *Archaeo News*, last accessed March 27, 2023, http://www.stonepages.com/news/archives/003061.html.

139. Original text German, as cited from: Klaus-Dieter Linsmeier, *Eine Revolution imgroßenStil*, "Interview mit Klaus Schmidt," *AbenteuerArchäologie. Kulturen, Menschen, Monumente* (Spektrum der Wissenschaft, Heidelberg 2006) 2. This English translation was, at the time of our initial research on this site in *Unearthing the Lost World of the Cloudeaters*, available directly from: "Gobekli Tepe," *Wikipedia*, under the heading "Interpretation," http://en.wikipedia.org/wiki/G%C3%B6bekli_Tepe#cite_ref-23.

140. Heun, Manfred, et al., "Site of Einkorn Wheat Domestication Identified by DNA Fingerprinting," *Science Magazine: Volume 278*, November 1997, 1312–1314; viewable here: http://www.ndsu.edu/pubweb/~mcclean/plsc731/homework/papers/huen%20et%20al%20-%20site%20of%20einkorn%20wheat%20domestication%20identified%20by%20DNA%20fingerprinting.pdf.

141. Scham, Sandra, "The World's First Temple," *Archaeology Magazine: Volume 61*, November/December 2008, last accessed March 27, 2023, http://archive.archaeology.org/0811/abstracts/turkey.html.

142. For those readers who may have heard the rumor that the Jericho wall was already fallen by the time of Israelite's famous war (when the walls tumbled down in the days of Joshua 2–6): Be aware that the dating of that catastrophic event was carried out in the 1950s and many glaring errors can be seen in the methods they applied in those days. This is a classic case of an "argument from silence," where a certain kind of ancient pottery—Cypriot bichrome ware—was not found at the site. The archeologist of the day, Kathleen Kenyon, then determined that the lack of this pottery argued for an earlier destruction, somewhere in the ballpark of a century and a half prior to the story of Joshua (1550 BC). However, archeological dating should *always* mirror what was found, not what was missing, and even then, the pottery Kenyon was looking for was found on the east side of the structure by British archeologist John Garstang back in the 1930s, where Kenyon failed to look twenty years later. In the 1930s, the significance of the Cypriot pottery was not yet established, so there is much reason to believe that Kenyon was unaware of this earlier find. Likewise, copies of Cypriot pottery was all over the place in ancient Jericho, showing that the original occupants had at least already been exposed to that style and design by that date. With this in mind—alongside the well-known fact that radiocarbon dating can be off with a margin of a hundred years anyway—the biblical timeline stands as the true date for the fall of the Jericho wall circa 1400 BC, as Garstang first attested.

143. "Revolutionary Karahan Tepe" September 14, 2022, *Archeology Worldwide*, last accessed May 5, 2023, https://www.archaeologyworldwide.com/post/revolutionary-karahan-tepe.

144. "Strange Phallic Pillars at Karahan Tepe," January 17, 2023, *Techzelle*, last accessed May 5, 2023, https://techzelle.com/karahan-tepe/; emphasis added.

145. "Karahan Tepe, Megalithic Supercivilization 11,400 Years Ago, New 3D Scans, Megalithomania," 2:35–3:15, YouTube video uploaded by MegalithomaniaUK on December 10, 2022, last accessed May 5, 2023, https://www.youtube.com/watch?v=3sQZLKd5nvY.

146. Ibrahim Ozcosar, as quoted in: Gunes, Muhammed Furkan, "Ancient Site Older than Gobeklitepe Unearthed in Turkey: Discoveries at Boncuklu Tarla in Southeastern Mardin Are around 1,000 Years Older than Those in Gobeklitepe, Says Professor," April 12, 2019, updated May 12, 2019,

Anadolu Ajansi, last accessed May 29, 2023, https://www.aa.com.tr/en/culture/ancient-site-older-than-gobeklitepe-unearthed-in-turkey/1664156.

147. Ibid.

148. Sincar, Halil Ibrahim and Ali Murat Alhas, "Archaeologists Unearth Ancient Settlement in SE Turkey: Sewer System Dating Back 11,800 Years, Over 20 Architectural Structures Found in Mardin Province," July 11, 2019, *Anadolu Ajansi*, last accessed May 29, 2023, https://www.aa.com.tr/en/culture/archaeologists-unearth-ancient-settlement-in-se-turkey/1638247.

149. Ibid.

150. "History," *The Baalbeck International Festival Official Website*, last accessed January 19, 2015, http://www.baalbeck.org.lb/index.php/en/the-festival/lang-enhistorylanglang-frhistoirelang; note that this site has been changed since we first recorded this quote in our study of Baalbek in 2015.

151. Ibid.

152. The spread of COVID-19 also staggered the success of the festival, though, at this time, there are efforts to return it to its glory days. Therefore, any present information regarding the festival, its attractions, and its practices of safety in large crowds will only reflect the operation of this event in the midst of a worldwide pandemic, and is not representative of how the festival has performed in the recent past or how it is expected to succeed in the near future.

153. Matthiae, Paolo, *Proceedings of the 6th International Congress of the Archaeology of the Ancient Near East* (Wiesbaden, Germany; Harrassowitz Verlag Publishers, 2010), 210.

154. Jidejian, Nina, *Baalbek: Heliopolis, "City of the Sun"* (Beirut, Lebanon; Dar el-Machreq Publishers, 1975) 15.

155. MacIsaac, Tara, "Largest Known Ancient Megalith Discovered—Who Really Made It?" December 20, 2014, *Epoch Times*, last accessed January 27, 2015, http://www.theepochtimes.com/n3/1154047-largest-known-ancient-megalith-block-discovered-who-really-made-it/.

156. Ruprechtsberger, Erwin, M. *Vom Steinbruch zum Jupitertempel von Heliopolis/Baalbek (Libanon)* [*From the Quarry to the Jupiter Temple of Heliopolis/Baalbek (Lebanon)*] (Linzer Archäologische Forschungen: 1990) 30: 7–56.

157. Hanauer, James Edward, *Folk-lore of the Holy Land: Moslem, Christian and Jewish* (London; Gerald Duckworth & Company: 1907), 74.

158. Paul Doyle, *Lebanon* (Buckinghamshire, England; Bradt Travel Guides: 2012), 213.

159. Ibid., among other sources with the same claim.

160. Shepp, Daniel B., *The Holy Land Photographed* (Chicago, IL: Globe Bible Publishing, 1894) 109.

161. Coulton, J. J., "Lifting in Early Greek Architecture," *The Journal of Hellenic Studies, Volume 94* (London; Hellenistic Society: 1994) 16.

162. Dienel, Hans-Liudger; Meighorner, Wolfgang, "Der Tretradkran," *Publication of the Deutsches Museum* (Technikgeschichte series) 2nd ed. (Bavaria, Germany; München: 1997) 13.

163. Lancaster, Lynne "Building Trajan's Column," *American Journal of Archaeology 103 (3)* (Archaeological Institute of America: 1999) 419–439.

164. Shepp, *Holy Land Photographed*, 110.

165. Original article appeared in: *Syria* 54:1–2 (1977): 31–63.

166. Michael Heiser, "Transporting the Trilithon Stones of Baalbek: It's About Applied Physics, Not Ancient Aliens," August 23, 2012, *MichaelSHeiser.com*, last accessed January 29, 2015, http://michaelsheiser.com/PaleoBabble/2012/08/transporting-trilithon-stones-baalbek-applied-physics-ancient-aliens/.

167. David Urquhart, *The Lebanon: Mount Souria. A History and a Diary, Volume 2* (London; Thomas Cautley Newby: 1860), 374–377.

168. As quoted by: Snyder, Michael, "Newly Found Megalithic Ruins in Russia Contain the Largest Blocks of Stone Ever Discovered," March 10, 2014, *The Truth Wins*, last accessed March 29, 2023, http://thetruthwins.com/archives/newly-found-megalithic-ruins-in-russia-contain-the-largest-blocks-of-stone-ever-discovered. The original article is available online at the following *Mysterious Universe* link, though it requires a sign-up to access: https://mysteriousuniverse.org/2014/02/super-megalithic-site-found-in-russia-natural-or-man-made/.

169. Jenson, John, "Super Megaliths," February 22, 2014, John Jenson's

personal blog online, *Earth's Epochs*, last accessed March 29, 2023, http://earthepochs.blogspot.com/2014/02/super-megaliths.html.

170. "Huge Mysterious Megaliths," *English Russia*, last accessed March 30, 2023, https://englishrussia.com/2014/03/06/huge-mysterious-megaliths/.

171. Google Classroom, "Prehistoric Art: Lesson 3: Neolithic Sites: Çatalhöyük," *Khan Academy*, last accessed April 26, 2023, https://www.khanacademy.org/humanities/prehistoric-art/neolithicart/neolithic-sites/a/atalhyk#.

172. Ibid.

173. Carlysue, "Explosive Evidence for the World's Oldest Map," January 15, 2014, *National Geographic*, last accessed April 27, 2023, https://blog.education.nationalgeographic.org/2014/01/15/explosive-evidence-for-the-worlds-oldest-map/.

174. Hodder, Ian, "Çatalhöyük: a 9000 year old town—Ian Hodder (Stanford University)," YouTube video, uploaded by Università di Catania—webtv on July 26, 2018, last accessed April 26, 2023, https://www.youtube.com/watch?v=vmFKBf5OVoI, 14:12–14:48.

175. Ibid., 26:01–26:41.

176. Ibid.

177. Google Classroom, "Prehistoric Art…Çatalhöyük."

178. Hodder, Ian, as quoted in: O'Brien, Jeremy, "New Techniques Undermine 'Mother Goddess' Role in Ancient Community," September 10, 2009, *The Irish Times*, last accessed April 27, 2023, https://www.irishtimes.com/news/new-techniques-undermine-mother-goddess-role-in-ancient-community-1.734909.

179. Ibid.

180. Coppa, A., L. Bondioli, A. Cucina, et al, "Early Neolithic Tradition of Dentistry," April 6, 2006, *Nature Magazine*, vol. 440, 755–756, last accessed May 1, 2023, https://www.nature.com/articles/440755a.

181. Richard Whitaker et al., *The Abridged Brown-Driver-Briggs Hebrew-English Lexicon of the Old Testament: From A Hebrew and English Lexicon of the Old Testament by Francis Brown, S.R. Driver and Charles Briggs, Based on the Lexicon of Wilhelm Gesenius* (Boston; New York: Houghton, Mifflin and Company, 1906), under the heading "תֹּהוּ" (*tohu*).

182. Ibid.

183. "reduce to," *Cambridge Dictionary Online*, last accessed March 31, 2023, https://dictionary.cambridge.org/us/dictionary/english/reduce-to.

184. Richard Whitaker et al., *The Abridged Brown-Driver-Briggs Hebrew-English Lexicon*, under the heading "בֹּהוּ" (*bohu*).

185. "American Worldview Inventory 2020—At a Glance…Release #11: Churches and Worldview," October 6, 2020, *Cultural Research Center, Arizona Christian University*, last accessed March 31, 2023, https://www.arizonachristian.edu/wp-content/uploads/2020/10/CRC_AWVI2020_Release11_Digital_04_20201006.pdf.

186. Swanson, James, *Dictionary of Biblical Languages with Semantic Domains : Hebrew (Old Testament)* (Oak Harbor: Logos Research Systems, Inc., 1997), under the heading "תֹהוּ" (*tohu*); bold in original.

187 Ibid., under the heading "בֹּהוּ" (*bohu*); bold in original; italics added.

188. James Strong, *A Concise Dictionary of the Words in the Greek Testament and The Hebrew Bible* (Bellingham, WA: Logos Bible Software, 2009), 123.

189. Ibid., 19.

190. "Gesenius Hebrew Bundle," *Logos Bible Software*, last accessed March 31, 2023, https://www.logos.com/product/6559/gesenius-hebrew-bundle.

191. Gesenius, William, *Gesenius' Hebrew-Chaldee Lexicon*, available online at: "תֹהוּ" (*tohu*), *Blue Letter Bible Online*, last accessed March 31, 2023, https://www.blueletterbible.org/lexicon/h8414/kjv/wlc/0-1/.

192. Gesenius, William, *Gesenius' Hebrew-Chaldee Lexicon*, available online at: "בֹּהוּ" (*bohu*), *Blue Letter Bible Online*, last accessed March 31, 2023, https://www.blueletterbible.org/lexicon/h922/kjv/wlc/0-1/.

193. Jamieson, Robert, A. R. Fausset, and David Brown, *Commentary Critical and Explanatory on the Whole Bible: Volume 1* (Oak Harbor, WA: Logos Research Systems, Inc., 1997), 17.

194. Ross, Allen P., "Genesis," in *The Bible Knowledge Commentary: An Exposition of the Scriptures*, ed. J. F. Walvoord and R. B. Zuck, vol. 1 (Wheaton, IL: Victor Books, 1985), 28.

195. Scofield, C. I. ed., *The Scofield Reference Bible: The Holy Bible Containing the Old and New Testaments* (New York; London; Toronto; Melbourne; Bombay: Oxford University Press, 1917), viii.

196. Bullinger, Ethelbert W., *The Companion Bible: Being the Authorized Version of 1611 with the Structures and Notes, Critical, Explanatory and Suggestive and with 198 Appendixes: Volume 1* (Bellingham, WA: Faithlife, 2018), 3; bold in original.

197. Richard Whitaker et al., *The Abridged Brown-Driver-Briggs Hebrew-English Lexicon*, under the heading "הָיָה" (*haya*); bold in original.

198. "הָיה," *Blue Letter Bible Online*, under "Outline of Biblical Usage," last accessed April 3, 2023, https://www.blueletterbible.org/lexicon/h1961/kjv/wlc/0-1/.

199. Ibid., under "Brown-Driver-Briggs Lexicon"; further under "STRONG'S H1961."

200. Bullinger, Ethelbert W., *The Companion Bible*, 3.

201. Ibid.

202. Vincent, Marvin Richardson, *Word Studies in the New Testament*, vol. 1 (New York: Charles Scribner's Sons, 1887), 704.

203. Brown, David, A. R. Fausset, and Robert Jamieson, *A Commentary, Critical, Experimental, and Practical, on the Old and New Testaments: Genesis–Deuteronomy: Volume 1* (London; Glasgow: William Collins, Sons, & Company, Limited, n.d.), 3.

204. Pember, George H., *Earth's Earliest Ages* (Crane, MO: Defender Publishing, 2012), 23.

205. Stearman, Gary, "The Dark Prophecy: Satan's Long, Long Story," Part 1, March 2023, *Prophecy Watchers Magazine*, 5; emphasis added in first paragraph; emphasis in middle paragraph appears in the original. Magazine subscription available at: www.prophecywatchers.com.

206. Brown, David, A. R. Fausset, and Robert Jamieson, *A Commentary, Critical, Experimental, and Practical, on the Old and New Testaments: Job–Isaiah: Volume 3* (London; Glasgow: William Collins, Sons, & Company, Limited, n.d.), 610.

207. Jamieson, Fausset, and Brown, *Commentary Critical and Explanatory on the Whole Bible: Volume 1*, 602.

208. As recorded by T. M. Perrin, *Annual Report of the Board of Regents of the Smithsonian Institution Showing the Operations, Expenditures, and Condition*

of the Institution for the Year 1873 (Washington, DC: Government Printing Office; Smithsonian Institution), 418.

209. As recorded by Dr. Augustus Mitchell, *Annual Report of the Board of Regents of the Smithsonian Institution Showing the Operations, Expenditures, and Condition of the Institution for the Year 1875* (Washington, DC: Government Printing Office; Smithsonian Institution), 395.

210. *Annual Report of the Board of Regents of the Smithsonian Institution Showing the Operations, Expenditures, and Condition of the Institution for the Year 1877* (Washington, DC: Government Printing Office; Smithsonian Institution), 260.

211. Ibid., 274.

212. *Fifth Annual Report of the Bureau of Ethnology to the Secretary of the Smithsonian Institution 1883–1884* (Washington, DC: Government Printing Office; Smithsonian Institution). See pages 19, 35, 52–57, 62–67, and 98.

213. *Twelfth Annual Report of the Bureau of Ethnology to the Secretary of the Smithsonian Institution 1894* (Washington, DC: Government Printing Office; Smithsonian Institution). See pages 113, 117, 273, 302, 335, 340, 362, 419, 426, 432, 437, 440, 453, 458, and 495.

214. Ibid., 436.

215. *The Weekly Democratic Statesman*, April 12, 1883. There is no author listed as this news is reported in general in the bottom paragraph of column two on page 6 of the paper. However, an image of the newspaper scan can be found at the following link, last accessed March 20, 2023: Library of Congress, "The Weekly Democratic Statesman., April 12, 1883, Page 6, Image 6," *Chronicling America*, http://chroniclingamerica.loc.gov/lccn/sn83021327/1883-04-12/ed-1/seq-6/.

216. "Giant Skeleton in Pennsylvania Mound," *American Antiquarian 7:52*, 1885.

217. "Monster Skulls and Bones," *The New York Times*, April 5, 1886. No author, as it is a short blip on page 5.

218. *American Antiquarian: Volumes 9–10: Jan. to Nov. 1887*, 176.

219. *The Baltimore Sun*, January 23, 1889. No author or article title, as it is a short blip.

220. *The Spokane Chronicle*, June 21, 1993, 35. No author or article title, as it is a short blip.

221. Heiser, PhD, Michael S., *Angels*, Kindle location 411.

222. Wenham, Gordon J., "Genesis," in *New Bible Commentary: 21st Century Edition*, ed. D. A. Carson et al., 4th ed. (Leicester, England; Downers Grove, IL: Inter-Varsity Press, 1994), 65.

223. Fee, Gordon D., and Robert L. Hubbard Jr., eds., *The Eerdmans Companion to the Bible* (Grand Rapids, MI; Cambridge, U.K.: William B. Eerdmans Publishing Company, 2011), 82.

224. David Flynn, "Seraphim, Cherubim & Ezekiel's Wheels: Aliens, Nephilim & the Days of Noah," *Watcher Website*. Quoted in: Putnam, Cris, and Tom Horn, *Exo-Vaticana: Project L.U.C.I.F.E.R., and the Vatican's Astonishing Plan for the Arrival of an Alien Savior* (Crane, MO: Defender Publishing; 2013), 90.

225. Kidner, Derek, *Genesis: An Introduction and Commentary: Volume 1*, Tyndale Old Testament Commentaries (Downers Grove, IL: InterVarsity Press, 1967), 91.

226. Pember, George H., *Earth's Earliest Ages*, 22.

227. Harrison, R. K., *Jeremiah and Lamentations: An Introduction and Commentary: Volume 21*, Tyndale Old Testament Commentaries (Downers Grove, IL: InterVarsity Press, 1973), 76–77.

228. Martens, Elmer A., "Jeremiah," in *Evangelical Commentary on the Bible: Volume 3*, Baker Reference Library (Grand Rapids, MI: Baker Book House, 1995), 525.

229. Brueggemann, Walter, *A Commentary on Jeremiah: Exile and Homecoming* (Grand Rapids, MI; Cambridge, U.K.: William B. Eerdmans Publishing Company, 1998), 59–60.

230. Pember, George H., *Earth's Earliest Ages*, 27–30.

231. Stearman, Gary, "The Dark Prophecy: Satan's Long, Long Story," Part 1," 4.

232. Ibid., 4–6; emphasis added.

233. "When Did Dinosaurs Become Extinct?" *United States Geological Survey*, last accessed April 25, 2023, https://www.usgs.gov/faqs/when-did-dinosaurs-become-extinct#:~:text=Dinosaurs%20went%20extinct%20about%2065,for%20about%20165%20million%20years.

234. Gilbert, Derek "NEW ONLINE SERIES: The Great Inception Part 1: The Mountain of Eden," January 28, 2017, *SkyWatch Television Online*, last accessed December 5, 2017, http://www.skywatchtv.com/2017/01/28/new-online-series-great-inception-part-1-mountain-eden/. Though this article has now been removed, many of Derek Gilbert's other works delve into this subject as well. I chose this source as it succinctly represented the *nachash* issue in a way most suitable for this book.

235. Augustine of Hippo, "Expositions on the Book of Psalms," in *Saint Augustin: Expositions on the Book of Psalms*, ed. Philip Schaff, trans. A. Cleveland Coxe, vol. 8, A Select Library of the Nicene and Post-Nicene Fathers of the Christian Church, First Series (New York: Christian Literature Company, 1888), 451; emphasis added.

236. Stearman, Gary, "The Dark Prophecy: Satan's Long, Long Story," Part 1," 5.

237. Gilbert, Derek and Sharon, *Giants, Gods & Dragons: Exposing the Fallen Realm and the Plot to Ignite the Final War of the Ages* (Crane, MO: Defender Publishing; 2020), 25–26.

238. Ibid., 26.

239. Heiser, PhD, Michael S., *Angels*, Kindle location 761.

240. Gilbert, Derek and Sharon, *Giants, Gods & Dragons*, 28.

241. Charlesworth, James H., *The Old Testament Pseudepigrapha and the New Testament, Volume 2: Expansions of the "Old Testament" and Legends, Wisdom, and Philosophical Literature, Prayers, Psalms and Odes, Fragments of Lost Judeo-Hellenistic Works, Includes Indexes* (New Haven; London: Yale University Press, 1985), 2:64. Quoted in: Putnam, Cris, and Tom Horn, *Exo-Vaticana: Project L.U.C.I.F.E.R., and the Vatican's Astonishing Plan for the Arrival of an Alien Savior* (Crane, MO: Defender Publishing; 2013), 91.

242. Karst, Josef, *Eusebius Werke*, 5. Band: die Chronik (Leipzig 1911). Quoted in: Putnam, Cris, and Tom Horn, *Exo-Vaticana: Project L.U.C.I.F.E.R., and the Vatican's Astonishing Plan for the Arrival of an Alien Savior* (Crane, MO: Defender Publishing; 2013), 91–92; emphasis added by Horn and Putnam.

243. Putnam, Cris, and Tom Horn, *Exo-Vaticana: Project L.U.C.I.F.E.R., and the Vatican's Astonishing Plan for the Arrival of an Alien Savior* (Crane, MO: Defender Publishing; 2013), 92.

244. Putnam, Cris, and Tom Horn, *On the Path of the Immortals: Exo-Vaticana, Project L.U.C.I.F.E.R., and the Strategic Locations Where Entities Await the Appointed Time* (Crane, MO: Defender Publishing; 2015), 53.

245. Black, Riley, "The Rise of Meat-Eating Dinosaurs Is More Complicated Than We Thought: Paleontologists Are Searching for How Carnivorous Dinosaurs Went from Pipsqueaks to Titans," May 11, 2020, *Smithsonian Magazine*, last accessed May 11, 2023, https://www.smithsonianmag.com/science-nature/meat-eating-dinosaurs-carnivorous-180974525/.

246. University of Bristol, "Scientists Discover What Was on the Menu of the First Dinosaurs," *Science Daily*, last accessed May 13, 2023, http://www.sciencedaily.com/releases/2022/12/221216142623.htm, emphasis added.

247. Geggel, Laura, "A Brief History of Dinosaurs," July 6, 2021, *LiveScience*, last accessed May 13, 2023, https://www.livescience.com/3945-history-dinosaurs.html.

248. Gilbert, Derek and Sharon, *Giants, Gods & Dragons*, 29.

249. Charles H. Dyer, "Ezekiel," in *The Bible Knowledge Commentary: An Exposition of the Scriptures*, ed. J. F. Walvoord and R. B. Zuck, vol. 1 (Wheaton, IL: Victor Books, 1985), 1246.

250. Knuth, Stacy and Douglas Mangum, ed. John D. Barry et al., *The Lexham Bible Dictionary* (Bellingham, WA: Lexham Press, 2016), under the heading, "Cherubim."

251. McGuire-Moushon, J. A., ed. Douglas Mangum et al., *Lexham Theological Wordbook*, Lexham Bible Reference Series (Bellingham, WA: Lexham Press, 2014), under the heading, "Divine Beings."

252. Heiser, PhD, Michael S., *Angels*, Kindle location 736.

253. Barry, John D., et al., *Faithlife Study Bible* (Bellingham, WA: Lexham Press, 2012, 2016), under Job 41:1; emphasis added.

254. Ibid., under Isaiah 27:1.

255. Butler, Trent C. and Douglas Mangum, *The Lexham Bible Dictionary*, under the heading, "Dragon and Sea."

256. Ibid., under the heading "Chaos."

257. Wyrick, Steve, ed. Chad Brand et al., *Holman Illustrated Bible Dictionary* (Nashville, TN: Holman Bible Publishers, 2003), 1028.

258. *The NET Bible First Edition Notes* (Biblical Studies Press, 2006), Job 3:8.

259. Clines, David J. A., *New Bible Commentary: 21st Century Edition*, ed. D. A. Carson et al., 4th ed. (Leicester, England; Downers Grove, IL: Inter-Varsity Press, 1994), 481, under Job 41:1–34.

260. Bruckner, J. K., ed. Mark J. Boda and Gordon J. McConville, *Dictionary of the Old Testament: Prophets* (Downers Grove, IL; Nottingham, England: IVP Academic; Inter-Varsity Press, 2012), 299.

261. Heiser, Michael S., PhD, *I Dare You Not to Bore Me with the Bible*, ed. John D. Barry and Rebecca Van Noord (Bellingham, WA: Lexham Press; Bible Study Magazine, 2014), 139.

262. Heiser PhD, Michael S., *The Unseen Realm: Recovering the Supernatural Worldview of the Bible* (Kindle ed. Bellingham WA: Lexham Press; 2015), Kindle locations 6557–6566.

263. Stearman, Gary, "The Dark Prophecy: Satan's Long, Long Story," Part 1," 16.

264. Siliezar, Juan, "The Cataclysm that Killed the Dinosaurs," February 15, 2021, *Harvard Gazette*, last accessed April 25, 2023, https://news.harvard.edu/gazette/story/2021/02/new-theory-behind-asteroid-that-killed-the-dinosaurs/.

265. Ibid.

266. Jones, Meghan, "10 Biggest Unsolved Mysteries About Planet Earth," August 4, 2021, *Reader's Digest*, last accessed May 1, 2023, https://www.rd.com/list/unsolved-mysteries-planet-earth/.

267. Barrett, Paul, quoted in: Osterloff, Emily, "How an Asteroid Ended the Age of the Dinosaurs," *Natural History Museum*, last accessed April 25, 2023, https://www.nhm.ac.uk/discover/how-an-asteroid-caused-extinction-of-dinosaurs.html.

268. Howell, Donna, *The Mystery of Jesus: From Genesis to Revelation: Volume Three: The Apocolypse* (Crane, MO: Defender Publishing; 2022), 198–199.